Antigone in the Americas

SUNY series in Gender Theory
—————
Tina Chanter, editor

Antigone in the Americas

Democracy, Sexuality, and Death
in the Settler Colonial Present

ANDRÉS FABIÁN HENAO CASTRO

Cover photo is "Daniel/Daniela 2." Lenticular photograph from Juan Manuel Echavarría's series *Requiem NN* (2006–2013), reproduced with artist's permission.

Published by State University of New York Press, Albany

© 2021 State University of New York

All rights reserved

Printed in the United States of America

No part of this book may be used or reproduced in any manner whatsoever without written permission. No part of this book may be stored in a retrieval system or transmitted in any form or by any means including electronic, electrostatic, magnetic tape, mechanical, photocopying, recording, or otherwise without the prior permission in writing of the publisher.

For information, contact State University of New York Press, Albany, NY
www.sunypress.edu

Library of Congress Cataloging-in-Publication Data

Name: Henao Castro, Andres Fabian, author.
Title: Antigone in the Americas: democracy, sexuality, and death in the settler colonial present / Andrés Fabián Henao Castro.
Description: Albany : State University of New York Press, [2021] | Series: SUNY series in Gender Theory | Includes bibliographical references and index.
Identifiers: ISBN 9781438484273 (hardcover : alk. paper) | ISBN 9781438484280 (pbk. : alk. paper) | ISBN 9781438484297 (ebook)
Further information is available at the Library of Congress.

10 9 8 7 6 5 4 3 2 1

Contents

LIST OF ILLUSTRATIONS — vii

ACKNOWLEDGMENTS — ix

INTRODUCTION
Slaves, *Metics*, Citizens — 1
  The Ancient Drama of Political Membership: Slavery, *Metoikia*,
    and Citizenship in Sophocles's Antigone — 1
  The Modern/Colonial Drama of Political Membership,
    SettlerColonial Capitalism, and the Slave–*Metic*–Citizen
    Triad — 7
  Redefining the Political Through Its Subtending Racialized
    Logic of Valuation — 12
  From *Antigone* in the Americas to the Americas in *Antigone* — 17
  From Classicization to Decolonial Rumination — 20
  Chapter Overview — 24

CHAPTER 1
Antigone in Colonial Antiquity: A Critique of Democratic Theory
in Ancient Athens — 29
  The Democratic Disavowal of Slavery and *Metoikia* — 29
  Tragedy's Misinterpellated Anarchy — 34
  Toward a Political *Antigone* — 36
  What If Antigone Was a *Metic*? — 42
  What If Polyneices Was a Slave? — 50

CHAPTER 2
Antigone in Colonial Modernity: A Critique of Feminist and
Queer Theory in North America ... 59
   Slavery, *Metoikia*, and Citizenship in Colonial Modernity ... 59
   From the Queer Equivocality of Kinship Positions to the
      Racial Equivocality of Social Positions ... 63
   Whose Ethical Act of Sublimation? ... 79
   Tiresias's Gender Complementarity and the Fungibility*cum*
      Fugitivity of Black Transness ... 90
   Whose Future? ... 96
   Fear of a Quare and TwoSpirit Planet ... 102

CHAPTER 3
Antigone in Colonial Postmodernity: A Critique of Biopolitics
in Latin America ... 109
   Slavery, *Metoikia*, and Citizenship in Colonial Postmodernity ... 109
   A Modern Biopolitical *Antigone* in Europe ... 117
   Postmodern Necropolitical *Antigones* in Latin America ... 128
   From Modern Melodrama to Postmodern Decolonial Cacophonies ... 140

CHAPTER 4
Antigone in the Settler-Colonial Present of the Racial Capitalocene:
A Critique of Deconstruction in the Americas ... 155
   Antigone in the Age of the Racial Capitalocene ... 155
   The Racialized Burial and the Human Border ... 159
   A Specter Is Haunting the Americas ... 172
   Decolonial Mourning at the Level of WorldHistorical Events ... 177
   Black and Indigenous Wakeful Mo'nin ... 181

CONCLUSION
What Is There Instead of Being Born? ... 195

NOTES ... 203

BIBLIOGRAPHY ... 247

NAME INDEX ... 267

SUBJECT INDEX ... 271

Illustrations

Figure 3.1   "Puerto Berrío's Mausoleum." Lenticular Photograph from Juan Manuel Echavarría's series *Réquiem NN (2006–2013)*, reproduced with artist's permission.   144

Figure 3.2   "Daniel/Daniela 1." Lenticular Photograph from Juan Manuel Echavarría's series *Réquiem NN (2006–2013)*, reproduced with artist's permission.   148

Figure 3.3   "Daniel/Daniela 2." Lenticular Photograph from Juan Manuel Echavarría's series *Réquiem NN (2006–2013)*, reproduced with artist's permission.   148

Acknowledgments

Antigone in the Americas took forever to finish and traveled a long distance. The idea of using Sophocles's tragedy to dramatize contemporary problems of political membership took form after I participated in Bonnie Honig's brilliant seminar on *Antigone*, during my attendance at the 2010 Summer School of Criticism and Theory at Cornell University. To all the participants in that seminar and especially to Bonnie, I owe an enormous debt. To frame the politics of burial of contemporary undocumented immigrants on the U.S. border through the tragedy of *Antigone* became the subject of my PhD dissertation, which I defended in 2014 at the University of Massachusetts Amherst. My adviser, Nicholas Xenos, and the other members of my committee, Ivan Ascher, Adam Sitze, and Jim Hicks, supported this project since the very beginning. For the generosity of their intellectual engagement I only have the highest gratitude. My network of interlocutors at UMass Amherst was, however, much larger and I was able to discuss some of the ideas that would eventually make it into the book with other superb faculty and graduate students. I should have recorded many more names here but I would like to especially thank Roberto Alejandro, Angelica Bernal, Barbara Cruikshank, Sonia Alvarez, Agustin Lao-Montes, John Brigham, Jane Anderson, Leah Wing, Elva Fabiola Orozco Mendoza, Ruchika Singh, Martha Balaguera, Carlos Valderrama, Julieta Chaparro, Antonia Carcelen, Carmen Cosme, Andrés Jiménez, Leidy Hurtado, John Gibler, Aurora Vergara Figueroa, Bilal Gorguluoglu, Seda Saluk, Claire Sagan, Mike Stain, Alix Olson, Manuel Matos, Javier Campos, Hrvoje Cvijanovic, Dunya Deniz Cakir, Sid Issar, Kevin Henderson, Gabriel Mares, Luz María Sánchez, Tyler Schuenemann, Kanchuka Dharmasiri, Ivelisse Cuevas-Molina, and Ghazah Abbasi. Melissa Mueller deserves a special mention, as she was willing to engage in a close textual analysis of Sophocles's original with me for a whole semester, just out of love for the tragedy. The same goes for Marios Philippides, Rex Wallace, and Debbie Felton who generously allowed me to join their classical Greek language courses, for me to be able to read *Antigone* in its original.

By the time I was about to defend my dissertation in 2014 I had become increasingly interested in another positionality, that of the enslaved. Such an interest coincided with my move to Amherst College, when I was selected as the Karl Lowenstein Fellow in 2014. The intellectual environment in Amherst was as stimulating, and I would like to express my deepest gratitude to Adam Sitze, Thomas Dumm, Andrew Poe, Austin Sarat, Pooja Rangan, Simon Stow, and Manuela Picq, and to the students who suffered through my seminar on *Antigone* for their creative interpretations and critiques of some of the texts that I engage in this book.

The tripartite system of political membership, as well as the reinterpretation of *Antigone* through the lenses of settler colonial critique that I offer in this text, fully formed during my research as an assistant professor of political science at the University of Massachusetts Boston, since the fall of 2014. Again, I should probably record many more names in here, but I would like to especially thank Heike Schotten, Leila Farsakh, Elizabeth Bussiere, Erin O'Brien, Joe Brown, Luis Jiménez, Ursula Tafe, Paul Watanabe, Shuai Jin, Caroline Coscia, Travis Johnston, Michelle Jurkovich, Paul Kowert, Rajini Srikhant, Meredith Reiches, Maria John, Denise Khor, Mickaella Perina, Karen Suyemoto, Elora Chowdhury, S. Tiffany Donaldson, Christina Bobel, Sofya Aptekar, Nedra Lee, Rakhshanda Saleem, Steven Levine, and Linda Uch for their intellectual camaraderie, collegiality, and friendship. As we all know, many ideas are first explored in the classroom, so I would also like to thank all of my students, especially Altan Atamer, Ezra Brown, Lucas Goren, Erin Mahoney, Kosar Mohamed, Bridget Mutebi, Brittany Orange, Lina Rubiere, Tatyana Shallop, Hadass Silver, and Sumaiya Zama, for their confidence in my teaching and for their very sharp observations about many political theories I address in this work. Finally, I would like to express my gratitude to my friends and comrades in the abolitionist organization *Black & Pink*, especially to Anja Bircher, Michelle Jane Tat, Jason Lydon, and Johannes Mosquera.

I finished *Antigone in the Americas* in Bologna, after I was selected as the Post-Doctoral Fellow by the Academy of Global Humanities and Critical Theory (AGHCT) in 2018. Here, I would like to express my deepest gratitude to AGHCT Director Raffaele Laudani, for facilitating a great environment for the last part of my research. For their hospitality and our conversations, I would also like to thank Paolo Capuzzo, Davide Domenici, Carla Salvaterra, Maria Elena de Luna, Sandro Mezzadra, Antonio Schiavulli, and all the students who took my graduate seminar on "The Mis-Interpellated Subject."

I undertook the final revisions of the book during my one-year residence at the John Hope Franklin Humanities Institute (FHI) at Duke University, during the second year of my Fellowship with AGHCT, where I was able to organize another reading group on *Antigone*. Here, I would like to express my deepest gratitude to the FHI Director, Ranji Khanna, as well as to Chris Chia, Sarah Rogers, Nima Bassiri, Roxana Bendezu, Carolyn Fulford, Pedro Gravatá Nicoli, Eva Wheeler, Riika Prattes, Magda Szczesniak, Marcelo Maciel Ramos, Eli Meyerhoff, Miriam Cooke, Veronica Davis, Charles Joseph del Dotto, Nick Hoff, Ryan Johnson, Saskia Cornes, Jennifer Zhou, and Claudia Milian.

Chapter 1 is a significantly modified version of a paper that I first presented at the 2014 NPSA Annual Meeting, under the invitation of David McIvor, who generously nominated the paper for the NPSA/McWilliams Best Paper prize in political theory, which I was awarded in 2015. I have most recently presented an updated version of this research at the lecture that I was asked to deliver for the *Dipartimento di Storia, Culture, Civilitè* at the University of Bologna in March 2019, under the invitation of Carla Salvaterra. Chapter 2 I first presented as a lecture for the *Political Theory Workshop* at UMass Amherst in October 2015, under the invitation of Barbara Cruikshank. That chapter underwent various revisions as a result of the conversations that for two years I had with Heike Schotten and Nedra Lee, when we decided to organize a reading group on Afro-pessimism in Boston. Chapter 3, finally, benefited enormously from the discussion that it generated during my intervention at the XXXV International Congress of the Latin American Studies Association in Lima, Peru (2017). In these and other spaces, scholars engaged with my work with genuine care and outstanding generosity and I would like to thank all of those who participated in these academic spaces for their feedback.

Almost a decade in the making, nourished by the academic communities and financial support of at least six institutions and two Fellowships, this book has also been the consequence of many more conversations and exchanges with other researchers and comrades. This list will be inevitably incomplete, moreover one in alphabetic order, but I would here like to express my heartfelt gratitude for their impact on my political theorizing, and my understanding of specific political contexts, to Aliyyah Abdur-

Rahman, Gustave Akakpo, Alejandra Azuero, Farid Abud Hoyos, Maria del Rosario Acosta, Minou Arjomand, Manuela Badilla, Ekin Bodur-Bayraktaroglu, Flor Emilce Cely, Joseph Cermatori, George Ciccariello-Maher, Laura Cull, Nijah Cunningham, Bernardo Correa, Iyko Day, Serap Erincin, Henrik Ernstson, Jeanne Etelain, Katie Feyh, Moira Fradinger, Armando García, Miguel Gualdrón, Kristina Hagström-Stahl, Lawrence Hamilton, Ryan Hatch, Nathalia Hernández, Alexander Hirsch, Murad Idris, Steven Johnston, Camille Joyeux, Kareem Khubchandani, Wangui Kimari, Mathias Klitgard, Premesh Lalu, Robyn Marasco, Francia Márquez, James Martel, David McIvor, Bernadette Meyler, Rita Kantu, Gil Morrejón, Leopoldo Múnera Ruiz, Allison Myers, Ianna Hawkins Owen, Diego Paredes, William Paris, Laurence Piper, Martin Puchner, Leslie Quintanilla, Nicholas Ridout, Sonia Ristic, Takeo Rivera, Freddie Rokem, Jacqueline Rose, Jennifer Row, Michael Sawyer, Suraya Scheba, Jade Larissa Schiff, C. Riley Snorton, Antonio Vázquez-Arroyo, Jasmine Wallace, Astrid L. B. van Weyenberg, and Stephen Wilmer. I apologize, in advance, for those whose names I failed to include.

My debt to Sarah Gray, who painstakingly copy edited this text before I submitted it to SUNY, has no equal. That is the case, too, with Juan Manuel Echavarría, who generously granted me the permission to reproduce three photographs from his beautiful *Réquiem NN* (2006–2013), in itself an Antigone-like political intervention in the context of the ongoing Colombian armed conflict. Working with SUNY Press has been wonderful; many thanks to my editor Rebecca Colesworthy and to the Gender Theory series editor Tina Chanter, for believing in this project. Thanks too, to the excellent work of the editorial team at SUNY: James Peltz, Diane Ganeles, Catherine Blackwell, and Alan Hewat, and to the four anonymous reviewers of this book, for their helpful comments.

For their unconditional love, thanks to my family (Marlene, Juan, Felo, Astrid, Antonio, and Jacques) and to my friends (Natha, Mao, Lulu, Laurita, and Clau). Thanks, finally, to Ashley, for her inspiring activism, groundbreaking scholarship, and infinite love. Without her support, I would have never finished this book.

Antigone in the Americas was written between two years whose events symptomatize the settler colonial capitalist violence this book seeks to theorize and contest. In 2014, the year I started writing this book, police officer Darren Wilson killed Michael Brown and the police left his body desecrated for hours in the streets of Ferguson. That same year, forty-three students from the Ayotzinapa Rural Teacher's College were forcibly disappeared by the Mexican police in coordination with organized crime. In 2020, the year I finished the revised version of this book, the structurally differentiated impact of Covid-19 led to the exposure of corpses in the streets, as happened in Guayaquil, as well as to the greater vulnerability of black and brown people to suffer death in solitary confinement in prisons and detention centers. Public acts of dissident mourning followed the killing of Michael Brown, the disappearance of the students in Iguala Guerrero, and the failure of governments around the world to adequately respond to the racially differentiated impact of the pandemic. In all cases, militant mourners faced some kind of state violence in response. *Antigone in the Americas* is a book that seeks to unpack the racialized and gender-differentiated logic of such violence, and the politics of militant mourning in response.

Thus, I would like to begin by humbly joining Toni Morrison and Leslie Marmon Silko, in dedicating this book to the sixty million and more black people, and to the sixty million and more indigenous people, who have lost and continue to lose their lives to settler colonial capitalist violence.

Introduction

Slaves, *Metics*, Citizens

> For us, there is no going back to the original text of Antigone, no return to a pure Sophoclean drama that would be shorn of all the translations and adaptations it has inspired. There is no returning to a Greek text somehow outside the political genealogy of its multiple translators. There is no pre-political text named Antigone. There are only the multiple resonances, between Sophocles and Heaney, between Heaney's Sophocles and McDonald's Sophocles, between McDonald's Sophocles and Fugard's Sophocles, and so on, ad infinitum.
>
> —Tina Chanter, "Antigone's Political Legacies: Abjection in Defiance of Mourning"

The Ancient Drama of Political Membership: Slavery, *Metoikia,* and Citizenship in Sophocles's Antigone

Sophocles's *Antigone* (441 BCE), which narrates the story of the title character, is both globally the most frequently performed classical tragedy in contemporary theaters and a foundational text for political theory.[1] Antigone is the oldest daughter of Oedipus, the previous sovereign of Thebes, well known for having committed parricide and incest after solving the riddle of the Sphinx. Her brother Polyneices, having been ostracized by their other brother Eteocles, who was unwilling to share the throne, sought to destroy and enslave the city. Polyneices and Eteocles kill each other in battle, but Creon, their uncle and the new sovereign of Thebes, grants proper burial only to Eteocles, who fought on behalf of the city. Creon decides to keep

Polyneices's corpse unburied and exposed for citizens to see it ravished by dogs and birds. And Creon would not treat disobedience lightly, as death awaits whoever dares to bury Polyneices. Keeping Polyneices's corpse above ground, subjected to the indignity of exposure, ends up contaminating the whole scene of the living with that of the dead. Antigone buries Polyneices, against Creon's edict and in disobedience of her confinement to the *oikos* (household) on the basis of her gender. Antigone, Haemon (Antigone's fiancé and Creon's son), and Eurydice (Creon's wife) all commit suicide. By the end of the play, Creon regards his own life as lived in death. Only Ismene, Antigone's sister, survives, deprived of her kin.

Most summaries of the play end here, showing how Antigone orbits around two interrelated contestations of political membership. First, she contests who can or cannot be buried, when she performs the forbidden burial for her brother, declared an enemy of the state. Second, she contests the gender regulations that determine who can act and speak in the city, when she enacts the forbidden ritual by occupying the public space from which she is excluded for being a woman. This exclusion is representationally mimicked by the fact that a male actor originally had to play her role in the stage, as ancient Greek women were not allowed to perform in the theater or, according to some, even attend as spectators.

Antigone, however, is also about coerced migration. This subject becomes clearer if one reads *Antigone* in connection to the two other surviving plays by Sophocles on the same Theban myth, often published as a cycle: *Oedipus Tyrannos* (429 BCE) and *Oedipus at Colonus* (406 BCE). Both refer to events that precede those narrated in *Antigone*, according to the chronology of the story. In *Oedipus Tyrannos,* we learn that Oedipus left Corinth fearing the prophecy of parricide and incest and still believing the Corinthian rulers, Polybus and Merope, to be his parents by blood. Corinth, it is worth mentioning, was known as an important slave port in Greek antiquity, and Sophocles symbolically places Thebes in between it and the democratic city of Colonus, where Oedipus arrives with Antigone as two refugees seeking asylum. *Oedipus at Colonus* thus comes second in the chronology of the story. And Sophocles extends the migratory journeys of the main characters in the Theban cycle, since it is in Colonus that an aged Oedipus is officially granted the Athenian status of *metoikia* (which should be translated as "foreign residence" or "home-changing," but is often translated as "alien residence,"; the noun referring to the human who has the status is *metic*). But Antigone does not remain in Colonus. *Antigone*, the last play in the chronology of the story (but the first one to be written), places Antigone in her native Thebes, where Polyneices is subjected to the indignity of exposure after death. Polyneices is treated, Antigone's speech suggests, as only slaves could be treated (A, 517 [181]); and it is in Thebes, once she learns that she will be put in a rockbound cave for daring to bury her brother, that Antigone refers to herself as a *metic* (A, 850–53 [194]).

To focus on the question of coerced migration is to focus on the problem of Athenian exceptionalism, that is to say, on colonialism, and on its impact on democracy's reliance on blood-based membership to restrict the recognition of political subjectivity. Oedipus was originally a native of Thebes, but his parents asked their servants (arguably slaves) to kill their son, fearing the fulfillment of the prophecy. Instead, the servants subversively removed him to Corinth to save his life. Raised in Corinth, a known slave center, Oedipus leaves and kills his biological father, unknowingly, at the crossroads, fearing the prophecy. He then solves the riddle of the Sphinx and, unknowingly, marries his mother, Jocasta, as a result. He thus moves from Corinth back to Thebes, and unknowingly becomes, as I will argue in the next chapter, the *metic* sovereign of his native land (OT, 452–53 [30]). He discovers his Corinthian parents not to be his parents by blood and is anxious to prove that he is not a slave (OT, 1063 [57]), but learns that he was a native of Thebes, and of his heinous deeds. Thus, as a self-imposed punishment, he blinds himself and leaves Thebes. It takes him a long time to arrive at Colonus, where he engages in supplication, following the protocols for the acquisition of *metoikia* according to the standards of democratic Athens. It is granted. When he dies, he is buried in an unmarked gravesite at the border of the Athenian *polis,* where the open, hospitable and democratic Athenians will defeat the aristocratic, enclosed Thebans (an enclosure hyperbolically dramatized through the incest).[2] Oedipus's migration is thus a traveling between citizenship, slavery, and *metoikia*.

Antigone's migratory drama equally travels across these positionalities. Antigone is forced to leave her homeland with Oedipus in order to become his eyes through foreign lands. But she does not reside at Colonus as a *metic*. No longer a sovereign of Thebes, the ostracized Polyneices marries Argeia (Adrastus's daughter) and assembles an army in Argos in order to fight against his brother. He is told that he needs Oedipus's favor in order to win the battle; so he solicits an audience with his aged father in Colonus. Antigone is the only one able to persuade her father to listen to Polyneices (OC, 1181–1205 [134]). Instead of giving his favor, though, Oedipus curses his sons to kill each other in battle (OC, 1373–75 [140]). Antigone has to return to Thebes to stop what seems unstoppable: the fratricide of her brothers. There she decides to bury Polyneices because it was Eteocles's brother, "not his slave" (A, 517 [181]) she claims, who died in the battlefield. And it is in Thebes, after Creon commands her to be displaced to a cave with enough food to give time for the gods to save her, that she regards her condition as that of a *metic*. Polyneices's and Antigone's forced migrations, like Oedipus's, travel across the positions of the slave, the *metic,* and the citizen.

It is my argument in this book that what *Antigone*'s coerced migrations between Corinth, Thebes, and Colonus dramatize is the conflictive, triangular organization of political membership between the positionalities of the slave (full exclusion), the *metic* (partial inclusion/partial exclusion), and the citizen (full inclusion). Political membership is only intelligible against the logic that relationally sustains these different positionalities, and it is the colonial dimension of such logic that I seek to interrogate in this book.

In revisiting *Antigone*'s tragedy, however, I am not interested in giving a different picture of ancient democracy by emphasizing the constitutive modes of exclusion that value citizenship on the basis of fully devaluing slaves and partially including *metics*. My real interest lies in exploring how this triangular model of political membership informs our modern/colonial world, which is drastically affected by the racialized logic that settler-colonial capitalism produced through the European conquest of the Americas and the institutionalization of modern slavery via the trans-Atlantic slave trade. In other words, this is a book about *Antigone* in the Americas and a book about the Americas in *Antigone*, which openly and anachronistically seeks in a different time, a time foreign to Sophocles, for a problematic that might help us to politically reinvent *Antigone* for our times.

The assumption of this book is, of course, that the very *Antigone* deprived of the Americas to which we have access—that is, the *Antigone* that we have received through its multiple translations by Hegel, Lacan, etc.—is already an *Antigone* remade by the conquest of the Americas and the trans-Atlantic slave trade. *Antigone* can play the mediating role that it plays in Hegel and onward, because the intimacies between four continents, to echo Lisa Lowe's work, brought up by the European conquest of Africa, Asia, and the Americas, already speaks through him, if in disavowed form.[3] The Spirit can move from the unintelligible Egyptian hieroglyph to the rational solution of the riddle of the Sphinx by Oedipus, which is said to inaugurate the symbolic order of the West, because modern colonialism has already redistributed knowledge and deprived black and indigenous peoples of history and recognizable humanity.

This is not, however, a book about the ways in which the conquest and the slave trade speaks through Hegel, Lacan, etc. It is a book that attempts to articulate an alternative political interpretation of the tragedy, by voicing what that colonial genealogy of translations has thus far silenced. Hence, rather than look to Greek antiquity in order to illuminate the political inclusions and exclusions of modernity, my book operates in the opposite direction. Given the disavowed role of the conquest in the colonial formation of a dominant literary and theoretical interpretation of classical texts, such as *Antigone*, why not look to settler colonial critique, black and women of color feminisms, and queer and trans of color critique in order to illuminate the political inclusions and exclusions of Greek antiquity, to which our Western political theory and its main conceptual vocabulary remain committed? This explains why the emphasis is on *Antigone* in the Americas, with only one chapter on Greek antiquity. Such emphasis leads me both to confront ancient democracy with its hierarchized and quasi-naturalized system of blood-based political membership but more importantly, to confront the ways in which that colonial history remains unchallenged in contemporary democratic, feminist, queer, biopolitical, and deconstruction theory's turn to the ancient Greeks for a contemporary re-politicization of *Antigone*.

By situating *Antigone* in the Americas, I want to offer an alternative genealogy to the multiple translations that mediate our engagement with the play. Doing so, I am not trying to make Greek antiquity into the origin of the Americas, in the way in which Hegel, and arguably the whole Romantic and post-Romantic tradition of German Idealism, can be said to have made Athens the birthplace of Germany. That is not the point of *Antigone in the Americas*. More *anti*-gone—as in against *genos*/genealogy/ generation—I want to tell the story of a decolonial disaffiliation. Hence, I want to explore the tragedy through a more contentious historiography, what I would call, following Mieke Bal, a "preposterous history" of *Antigone in the Americas*.[4] What I want to write, even perhaps to invent, is more the history of a rupture than of a continuity, to document not a passage (i.e., from Europe to the Americas) but the violent history of a "middle passage," the one that connects the four continents together and yet remains politically undertheorized.

To focus on the *metic* and the *slave*, is to think about this tragedy anew, and thus to accentuate other passages that have not received the same level of commentary. Most interpreters of the play (Hegel, Lacan, Irigaray, Derrida, Butler, Honig, etc.) focus their attention on two passages that appear, at first sight, contradictory. In the first passage, Antigone justifies her burial of Polyneices on the basis that "the god of death demands these rites for both" (A, 519 [181]). This is the claim that, as we know, champions the civil disobedience of Antigone as a figure of universal humanism. Death is the grand equalizer and marks a limit to politics; all bodies are, in principle, exempt from state instrumentalization post mortem. The second passage refers to Antigone's controversial answer to the question posed by the Chorus, vis-à-vis the law that backs her up, when she cites the Persian story of Intaphrenes's wife's reasoning: "If my husband were dead, I might have had another, and child from another man, if I lost the first. But when father and mother both were hidden in death no brother's life would bloom for me again" (A, 909–12 [196]). Singularity, rather than universality, is what gets emphasized in this case. She would only do it for her brother, who is uniquely irreplaceable. The dominant political-theoretical interpretations of *Antigone* all focus on these two reasons. Democratic theory, psychoanalysis, feminist and queer theory, biopolitics, and deconstruction, all offer different answers to the puzzle of Antigone's move from universality to singularity, a puzzle whose solution enlists other oppositions in its wake.

There is, in short, a vast theoretical tradition that one could trace back to the Hegel-indebted opposition between the family (*oikos*) and the state (*polis*), the divine and the civic, life and death, and the feminine and the masculine, that comes to supplement the incompatibility between these two justifications for her acts: the god of the dead demands the rites for all and I would only do it for my brother. There is, however, a new theoretical tradition, to which my book belongs and contributes, that makes the question of freedom and slavery central to the literary adaptations of *Antigone* in the Global South. This tradition, which Tina Chanter inaugurated through her excellent analysis of the Hegel-indebted marginalization of slavery in the political interpretation of Greek tragedy, focuses instead on Antigone's claim to have buried Polyneices because "it was [Eteocles's] brother, not his slave, that died" (A, 517 [181]).[5] According to the logic of that claim, some bodies could presumably be treated under some undignified manner by the sovereign without eliciting the same kind of public response that Polyneices's mistreatment does, namely, the bodies of slaves who were also spoils of war. But slaves have not been the sole ones neglected, as Antigone's reclamation of *metoikia*, otherwise misunderstood as only a rhetorical flourish, has also been only marginally touched upon by the vast readership of this play. And yet, Antigone refers to herself three times as a *metic* (A, 852, 867, and 890 [194–95]), as does Creon, when he calls on the guards to confine her in a cave, in order to deprive her "of her metic status on earth" (A, 889–90 [194–95]).[6]

Reading is a performative act, and the theoretical texts with which we interpret a text inevitably modify it. *Antigone in the Americas* is the performance of such transformative reading. I am well aware that the *Antigone* I offer in this book will be unrecognizably classical. That is not a problem for me. What I hope is that it will also be uncomfortably modern. Moreover, I hope it will be, if not anticanonical—as the repetition of *Antigone* cannot help but to solidify the position that the play already occupies in the Western canon of political theory—at least alter-canonical.

The Modern/Colonial Drama of Political Membership, Settler-Colonial Capitalism, and the Slave/*Metic*/Citizen Triad

As an authorized immigrant in the United States, my interest in *Antigone* first emerged from the parallels I noticed between the double contestation of political membership in the play and the double contestation of political membership often led by unauthorized immigrants in the U.S. Organized unauthorized immigrants are subjects who are not allowed to speak politically because they lack proper documentation, yet often occupy the public spaces of the city to protest the terms of their social marginalization. The bodies of dead unauthorized immigrants are also routinely subjected to improper burial in the United States, and the group Humane Borders reports that such improper burials are not exceptional but a normalized act of sovereign violence.[7] Improper burial is, in fact, the last injury in a series of acts of violence that facilitate disregard for the dead by the sovereign institutions of the inhospitable city. These series include, but are not limited to, the militarization of the border, the criminalization of the crossing, and the capitalist marginalization of labor conditions in the immigrants' cities of origin and arrival, which forces them into such dangerous crossings in the first place.[8] The colonial organization of labor movement then gives continuity to the endangering of peoples' lives and facilitates the potential desecration of their deaths, afterward.

When I set out to translate the politics of unauthorized immigrants' burial onto the political drama of membership in *Antigone*, I realized that the dominant secondary literature on the play analyzes its political value as an allegorical commentary on democracy from the standpoint of Athenian citizens.⁹ Though they composed the main audience of the play, when it was first performed at the Festival of Dionysus in 441 BCE they were not the sole spectators; *metics* and at least eight slaves (those who served the Council) attended them as well.¹⁰

Inspired by what James Martel calls a "yet more minor" literature, (echoing Gilles Deleuze and Félix Guattari's work), I wanted to read *Antigone* from the perspective of those who are "misinterpellated" by its message, to use Martel's term.¹¹ I wanted to read the play from the positions of the *metics* and slaves who were not its intended audience and who heard Antigone claiming *metoikia* to inform her condition and justify her heroic disobedience on the basis that Polyneices was not a slave. The substance of my interpretation, however, does not rest in simply claiming that the references to the *metic* and to the slave convey empirically accurate statutory conditions in Greek antiquity. Rather, the substance of my reading lies in Sophocles's own metaphorical use of these terms to frame the politics of Antigone's burial. In other words, if Antigone can instrumentalize *metoikia* and *slavery* to frame the differential exclusion to which she and her brother were subjected, why not make it possible for *metics* and slaves to instrumentalize her agency as well.

I do not claim my reading to be the right one and that all the other readings that have missed the political potential of these metaphorical associations are wrong. If anything, like Martel, I want to deliberately "not get the reading right," so as to gain access to "undertext(s) that normally would escape our attention."¹² Those undertexts refer to the buried history of a colonial drama, one replayed in modernity and intensify in what I characterize as neoliberal postmodernity. I thus argue in this book for a more complicated dramatization of political membership in *Antigone*, one better equipped to explain why Antigone claimed the position of *metoikia* to inform her condition at Thebes and why she claimed to have performed the disobedient deed on the basis that Polyneices was Eteocles's brother, not his slave.

The inclusive exclusion of the *metic*, I realized, occupied a middle position in the structural organization of political membership in Greek antiquity—between the full inclusion of the citizen and the full exclusion of the slave—making any interrogation of *metoikia* inseparable from a confrontation with both citizenship and slavery.¹³ Given the dominant association of ancient citizenship with the political, my interpretation constitutes a critical intervention that, by addressing the structural relation of citizenship to *metoikia* and slavery, displaces citizenship as the dominant locus of the political. Thus, I do not offer a reading of *Antigone* from the exclusive perspective of the citizen; I focus instead on the subordinated and misinterpellated *metic* and slave as positions from which to rethink the politics of this play.

My main interest, however, lies not in Greek antiquity but in the modern/colonial configuration of political membership in the Americas. An interrogation of political membership in the Americas is, however, inescapably mediated by the racialized logic of social (de)valuation that modern capitalism inaugurated. Race, however, "in no way pivots around 'whiteness' and 'blackness' in antiquity, despite the centrality of those categories to racial thought today," as Denise Eileen McCoskey claims.[14] "The closest parallel in antiquity to the modern racial binary of 'black' and 'white,'" McCoskey rightly affirms, would be that of "Greek versus barbarian."[15] The problem, however, lies not only in the difficulty—if not impossibility—of equating the more ethnic Greek-versus-barbarian division to the racialized one of white versus black. The problem lies in the fact that, despite contemporary efforts to trace modern racism back to ancient attempts at naturalizing slavery, most notably in the political theory of Aristotle, such genealogical efforts often obscure the role that modern capitalism played in the biological construction of race as a heritable trait, in opposition to other ancient modes of naturalizing social hierarchies among peoples regarded as different.[16]

That is not to say that in the ancient world bodies were not "othered" and even physically marked as different in ways almost identical to those in modernity.[17] From Solon's law forbidding slaves from exercising at the gymnasia, thus producing "visible" somatic differences of "otherness," to the identity trials of the *dokomasia* (membership test) and the Periclean prescription of double endogamy to grant Athenian citizenship in 451/450 BCE, male, able-bodied Greek lives were valued based on devaluing physically marked others.[18] Those lives were marked as more essentially linked to their socially constructed corporal traits in what Lape has justifiably characterized as "racial citizenship."[19] Democratic tragedy itself, as Edith Hall demonstrated, was an important representational effort at reproducing that hierarchy through the literary invention of the barbarian, one sustaining the cultural superiority of the Greek over that of the non-Greek.[20] Yet, by simply regarding the invention of the "barbarian" as an early mode of racialization, we obscure processes characteristic of modern capitalism, such as the trans-Atlantic construction of a global market that expropriated workers from their means to socially reproduce their own communities. In other words, the race that is presumably traceable to Greek antiquity takes for granted the incommensurability between times and the ways in which different colonial modes of production affect the social regulation of differently marked bodies. In this book, I focus on the invention of the Americas through the violence of the conquest and the trans-Atlantic slave trade, as well as in its historical disavowal, as the most important events affecting political membership in modernity. This is the rupture that brings four continents (Asia, Europe, Africa, and America) into intimate contact with each other, and makes capitalism into a world-historical and highly differentiated system of labor exploitation and land expropriation.

Thus, in this book I follow the persuasive thesis of Iyko Day vis-à-vis the explanatory framework for understanding different logics of racialization in the Americas as the products of subtending logics of settler-colonial capitalism. To those logics I trace the colonial effort at distinguishing full inclusion (citizenship) from full exclusion (slavery) via the differential inclusion/exclusion of some (*metoikia*).[21] Day explores those logics through the migratory characteristics of the positionalities involved, generating a triangular understanding of settler colonialism that distinguishes the native (indigenous to the territory) from the alien (coerced to migrate as exploitable labor force in place of the native) and the settler (who voluntarily migrates in order to appropriate the land of the native and exploit the labor of the alien). Day's triangular account of settler-colonial racialization in the Americas allows us to interrogate the different logics by which this triad is organized. Those logics are the logic of elimination, which subtends the relationship between the settler and the native organized around the appropriation of the latter's land, and the logic of exclusion, which subtends the relationship between the settler and the alien organized around the exploitation of the latter's labor. Elimination and exclusion, Day also clarifies, are often used in conjunction with each other but they characterize different modalities of settler-colonial capitalist accumulation. They distinguish the settler interest in accumulating the land of indigenous peoples (thus seeking a claim to territorial indigeneity that wants to replace the native population with that of the settlers) and appropriating the labor power of the black people, as the original aliens of the Americas (thus seeking a disclaimer to the extreme condition of excessive exploitability). Through this distinction, Day argues, the assimilation of indigenous peoples to whiteness constituted a logic of elimination—unlike the "one-drop rule," which "relegated to blackness a biological permanence that would survive any amount of interracial mixing."[22]

The triangulation I focus on here—citizen, *metic*, and slave—does not seek to contest Day's; rather, it is inspired by it. And if I speak not of settler, native, and alien positionalities but of citizen, *metic,* and slave ones, it is in order to translate the settler-colonial logic of racialization into the hierarchical organization of political membership in the settler state. Thus, I further extend Day's claim that "blackness was not the only condition for enslaveability" in the Americas, as indigenous peoples were also enslaveable, to account for settler colonialism's necropolitical formula: "Take life and let die."[23] In my account, the settler first subjected the native and the alien both to slavery, in order to more effectively enforce the elimination of indigenous peoples and the hyperexploitation of black people, the original aliens of the Americas. Slavery's capacity to subhumanize the subject, who was targeted with extreme state violence, made it possible for settlers to commit genocide against both black and indigenous peoples, as it was considerably easier to annihilate a population that was not endowed with recognizable rights. Genocide, however, performed very different functions: it allowed the expropriation of indigenous peoples' land, and the intensification of black people's labor exploitation. Citizenship was the settler's privilege and when slavery was eventually abolished, it was not citizenship but something akin to *metoikia,* an in-between position, that was first extended to natives and aliens. Recall, also, that manumitted slaves did not become citizens in Greek antiquity, but *metics*.[24] As I will also demonstrate in this book, however, even when black and indigenous peoples were eventually de jure recognized as equal citizens in the Americas, they continued to be subjected to the racialized stratification of membership that these logics engendered, thus giving slavery an aftermath. I am, in short, interested in translating this racialized logic of settler-colonial capitalism into the dominant organization of political membership through the hierarchical distinctions among the citizen (full inclusion), the *metic* (half-inclusion/half-exclusion), and the slave (full exclusion). I am interested in that translation, in order to rethink the severity, obscurity, and historical indebtedness of contemporary forms of state and parastate violence to settler colonial capitalism.

My terms, not unlike Day's, are theoretical abstractions, categories by which to make a problem visible, rather than accurate representations of an empirical reality. There is, obviously, neither a single and monolithic modern slavery, any more than there was a single ancient one. Nor is there a single modern citizenship, anymore there was one in Greek antiquity. Citizenship, *metoikia,* and slavery, even as analytical terms, are changing historical categories, the unstable result of socially contested practices. My preposterous historical use of these categories is not trying to flatten history and deny the vast modifications in the meaning of these terms. Why, then, turn to *Antigone* and continue to employ this triad? First, because *Antigone*, as one of many classical texts that Europeans used in order to "modernize" the colonized subjects they retroactively constructed as "primitive," already participates in the coloniality that its theoretical reception often disavows. Second, because *Antigone* has already been reappropriated in the Americas, made to voice the cry of a different mourning. Finally, because the problem that interests me, the political problem of the *polis*'s ground, or more adequately, of the lack of ground, is what is at stake in this play. The unburied body is, to put it differently, not just a symptom but perhaps *the* symptom of the political.

The slave/*metic*/citizen triangulation that I offer in this book, as a complement to Day's triangulation of native, alien, and settler positions, seeks to redefine how contemporary political theory draws from ancient political thought in general, and Sophocles's *Antigone* in particular, in order to rethink the political in ways that foreground its subtending racialized logic of social (de)valuation. This is a relational logic that values citizenship by devaluing slavery, inventing the *metic* as the malleable in-between position. By means of this logic, black- and brown-marked bodies are kept from full membership in the colonial and postcolonial states of the Americas. Just as emancipated slaves in antiquity did not become citizens but *metics*, emancipated black and indigenous peoples in the Americas do not become full citizens either, even when citizenship is eventually extended to them. Other alien labor forces are subjected to a more compartmentalized system of *metoikia*, but some citizens and *metics* in fact continue to be subjected to slavery's aftermath. The abolition of modern slavery, however, does not end it. The "racial calculus and political arithmetic" that settler colonial capitalism engendered survives it, in what Saidiya Hartman has adequately named slavery's aftermath.[25]

Redefining the Political Through Its Subtending Racialized Logic of Valuation

One might explain the significant marginalization of *metoikia* and slavery—as two alternative subject-positionalities for interpreting *Antigone*'s drama—in political theory's long investment in this ancient tragedy, based on the fact that neither *metics* nor slaves, irrespective of gender, could participate in the *agora* (assembly). Unlike citizens, slaves were not allowed to speak in public, or own property, as they were the property that others owned.

Metics, who were allowed to own property, except land, were also excluded from proper political participation. *Metics,* however, could still influence political outcomes, either through forms of legal ghostwriting and political advising, or by pretending to be citizens, a practice common enough as to merit legal regulation. *Metics* and slaves were, thus, differentially deprived of *lexis* (speech) and *praxis* (action), and differentially subjected to the private sphere—as animated objects for the master, in the case of slaves, and as nonproprietors of the land, in the case of *metics.* If citizens were free and slaves were unfree, *metics* were "free," in that they were not under another master's rule, ruled their own *oikos,* and yet, had no political rights to participate as equals in the government of the city, which is what freedom really meant in Greek antiquity.

Prior to Pericles's 451/450 BCE Citizenship Law, and during its suspension (from 430 to 403 BCE, according to some sources), *metics'* children could become citizens if the other parent was a citizen. Things get more complicated when we understand that *metics* were also manumitted slaves, rendering all of these boundaries permeable through the reproductive politics of democracy. In other words, citizens and slaves met in *metoikia,* making the regulation of *metic* sexuality in particular, a subject of great anxiety in Greek antiquity. As Rebecca Futo Kennedy argues, *metic* women were "the ultimate Other and the gravest threat to Athenian exceptionalism and democracy."[26] The equation of the citizen with the political, thus, rested on the compromised prepolitical exclusion of *metics* and slaves from blood-based membership, reconfigured by Pericles's Citizenship Law, and the differential subjection of all women to such stratified regulation.

But this exclusion did not affect all women equally, either, as women's status depended on their genealogical filiation, making women married to citizens differently regulated from those married to *metics* and those enslaved. As Kennedy argues, *metic* women were subjected to taxes and to the law courts "in ways that no citizen woman ever would be."[27] *Metic* women were subjected to the charge of *graphê xenias* (pretending to be a citizen), *graphê aprostasiou* (failure to register and pay the *metic* tax) and *dike apostasiou* (disregard of their *prostates*). If found guilty of the first charge, the punishment could be as harsh as a death sentence, if guilty of the second and third charges, they could be sold into slavery. A portion of the profits from the sale, furthermore, went to the prosecutor, rendering independent *metic* women "extremely vulnerable," "a legal non-entity" "as far as private law was concerned."[28] Because the most radical difference between the free and the unfree, between citizens and slaves, could be undone through *metic* reproduction, it became crucial for democracy to control their sexuality, and police their intimacy.

A different understanding of the political, however, inverts the terms of that exclusion. If one were to qualify an action as political, not because it happens in a specific (public) space but because it troubles the logic of the "proper" that governs the location of some bodies within specific spaces and the dislocation of others, *metics* and slaves, rather than citizens, would become the primary subjects of the political. Jacques Rancière seems to have proposed such an understanding of the political. According to Rancière, what we normally understand by "the political," as in the official public institutions of the ancient city-state, or the modern state, should rather be understood as "the police" instead: the regime that determines what is sensible to the community by distributing and assigning bodies to particular places.[29] In this logic, the community is distributed in parts that belong to different spaces: some to the public sphere, others to the private. The political, Rancière argues, occurs when the part that has no part, that is incommensurable with any of the already identifiable parts, takes the part of the whole as its part, and thus breaks with the idea that property (*arkhê*) is needed to participate.

To the extent that neither *metics* nor slaves, irrespective of their gender, nor "free" Athenian women could attend the assembly because they lacked the *arkhê* to do so, this most iconic political space should rather be understood as a policing space. But this was not the part that Rancière had in mind, when he defended democratic an-*arkhê* against birth and wealth (the two main policing forms of *arkhê* in Greek antiquity). Rancière, like many contemporary democratic theorists who turn to the ancients, fails to confront the ethnic/gendered logic of blood-based status, through which democracy also regulated membership in the *demos* (people). Thus, Rancière might have been able to translate the ancient part that has no part (the *demos* of Greek antiquity) into the modern proletariat—as the class that dissolves all classes—but it is unclear how such historical translation includes the differentiated racialized and gendered working class of modernity.[30] For that to happen, I contend in this book, one must confront racial/sexual capitalism, that is to say, the logic of social (de)valuation that causes the political integration of the settler to rest on the sexually differentiated expropriation of native land and exploitation of alien labor.[31] This triangulation is my own way of redefining the political in ways in which the racialized and gendered logic of value that members some through the dismemberment of those that the ongoing settler state "others," stays at the foreground of the analysis and at the center of the radical political claim for equality.

Creon, Antigone, and Polyneices, as the main characters of the political conflict that *Antigone* dramatizes, stand for the interrelated positionalities of the citizen, the *metic*, and the slave, as the positions through which political membership was hierarchically organized and relationally sustained in colonial antiquity. The full visibility and audibility of Creon, as carrier of sovereign speech, here contrasts with the partial visibility and audibility of Antigone, confined to the *oikos* on the basis of her gender. Both contrast with the full invisibility and complete silencing of Polyneices, mistreated after death in ways that, as Antigone's speech suggests, only slaves could have been treated.[32] Actually, this extension of *metoikia* and slavery to those previously immune to it, might very well be what makes this play politically relevant for citizens in the audience. Had Antigone truly been a *metic* and Polyneices truly been a slave, there might have been no *Antigone*.

The social legibility of the citizen body, which moves from aboveground in life to underground in death, here contrasts with the enslaved body, which moves from underground in life (intensively employed in the mines for the extraction of metals) to aboveground in death (exposed to the indignity of nonburial). The *metic* lies somewhere in between, and the equivocal placement of Antigone in a cave with enough food to survive, after she self-identifies as a *metic*, manifests the worse forms that such liminal inclusion can take. The selective inclusion of the *metic*, however, differs from the extreme desecration of the slave, of Polyneices's corpse, left to rot and be chewed by dogs and birds under the coerced gaze of citizens. Whether or not this was a historically accurate representation of the ways in which despised slave burials were desecrated in Greek antiquity is less important than the fact that Antigone considers that distinction to be of value. Equally important to me is the fact that it has played a rather minor role in the dominant political interpretations of this play.

The sensible distribution of visibility and invisibility through burial mimics the sensible distribution of audibility and inaudibility in speech. Creon delivers his speech standing aboveground, and his position is most radically contrasted by the silent body of Polyneices, exposed while dead when he should have been underground. Antigone delivers her speech from the ground, but her grounds are not stable enough for her to be "above" and she risks being displaced to the underground precisely when she renders that ground contingent, through the fierceness of her speech. As Kennedy argues,

"The metaphorical use of metic in *Antigone* gives us the first real hint that to be a metic is to be without secure status, rights, or even visibility."³³ Her public speech is only partially audible and almost immediately disqualified by the sovereign as "mad." Polyneices, altogether expelled from the acoustic realm through the extreme silencing of his claims that the desecration of his death performs, in death is further invisibilized through the hypervisible exposure of his dead body as a debased spectacle. Overground (citizen), not quite in the ground (*metic*), and unable to rest underground (slave): *Antigone* dramatizes the refusal of these bodies to occupy the locations assigned to them, and the contingency and instability of the grounds that is *the political*, when it is the coloniality of the *polis* that gets accentuated.

What interests me the most about this triangular relationship, however, is the relational structure, the one that explains why Antigone's need to revalue Polyneices into the human order of the citizen—she claims to have lost herself, through her own references to *metoikia*—can only take place via her devaluation of the slaves, for whom she would not have protested this injurious treatment. Based on Lindon Barrett's groundbreaking work, I make the disjunctive dynamic of racialized valuation—which members settler lives by devaluing native and alien lives—into the logic that supports and reproduces the hierarchical distribution of political membership in the contemporary theoretical reception of the play.³⁴ Thus, in this book I redefine the decolonial politics of the tragic as the confrontation between two modes of re-membering: one that members the lives it values through the settler colonial devaluation of those it "others," and one that values those devalued "others" by decolonially dismembering the subtending racialized logic of value.

The preposterous history of *Antigone* in the Americas that I offer does not work by establishing a simple correlation between terms, making the citizen, *metic*, and slave of antiquity equivalent to the ways in which those statuses are regulated in modernity. Nor, do I want to suggest that the colonial forms of domination that explain such stratification in antiquity, rather than the terms themselves, are equivalent to the relations of power by which colonial capitalism founds modernity. This is not what this book is trying to do, even when I continue to use citizen, *metic*, and slave in order to tell the story of abyssal political ground. My preposterous history seeks neither to force the colonial modernity of the Americas into the ancient tragedy of *Antigone*, nor to impose *Antigone* as a meta-framework by which to understand the history of the Americas. This book is trying to understand, complicate, and problematize why *Antigone* is in the Americas, and suggest how it can be otherwise. This is not unrelated to what a different interrogation of the play might help us to undo here, to unbury, where the very stability of the "here" is already what is at stake. After all, the very literature and politics from which I draw connect the naturalization of the Americas to the violent burying of *Abya Yala*.[35] To unearth that history is to confront the colonially interdicted memory, which forbids us to mourn the sixty million and more black people, and the sixty million and more indigenous people, who continue to lose their life to settler colonial capitalism violence.

Antigone in the Americas is thus structured via a double journey between the past and the present that in fact entails a multiplicity of travels. I thus move back and forth between the classical tragedy of Sophocles in the democratic order established by Pericles in ancient Athens, and contemporary adaptations/recreations and theoretical reception of *Antigone* in the Americas under the ongoing structure of settler-colonial capitalism. This movement in time, through time, also distorts time. What I am proposing is more a series of Nietzschean leaps than a Hegelian dialectics of history. I am not trying to offer the Americas as an alternative location for Minerva's owl, for another worldview retrospective that can reintegrate the previous moments of a universal spirit under a grammar that finally confronts the colonial violence of Eurocentric progress. More Nietzschean than Hegelian, I am trying to use history as nourishing food, to chew on the corpse of ancient Greek tragedy and, like the birds in the play, disperse its message to noncanonical places, thus intensifying the pestilence of a corrupt reading. The problematization of the Americas, then, comes first in this book. But the ancient *Antigone* that follows does not follow in any linear way. That is the sense of a double journey, of a preposterous history, of a different relationship between the past and the present that takes neither as stable and both as interactive. The very ancient *Antigone* that a certain problematization of the Americas helps to make readable anew also affects our understanding of the Americas, where *Antigone* metamorphoses and takes new shapes, pluralizing the literary journeys of the classical text in order to dig out what a certain reading of the political has improperly buried underneath.

From *Antigone* in the Americas to the Americas in *Antigone*

Martin Bernal's groundbreaking *Black Athena*, as its subtitle indicates, explores the Afro-Asiatic roots of classical civilization; or, in more specific terms, the Semitic and Egyptian origins of Greece in the Middle and Late Bronze Eras.[36] By genealogically tracing Greece back to its disavowed Afro-Asiatic origins, Bernal troubles the romanticized circumscription of Greece as the origin of Europe, geographically displacing the imaginary that sustains the study of classical civilization. The force of the Eurocentric circumscription that *Black Athena* troubles is quite noticeable in Hegel's *Phenomenology of the Spirit*, arguably the most theoretically influential interpretation of *Antigone*. Recalling Hegel's *Philosophy of History*, Baillie calls attention to Hegel's rewriting of history via Sophocles's tragedies, as if signifying the geopolitical transition of the spirit from the East to the West and from the South to the North, purging the classics of their Afro-Asiatic roots. From Egypt's inability to solve the riddle of the Sphinx to Oedipus's satisfactory solution in Sophocles's classical text, Hegel champions ancient tragedy as the founding of the "humanities" in the West. And, as Chanter proves, Hegel also proceeds, primarily through his reading of *Antigone*, to exclude slavery as an inappropriate topic for tragedy, passing that prohibition onto contemporary critical theory.[37]

Classical scholarship has thus troubled Eurocentrism in two interrelated ways: first, by no longer giving us a Greece purged of its Afro-Asiatic roots; second, by interrogating the complementary process that follows that erasure, one by which Egypt is then Hellenized.[38] The double gesture of such a critique, originated by *Black Athena*, has made it possible to interrogate the colonial roles of the classical tradition, as well as to explore the role of the classics in general, and ancient tragedies in particular, in the symbolic constitution of postcolonial worlds.[39] *Antigone in the Americas*, albeit inspired by this tradition, looks elsewhere, in the direction of the Americas in *Antigone*. I am neither a classicist nor interested in giving a yet more historically contextualized interpretation of the play that focuses on its otherwise disavowed Afro-Asiatic roots. Rather, I am interested in the ways in which the conquest of the Americas and the trans-Atlantic slave trade, as well as their disavowal, affect the theoretical interpretation of *Antigone*, inclusive of the Eurocentric circumscription of the classics.

This is a book about the political interpretation of *Antigone* in contemporary critical theory, not in Greek antiquity. It is also a book about how focusing on the disavowed conquest of the Americas and the trans-Atlantic slave trade affords us a vantage point of view by which to question the limits of the most dominant theoretical interpretations of the play. It is, finally, a way of reinventing *Antigone* for our settler colonial present, through the disavowed perspectives of *metics* and slaves. I thus follow one of decolonial theory's main theses, by foregrounding the coloniality of modernity, in claiming race as "the most effective and long-lasting instrument of universal social domination."[40] By emphasizing race as a political structure of social (de)valuation, I do not claim that race holds a more significant role in the distribution of political membership than gender does. Like many contemporary decolonial and critical race theorists, I regard race as an intersectional category, always informed and constructed by other differences that it helps, in turn, to construct as well.[41] Yet I am sympathetic to Chanter's main criticism of the reception of *Antigone* in contemporary critical theory: its inability to interrogate race.[42] I am, thus, as concerned with *Antigone* in the Americas—the reception, translation, adaptation, and rewriting of the play in the continent—as I am with the Americas in *Antigone*—how the colonial invention of the Americas affects our interpretation of the play by forcing us to foreground the racialized logic of social (de)valuation that regulates the distribution of political membership.

Antigone in the Americas by no means suggests that, from now on, there needs only be the Americas in *Antigone*. Ancient slaves, *metics,* and citizens were subjected to very different forms of state violence from those targeting modern slaves, *metics,* and citizens. There is a historical *Antigone* that is as unrelated to the Americas as it is to Europe. But the *Antigone* to which Europe traces a genealogic origin, and the one on which critical theory focuses in order to say something universal about the human condition, is not. This book offers one interpretation, of how the conquest of the Americas and the trans-Atlantic slave trade that founded colonial modernity, affects the political interpretation of *Antigone* and troubles what critical theory regards as Antigone's politics. This book, in short, is an answer to two interrelated questions: First, what would happen if one resituated the dissident mourning of Antigone under settler-colonial conditions that make the interdiction of native and alien burials into the condition of possibility for the humanization of the settler's dead? Second, how does such recontextualization of *Antigone* affect the political interpretation of the play in critical theory (democratic theory, feminist and queer theory, the theory of biopolitics, and the theory of deconstruction)?

To read the Americas in *Antigone* is, in short, to understand the role that racial/sexual capitalism plays in regulating who counts and who does not count for the settler *polis*. I thus move back and forth between the ancients and the moderns, between Sophocles's *metic* Antigone and the slave for whom she would not have protested the violence to which Polyneices's corpse was subjected, and the ways in which today's black and indigenous peoples in particular, are forced to occupy these positions in the Americas. This movement back and forth does not assume that these positions are eternal. These positions are historical and have themselves changed. Acknowledging those changes, their relationality persists, and it is the colonial aspect of that persistence that I want to offer as the main object of political critique.

From Classicization to Decolonial Rumination

Since *Antigone* is the most frequently performed ancient tragedy in contemporary theaters around the world, there is an obvious appeal in framing a current political problem in its script.[43] The literary status of the play offers contemporary adaptations the possibility to enlarge the scope of its audience and, perhaps strategically, to present the problems in which the audience is invested within a frame that makes the localized plight more universal, as Ariel Dorfman puts it.[44] However, the aesthetic claim to universality, to evoke James Porter's influential distinction between classicism and classicization, is empty if all that supports that claim is a mere effacing of the conditions of production of the original text, by which such text is ultimately rendered a "classic."[45] Against empty claims to the universality of classicism, Honig interprets Porter's classicization as an interpretative technique that, while focused on the present, "turns for understanding to ancient circumstances, scripts, or images for analogies that might illuminate our condition or even mirror our circumstances."[46] Building on this, Honig adds that such an interpretation should treat "the classical past as alien and resistant to appropriation" in order to become "more instructive than the sort that seeks and finds our stammering selves in the mirror."[47]

Refusing to efface the historical conditions of production of the original text, by which the political theorist recognizes the foreignness of the past, onto which such theorist tries to map the present, Honig remains sensitive to the deconstructive understanding of that interpretative mirroring as inescapably equivocal. According to this interpretive tradition, the very originality of the ancient text is troubled, as there is no access to the past that is not already mediated by a cumulative set of readings, commentaries, and interpretations. But these mediations not only make the past more or less alien, they also make it as *the* past to turn to, for a mirroring of "our" contemporary circumstances. In other words, there is always more than one past, as the past of the citizen is not the same as the past of the *metic*, or that of the slave.

The question of which texts to turn to, and how to turn to those texts—that is, by which set of mediations—problematizes *whose* past is rendered as alien and resistant to appropriation. It also problematizes whose selves are reflected in those mirrors. These are questions that both classicism and classicization, in my view, leave insufficiently answered, but that Marxist literary criticism has taken to task. That is the case, primarily, in Pierre Macherey's work, who speaks of literature—and by extension, classical literature—not as the ancient mirror in which we look for analogies to illuminate our present condition, but as the broken mirror that reflects the ideological contradictions that condition what can and cannot be said in the literary text.[48] As Macherey puts it in a remarkable passage that gives the interpretative key to Gayatri Spivak's way of subalternizing deconstruction and deconstructing the project of the subaltern studies:

> What is important in the work is what it does not say. This is not the same as the careless notation "what it refuses to say," although that would in itself be interesting: a method might be built on it, with the task of *measuring silence,* whether acknowledged or unacknowledged. But rather than this, what the work *cannot say* is important, because there the elaboration of the utterance is acted out, in a sort of journey to silence.[49]

The utterance in which Antigone reclaims *metoikia*—a social positionality silenced by the extensive interpretative archive devoted to this play—can only be acted out based on Antigone's devaluation of slaves, on whose behalf she would not have protested Creon's undignified treatment of the dead. In a way, the interpretative method of *Antigone in the Americas* could be summarized by the image of such a journey into silence, if only by emphasizing that such silence results not from that which is not said in the text, or refused to be said, but from that which cannot be said, even when it is explicitly enunciated. This book constitutes a journey into the silenced position of *metoikia* that Antigone claimed for herself and into the other silenced position of slavery, which she could not have claimed, as her reclamation of Polyneices into the order of the human rested on her devaluation of slaves. *Antigone in the Americas* is an effort to tell the story of that silence by confronting the ancient Greek drama of political membership with the modern/colonial racial drama that distributes political membership by separating settlers from natives and aliens today.

Honig's greatest methodological challenge, however, came from Rajeswari Sunder Rajan, who, against Honig, claimed the necessity of decentering Antigone as a model in order to "draw on other non-Western models of female agency who may also offer more empowering narratives and tactics."[50] Honig agrees with Rajan on the need for such a decentering, but also claims that it is important to pluralize Antigone in ways that escape the heroic isolation of her individual act and propose a yet unexplored version of collective action in the play, such as the one taking place in the sororal conspiracy between Ismene and Antigone that she so splendidly unpacks. There is, I argue, another way of pluralizing *Antigone* that responds more directly to Rajan's postcolonial challenge to classicization: a way of pluralizing *Antigone* that also decenters *Antigone* in order to draw on non-Western models of female agency.

Doing this requires us to move from classicization, as a temporal relation between the present and the past text, into textual nomadism, as an inseparable spatial relation that troubles the imagined geographies of that past and that present text. After all, *Antigone* has already traveled outside the West and her character already signifies non-Western models of female agency. *Antigone* is, in other words, irreducible to the Eurocentric origin to which classicism—and sometimes classicization, too—might want to confine her. Thus, Steiner pluralizes *Antigone* and publishes *Antigones* instead, in proper recognition of the plurality of texts by which the play is classicized. Yet Steiner's *Antigones* remains dominantly circumscribed to the Global North, making that pluralization liable to the decolonial critique of Rajan. Moira Fradinger's nomadic *Antigone*, by contrast, travels not only through the Global North but most significantly to the more extensive yet continuously invisibilized Global South, joining other studies (mentioned above) that focus on the reception of the classics in postcolonial contexts.[51]

Following the classical text into less proximate topographies to the geopolitical sites in which the canon is invested, Fradinger's pluralization of the text realizes the insufficiency of classicization as an interpretative strategy that looks for mirrors. The *Antigone* in the Global South faces not a mirror in Porter's sense, but a broken mirror, in Macherey's. In order to account for the colonial brokenness of that mirror, Fradinger expands on the Nietzschean idea of rumination and understands the decolonial pluralization of *Antigone* as a sort of double process of digestion of the classical text. According to this process, the decolonial interpreter first "ingests" the colonial frame in order to "regurgitate" it: that is, decolonially displace it from its temporal and spatial hegemonic sites of knowledge production, so as to fully digest it as no longer a Western imposition. Fradinger's decolonial definition of *rumination* is

> to turn over and over something that has already been "ingested" (and not properly digested) physically or mentally. The metaphor of cannibalization stresses the first moment of the violent encounter with that which is foreign and external to the body; that first bite, which tastes of rebellion (with regard to the European canon). This metaphor may no longer suffice to account for certain aspects of the rewriting of New World *Antigones*. Come to think of it, cannibalism is limited as an image in comparison to rumination.... The "ingested" *Antigone* is cannibalized as a foreign artifact, a colonial legacy, in the early nineteenth century. But, having ceased to be *external* to the Creole symbolic-digestive system, it returns from within the system to be re-created in the twentieth and twenty-first centuries.[52]

Neither classicism (with its empty claims to universality) nor classicization (a historically attentive way of mirroring the contemporary to the ancient), my reading operates through decolonial rumination: the constant turning over of *Antigone*'s frame, which reinvents her as irreducible to one topography, and politically finds the proper place of the classical text in the place of the improper. The preposterous history of *Antigone* in the Americas that I offer is, in short, the story of just such decolonial rumination on the play.

Making the past not only more alien and resistant to appropriation but also more literally alien—that is, more slave and *metic* than citizen—my decolonial rumination of *Antigone* seeks to trouble the most radical absence of speech that serves as the prior condition of all speech in colonial modernity: the logic of value that makes *metics* audible—even if always in the subordinated manner of unintelligible speech—by making slaves into the ultimate embodiments of mere noise, entirely inaudible. From democracy and citizenship, as the traditional locus of the political, my own way of politicizing *Antigone* moves to what figures perhaps as the most radical "other" side of the political, to *metoikia* and slavery, in order to rethink both the aesthetics of the political and the politics of the aesthetic from these positionalities.

Chapter Overview

In chapter 1, I discuss Rancière's radically innovative theory of democracy and show how his theory, despite its potential, remains unable to properly politicize the agency of slaves and *metics*, on whose disavowed histories the politicization of the *demos* relies. In the polyphony of the tragic genre and its capacity to imagine the agencies of those the *polis* disavowed, I see the paradoxical confrontation of another an-*arkhê*, one that goes against the statutory limits of the *demos* itself. Here I show how the politics of aesthetics, in the tragic text, might help us to trouble the aesthetic of the political, in the democratic one. In what I characterize as tragedy's misinterpellated anarchy, I see the possibility for the tragic genre to open up its political messages for the unintended positions of the *metic* and slave, and not just inform the dramas of the democratic citizen. I critique the perhaps unintentional reproduction of that republican assumption in democratic interpretations of *Antigone*, according to which tragedy's politics rest on its pedagogical function for civic training. I see Helen Foley and Bonnie Honig, in my view the two most interesting political interpreters of *Antigone* in contemporary democratic theory, as potentially collapsing the *demos* of antiquity into the majoritarian citizenry of the audience both of their theories sought to pluralize. By foregrounding the political confrontation between a democratic and an aristocratic ethos in the regulation of funerary practices as the political entry point to this tragedy, I claim that their democratic theories overlook other politically salient aspects of the tragedy. *Metics* and slaves could not negotiate both of these *ethos* in other public spaces, from which they were also excluded. I conclude that chapter by offering an alternative reading of Antigone as a *metic* rather than a citizen figure, yet one that in its own efforts to speak on behalf of the other nevertheless reinscribes the devaluation of slavery.

Chapter 2 performs various moves, as the subject-positionality in which I focus here is no longer the *metic*, as in chapter 1, but that of the slave. But it is modern slavery rather than ancient slavery that I explore during my critique of the reception of *Antigone* in contemporary U.S. feminist and queer theory. I show how U.S. feminist and queer theory draws from the real history of modern slavery to infuse their politics with a radical political message. Yet that message nonetheless obscures the social death that characterizes modern slavery, as the failure of these theories to foreground colonial racial valuation means that they are ultimately invested elsewhere. I do value, particularly in the case of Judith Butler's interpretation, the effort of queer theory to repoliticize the *oikos*, not only as a space but as the framework of social intelligibility through a critique of the equivocality of kinship positions. Yet I explain how the equivocality of kinship positions only works against the background of a more difficult to discern and politicize colonial equivocality of kinship's sociality. I thus criticize Judith Butler's, Joan Copjec's, and Lee Edelman's interpretations of *Antigone* for their failure to interrogate the forms of racial valuation that settler-colonial capitalism inaugurated in the United States. Based on black feminist theory, decolonial theory, and queer and trans of color critique, I thus contrast the celebrated death drive Antigone is called to represent when she occupies the space between two deaths with the social death of slavery. Such contrast allows me to explain the very different economies of violence to which "free" ancient Greek women and modern enslaved women are subjected, when they are differentially dispossessed from control over their own bodies. Not overlooking the colonial history of that differential subjection to death in life, I conclude, is crucial when it comes to understanding the radical politics of the black *quare* (to borrow from Patrick Johnson) and the indigenous two-spirit against settler-colonial heteronormativity, and beyond the otherwise universal heroization of the racially unmarked queer subject.

Although both enslaved Africans and indigenous peoples were subjected to slavery in the Americas, settler-colonialism explains why black people, as the original "aliens" of the Americas, were subjected to this form of violence longer, as it was their exclusion rather than their elimination that oriented the logic of the settler vis-à-vis the exploitation of their labor. Thus, in chapter 2, I focus primarily on the experiences of black people and the problematic gestures of feminist and queer theory to draw from those experiences without ever fully making them the focus of their otherwise radical interpretations. I raise that critique by drawing from black and trans feminist theory in particular, primarily from the work of Hortense Spillers, Saidiya Hartman, and C. Riley Snorton. In contrast, I turn in chapter 3 to the subject-positionality of the native and the contemporary forms of elimination by which their enslavement survives the official abolition of slavery in postcolonial Latin America.

I thus move, in chapter 3, to the second half of the twentieth century and hold the theory of biopolitics accountable for its failure to properly theorize the forms of racialization, to which this theory traces the genocidal violence of the modern state, to the settler-colonial logics of capitalist accumulation. Situating *Antigone* in neoliberal Latin America, which originates with the U.S. imperially supported military dictatorship of Augusto

Pinochet in Chile during the early 1970s, here I show the ways in which slavery, despite its formal abolition in Latin American postcolonial states, persists in the extreme forms of institutionalized violence to which the dissident actors of nominative democracies are subjected. Such is the violence of enforced disappearances, which I trace to the differential subjection of indigenous peoples to conditions of slavery, under a logic of accumulation interested in their elimination, and not only on their exclusion. Inspired by settler-colonial critique, in the logics of elimination and exclusion I seek a broader historical explanation to the widespread use of enforced disappearances, by which the state and the parastate apparatuses target the dissident agency of the people they mark as rebellious in different countries of Latin America.

I support my interpretation of *Antigone* in neoliberal Latin America, by reading the ancient text together with Jean Anouilh's *Antigone* and three Latin American *Antigones*, all of which focus on contesting the normalization of enforced disappearances as the signature of postmodern sovereignty: Ariel Dorfman's *Widows* (1981) in Chile, Sara Uribe's *Antígona González* (2012) in Mexico, and Patricia Nieto's *Los escogidos* (2012) in Colombia. Enforced disappearances are the vehicles by which the state both repeats the elimination of the subjects who most radically question the historical illegitimacy of the settler state and disavows that violence, since it officially recognizes them, at least nominally, as citizens or *metics* and can no longer legally subject them to a previously legally institutionalized eliminatory violence. Enforced disappearances are, in short, the horrifying solution by which various postcolonial Latin American states can both self-represent as democratic and continue to enforce the racialized structure of settler-colonial capitalism and its most lethal forms of necropower.

In chapter 4 I situate Antigone's mourning in a more difficult to comprehend historical-political context, that of the "racial Capitalocene."[53] What would it mean to mourn the millions that were lost as a consequence of the European conquest of indigenous territories and the trans-Atlantic trade of enslaved Africans, not as losses safely displaced in the past but as ongoing losses, active in the present? That these losses should continue to haunt us, makes *Antigone in the Americas* into a deconstructive device by which to trouble the "present" history of the Americas. In that sense, my book constitutes a deconstruction of the Americas, but I clarify the ways in which my decolonial deconstruction of the *Americas* both relates to but also differs from the hauntology that Jacques Derrida proposes in *Specters of Marx* (1994), as the science of deconstruction. Based on Ian Baucom's and Avery Gordon's work, I give to the power of specters to haunt us a more materialist foundation. Thus, I take spectral haunting into a more political than ethical destination, in contrast to Derrida's project. Following Barrett's insights, the politics of this tragic form of revolutionary remembrance makes the ethical re-membering of the settler-colonial lost "other" inseparable from the political dismembering of the capitalist law of racialized valuation. Exhuming the grave rather than digging it, decolonial mourning would no longer seek to value the citizenship into which Antigone would like Polyneices to be included by devaluing slaves. And militant mourning, in the differential form of black and indigenous mo'nin, becomes not an ethical but a political condition for the formation of a New International against the racial Capitalocene.

In the conclusion of this book, I revisit the citizen/*metic*/slave triad. Here, I demonstrate that to decolonially ruminate in this play is not to fix the meaning of *Antigone*'s text once and for all, but to open up a new interpretative possibility for the play that helps us to confront racial/sexual capitalism. My objective, in other words, is not only to reinvent the ancients for our times, but to voice the otherwise disavowed settler colonial past-present-future at work in the theoretical reception of *Antigone*. To reach the ancients through the path of the Americas is to make the ancients less ancient, less stable as classical texts, and "our times" less familiarly "ours." Defamiliarizing the Americas in such way, I offer a different interpretation of Antigone's puzzling name, and a new solution to the riddle of the Sphinx.

Antigone in the Americas is thus a critical intervention in democratic theory (chapter 1), feminist and queer theory (chapter 2), the theory of biopolitics (chapter 3), and deconstruction theory (chapter 4). *Antigone in the Americas* is also an intervention on the study of ancient political theory as inevitably affected by the concerns of contemporary political theory, since there is no original text—and no return to the Greek text—that is not, as Chanter says, "somehow outside the political genealogy of its multiple translators." The otherwise deceptively simple division of this book between antiquity (chapter 1), modernity (chapter 2), postmodernity (chapter 3) and a "present," that extends all the way from the long sixteenth century onward (chapter 4), seeks not to offer another metanarrative of history. Rather, my preposterous historical leaps seek to emphasize the rupture that the conquest of the Americas and the trans-Atlantic slave trade signified for our mediation of that genealogical history of translations. *Antigone in the Americas* is, finally, an epistemic and political intervention in the subversive and emancipatory potential of critical theory if it is more properly understood as critical race theory.[54] To further develop those potentials, as I conclude this introduction, implies not only reading canonical texts such as Sophocles's *Antigone* under misinterpellated lenses, as Martel suggests, but also to decolonially ruminate on the tradition that has canonized those texts in order to amplify its yet unattended-to subversive messages.

1

Antigone in Colonial Antiquity

A Critique of Democratic Theory in Ancient Athens

> I am a [*metic*]! O dear brother, doomed in your marriage—your marriage murders mine,
> Your dying drags me down to death alive!
>
> —A, 850–53 [103/194]; translation modified[1]

> It was his brother, not his slave, that died.
>
> —A, 517 [181]

The Democratic Disavowal of Slavery and *Metoikia*

From *Proletarian Nights* (1981) to *The Politics of Aesthetics* (2004) and from *Disagreement* (1999) to the *Hatred of Democracy* (2013), Jacques Rancière has become a—if not the—canonical author of the aesthetic turn of the political.[2] He has also emerged as the most innovative advocate of radical democracy beyond the historical debates between liberals and republicans, deliberative and agonistic theorists of democracy.[3] Critically echoing Walter Benjamin's thesis on the relationship between politics and aesthetics, Rancière writes that "there never has been any 'aestheticization' of politics in the modern age because politics is aesthetic in principle."[4] *Aesthetic* here refers to a certain redistribution of the sensible (*partage du sensible*), a shifting of bodies from the place that a policing order assigns to them. Politics here refers to the conflictual occupation of the unassigned place, by which such bodies interrupt the governing logic of that assignment, making "visible what had no business in being seen, and mak[ing] heard a discourse where once there was only place for noise."[5] The embodied disruption of this ordering of specific bodies to specific places, which throws the order back to its irreducible contingency, Rancière then links to democracy. Thus, Rancière redefines democracy neither as a procedure nor as a regime or social way of life but as "the institution of politics itself."[6]

Like other contemporary political theorists, Rancière's concept of the political rests on his interpretation of democracy in Greek antiquity. According to him, unlike the aristocratic and oligarchic political regimes, which distributed power on the basis of stable property (*arkhê*)—the noble birth of the *aristoi* (nobles) and the wealth of the *oligoi* (rich)—democracy could not be considered a proper regime of power. That is the case because, as the government of the poor, the stable property of the *demos* was actually a nonproperty: freedom (*eleutheria*). Freedom is a nonproperty because it belongs to the community as a whole and not just to one of its parts. But precisely because the only part that the *demos* could take, in the event of their rule, was that of the whole—the freedom that belonged indistinctively to all parts—the rule of the *demos* was equivalent to a break with the very idea that having properties was necessary to rule.[7] Hence the identity that Rancière establishes between democracy and *an-arkhê*.

Antidemocratic regimes of power, such as oligarchy, aristocracy, and tyranny, wrong (*blaberon*) the community by miscounting the "parts" in which these regimes distribute it. This is another name for what we now call structural inequality, which all regimes of power (aristocratic, oligarchic, or tyrannical) enact when they deny, through their way of counting parts, that one part had no part and was supplementary to the count. But the implication of the equality of all in democratic freedom was only historically valid in the case of the Athenian *demos,* and against the background of a more radical form of inequality that remained prepolitically displaced. Thus, Rancière first echoes the establishment of freedom in Athens as the positive property of the people through the institution of *seisachtheia* (literally "the shaking of the burdens"). *Seisachtheia* historically refers to forbidding the enslavement of poor people who could not pay their debts—which was finally institutionalized through Solon's reforms. But Rancière does that only to distinguish Athenian democratic freedom from another form of slavery that remains impervious to political translation: that of the Scythian slaves' revolt, as told by Herodotus.

In other words, *eleutheria,* that is to say, political freedom, distinguishes the government of the *demos* from that of the *oligoi* and the *aristoi.* Foundational to that distinction, however, is the expulsion altogether from equal membership in the *demos,* of another form of slavery that Rancière considers incapable of transforming equality in war into political freedom. Scythian slaves (*doulos*), according to Herodotus, were brutally blinded by their masters at birth, in order to better restrict them. A whole generation of Scythian slaves, however, could for the first time see, because their masters were unexpectedly delayed in Asia while seeking to colonize it. They decided to declare their equality with their masters on the basis of bearing the same corporeal attributes. Knowing that their masters would try to enslave them again, upon the masters' return, the slaves armed themselves and successfully held their ground. Things changed, as Herodotus reports, when one of the masters came up with the plan of facing them not with arms—weapons that implied some recognition of equality—but with the whip, successfully bringing the slaves to heel without a fight.[8] The whip is thus endowed with powers far greater than those ever granted to the commodity-form in modernity, as not even its use nor even its appearance (as this was the first generation of slaves who could actually see the whip), but its mere rhetorical evocation seems to have provoked the genuflecting effect of submission.

The egalitarian demonstration of the Scythian slaves fails to reach the status of a political interruption, says Rancière, because "when the [masters] once more show the signs of their difference in nature, the rebels have no comeback."[9] Beyond the obvious inconsistencies of Herodotus's story and their repetition in Rancière's uncritical acceptance of it, what I want to highlight is that the foundational *blaberon* the Athenian *demos* fought rested not only in the interruption of the policing *arkhê,* but also in the prepolitical displacement of another wrong—the one experienced by the Scythian slaves—to the politically neutralized site of "natural" differences, for which no political translation was possible. The sign-deprived experience of the *doulos,* conspicuously requiring a supplemental ethnic difference—a geopolitical move from Athens to Scythia—reveals civil war and colonialism as the politically enabling sites for the coherence of the commons inside the civic order of the Athenian *polis.*

In other words, through the paradoxical status of freedom as the improper property of the *demos,* democracy undoes the existence of a proper count on the basis of this *an-arkhê.* But in doing so, democracy also becomes the one count of the community in which the *demos* are no longer a supplement. Contrary to what Rancière argues, this undoing of property did not extend into counting the uncounted. Slaves, *metics,* and

Athenian women counted neither in aristocracy nor in oligarchy nor in democracy, and in all of these cases they constituted the majority. They were all relegated by all regimes, and by the nonregime that is democracy, into a depoliticized space, notwithstanding the material dependency of all these political formations on their coerced productive and reproductive labor.[10]

I am by no means the first to critique Rancière's radical theory of democracy on the basis of a rereading of ancient tragedy that focuses on democracy's own way of regulating political membership. In an excellent book on the figure of the *metic,* Demetra Kasimis critiques Rancière's interpretation of Plato, which Rancière has turned into the archetypical antipolitical philosopher of the police order, for failing to address democracy's constitutive exclusions. According to Kasimis's compelling reading, Plato's *Republic* was a historical-political meditation on the limits of Athenian democracy, rather than the thought-experiment of an aristocratic and antidemocratic philosopher.[11] Kasimis thus shows the political significance of Plato's decision to set the *Republic* in the house of a rich *metic,* Cephalus, in the Athenian harbor of Piraeus, reframing the whole dialogue as a historically situated critique of ancient democracy. She also calls our attention to the rhetorical aspects of Plato's text and reinterprets his most unredeemable "noble lie" as, in fact, his best guarded "open secret," a dramatic strategy by which he rendered democracy's own noble lie of blood-based membership open to dialectic critique. Even Plato's critical view of *mimesis* in Book VIII of the *Republic,* whereby he shows the difference between copies and originals to be "potentially unrecognizable," Kasimis reconsiders as democratically instructive, as Plato's view in fact challenged "the autochthonous premise that Athenianness is self-evident and autochthony always successful."[12] Criticizing ancient democracy's attempt to ground Athenian exceptionalism "on a fictional foundation in nature," via its recourse to blood-based membership, Kasimis also turns to tragedy.[13] Her problematization of democratic theory's overlooking of secrecy in the politics of Euripides's *Ion,* as well as her analysis of Euxitheus's trial, shows the failure of blood to secure citizenship and thus to restrict the popular composition of the *demos.* The regulation of blood, on which ancient Athenian democracy—and most, perhaps all, modern democracies, too— relied for the distribution of political membership, she convincingly argues, constantly fails "to accomplish what it is tasked to do."[14] Such failure, she adds, often turns into an intensification of class and ethnic policing, as in the case of Euxitheus, but also of gender. Because *metic* women had been able to reproduce citizens, which they did prior to Pericles's

451/450 Citizenship Law, and then again when exceptions to the law were introduced (430 and 403BCE), their sexuality became the object of greater policing scrutiny.

From Kasimis we get a fresh and timely political theorization of the tragic effort of democracy to secure citizenship as a status predetermined by blood, while tragedy helps us to see that the lines between citizens and aliens are "impossible to settle once and for all," and thus reveals "their adaptability for alteration, manipulation, and strategic adaptation."[15] But Kasimis focuses on the liminal position of the *metic*, in great part moved by a desire to overcome "the oppositional frames that govern the study of membership in Athenian thought and politics"—such as free/slave and male/female.[16] Given that Athens classified both resident aliens and manumitted slaves as *metics*, I think it is necessary to explore the political meanings of the citizen/*metic* relation together with, rather than in lieu of, the *metic*/slave one, as Kasimis does. Thus, rather than taking the *metic* as the "critical figure of our time," as Kasimis argues, in this book I argue that it is the tripartite relationship that links the valuation of the citizen to the differential (de)valuation of the *metic* and the slave, that should become our analytical tool instead.[17]

Metic and slave agency haunt the political imaginary of democracy.[18] Their agencies trouble the stability of policing regimes (aristocracy and oligarchy) seeking to distribute bodies according to their properties but also, and more radically, the instability of the nonregime of the *demos*, from which they are also excluded. Tragedy, however, is one of those textual spaces in which those agencies continues to emerge, even if not necessarily shown through a heroic lens. Here, I find Rancière's theorization of the literary animal to be useful, as it helps us to contest the blood-based restrictions constitutive of the Aristotelian *zoon politikon* (political animal).

According to Rancière, where the Aristotelian political animal (citizen) polices the boundary between intelligible and unintelligible speech, the literary animal undoes that boundary through the production of a common *aesthesis* between political and depoliticized animals.[19] Not only citizens but also foreigners, *metics*, slaves, and Athenian women speak in tragedies, addressing the public and, via the artificial mediation of the Festival literature, make it possible for their *phôné* (voice) to travel into *logos* (speech). This is what Rancière refers to as the mutual implication of politics and aesthetics in the redistribution of the sensible. But this redistribution, this "making what was unseen visible" and "what was audible as mere noise heard as speech," concludes not with democracy but with the theatrical performance of imagined agencies taking the democratic challenge to the *arkhê* beyond the limits of the *demos* itself. It takes place, one could argue, when the meta-supplementary part of those who could not even be considered as the "no part," produce the political partition of three, rather than two, worlds in one. The most fully depoliticized contest, not just the world that seeks to naturalize inequality (the world of the *oligoi* and the *aristoi*) but also the world of the *demos*, which naturalizes inequality by attributing to its political organization the already realized world of equality—both of these worlds stand in differential contradiction to the radical world of equality enacted through the subversive agency of slaves, *metics*, and Athenian women, whose agency challenges the silent qualifications of gender and ethnic differences that inform blood-based democratic membership in Greek antiquity. That agency, which was prohibited in the *agora*, was given a different public space—not quite the public Festival of Dionysia, but the unintended political destinations of tragedy's errant literarity.[20]

Tragedy's Misinterpellated Anarchy

Edith Hall argues that "taken as a whole, tragedy [legitimized] the value-system necessary to the glorification of Athens and the subordination of the slaves, Athenian women, and other noncitizens who constituted the majority of her inhabitants"; at the same time, she claims that tragedy also "[challenged] the very notions which it simultaneously [legitimized]" by imagining the powerful agency it sought to disavow.[21] The tragic template's propensity to mimetic inversion and transgressive repetition is a result of what Hall calls tragedy's "relentless polyphony," an irresolvable coalescence of different voices and linguistic registers. Tragedy offered a dramatic space of public visibility to enact the otherwise invisible agency of foreigners, *metics*, Athenian women, and slaves.[22] In doing so, it provided a political script for the otherwise voiceless agency of those lacking speaking rights in the city, to transform their disavowed *phôné* into legitimate *logos*.

Furthermore, foreigners, *metics*, and (according to some interpretations) elite Athenian women and, at least, the eight slaves who accompanied the members of the Council were allowed to attend the Festival of Dionysia. I do not want to romanticize their presence in the Festival, as their attendance remained obviously policed and severely subordinated—particularly in the case of slaves, who were not there to enjoy the play but to provide coerced labor for their masters. Potentially responsive to the tragedy's calls that were not meant for them, as Martel argues, they could cause "politically radical forms of subversion."²³ And even if, as Goldhill has shown, citizens outnumbered them—justifying his warnings about the proto-nationalist aspects of ancient drama—tragedy rested in the very possibility of this common *aesthesis,* which was fully denied in other civic spaces.²⁴ Likewise, Hall, for whom tragedy was an ideological laboratory to reproduce and perpetuate the xenophobic, patriarchal, and imperialistic character of Athenian democracy, recognizes that the tragic genre represented a wide variety of ethnicities. Finally, tragedy also negotiated and frequently suspended the boundaries between the "Greek" and the "barbarian" through a fantastic inversion of gender and ethnic hierarchies.²⁵

If tragedy, as Hannah Arendt suggests, is the genre that best captures the spirit of revolution, as it establishes the cognitive conditions of its remembrance, I believe tragedy to be revolutionary in yet another sense.²⁶ In my view, and despite tragedy's most obvious reactionary proto-nationalist, xenophobic, patriarchal, and imperialist interpellations, its relentless polyphony makes room for the misinterpellated imagination of these other more insurgent agencies. This is done not by showing minor characters such as *metics,* slaves, and Athenian women to be secretly great, but by rendering contingent, revisable, and transformable the conditions of their exclusion.

This understanding of tragedy was not foreign to Rancière, who celebrates in the theater precisely this capacity to move into the *polis* that which the social order otherwise relegated to the domestic space of the *oikos*. Rancière's commitment to the *demos,* however, continues to substantiate political subjectivity in the workers' representation of their productive activity to themselves on the stage.²⁷ Rancière thus fails to translate the political into the social question beyond class, most notably through the other co-constitutive differences of gender and ethnicity in his own interpretation of Greek antiquity.

Only once, to the best of my knowledge, does Rancière refer to *Antigone*. He does it during his critique of the ethical turn, where he praises a political Oedipus against an ethical Antigone, for whom the *atè* (misfortune) becomes not a historically transformable trauma in political dissidence, but an inescapable curse.²⁸ Rancière thus fails to interrogate Antigone's politics—or, more accurately, the policing that dismisses Antigone's speech as nonpolitical. And if politics is, as Rancière suggests, a conflict between two speeches that disagree on the correspondence between the names that they use and the populations that they name, Rancière overlooks how Antigone's names defy the social positions assigned to the different characters in the play. He misses the fact that her naming, just as much as the names by which she is named, troubles any simple correspondence between names and populations. These are not only, as feminist theory has shown, the names of Athenian women, but also (and more difficult to discern) the names of the *metic,* which she claims for herself, and that of the slave, which she disclaims for Polyneices.

Toward a Political *Antigone*

A political rather than an ethical interpretation of the play consolidated during the debate that *Antigone* motivated between Christiane Sourvinou-Inwood on the one hand and Larry Bennett and Blake Tyrrell on the other.[29] Both interpretations were influenced by the French school of structuralism in classics, which reinterpreted Attic tragedies as the cultural device by which Athenians negotiated the tension between the old religious values of Homeric aristocracy and the new political institutions introduced by Pericles's democracy.[30] Thus, they both interpreted the mythical history of Laius and Jocasta's family as the literary mediation of Sophocles's historical *polis.*

Helene Foley analyzed this debate in her influential essay "Tragedy and Democratic Ideology: The Case of Sophocles' *Antigone*," originally given as a lecture at the 1992 conference "History, Tragedy, Theory."[31] The play orbits around the interdiction of burial, and both historical interpretations, according to Foley, emphasize ancient Attic funerary practices—from Solon's sixth-century prohibition of women's excessive lamentation in funerals onward—as the proper hermeneutic context for discerning the political orientations of the main characters. Following such historical contextualization of the politics of burial, Sourvinou-Inwood claims that the fifth-century BCE democratic audience would have seen Antigone as a "bad woman" (representative of an aristocratic ethos) and Creon as representative of the (democratic) values of their own *polis.* Bennett and Tyrrell arrive at the completely opposite conclusion. For them, Antigone is a champion of democratic ideology in Greek antiquity, further confirmed by her praise of a hospitable Theseus in *Oedipus at Colonus.* Neither position, however, ever questions the assumptions governing the fantasy of their own capacity to transport themselves transparently to the fifth-century BCE audience of the play. As a consequence, Foley justly critiques Sourvinou-Inwood for treating the audience as an undifferentiated collectivity with a unified cultural ideology. Relatedly, she criticizes Bennett and Tyrrell for basing their reading on the authorial intention of Sophocles, despite the inability of any author "to control his or her text."[32]

Foley's critique richly illustrates how selective both readings are by showing how each brackets the passages that conflict with their reductive "bad versus good" versions of the play, in which characters are singled out as exclusively for either Homeric aristocracy or Periclean democracy. I have no objections to her criticism of these texts. What I want to do here, however, is to further problematize Foley's most deconstructive conclusion: that tragic characters cannot be analyzed from the "clearly defined, logically consistent and easily assimilable viewpoint" that only results from dismissing "those elements in the text that apparently create a complex dialectic between points of view or even within one position in the play."[33] This argument helps Foley deliver her own conception of ancient tragedy as the "dramatic narrative" that "requires its audience (each different member of it) not to uncover a message, nor to leave the theater in a state of helpless *aporia* (inability to make a judgment), but to negotiate among points of view just as it would in a court of law or an assembly."[34]

This statement represents Foley's deconstructive reading at its best while also revealing its political limitations. It shows that Foley recognizes that the audience contains a plurality of perspectives; tragic texts, like all texts, are ambiguous and unstable, and tragedy "is a complex dialogue that evolves in space and time."[35] But then Foley proceeds to reproduce at another level the homogeneity she wanted so much to contest. By putting the tragedy in parallel with the democratic assembly, thus solving the helpless *aporia* with a negotiation in which the audience would engage "as it would in a court of law or an assembly," Foley restricts tragedy's addressee. She reintroduces homogeneity into the very audience she was trying to pluralize. By turning the tragedy into a mirror of the assembly, she overlooks the presence in the audience of many subject-positions that could not have participated in the assembly. Slaves, *metics,* and Athenian women had access to the play's plot and its messages, without its problems ever resulting in a chance for them to negotiate viewpoints in the assembly.

Such is the critique raised by Nicole Loraux, who questions transforming the theater into a "double of the assembly (*ekklesia*)," because it overlooks the significant presence of foreigners, *metics,* and Athenian women, who were never forgotten by Attic orators.[36] As Bonnie Honig has shown, Loraux goes on to claim a very suspicious universality based on separating the partisan text from the presumably universal status of the song through which Attic orators reached beyond the *demos*.[37] I agree with Honig's critique. Loraux's claim, that such phonetic displacement is not political, does not follow from her argument, given that different social positions are already articulated in the text and not merely displaced into the presumably all-inclusive and nonrepresentational mode of the song. Yet something of Loraux's claim is nonetheless lost in Honig's own politicization of Antigone, as the politics of *Antigone* get subsumed in the contrast between two ideological ethos that are also inaccessible to slaves and *metics* in particular—if perhaps still operative for Athenian women, who had political responsibilities as vehicles in the transmission of citizenship and caregivers for the dead.

In Honig's earlier accounts of the play, she argues that Antigone substantiated aristocracy through excessive lamentation and the emphasis on the singularity of Polyneices, while Creon metonymized democracy through an economy of exchange and the emphasis on replaceability.[38] This perspective falls prey to Foley's critical charge of providing versions of the characters that are too clearly defined and logically consistent. Honig revised both essays in her excellent book *Antigone, Interrupted* (2013), where she gives a more complex picture. Sensitive to the evolution of the characters in space and time, Honig reads Antigone and Creon as constituting two different elitist ways of accommodating democracy and aristocracy at different instances in the play. In her view, however, only Antigone is finally able to "traverse the interval" as she moves from the presumably universal claim that "the god of death demands burial for all" to the opposite one of exclusive singularity, in which "she will only do it for her brother."[39]

Like Foley, Honig also considers that *Antigone*'s relevance for contemporary democratic theory rests, paradoxically, in understanding the character's antidemocratic commitments to an aristocratic form of lamentation that democracy was seeking to replace through the articulation of a different ethos in relation to funerary practices in ancient Athens. Beyond Foley, however, she also explores a different and more difficult to discern form of collective action in *Antigone*, in the form of a sororal conspiracy. As Honig persuasively claims, against practically all interpretations, it was Ismene, Antigone's sister, who first buried Polyneices at night, as Ismene claims at one point in the play.[40] Admittedly, the relative secrecy of Ismene's nocturnal burial is perhaps not as subversive as the public one Antigone performs in broad daylight, but Ismene's public reclamation of her deed is deeply subversive, as is the sororal agonism that ensues. "From the perspective of sororal agonism," Honig argues, "Antigone's accusations against Ismene operate as a double entendre that is nothing short of brilliant."[41] It is brilliant because, in her public accusation of her sister and Ismene's understanding of her *sotto voce* message, Antigone succeeds not only in protecting and ultimately saving Ismene from the death-grip of Creon's sovereign right to kill (Ismene is the only character who remains alive, as even Creon regards himself as dead), but also opens the play up for a more collective and political interpretation.[42]

In producing the two most influential political interpretations of *Antigone*, Honig and Foley were trying not to delimit the clearly defined and logically consistent positions of each character in the play as either aristocratic (bad) or democratic (good), but to explore the role of democratic debate in tragedy by attending to the ambiguity of its messages and the instability and the slipperiness of the tragic form. Both were looking for democratic ideology in *Antigone*, rather than in Antigone. Both accentuated the inescapable negotiation among different points of view with which the spectators are confronted in the theater, rather than the deliverance of the solution by the strong vindication or vilification of the tragic heroine.

What in my view neither Honig nor Foley does is to question their own erasures of a more contentious plurality in the audience, when the interpretation slips from the representational space of the theater to that of the political, and the supplement of institutional places is invoked in order to resolve the helpless *aporia* introduced by the literary animal of tragedy's more anarchic destination. Athenian women, *metics,* and slaves, none of whom were allowed to negotiate points of view in the assembly, as Foley argues, were nonetheless spectators of the tragedy, as Loraux claims. And although Foley's and Honig's political interpretations of *Antigone* open up the play for Athenian women, the openness their readings perform reinscribes the depoliticization of *metics* and slaves, restricting the pluralization they intended.

What if, then, one were to take Foley's insight on the slippage between theater and politics in a different sense, in order to address democracy as it might have informed those who were neither allowed in the courts of law nor in the assembly, yet were present at the Festival? What is the political message of this tragedy for those who did not attend it in order to receive proper pedagogical training in civic action? Were democratic ideology and the regulation of funerary practices what those who could not attend the Festival but probably heard the story understood to be the politics of this play? Did Antigone's reclamation of *metoikia* to qualify her condition affect *metics* in different ways than the citizens in the audience? Did the same happen with her references to slavery, for those slaves sitting in the audience, or hearing about the play when their masters returned from the Festival and talked about it in the *oikos* to which they were confined?

We cannot know how they perceived democracy through the lenses of this play because we cannot even know—as Foley rightly claims, vis-à-vis Sourvinou-Inwood's and Bennett and Tyrrell's interpretations—how democratic citizens themselves perceived it. Who knows if slaves and *metics* were indifferent to the political messages of tragedy in general and this tragedy in particular? Who knows whether, as I think Loraux wrongly assumes, most of them only enjoyed the beauty of the song and paid no attention to the semantic content of the plays and their distinctive political vocabulary? Who knows how some of them might have heard a song they were forbidden to hear? Who knows if they listened from a distant place to disguise their transgression or heard the song recited in the untrained voices of some of their masters? Who knows whether or not *metic* and enslaved women found tragedies that moved citizens to tears ideologically ridiculous, more comic than tragic, as men pretended to act like women and claimed to suffer the injuries to which they themselves were constantly subjected? Who knows what kinds of prejudices, histories, and legends from their cities of origin mediated their receptions of *Antigone*?

It is this much larger plurality of the unintended audience, of the misinterpellated subject of tragedy's anarchic message, that interests me. I do not want to suggest that either Foley or Honig is not interested in this audience; they are. I could not have performed my reading without their insights, primarily their excellent use of deconstruction's analytical tools to pluralize the text. Yet neither sufficiently explores how reaching toward those unintended audiences problematizes the politics of *Antigone*, and its implications for democratic theory.

To clarify this point about misinterpellated audiences, let us turn to the opening scene of *Antigone*. In the prologue, we learn of the mutual fratricide between Eteocles and Polyneices and Creon's prohibition of Polyneices's burial. Antigone tells all of this to Ismene in secrecy, in a place where they are not allowed to be without a male guardian. Democratic speech arrives at the audience that it excludes from its scope, banned as Antigone and Ismene are from the public domain. It circulates rapidly through a multiplicity of voices that are not always accorded proper political status within the city but whose participation, as reproducers of that very same speech, it cannot curtail. There is, in democracy, a profound tension between the unrestrictive potential of the speech that it solicits—its polyphonic *an-arkhê*, its literarity—and the positional restriction of legitimate speakers to perform it.

In the tragedy, Sophocles tells us, Antigone is the first to pronounce Creon's speech. The authorial source is reversed because the literarity of the play confounds it within the errancy of speech itself. The force of the speech depends on its repetition, on the iterability of the *kerugma* (edict), but the power of this particular iteration threatens, in return, the predemocratic enclosure of speech and its presumed authorial origin in both proper subject-positions and properly institutionalized spaces. In other words, while the life-source of democracy is the free mobility of speech throughout the city, this mobility threatens the boundaries of the *demos* it also legitimizes and seeks to secure. Linking the tragic genre to democratic ideology, we might conceive of this phonetic errancy in democracy as the dramatization of tragedy's political slippage, in which the unintended participation of noncitizens as "equal" spectators of the play problematizes the rational foundation of their exclusion from the political sphere. In other words, tragic signs of politics do not end in the assembly but are radicalized in the troubling of the *agora*'s limits, through the literary imagination of the unaccounted agencies of those on whose differential productive and reproductive labor democracy materially depended. The unrealized potential of equal spectatorship at the Festival dissents with the continuing exclusion of the majority from democratic institutions that were supposed to enact equality. In short, the politics of aesthetics of the tragic genre troubles the aesthetics of politics of the democratic *polis,* with the unrealized potential of its radical claim to equality.

It is this other, more subversive function of tragedy as a public literary mode of address, in what was otherwise a deeply conservative aesthetic form in Greek antiquity, that interests me. The theatricality of tragedy amplifies and pluralizes this confusion between proper and improper subjects. Drama emerges precisely because of the impossibility of ever closing such a gap, notwithstanding the fact that ancient theater was far from sustaining something that could resemble equality. As the improper speaker who nevertheless speaks first, Antigone reveals the fabricated nature of the boundary that limits the *demos* to the field of "proper" speakers. Speaking from a subordinated position despite being a member of the royal family, Antigone also metonymizes—as a *metic* princess, as I will argue shortly— the irreducible slippage of speech back into its improper sites, beyond the courts and the assembly, to make yet unattended subversive agencies visible.

Seen from one of these disavowed subject-positions, is it possible that *Antigone* carries yet another politically unaddressed message? Making her political legacies irreducible to the democratic versus aristocratic ideological dispute, could this character represent a prior political contestation over the membership in the political itself, one that already represents this ideological dispute as a way of displacing a more troubling political schism at the heart of the *polis*? Is it possible that rather than politicizing two ethos, *Antigone* confronts, against itself, the politicization of two *demos*? Is there room for a *metic* Antigone, as she claims that identity for herself in the play?

What If Antigone Was a *Metic*?

The earliest definition of *metoikia*, given by Aristophanes of Byzantium, defines a *metic* as "anyone who comes from a foreign (city) and lives in the city, paying tax toward certain fixed needs of the city. For so many days he is called a *parepidemos* (sojourner) and is free from tax, but if he outstays the specified time he becomes a *metoikos* and is liable to tax."[43] As Whitehead documents, *metics* were not only immigrants subjected to a special mode of taxation (the *metoikion* tax), without rights of political participation or ability to own land, but also freed slaves, who did not become citizens after their liberation. If liberated slaves (*apeleutheros*) decided to remain in the same city of their ex-masters, they were "placed in the category of the *metics* or resident foreigners."[44]

Resident foreigner is a good translation of *metic*, which should perhaps be more literally translated as "home-changer" and has also been translated as "resident alien." Benjamin Jowett's choice to translate *metoikos* as "resident alien" in the lexical translation of Aristotle, under the editorship of W. D. Ross for Oxford University Press in 1941, "bears interesting traces of modern, twentieth-century configurations of Anglo-American immigration policy."[45] Rightly criticized by Avelar for the historical erasures that such mistranslation produces, one could also reappropriate it in order to facilitate a misinterpellated and probably more subversive interpretation of the play, as if referring to the public agency of noncitizens instead. After all, not only are contemporary unauthorized immigrants in the United States, for instance, associated constantly with national security threats, their corpses are exposed more often than others' to state violence. As I claimed in the introduction, unauthorized immigrants in the U.S. also suffer both types of exclusion experienced by noncitizens in Athens: political exclusion, which deprives them of legitimate speech in the city, and representative exclusion, which obliges others to speak on their behalf (as with the representation of Antigone's character by a male actor in the ancient theater).[46]

My point is not that Benjamin Jowett's translation is correct, nor that when we talk about resident aliens today and *metics* in ancient Athens we are talking about the same figure. My point is that such translation opens up an interesting and potentially productive misreading of the play, a misreading that allows us to read something else that has not been sufficiently explored, a stratified system of political membership insufficiently interrogated by contemporary democratic theorists invested in this play. By connecting the problems of participation and representation that resident aliens face in today's democracies with the problems that *metics* faced in Greek antiquity, I am not saying that these problems are the same but that their connection allows us to confront politics in a prior scene, on a more foundational level, about who counts and who is unaccounted for in the *polis*. This prior scene, I further contend, contemporary democratic theorists (with some exceptions) have failed to properly theorize.

Antigone claims to be a *metic* when she can no longer find a home in common either with the living or with the dead (A, 853 [194]). She claims to be a *metic* when she inhabits the liminal condition of living death that characterizes those today who are actively disqualified from citizenship on the basis of their racial and gender subordination. As Jutta Gsoels-Lorensen argues, Antigone's use of the term *metoikos* cannot be taken as a "rhetorical flourish" and should be understood as "consciously calling upon a vocabulary of hierarchically stratified membership in the polis to help frame her situation."[47] Making a similar connection to the one for which I argue in this book, Gsoels-Lorensen focuses on the cave that Creon builds for Antigone as the iconic non-place that corresponds today to the detention centers in which undocumented immigrants are endlessly confined while undergoing forcible removal. Such a liminal condition refers neither to being parts of the city, nor to being the part that has no part. And yet this unaccounted part also publicly demonstrates that it participates in a common *aesthesis* when it attends the theater. Occupying the equal position of spectatorship, this part understands that Antigone substantiates neither aristocracy nor democracy, but the prepolitical exclusion that still delimits the *demos* against the background of a more radical commitment to its operative *an-arkhê*.

The Temporal and Spatial Unfolding of Antigone's Character

Antigone's *metoikia* is allegorical, but her recourse to that vocabulary in the play, to frame her situation, is understandable if we read the play together with Sophocles's other two plays on the Theban family. The paratextual effect of assembling the plays in a cycle is crucial for the interpretation that

I develop here, in which the audience might look for something missing in one play to be explained in the other.[48] By means of that erroneous (or, more accurately, misinterpellated) contextualization, Antigone's reclamation of *metoikia* becomes a conscious reflection of her unstable membership, rather than a rhetorical image by which to dramatize her exclusion. These stories could, however, be taken as unrelated, and I am overlooking the contradictions among them when taking them together not as variation but as constitutive parts of the same myth. Against those challenges I would only say that I do not invoke the paratextual interpretation that I offer here as the valid or definitive interpretation, and would even accept that it is a deliberative effort *not* to get that reading right. Yet, as Martel argues, it is precisely through those practices of misreading that canonical texts become open to more subversive ends, like the ones I seek in my reading of *Antigone*.

Having said that, my interpretive strategy does not lack precedents. For example, it informed the 1999 production of *Oedipus Tyrannos* in the Odense municipal theater in Denmark. A collaborative project between the Swedish director Leif Stinnerbom and the literary scholar Freddie Rokem, this iteration of the play portrayed an Antigone who was dramatically split into two temporally related subjects: the seven-year-old child who had to leave Thebes with Oedipus at the end of *Oedipus Tyrannos* and the woman who was forced to return to her native land at the end of *Oedipus at Colonus* in order to stage the tragedy of her own name.[49] On the other hand, this way of reading *Antigone* in conjunction with the other two plays is also part of the theoretical tradition. Mary C. Rawlinson suggests a similar split to Stinnerbom and Rokem in her more historically grounded analysis of Antigone's character as one that develops through time. According to her, the laws of property, the frequency of death at childbirth, and the common practice of mature men marrying young girls make it possible to speculate that both Antigone and Ismene should have been in their mid-twenties in *Antigone* and *Oedipus at Colonus*. That is the case, Rawlinson argues, if one makes Oedipus as young as possible and Jocasta "no older than we must" in *Oedipus Tyrannos*.[50] By her counts, Jocasta would have been fourteen when she married a forty-five-year-old Laius. In *Oedipus Tyrannos*, however, Laius's death is referred to as having occurred "long ago," and in *Oedipus at Colonus*, Oedipus has reached old age, making Rawlinson suggest that at least twenty years passed between the two plays.

By investigating the material conditions of Antigone's agency through the spatial-temporal unfolding of her character, we can analyze the other intervals that a misinterpellated Antigone travels, vis-à-vis her unstable political membership. Here, I argue that a silent character in *Oedipus Tyrannos* (429 BCE) becomes the most important and vociferous agent in *Antigone* (441 BCE), because the regulatory mechanisms that distributed *phônê* and *logos* so as to allocate voice and action in a particular gendered and ethnic subject were not only temporally suspended but inverted, in *Oedipus at Colonus* (405 BCE).

The Antigone from *Oedipus at Colonus* is closer in age to the Antigone of *Antigone*. She is no longer a child, even though Creon continues to refer to her in infantilizing terms, hyperbolically demonstrating the ancient Greek understanding of women's rationality as if in a perpetual state of infancy. Yet, as Rawlinson argues, Antigone and Ismene are "long past the usual age of marriage."[51] Twenty years have passed between *Oedipus Tyrannos* and *Oedipus at Colonus*. In *Oedipus at Colonus*, Oedipus is now an old man and Polyneices has already been ostracized by his brother, married Argeia, and assembled an army in Argos to invade, enslave, and destroy his native city. Antigone is no longer the child cast out with her father. She has become a woman who speaks, argues, and achieves what no other character was able to achieve in *Oedipus Tyrannos*: she persuades her father to receive Polyneices at Colonus.

This means that the most important years of Antigone's pedagogical and political training took place under exceptional conditions. She dealt with very difficult and demanding tasks at an early age. Not only did she learn of the suicide of her mother when she was only seven, she also learned that she was the product of incest—a heinous crime for the community into which she had been socialized—and that she was entrusted with the mission of leading her damaged and morally repulsed father through foreign lands for close to twenty years. She performed this leading role while haunted by her incestuous origins. Antigone is the only one forced to spend every day of her life with Oedipus, who blinded himself violently and who knows that no citizen nor foreigner will ever welcome him again in their houses. Antigone has been severed from her own family and uprooted from her native city, spending more years of her life as a foreigner outside of Thebes than inside it. Thus, she is not exposed primarily to the cultural codes and social norms of Thebes, but to the relative and changing ones in the different towns and cities that she visits with Oedipus while wandering, like foreigners, on their way toward Colonus. Antigone's political upbringing is thus not a Theban product but a foreign one. It is in Colonus that she finally calls foreigners friends (OC, 844 [119]), and when she is forced to return to her native land by the end of *Oedipus at Colonus*, she no longer considers it her home (OC, 844 [119]). She is uprooted a second time, taken away from her long nomadic journey to a forced settlement in the city of her origin, now foreign to her. And if parricide and incest forced her to exit Thebes, filicide awaits her when she enters it again (OC, 1743 [155]).

It is also at Colonus that Antigone promises to bury Polyneices. Sophocles makes the promise of burial explicit. The promise binds her, and she makes it from a dispossessed site of those seeking refuge. Such foreignness actually better explains the rationality of her act. Seen from this perspective, one might argue that her years of exile with Oedipus and her own experiences depending on the solidarity of strangers prepared her to see that even those most disgraced in the eyes of others also need someone to speak on their behalf. Antigone knows what it means to be regarded as abject, to be received with suspicion for bearing the mark of divine hate. She is better situated than other characters in the play to respond to Polyneices's request—and such might be the case, too, with noncitizens in the audience.

Antigone's character also shatters gender arrangements in the story. Ismene stays in Thebes and tries unsuccessfully to persuade her sister not to disobey Creon's edict, arguing that they are "only women, not meant in nature to fight against men, and . . . ruled by those who are stronger" (A, 61–63 [163]), but Antigone knows otherwise. She knows that nothing in her gender makes her naturally unfit to argue against men. She has been leading Oedipus in foreign lands for years. She has learned how to speak and persuade where men have failed. Her experience tells her that there is nothing natural in women's subordination to men and that a change in circumstances, as in her own case, proves the opposite. In their wanderings, Oedipus was subordinated to Antigone. She was the one telling him where to go, where to step, with whom to talk, which places to avoid. The regulatory mechanisms of the city allocating legitimate speech to a particular gendered subject were perhaps operative for Ismene, who stayed in Thebes, but not for Antigone, who wandered for years.[52] Gender hierarchies were suspended, if not inverted, and she was able to perform a different role as a result. Despite all the difficulties, Oedipus and Antigone survived, and she managed to bring them both safe to Colonus. Antigone knows strength and leadership are contingent attributes, dependent on the transformation of the social conditions under which gender roles are politically constructed.

Metic women in the audience might also have been better situated to attend to the variability of gender arrangements for which Antigone's actions have now become iconic. Kennedy, for instance, argues that elite *metic* women often engaged in a lifestyle that Athenian citizens associated with masculinity, thus leading to their pejorative characterization as prostitutes.[53] The ethnically constructed masculinity of *metic* women is also evident in Lysias's funeral oration, who considered the courage of the Amazons "more like men than women in their nature."[54] Antigone's own transgression of conventional gender roles might, in fact, reflect the exceptional socialization to which she was subjected as a foreigner, despite her native status.

AN-ARKHÊ BEYOND THE DEMOS

Let's imagine, then, that in *Oedipus the King*, written some fifteen years after *Antigone*, Sophocles develops Antigone's origins, modifying our perception of this character. Antigone was not only born from an incestuous union, as the audience already knows, but from a Theban mother and a Corinthian father. As Tiresias's character tells us at the beginning of the play, Oedipus "is a stranger (*metic*) among citizens [who] soon will be shown to be a citizen true native Theban, and he'll have no joy of the discovery" (OT, 452–53 [30]). Classics scholar R. C. Jebb argues that until Tiresias's revelation, Oedipus held the status of a *metic* in Thebes for an Athenian audience. I agree, given that Oedipus arrived from Corinth and thus far knows nothing about his Theban origins. The play was performed years after the Periclean Citizenship Law of 451/450 BCE prescribed double endogamy to confer citizenship, which made Antigone's status closer to her father's than to her mother's in Athenian eyes.[55] Exceptions to that law had not yet been introduced.

Moreover, Oedipus's political education and the cultivation of his morality and ethics were not of Thebes but of Corinth. The new context would have undoubtedly impacted Oedipus's Corinthian background but would not have erased it. One might expect a complex mixture of both cultural frameworks in Oedipus's political decisions as the Theban sovereign and as the *kyrius* (ruler) of the royal household. One could also expect such migratory experiences to have affected Oedipus's children, raised in a culturally mixed family.

Sophocles fills the gaps between *Oedipus Tyrannos* and *Antigone* in *Oedipus at Colonus*, his last surviving tragedy about the Labdacids family. The tragedy begins with the long journey of Oedipus and Antigone through foreign lands on their way to Colonus, a *deme* (district) of Athens. This means that Antigone, who would have been perceived as a *metic* in *Oedipus Tyrannos*, learns that she is a native citizen of Thebes only to have to immediately leave, in order to become Oedipus's eyes through foreign lands. Here, it is also important to notice that Vidal-Naquet, in his famous analysis of Oedipus's political status in *Oedipus at Colonus*, argues that Oedipus did not acquire Athenian citizenship by the end of Sophocles's last play, serving as an iconic representation of the process by which the status of *metoikia* was granted in Athens.[56] Oedipus's story actually follows the standard political procedure to request this type of residency. Oedipus engages in *aitesis* (a formal request). By means of a *prostates* (a patron, in this case, a man from the *deme* of Colonus), Oedipus presents his solicitation to Theseus. The *prostates* then advocates for Oedipus's credentials, for his advantages (*kerde*) as a benefactor for the city (*euergetai*). Then he engages in supplication to Theseus and is granted residency, but not equal membership. As Vidal-Naquet says, Sophocles wrote *Oedipus at Colonus*, not *Oedipus from Colonus*.[57]

The Antigone of *Antigone*, already transformed by the Antigone of *Oedipus Tyrannos* into a *metic* princess, brought up in a bicultural family, becomes further transformed into a *metic* refugee in *Oedipus at Colonus*, when her father is granted *metoikia*. If we follow the migratory structure of this play, and the ways in which Thebes is used to allegorize Athenian political membership, Antigone is only ever nominally a native of Thebes. All of her life, however, she has in fact been treated as either a *metic* or as a foreigner, so it is not surprising that her social and political agency reflects not the gender codes associated with citizens but those attributed to foreign and *metic* women.

As Sue Blundell's important work on women in antiquity affirms, even though "we know very little about the lives of *metic* women . . . as they were not in most cases vehicles in the transmission of citizenship, it is possible that masculine control over their behavior was less rigorous than in the case of Athenian women."[58] Independent *metic* women in particular, who were liable for their own *metoikion* (tax), had to live more public lives since they needed to work to support themselves and worked in trades deemed inappropriate for citizen women. Actually, *metic* women were crucial for the Athenian economy, working as nurses, market vendors, wool workers, seamstresses, musicians, midwives, healers, priestesses, sophists, and prostitutes.[59] Thus, even though Blundell might be right, in that *metic* women might not have been subjected to such masculine control, such public exposure in fact made them more vulnerable to gender-based violence and prejudice. Perhaps we can reinterpret the severity of Creon's trial and punishment of Antigone as indicative of such differential treatment and hear something else in Creon's claim to have dispossessed Antigone of her *metic* status in the earth (A, 889–890 [195]). As Kennedy argues, Creon's claim could be an indication that her right to dwell among them was something that he could revoke, "not an inherent right, but contingent and within the power of the state and society to decide."[60]

One likely consequence of such revocation, as I explained in the introduction, was the selling of the *metic* into slavery, and Creon's comparison of Antigone with a horse he needed to break (A, 476 [179]) might have suggested just that transformation, as Chanter argues.[61] Chanter makes that connection based on Cartledge's analysis of the term *andrapodon*, a term that "unambiguously" designated slaves, "formed by analogy with a standard Greek world for cattle, *tetrapoda* or 'four-footed thing,'" and one that illustrated the ways in which the Greeks construed slaves "as subhuman creatures."[62] Slaves were animalized, and Creon's reference to another four-footed animal, the horse, to degrade Antigone, might have been indicative of his effort to move her from *metic* to slave.

Thus, as much as Antigone's family is haunted by filial transgressions, it is also haunted by status-anxiety, territorial unrest, and border-crossings. From the point of view of the state, which epitomizes biological reductionism in the law of Pericles, Antigone belongs to Thebes as much as she belongs to the household, and not to the public domain of *logos* and action, which is made clear in Creon's *agon* (confrontation) with her. From her point of view, such a fixed territoriality was probably never operative, nor was the conventional role associated with her gender, or the a priori exclusion of her speech. Foreignness represents for Antigone the temporal suspension of the Theban status quo, whose distribution of agency and speech in a gendered and ethnic subject are no longer at work. If we reinterpret her as a *metic*, Antigone's performance, in comparison to the one conventionally attributed to her sister Ismene, becomes more intelligible. Antigone's strong voice had specific conditions of possibility linked to how her *metoikia* and foreignness, not her citizenship, opened up a space for her to perform a different role. As a foreigner, Antigone learns to assume risks that she might not have otherwise taken. She is exposed to a unique experience of the contingency of political orders, in which no solid foundation can be uncontestably established.

As an unmarried *metic*, who mourns the children she will not have, she thus strategically invokes the case of Tantalus's daughter Niobe, whom she names the "Phrygian stranger" (A, 826 [193]) to frame her case. Niobe is, rather significantly, a foreign deity and the wife of Amphion, who was considered a second founder of Thebes. Such reference is all the more crucial, if one considers Thebes's mixed foundation, in contrast to Athenian autochthonous identity. As Stefani Engelstein argues, the foundation of Thebes actually combined the two common Greek myths for the foundation of the *polis*: "Cadmus, of the royal family of Phoenicia, founded the city of Thebes with the help of the Spartoi, warriors who sprang from the ground as offspring of the teeth of a dragon Cadmus had slain (Spartoi means "sown")."[63] Even her citation of the Persian story of Intaphrenes's wife, when she announces her intention to transgress the civic law and perform the burial with the otherwise scandalous claim that her brother is irreplaceable, makes more sense.[64]

Noncitizens in the audience at the Festival of Dionysia, or hearing secondhand reports of the story from those who were authorized to attend it, might have been particularly sensitive to Antigone's reclamation of *metoikia*, her invocation of foreign divinities such as Niobe, and foreign stories like that of Intaphrenes's wife. It is thus possible to think of an Antigone who speaks with a foreign accent in the theater in order to further convey that her political skills are not a Theban gift but result from the nomadism of her border-crossings.[65] More importantly, we can open up this classical tradition again by imagining not only a different type of female agency but the political meanings that such agency might bear for those subject-positions that were a priori excluded from the *demos* and did not attend the theater, in order to put those skills in practice in the *agora* and the law courts.

What If Polyneices Was a Slave?

But *metics* are not the only subject-positionality Antigone references to convey the historically stratified form of membership by which her speech is rendered unintelligible in the play. During her *agon* with Creon, when Creon ventriloquizes Eteocles, claiming that Antigone's act would be impious in his sight because she would be putting "him only on equality with one that was a desecrator" (A, 516 [181]), Antigone reacts by saying, "It was his brother, not his slave, that died" (A, 517 [181]). As Honig claims, in this line "Antigone practices a politics of differential grief" as she demands equal treatment for both brothers—challenging Creon's friend/enemy distinction through a more inclusive form of grievability—only to then "contrast her brothers with slaves on whose behalf she would never protest the indignity of exposure."[66]

This indignity plays a crucial role in Honig's argument against Judith Butler's move from the partisan politics of speech acts in *Antigone's Claim*

(2000) to the universal ethics of grief in *Precarious Life* (2004).⁶⁷ Antigone's laments are not universal, Honig argues, not even in the first law that presumably enacts that universality, as slaves are not included within the scope of Divine law. The indignity of slavery, however, is as unexplored as *metoikia* in Honig's otherwise exemplary political reframing of *Antigone*. I am not, however, the first to call for the political significance of foregrounding slavery in our analysis of *Antigone* (and ancient tragedy more broadly). My own interpretation was inspired, in this case, by Tina Chanter, who follows a long tradition of critical scholars seeking to problematize the romantic idealization of ancient Greek democracy by focusing on how the privileges of citizenship depended on the devaluation, labor exploitation, and physical violation of slaves in particular.⁶⁸

If *metics* may have been better located than citizens to respond to how Antigone's foreignness, rather than her citizenship, helped her to denaturalize sexual and ethnic hierarchies and perform her disobedient speech-acts, slaves could have been better located to notice how such political denaturalization could then renaturalize other hierarchies in the process. Chanter's book holds accountable an extensive repertoire of political theorists, playwrights, and other scholars for failing to address how Antigone contests Creon's account of Polyneices as an enemy and traitor at the cost of "re-inscribing the inferior—and unquestioned—status of slaves."⁶⁹ Despite her radical critiques of Hegel, Lacan, Butler, Mary Beth Mader, Giorgio Agamben, and Luce Irigaray, and her excellent interpretations of Athol Fugard, Winston Ntshona and John Kani's *The Island*, and of Fémi Òsófisan's *Tègònni: An African Antigone*, Chanter's thesis has received, in my view, no major follow-up. *Whose Antigone?* remains, to the best of my knowledge, the sole book entirely devoted to a serious interrogation of slavery and racism as they happen in the play and are disavowed in its large archive of theoretical reception, which continues to limit our ability to rethink the political. I would like to think about this book as a further exploration of Chanter's critical project, as following her in the politicization of *Antigone* by exposing, as she claims in her concluding remarks, "the limits of what a given society finds it tolerable to represent to itself."⁷⁰ Beyond Chanter, I have tried to politicize not only slavery but also *metoikia,* and have turned to the Americas, rather than to Africa, as an alternative site for the political interrogation of colonial racism and the ways in which its disavowed history frames critical theory's meditation on classical tragedies.

So, what if Polyneices had been a slave? First of all, in my view, the subject of slavery is rather central to the Theban cycle as a whole. The fact that Oedipus was saved and not killed by Laius and Jocasta's servant, as that servant was ordered to do, already demonstrates that this whole drama is actually the political result of slave's dissident agency.[71] Slaves are not, in other words, secondary to the story. Read through this lens, the whole Theban cycle is the subversive consequence of a slave's disobedience. Instead of killing Oedipus, as he is ordered to do, the Theban servant gives him to a Corinthian shepherd, who then gives the child to Polybus and Merope, the rulers of Corinth, a known slave center in Greek antiquity. Unable to have children of their own, Polybus and Merope hold Oedipus's origins secret and raise him as their own. But Oedipus learns about the prophecy and, in order to avoid fulfilling it, leaves the city, not knowing that Polybus and Merope are the misinterpellated subjects of his actions. By leaving Corinth, Oedipus tragically fulfills the prophecy. He unknowingly kills his father and marries his mother, producing four *metic* children with her, as the new sovereign of Thebes. But the killer of Laius has not been brought to justice, so the gods send a plague to the city of Thebes that impedes all women from reproducing, thus marking the end of Thebes's future. And when Oedipus investigates what the gods want in order to overcome the plague, he learns that they want Laius's killer, who they claim still resides in the city, to be brought to justice.

Oedipus engages in a juridical-political investigation to find the killer of Laius, against warnings from practically every single character in the play, all of whom, knowingly or unknowingly, intuit that such investigation will bring him to his own demise. Blinded by his own power, the investigation has not even started when Oedipus curses the one he misinterpellates, as he will become the unintended addressee of that curse. Even after the Corinthian shepherd arrives with the news that his father Polybus has died—de facto giving him a way out—Oedipus continues the search. Confident that he has not fulfilled the prophecy after hearing the news, and still believing Polybus and Merope to be his parents by blood, he proceeds to interrogate the Theban servant and sole survivor of the scene in which he unknowingly killed his biological father.

The Theban servant and the Corinthian shepherd, I claim, were putting a play in front of the sovereign.[72] The two servants were also conspiring, articulating a secret in public, just as Honig argues Ismene and Antigone were. Honig concludes that it was Ismene who first buried Polyneices at night, I that it was because the Theban servant disobeyed the order of his masters that Oedipus fulfilled the prophecy. The Theban servant, in other words, held the key to the resolution of both Oedipus's identity and that of Laius's killer. But the Theban servant was a slave, so his testimony could have only been accepted as truthful if he had been subjected to torture. As Michel Foucault's own anti-Oedipal turn to Sophocles's tragedy in the 1970s demonstrated, in this violent encounter between the sovereign (Oedipus) and the slave (Theban servant) as the bearer of his secret, Sophocles's play actually dramatizes the historical technologies by which truth was produced in Greek antiquity.[73] The torture of the slave, as scholars of classics have analyzed, was not a capricious but a procedural requirement in legal cases.[74] Oedipus tortures the Theban slave in order to produce the truth about the identity of Laius's killer. The ancient Greek term for truth, *basanos*, as Page Dubois demonstrates in her excellent analysis of the production of truth in Greek antiquity, was the same word used for torture and for economic transactions.[75] *Basanos* was the stone against which other metals were rubbed, to determine whether it was really gold and not something else underneath. Tortured, the Theban servant confesses not only Oedipus's identity but his own active role in the story. This explains why he claims at one point, that he would "die far worse" (OT, 1159 [62]) if he confesses. Oedipus, furthermore, is aware of such a violation when he asks the Theban shepherd, "How was it that you gave it away to this old man?" (1179). The servant understands that Oedipus is not inquiring further into the details of the transaction but into the motivations underlying the disobedient act, and answers accordingly: "O master, I pitied it, and thought that I could send it off to another country" (OT, 1178 [63]).

I read something else in that "pity" than just the historical articulation of the juridical procedure by which torture was produced in Greek antiquity.[76] Something, in my view, more politically radical and subversive: I read the political traffic of Oedipus at the border, across three undecidable motivations, where Oedipus was simultaneously instrumentalized for political purposes and virtuously saved, for the collective and individual reconstitution of the slave's otherwise structurally damaged sense of selfhood. I do not want to overlook the fact that the prophecy turned Oedipus into a lethal weapon in the hands of the servant, who could thus instrumentalize the child in order to destroy the household of his master and, given their status as rulers, also the city of Thebes itself. But I also want to take that "pity" at face value, because the Theban servant could have felt responsible for a child with whom he shared conditions of marginalization. The child had been stripped of any kind of legal personhood and was now being disposed of by the sovereign, like slaves were. The Theban servant, I claim, was better positioned than anyone to become responsive to Oedipus's new marginalized condition. Finally, saving the child might have given the Theban shepherd a more narcissistic form of pleasure, a sense of self-esteem grounded in the heroism of that act.

I would like to further radicalize this interpretation with something that I missed in my previous account of the conspiratorial play-inside-the-play between the two slaves. In my previous interpretation, I claimed that when Oedipus, pointing to the Corinthian shepherd, asks the Theban servant if he had met him before, his opaque answer—"Not such that I can quickly call to mind" (OT, 1132 [60])—was his way of conveying to the Corinthian shepherd the risks of pursuing the investigation any further, risks that would result in his own torture. I also claimed that the Corinthian shepherd probably did get the message but refused the dis-identificatory gesture of the Theban servant in order to keep a polluted Oedipus safely at Thebes, rather than bringing him back to Corinth as their ruler. Here, I would like to suggest a different interpretation. What if these two servants were even more conspiratorially Honigian in their *sotto voce* exchanges? Perhaps they have in mind not only Thebes and its royal household but also Corinth when they instrumentalize Oedipus's prophecy for their own purposes. A known slave center, Corinth was arguably the city that they would have been more strategically interested in destroying. All we know is that both slaves had seen each other across a half-year, from spring until autumn, for at least three years prior to the subversive traffic of Oedipus across the border. But we do not know under what circumstances or what was discussed in those secret meetings. We do not know if something more revolutionary was being plotted.[77]

What if, more sensitive to the social equivocality of kinship positions, they knew that nothing in nature could ever fix the linguistic positions of father and mother in the form expected by the democratic law of Athens, which, as noted, prescribed double endogamy to confer citizenship? What if their own experience of slavery made them aware that a change in social conditions pluralized the destination of the prophecy so as to make Polybus and Merope, not just Laius and Jocasta, the misinterpellated addresses of Oedipus's terrible actions? What if they took advantage of the very system of slavery that allowed these rulers to claim this child as their own, in order to redirect the target of the prophecy to the rulers responsible for running one of Greek antiquity's slave centers? And what if part of what explains the unclear strategy crafted through those "open secrets," voiced in the play-inside-the-play, are fears about the consequences they could not have foreseen, since not only parricide and incest but general infertility resulted from their attempt to mobilize the will of the gods for their own subversive ends?

Had Oedipus been a slave, as he was anxious to demonstrate he was not, so would have been Polyneices. Benjamin Isaac claims that the inferiority of slaves was in fact inherited, not only through biological reproduction but also through physical nurturing, as that condition was passed as much from the seed as from the milk the child received, thus explaining Favorinus's discourse against the employment of wet nurses.[78] According to Blundell, however, in the Homeric age, to which the Theban cycle belongs, only women and children were enslaved. Male prisoners of war were killed, as in the *Iliad*.[79] That was not the case in 441 BCE Athens, when the play was performed, since "the growing use of slaves for agricultural and industrial purposes began to produce a much greater demand for males" ending the preponderance of female servants that had existed since the sixth century BCE.[80] By 431 BCE, Blundell claims, "it is estimated that there may have been as many as 100,000 slaves in Athens . . . while the adult male citizen population at the same time may have been about 40,000."[81]

At the time *Antigone* was performed, all slaves were treated as property. They could obviously pass no property onto their offspring, as they had none, and were themselves inherited by the heir of their master's *kyrius* in the event of his death. According to Cohen, "slaves could be set free in ways that are not documented for Athens," but we know that if able to secure twenty *minae,* they could sometimes purchase their own freedom and become *metics*.[82] So, what do we make of the subject of slavery, as Antigone's claim to bury Polyneices because he was Eteocles's brother, not his slave, is by no means the sole reference to slavery. As Chanter claims, not only was Oedipus anxious to establish "whether or not he was born a slave," Antigone's birth indicates a hereditary curse that "might be read as a reference to the heritability of slavery."[83]

Arguably, what makes the treatment of Polyneices unacceptable not only to Thebans, who ultimately champion Antigone's cause, but also to their enemies—to Argos, and according to Mark Griffith, Pantheropaios from Tegia, and Tydeus from Kalydon—is that enemies in battle have been treated as only slaves could be treated, according to the implications of Antigone's speech.[84] Thebes violated the boundary between the free and the unfree, which seems to overrule the friend-enemy distinction and thus appears to be more politically foundational. These enemies are willing, as

Tiresias eventually reports, to fight Thebes again in order to correct the injustice. What, then, about the slaves in the audience, who either see or hear that in this play, the one who was supposed to be a citizen—and not just any citizen but a member of the royal house—is forced to endure a violence that appears to be legitimate only if discharged upon slaves? Polyneices endures that violence only after death, but not while living; does the violence of slavery become politically relevant and deserving of tragic commentary only when it is a royal citizen and not an actual slave subjected to it? Was that message what the slaves in the audience, or those who disobediently attended the festivals in disguise, got from the play?

My analysis, in other words, relies less on whether Creon's particular mistreatment of Polyneices's corpse was actually historically characteristic of the one inflicted on slaves in Greek antiquity, than in the claim that the difference between citizens, *metics,* and slaves was marked as much in the regulation of their lives as it was in the differential regulation of their deaths. Burial, in short, was also an occasion in which stratified membership was marked, and thus one occasion in which the boundaries of the *demos* were policed and open to contestation. Not just, as democratic theorists have claimed, in the ways in which an excessive aristocratic burial—i.e., that of Patroclus in the *Iliad*—contrasts with the more economical burial that Pericles demands in the *Funeral Oration*, as a kind of ur-text of democracy. The politics of burial, I claim, does not exhaust itself in the ideological contestation over the form that the burial takes, between an excessive aristocratic ritual and a more economically democratic one. There is, so to speak, a prior politics of burial, more foundational, and more troublesome for the constitution of the *demos*. This political scene distinguishes between those burials that can articulate ideologically recognizable ethos, and those that can be desecrated or given no form at all.

In this chapter, I have tried to make room for Antigone's reclamation of *metoikia* as a historically alternative description of her condition, given the migratory journeys of her life and the political context of her conscripted agency. *Metoikia* informs Antigone's life in ways that slavery, however, does not inform Polyneices's. He is treated as a sovereign, marries the princess of another royal house—which he could not have done had he been regarded as a slave—and tries to enslave his native city after assembling an army. Creon refers to him, Antigone, and Haemon as slavish at different moments in the play, and Polyneices is treated in ways that, at least according to Antigone's speech, only slaves could be treated. But Polyneices did not live the life of a slave, and it was not only his sisters but the citizens of Thebes and those of other cities who were willing to fight against the violent treatment to which his corpse was subjected, who thus perceived him as no slave. For a slave they would have never intervened. Polyneices could have been a slave, but if he had been socially viewed thus, there would have been no *Antigone*. Slavery permeates the play, but must be disavowed, simultaneously acknowledged and denied, for citizens to purge their emotions on the stage.

Like most contemporary democratic theorists, I have also turned to the ancients while motivated by a desire to intervene in contemporary debates in democratic theory. The past does some work for us in the present. Rancière wanted to translate the litigious universalism of the ancient *demos* into the litigious universalism of the modern proletariat. Foley and Honig wanted to highlight the agonism between an aristocratic and a democratic mode of doing *burial* against the consensual emphasis of deliberative democracy, and the universal mortalism that feminism was trying to ground on *Antigone's* lamentation. Closer to Chanter and Kasimis, I wanted to highlight the interrelated forms of valuation that disqualify some from equal membership and thus from participation in the government of the city, in order to include others. The point of these time-travels, of this preposterous history, is not to suggest that nothing has changed, and that democracy has remained the same. The point is, rather, that we might be constantly reinventing the democracy of the ancients through the contentious ways in which we reinterpret the democracies of our times. Like Chanter and Kasimis, I am interested in the constitutive exclusions of democracy, and in replaying those exclusions to problematize contemporary democracy as well. Not, again, in order to claim that such exclusions are the same as the exclusions of today but in order to highlight, theoretically, the ways in which the inclusionary logic of the *demos* comes to rest on the prepolitical and differential exclusion of the *metic* and the *slave* as insufficiently addressed problems in democratic theory. Perhaps we can read, through the misinterpellated lenses of *metoikia,* the anxious racialized regulation of sexuality that sustained Athenian exceptionalism, and use that framework to complicate the ways in which contemporary "democratic" exceptionalisms continue to police racialized sexuality.

Slavery, rather than *metoikia,* is the subject of the next chapter, as I move from Athenian exceptionalism in Greek antiquity to European exceptionalism in colonial modernity, through the conquest of the Americas and the trans-Atlantic slave trade. The addressees of my critique there are U.S. feminist and queer theory, rather than democratic theory. In that chapter I also explore what has inscribed Antigone most forcefully in an ethical rather than a political paradigm: her confinement to the *oikos* and, more precisely, to the *atè* (misfortune) that runs throughout her family. Modern slavery, as I will show, complicates the subversive ways that Antigone renders kinship positions equivocal, as it shows how the coherence of kinship positionality comes to rest on the otherwise disavowed coloniality of gender.

2

Antigone in Colonial Modernity

A Critique of Feminist and Queer Theory in North America

> The place of slavery in queer studies work has yet to be reckoned with.
> —Sharon Patricia Holland, *The Erotic Life of Racism*

Slavery, *Metoikia*, and Citizenship in Colonial Modernity

In this chapter, I demonstrate how modern slavery is not simply denied but is actively disavowed in the positive reclamation of Antigone's unintelligibility in the anti-heteronormative politics of U.S. feminist and queer theory. U.S. feminist and queer theory draw from the language of social death, to radicalize the political character of its critique, without the violence of modern slavery ever coming into the foreground of this body of literature's main political preoccupations. Like Antigone, who contests one power structure by reinscribing another, and like democratic theory, which pluralizes Antigone's conspiracy with language only to restrain the addressees of her claims, U.S. queer and feminist theory animate their transgressions by reproducing exclusions of their own.

Contemporary decolonial theory traces the foundation of modern capitalism back to the European conquest of the Americas and the trans-Atlantic slave trade.[1] Decolonial feminism in particular analyzes the construction of gender identity and heteronormative regulation of sexuality as inseparable from the coloniality of power. Drawing from intersectional third world feminism and most significantly from the work of Paula Gunn Allen and Oyèrónkẹ́ Oyěwùmí, Maria Lugones troubles not only the often questioned "gender as cultural/sex as biological" binary, but the ahistorical naturalization of sexual differences, patriarchy, and normalization of heterosexualism that the failure to attend to the colonial history of gender production replicates.[2] Such naturalization has erased more egalitarian nongendered societies, like the Yoruba, as well as more egalitarian gynocratic societies, such as the Cherokee and Iroquois, from history. As Lugones claims, indigenous peoples "recognized more than two genders, recognized 'third' gendering and homosexuality positively, and understood gender in egalitarian terms rather than in the terms of subordination that Eurocentered capitalism imposed on them."[3]

In this chapter, I turn to the racialized form of sexuality that emerged in North America as a consequence of the settler-colonial system that originated with the European conquest of indigenous territories in the continent renamed "America," and their institutionalization of a transatlantic trade of enslaved Africans.[4] By situating the theoretical reception of *Antigone* in U.S. feminist and queer theory against the colonial background of modern slavery in North America, I want to reckon with the place of slavery in feminist and queer theory. I thus focus not on *metoikia* but on slavery in this chapter and explore how the agency of slaves is disavowed in U.S. feminist and queer theory. I say *disavowed* because slavery is both acknowledged and denied. It is acknowledged when feminist and queer theory contest the patriarchal and heteronormative dictates of the social order through the conditions of those who are forced to experience a social death. It is denied, however, when these theories fail to produce a political theory of racialized sexuality that foregrounds the slaves' agency within the broader history of the coloniality of gender.

But slavery is not the sole category that changes with the consolidation of modern racial/sexual capitalism. The ancient condition of *metoikia* disappeared from the European lexicon of political membership long before the European conquest of the Americas.[5] After the decline of ancient Greek democracy and the emergence of the Roman empire, other names were given to "resident foreigners." That status was conferred upon foreigners not by supplication but by other technologies of power. Citizenship changed, too, under a Roman empire that was territorially larger and more ethnically diverse than the Athenian empire ever was. Citizenship was no longer the collectively institutionalized power of the poor to govern the city on the basis of their *an-arkhê*, as I articulated in chapter 1, following Rancière's thesis. Instead, citizenship was transformed into a set of statutory legal guarantees protecting individuals from a compartmentalized imperial authority from which those individuals were now further estranged, and whose power over their lives many of them continued to experience as deeply oppressive.

All of these changes were intensified by the European colonization of Africa and the Americas: not only were entire indigenous populations expropriated from their land and forced into slavery in both Africa and the so-called New World, but the already existing slave-trade system in North and West Africa became a transatlantic slave system connecting four continents.[6] As a consequence, enslaved Africans were territorially alienated in new ways, simultaneously subjected to a logic of elimination that expropriated them of their land in Africa and a logic of exclusion that instrumentalized territorial alienation in order to subject them to more extreme forms of social exclusion in the Americas.[7] All competing European empires (Portuguese, Spanish, British, Dutch, German, and French) engaged in these logics. All expropriated indigenous peoples of their land in the "New World" through genocidal policies seeking to either eliminate or enslave them, at least during what Sylvia Wynter refers to as the first modernity.[8] As the indigenous population rapidly declined during this period because of genocidal European policies—including the diseases that Europeans spread, sometimes inadvertently, to a population who possessed no immunities to them—these empires then proceeded to replace their labor force with another.[9] This other "exploitable source of energy," as Robinson argues, Europeans considered "both mindless to the organizational requirements of production and insensitive to the subhuman conditions of work."[10] Thus, unlike ancient slavery, modern slavery situates the slave outside the domain of the human, and makes that exclusion central to the construction of "the human." If, in antiquity, the slave and the citizen could meet in the figure of the *metic*, who was both a freed slave but also a potential reproducer of citizens, that meeting point became impossible under the thoroughly racialized world of settler colonial capitalism in the Americas.

Mixing the expropriation of native land with the exploitation of alien labor, the European conquest of the Americas constituted a characteristic form of settler colonialism. This form, as Patrick Wolfe reminds us, should be understood as the ongoing structure of our present rather than as an event safely displaced to the past.[11] Although settler colonialism expressed itself differently in all parts of the Americas, the subordinated position of black and indigenous peoples, in contrast to the social valuation of white people, remains a constant effect throughout the whole continent.

In this chapter, I only discuss North America, and more specifically the experience of black people under slavery in the U.S. antebellum South. But I refer to North America rather than just to the United States, because the structural patterns of racialization that first subordinated black and indigenous peoples to slavery were common to the logics of exclusion and elimination in both the United States and Canada. It is true, however, that there was not a significant trade in enslaved Africans in Canada, in contrast to the trade in which the United States engaged primarily during the second modernity, after the settlers achieved their independence from England.[12] I am conscious of the fact that black people in the U.S. South were enslaved for longer, and that it is their experience of slavery more than the experience of indigenous peoples from which U.S. feminist and queer theory draw when it comes to their most radical interpretations of *Antigone*. I thus refer to North America, not just to the United States, and I include indigenous peoples, even if the literature that informs my critique refers primarily to the experience of black people in the U.S. South.[13] Indigenous peoples in the Americas and black people in Africa, nevertheless, were the first populations subjected to modern slavery—that is to say, to the form of total captivity that sought to confine entire populations to the politically constructed biological overdetermination of their bodies for the greater accumulation of capital and the self-definition of the human as settler's prerogative.

Like slavery in Greek antiquity, modern slavery also confined slaves to the two main spaces in which existence in the world was to be recognized: the *polis* and the *oikos,* the public and the private. Slavery continued to serve both spaces, as its radically structural other. Unlike ancient slavery, however, this radical exteriority also deprived slaves of their own bodies in unique ways. Capitalist conditions of exploitation, separating the exclusion of the modern slave from the integration of the modern citizen in the settler colony, radicalized the gap that existed between them. Orlando Patterson characterizes this permanent rather than transitory condition as a form of social death. Since slavery replaced physical death in the form of not a definitive pardon but a conditional commutation, and only for "as long as the slave acquiesced in [their] powerlessness," slaves "had no socially recognized existence outside of [their] master"; they "became a social nonperson."[14]

In order to guarantee the permanence of that condition during the second modernity, difference was reified on the somatically marked body. This newly marked body was not only subjected to the more sophisticated repressive apparatuses of the colonial empire—including the panopticon that was first tried in the slave ship before being incorporated into the modern prison—but also to an organized religious, scientific, pedagogical, economic, and punitive apparatus in charge of legitimizing and further naturalizing the exclusive and unmodifiable character of that subhuman condition.[15] The "animated tool" of the ancients became not only a commodity to be sold in the market but a body that marked the border between the human and the nonhuman and helped to define the legal contours of modern personhood as the exclusive prerogative of Europeans. Separating the citizen from the slave thus entailed a more ontological separation between two "species" that shared very little in common, since the ability to identify one as human came to rest on a series of technologies of power and rationalizations, invested in reducing the other to the commodified status of a dehumanized object of exchange.[16] To confront the colonial history of such separation is to complicate the political translation of Antigone's heroism in the Americas.

From the Queer Equivocality of Kinship Positions to the Racial Equivocality of Social Positions

It comes as no surprise that *Antigone* has been such an important text for feminist and queer theory.[17] After all, her disobedient burial of Polyneices breaks not only the law of the sovereign, Creon, but also the norms that regulate her social roles in Greek antiquity and confine her to the *oikos* on the basis of her assigned gender, while rendering her monstrous on the basis of her incestuous background. If not free, like able male citizens of a certain age, Antigone is not, however, a slave. She has civic duties vis-à-vis both the living and the dead. In Athens, "free" women were expected to reproduce citizens for the *polis* and participate in the fertility festivals, such as the Thesmophoria. Those festivals were political, meaning they had a public character and involved a concern for the futurity of the *polis* as a whole. They also had private significance for the women involved in them, but were not reducible to the practitioners' concerns with their own *oikos*. "Free" women were also expected to mourn the losses of the *polis* and actively participate in the funeral rites of members of their own families. The burial of citizens, too, had a public meaning beyond its distinctive significance for the individual family involved.[18]

To complicate things a bit further, Antigone is not the member of just any family but of the royal family. Her sovereign is also her uncle, and the brother on behalf of whom she disobediently speaks was a legitimate heir to the throne. Even if Athens was not a tyranny but a democracy, elite families—the main patrons of the Festival of Dionysia and the main owners of slaves in Greek antiquity—still held significant power, stressing the political significance of Antigone's nobility to a political account of the play. Antigone's disobedient action thus stands at the intersection of several borders: those between life and death, the *polis* and the *oikos*, democracy and aristocracy, man and woman, and the "free" and the unfree, rendering Antigone's transgression particularly significant for the various political projects of contemporary feminist and queer theory.

Antigone is also placed in an incestuous drama, in the mythical curse of her family. It is this *atè* (misfortune) that most radically deprives her of political significance. If the multiply transgressive character of her actions demonstrates that nothing in her gender could safely place her in the depoliticized site of the border, her *atè* depoliticizes those actions. Her *atè*, one might argue, reinscribes them in a metaphysical curse that dictates those actions as if from a transcendental source, immune to her agency. Kinship, in order words, haunts her, and the politics of her drama are overburdened by the metaphysical force of the incest taboo.

Judith Butler's *Antigone's Claim* (2000) represents, arguably, the most ambitious attempt by feminist and queer theory to repoliticize *Antigone*, precisely by attending to Antigone's sociosymbolic undoing of her *atè*, through the catachresis of her speech acts. Butler takes the challenge of reading politics where others had insisted on Antigone's presumably antipolitical assertion of blood and kinship—most notably Hegel, Lacan, and Irigaray. In the linguistic equivocality of Antigone's kinship-terms, however, Butler sees a critical opportunity to argue for historically transformable ways of doing kinship, rather than for the transcendental presupposition of kinship's heteronormative stability in the Symbolic order. Given that Antigone's father is also her brother, Butler argues, it is impossible to claim that Antigone's uncompromising fidelity to the singularity of her brother—as constituting the ethical law by which she acts—ever fixes her signifying chain in the form expected by Jacques Lacan's ethics of the Real, for instance. According to Butler, the political and social character of language, whose meaning cannot be subordinated to the intentionality of the author, betrays Antigone and thus "disperses the desire she seeks to bind to him [Polyneices] cursing her, as it were, with a promiscuity she cannot contain."[19] What Butler reads in the equivocality of Antigone's terms, then, is a failure of heterosexual closure in the Symbolic order. This gives Butler the opportunity to read the social (redefining Hegel's *sittlichkeit* [ethical life] here as the cultural framework of social intelligibility) through that which the social renders unintelligible within its Symbolic economy. In other words, what Antigone represents for Butler is a crisis of representation, because the heteronormative regulation of her desire faces an *aporia* when it confronts the equivocality of her terms— that "nothing in the nomenclature of kinship can successfully restrict its scope of referentiality to the single person, Polyneices."[20]

Butler is here referring to Antigone's most scandalous speech, the one that, as Lacan reported in his 1959–60 seminar on *Antigone*, Goethe wished "'that one day some scholar will reveal to us [was] a later addition.'"[21] It is the passage in which Antigone no longer claims to have buried Polyneices because the god of death demands the rites for all, the argument that champions her as a figure of universal humanism, nor because he was not Eteocles's slave, but because her brother is uniquely irreplaceable. As Antigone puts it: "What law backs me when I say this? I will tell you: If my husband were dead, I might have had another, and child from another man, if I lost the first. But when father and mother both were hidden in death no brother's life would bloom for me again" (A, 907–12 [196]).

This law, which the Chorus characterizes as *her* law, hence their reference to Antigone's autonomy, is the one at the center of Hegel's, Lacan's, Irigaray's, and virtually all theoretical interpretations of *Antigone*. It is this law that leads Hegel to claim that, despite being of the same blood, the unmixed brother-sister relationship makes it possible for the spirit to reach within the otherwise natural family, and in this relationship alone, its highest state of "*rest* and *equilibrium*."[22] It is by means of this law, too, that Lacan claims Antigone can freeze the signifier and purify (from purgation, that is, *catharsis*) her desire, otherwise free to perpetually circulate through metaphor and metonymy.[23] Antigone confronts her desire, and comes to represent for us an ethical fidelity to it, when having transgressed the limits of her *atè*, she establishes her duty toward her brother, ex nihilo, that is to say, beyond any historical content and despite whatever good or evil he may have done. And yet, it is the singularity of having shared the same womb, too, that leads Irigaray to mark, here, the patriarchal repression of a matriarchal lineage. Asking herself what draws Antigone and Polyneices into the singularity of this exchange, Irigaray speculates: "Could it be their complicity in the permanence, the continuance of blood that a matriarchal type of lineage ensures in its purest and most universal being?"[24] All of these answers, which situate Antigone within the realm of the ethical, Butler regards not only as insufficient, but also as the problematic erasure of a political displacement.

With Hegel, Butler returns to the social, to politics as the dispute over the cultural framework of social intelligibility. But she also problematizes the location, perhaps the confinement, of Antigone within Hegel's dialectics of the Spirit in the *Phenomenology of the Spirit*. As Irigaray had already argued, Antigone is not allowed to seek individuality in the public sphere and can only participate in that individuality indirectly, through the brother for whom she must perform the recuperative burial. In other words, Butler finds in Hegel a similar refusal of politicization as that which she questions in Lacan, although for different reasons. Butler questions Lacan's interpretation for potentially reifying heterosexuality in the transcendental organization of the Symbolic order, that ahistorically structures the psyche of all individuals, irrespective of their historically variable experiences of kinship formation and the incoherence of those terms in the case of Antigone. Butler questions Hegel's prepolitical exclusion of Antigone, which confines her to the family, for reifying the liberal private/public gendered division of labor. Hegel fails to account for the plasticity and historical variability of the norms that render the public/private border deeply unstable and prone to subversive transgression, as happens through Antigone's own performance. Finally, Butler questions Luce Irigaray's interpretation, which embraces a matriarchal priority to the order of patriarchy, as risking a problematic universalism that moving from the phallus to the womb risks reestablishing at another level the essentialism it seeks to contest. According to Butler, in all of these cases Antigone is forced to represent *"kinship as the sphere that conditions the possibility of politics without ever entering into it."*[25]

Hegel, Lacan, and Irigaray are the main targets of *Antigone's Claim*, and Butler's critique mobilizes against all of them a central feminist critique of Western political thought that troubles the gendered division of labor that separates the feminized *oikos,* as the space of the prepolitical, from the *polis,* as the exclusively masculine space of the properly political. But she also troubles the essentialization of Antigone's gender identity that such distribution presupposes. In all of these theories, Antigone's positionality within the universe of kinship is constructed as if outside of discursively contested practices and historically transformable norms. Butler's text thus facilitates the long journey of Antigone in queer—not just in feminist—theory, arguing that Antigone's claims expose "the symbolic itself [as] limited by its constitutive interdictions."[26] By means of that reading, Butler makes Antigone's drama more undecidable than transcendentally structured, shows her actions to be more performatively variable than naturally fixed, and underlines her citation of norms as more insubordinate than confirming an infallible structure.

Butler's way of resisting the prepolitical displacement of kinship, however, complicates the psychoanalytic distinction between the Symbolic and the social. In problematizing such a distinction, Butler realizes that kinship is positioned in relation to not only a sexual difference but also a racial one, and she goes on to cite how heterosexual monogamy is used to render black urban kinship arrangements dysfunctional, quoting Carol Stack's *All Our Kin* and Orlando Patterson's *Slavery and Social Death*. Race and sexuality, however, hardly come together in Butler's undoing of the binary between the Symbolic and the social in *Antigone's Claim*. They cannot, I argue, because the discursive and political rupture that the socially dead represent challenges not a dominant way of doing kinship but the sociality that kinship arrangements presuppose in colonial modernity. To put it differently, the kinship equivocality of the unacknowledged white feminist and queer subject cannot be translated into the kinship equivocality of the socially dead one, because black and indigenous peoples' kinship formations were, as Hortense Spillers argues, invaded by property rather than protected by personhood.[27] Actually, the enslaved became one of the forms of property that actually qualified the personhood of modern citizenship.[28] It is this colonial relation, too, that allows the very unfreedom of slavery to also be appropriated by the citizen to inform their condition instead. It is the disavowal of that relation, in other words, that allows feminist and queer theory to take historical variability from the socially dead subject, without the colonial conditions of the socially dead ever becoming the dominant framework of their theorizing. After all, the conditions of social death—in Patterson's formulation: natal alienation, gratuitous violence, and general dishonor—trouble not only the prepolitical displacement of kinship that interests Butler, but the very idea of the social that is assumed for something like kinship to be predicated in the first place.

As Sharon Patricia Holland argues in her critique of Butler's *Antigone's Claim*, claims "to kinship—in black and white—were and are obliterated by liaisons created as a result of slavery's economic structure."[29] The incest taboo, which haunts the heterosexual matrix with the equivocality of its terms, haunts the Southern imaginary of the settler-colonial United States differently, since chattel slavery in North America makes it impossible to "separate the practice of incest and the occurrence of miscegenation."[30] Butler was, however, by no means inattentive to that history. Thus, she rightly criticizes Patterson for suggesting that slavery's "primary offense against kinship was the eradication of paternal rights."[31] Following a long tradition of black feminist theorizing, Butler recenters black women's vulnerability to rape as slavery's primary offense to kinship. In this case, Butler draws her knowledge from Angela Davis's essay "Race, Racism and the Myth of the Black Rapist," and concludes her critique with a reference to Kath Weston's anthropological analysis of how black families replaced destroyed blood ties by consensual affiliation in an alternative way of doing kinship under the political-economic conditions of chattel slavery.

The limit of Butler's critique lies elsewhere, in properly addressing the ways in which that vulnerability to rape came to define the identity of the female enslaved as the bearer of a "negligible injury," as Saidiya Hartman argues.[32] Here, black feminism troubles Patterson's definition of social death by showing how natal alienation happened through forced reproduction, rather than through its denial. The enslaved are alienated from their natality, from giving birth to a socially recognized and valued member of the social order, to whom culture, history, knowledge, etc. are passed on, because enslaved women in particular were forced to pass the condition of total dispossession to which they were themselves subjected. Slavery was regulated through the line of the mother (*partus sequitur ventrum*), and social death meant that the coloniality of gender forced the inheritance of a "disinheritance," to use Patricia Williams's term.[33] Enslaved women were forced to pass down to an offspring that they could no longer claim as theirs, precisely because of the illegibility of their sexual violation as violence, the foundational inability to own themselves. The two taboos are, in other words, incommensurable. Because of the incest taboo, Antigone is socially fated to pass a curse onto her future generations, and what she passes dispossesses her of her ability to control the symbolic terms that she uses. But Antigone was not a slave, so she was not forced to pass the condition of total dispossession that slave women were forced to inherit.

Antigone's Claim, it is worth noting, was not Butler's first theoretical challenge to psychoanalysis on the basis of race. She performed that critique during her reading of Nella Larsen's *Passing* in *Bodies That Matter* in 1993. There, Butler mobilizes racial differences in order to contest the ontological priority that psychoanalysis grants to sexual difference, while considering both race and sexual assignation to be the sedimented consequences of performative actions. "How might we understand homosexuality and miscegenation to converge at and as the constitutive outside of a normative heterosexuality that is at once the regulation of a racially pure reproduction?" Butler asks, not to declare race as more ontologically determinant than sex but to articulate the racialized modality of power by which sexual differences were historically articulated and assumed as transcendental.[34] She even echoes Karl Marx when, seeking to understand the convergence of homosexuality and miscegenation as the constitutive outsides of heteronormativity, Butler remembers that "the reproduction of the species will be articulated as the reproduction *of* relations of reproduction, that is, as the cathected site of a racialized version of the species in pursuit of hegemony through perpetuity that requires and produces a normative heterosexuality in its service."[35] But when Butler proceeds to extend the racialized figure of the socially dead, which structures Larsen's story, to inform the condition of a racially/ethnically undifferentiated queer subject in *Antigone's Claim*, such materialist attention to the racialized reproduction *of* relations of reproduction gets lost. Larsen's recession into anonymity, which Butler laments in the conclusion of that chapter, is unintentionally repeated as the psychoanalytic challenge of *Passing*, on the basis of race, does not pass *Bodies That Matter*. The colonial history of enslaving black women in Africa in order to transport them as cargo to the Americas, the very history with which Butler troubles the ahistorical stabilization of the Symbolic order in psychoanalysis, never really enters Butler's broader queer theorizing.

Butler does return to the convergence of homosexuality and miscegenation as the constitutive outsides of heteronormativity in *Undoing Gender* (2004), where she properly addresses the racialized supplement that problematically makes the incest taboo into the basis of cultural intelligibility. In that text, Butler stresses how the prohibition not only mandates exogamy (marriage outside the "clan") but also restricts it, thus cornering the prohibition "between a compulsory heterosexuality and a prohibited miscegenation."[36] Her critique, in this case, was inspired by none other than Hartman, from whom Butler takes the idea that "slavery is the ghost in the machine of kinship."[37] But her confrontation with miscegenation, and of the different ways in which kinship was coercively (un)done, never truly intersects with the historical confrontation of the settler colonial history by which the social order, into which the queer subject seeks entry through transgressive catachresis, sexually reproduces itself through the differential subjection of racialized women to the condition of negligible injuries. Here, we should also notice how the sexual reproduction of indigenous women was regulated so as to eliminate them from history, as the child was dispossessed of their indigeneity. The prohibition that establishes cultural intelligibility operates as much through its "inclusive" forms of exogamy, when that inclusion can be made instrumental to the elimination of the native. Exclusion and inclusion can work together in order to strengthen the settler's endogamy.[38]

The socially dead provide Butler with the key historical event-*cum*-structure by which to trouble the Symbolic/social distinction, historically undone with the sexual horrors of slavery, since it is in slavery that kinship positions become more radically equivocal. But it does that in order to then immediately disappear, because that colonial history is not foregrounded in her political theory of sexuality. Butler, despite her attention to that history and evident and outspoken antiracist camaraderie, risks replacing the psychoanalytic abstraction with one of her own. What she fails to interrogate in her otherwise important critique of psychoanalysis is the fact that, as Hartman claims, the "decriminalization of rape" did not dispossess enslaved women of their gender but differentially produced their gender identity in ways that feminist and queer theory have failed to interrogate, and still need to reckon with.[39]

Other Kinds of Aberrant Transmissions

Undoing Gender is the title of Butler's work, but it could easily have been the title of Hortense Spillers's critique of Daniel Patrick Moynihan's infamous "Moynihan Report" of the late sixties entitled *The Negro Family*. In that report, as Spillers puts it, "the missing agencies in the essential life of the black community" are made into "the fault of the daughter, or the female line."[40] Like Butler, Spillers opens with the order of the signifier, with an injurious grammar whose excess demonstrate a failure to name. The American grammar fails to name, because the subject position the symbolic order tries to name—that of black woman in the United States—confronts the radical expulsion of black women from the modern order of the human. That historical expulsion ultimately renders all signifiers equally inadequate and propels the symbolic order's need for more injurious ones. That is the case because the sign is not the performative event of a subjectivity in motion, but the extended scene of captive flesh. "Peaches," "Brown Sugar," "Sapphire," "Earth Mother," "Aunty," "Granny," and so on are the overdetermined signifiers with which Spillers opens her most influential essay "Mama's Baby, Papa's Maybe: An American Grammar" (1987). The excessive nomination of this American grammar symptomatizes not the void of the

Real, but the modern/colonial construction of "woman" as passive, virtuous, and submissive, which came to exclude black and indigenous women from its humanistic field, in order to construct it from underneath. As Spillers, Davis, and Lugones argue, black and indigenous women were cast as overtly sexual and bestial, and their abjection helped to construct, in return, that social positionality from which they were most radically excluded.[41]

What Spillers, Davis, and Lugones add to the Butlerian challenge of psychoanalysis is a materialist critique of psychoanalytic abstractions that foregrounds the history of kinship formation and gender production under colonial logics of capitalist accumulation. Like Butler, they also understand the symbolic structure as the sedimented result of historically contingent social practices, practices whose repetition raises some signifiers to the position of mastery precisely by repressing or disavowing the structural violence committed against differently marked bodies, including the violence of the marking itself. Unlike Butler, however, they seek that history in a more inscrutable scene of racial subjection, in which linguistic signification literally cuts the flesh of the subject in order to extend the scene of appropriation over the injuries themselves. The linguistic cut does not produce a subject, as Lacanian psychoanalysis might suggest; rather, it excludes the object that it differentially produces from the human order of subjectivity.

Lacan, it should be noted, turned to language in order to overcome the limitations of Freud's psychoanalytic understanding of sexual difference. By claiming that the "unconscious was structured like a language," that "desire is the desire of the Other," and that "the signifier represents the subject for another signifier," Lacan considers the subject irreducibly social. In Lacan's theory, the individual becomes a subject via the cut that linguistic signification performs, one that individualizes what is not, prior to language, differentiated.[42] In looking for signifiers in the Symbolic order to satisfy desires that should by no means be considered independent from the linguistic process of signification, the subject develops their social identity. That is because none of those signifiers is ever exhaustive, setting in motion the machine of social subjectification that eventually makes the individual into who they are through their unique ways of trafficking through signs. The subject, in other words, is always the narrative outcome of a struggle with that which can have no name, the material outcome of confronting the unwritable desire with words.

There is one historical case, however, in which that linguistic cutting of the subject is neither a psychic abstraction for the process of subjectification nor the exceptional occasion of a traumatic event in the biography of the subject, but the structural reality of an ongoing historical scene of racialized subjection. That is the case of the enslaved in modernity. Because the colonial order engraves that symbol in the flesh of the slave, the cut of the signifier does not turn the individual into a subject but forever expels the slave from the order of subjectivity "proper." Such expulsion, then, comes to define proper subjectivity as the prerogative of the unmarked body. Thus, when the (master) signifier first faces the subjectivity of the slave, the result is a wounding of the flesh, a somatic branding of the body. The sign collapses Symbolic inclusion with social death, as the symbolic mark is what registers the slave not as a person but as the property of the master. Captivity, the inclusion of the enslaved into the order of the signifier, is always mediated by the brutal laceration of the flesh, making the flesh bear the sign of an endurable exclusion. Hence Spillers's influential distinction between the body and the flesh.[43] Given that no system of slavery can ever extinguish the subjectivity that it both denies and yet cannot help but also recognize, the cut of the flesh is never an exceptional event in the life of the enslaved. First of all, the branding that marks the enslaved as a commodity turns into a constant threat against the very subjectivity that it cannot fully de-animate. Such violence looms over the enslaved and reinforces the brutality of their coercion with the anticipation of pain in the event of their resistance. Second, cuts are also randomly inflicted in order to police the confinement of all the enslaved into the site of the object. The cuts in the flesh of a gratuitous violence is the exercise of a sort of preemptive technology of de-subjectification of the enslaved, as the cuts themselves recognize in and through the very violent act that which they try to deny. I say *all the enslaved* because the lacerating cut was always performatively staged, multiplying the addressees of the scene of subjection: other slaves were forced to watch and to watch in coerced docility. Finally, the reiterative cut naturalizes the abjection by making the skin itself, not just the act, become the bearer of the abject condition.

Racism is first and foremost articulated through the physical wounding of the flesh (Real), a wounding that becomes a reiterative activity through the gratuitous violence that polices the place of the enslaved in the social order. The violence of the social order, however, eventually transposes the active wounding into the very phenotypical marking of the body as colored (Imaginary). In the end, the coloniality of gender secures the symbolic association of blackness with inferiority at the linguistic level (Symbolic) through the injurious name. The American grammar that makes up the Symbolic order is thus the sublimated achievement of the reiteratively wounded flesh of the enslaved and of its historical disavowal. In the end, the "n" word can wound the flesh and become a sort of material replacement for the absent whip.[44] Actually, not only the "n" word but "black" and "African," at least until the decolonial revolution of the 1960s, as Angela Davis claims, were "just as bad in those days," "both of which were considered synonymous with 'savage.'"[45]

It is crucial to understand that Symbolic violence exercises a psychic function of subject-constitution for the white settler citizen in modernity, because it exercises both a psychic and an additional physical function for the racial subjection of black and indigenous slaves, indistinctively "savage." Such function is not unrelated to the unmarking of whiteness, or the performative construction of "white" as precisely the unmarked. Nonwhites are all people of color, and to be white is to not be "of color." The signifier that cuts these nonwhite bodies does not turn them into subjects but more fully confines them to its terms. The recognizability of white subjectivity, as a linguistic body, comes to rest on the greater vulnerability of all other marked bodies to the wounding of their flesh.

Yet slaves also resisted that form of signification. Here I believe that Spillers both anticipates and radicalizes Butler's crucial insights on the mimetic insubordination of queer agency via catachresis. Actually, Spillers's text address the subversive capacity of the enslaved to perform a more aberrant form of transmission than the one that Butler discerns in the proto-queer equivocality of Antigone's terms. Slaves could mobilize the horrifying mark by which they were recorded as property and denied personhood in order to insurgently reconstitute themselves as human, beyond the social norms of liberal humanism. By means of the mark that identified them as property, like commodified animals, slaves were also able to subversively discern their location as "persons" in the otherwise brutally violated universe of kinship, socially reinventing themselves outside of the white supremacist Symbolic terms of recognition.

Such agency is well articulated in Toni Morrison's *Beloved* (1987), where slaves resist the violent conditions of their objectification precisely by mobilizing the ways that their bodies had been marked for transgressive purposes of their own. Slaves arrest the symbolic use of that mark, expropriating their masters from the objectifying intentions they attribute to that signifying chain, and mobilizing the sign for socially reconstitutive purposes of their own, generating a different story to be transmitted (through, among other avenues, Morrison's novel itself). This redeployment of the signifier constitutes a more aberrant way of reconstituting their otherwise impossible intersubjective humanity under the hellish conditions of chattel slavery, and through the very sign that recorded them as property rather than persons.

As Sethe, the heroine of *Beloved*, claims, the only thing that her mother did to inscribe herself in the order of kinship—in contrast to all the actions she was not allowed to do as a captive body (fix her hair, sleep in the same cabin, and generally perform motherhood per the gestures that support motherhood's Imaginary in the social order)—was to show her the distinctive mark by which she could be identified if dead:

> Back there she opened up her dress front and lifted her breast and pointed under it. Right on her rib was a circle and a cross burnt right in the skin. She said, "This is your ma'am. This," and she pointed, "I am the only one got this mark now. The rest is dead. If something happens to me and you can't tell me by my face, you can know me by this mark."[46]

It is that powerful agency of slaves, who were capable of reinventing their sociality by arresting the signifying chain of the American grammar, from the most brutal dehumanizing history of the coloniality of gender, that also resounds in Spillers's concluding reclamation of "Sapphire" as a radically different signifier of "female empowerment."[47] And it resounds, too, in the celebration of blackness in the poetics of *Negritude*, in the Black Power of the Panthers, and the Civil Rights Movement, all the way to black people's subversive reclamation of the "n" word.

Butler, as I have noted, is neither ignorant nor insensitive to that history. She understands that the light-skinned characters in Larsen's story are able to pass as white "because what can be seen, what qualifies as a visible marking, is a matter of being able to read a marked body in relation to unmarked bodies, where unmarked bodies constitute the currency of normative whiteness."[48] But she then fails to mark the queer subject that her theory is invested in politicizing through her reinterpretation of Antigone's equivocal terms, as if rewriting the terms of livability for the first time.[49] Thus, Butler risks reproducing the normativity that she previously decried in her analysis of Larsen's story, limiting the politics of her otherwise subversive call to undo gender under colonial conditions in which such an undoing proves to be a certain redoing of gender for symbolically marked flesh.[50]

Protected by Personhood Rather than Undone by Property

What more radically complicates the translation of Butler's "aberrant queer" into the black-feminist-redefined domain of Patterson's "social death," is the fact that Antigone was an *epikleros* (which literally means "with the property"). To the best of my knowledge, Foley first argued for such a condition to inform Antigone's case in Sophocles's tragedy, which Roger Just describes in the following terms:

> A man could bequeath his property and his *oikos* to whomsoever he wished, provided that he married his daughter to that man, who, of course, also became his adopted son and direct heir. If, however, he failed to bequeath his property by adopting the man to whom he married his daughter, or if he died before arranging the marriage of his daughter, then the fate of the *epikleros* was practically the same as the fate of the property in the case of intestate succession: i.e., the daughter could be claimed in marriage along with the property to which she was attached by her father's closest male relative within the *anchisteia* [set of relatives].[51]

According to Athenian practice, the first claimant of the *epikleros* was her father's brother and the second her mother's brother (Creon, in Antigone's case). Her mother's brother would be obliged to marry her, unless he was already married, as Creon was to Eurydice. The next claimant was the next male kin, her mother's brother's son, Haemon in Sophocles's tragedy. Respecting the legal customs of the audience for which the tragedy was performed, Antigone is to marry her cousin and pass on Oedipus's property. The institution of the *epikleroi*, however, also implied that the next-of-kin

> who claims the *epikleros* in marriage, becomes merely the caretaker of the *epikleros*' father's property until such time as she supplies by her marriage with him a male heir for her father's *oikos*. Hence the regulations which demand that the husband of an *epikleros* should have sexual intercourse with her at least three times a month, or, if he was incapable of this, that she should be allowed to "consort" with her husband's next-of-kin.[52]

As Just notes, in this way, the *epikleros* guarantees the patrilineal succession of the property through a de facto matrilineal succession, which further strengthens Antigone's bargaining power in her *agon* against Creon. As an *epikleros*, Foley thus claims, "[Antigone] may even be going so far as to suggest that Creon is illegitimately attempting to deprive her future offspring of their rightful leadership of Thebes."⁵³

One could also argue that in privileging Polyneices over Haemon, within the cultural horizon of property relations that regulate gendered inheritance in this Theban allegory of the Athenian *polis*, Antigone's semantic promiscuity troubles the symbolic order under conditions beyond the scope of Butler's framework. Opting for her natal rather than her conjugal family (a distinction first drawn by Foley) might perhaps be Antigone's own way of undoing the *atè*. As an *epikleros*, her marriage to Haemon would have continued Oedipus's rather than Haemon's offspring, and thus the curse of Oedipus's blood. Within the Symbolic context of property relations, which in this case endows Oedipus with a futurity through the figure of the *epikleros*, Antigone's privileging of the natal over the conjugal becomes, paradoxically, the opposite: a schizophrenic anti-Oedipal action, to riff on Gilles Deleuze and Félix Guattari's work.⁵⁴ Here, it is worth remembering that marriage and burials are the two civic functions for "free" women, who were otherwise excluded from the public, to perform as a public action in the Greek *polis*: reproducing the living citizen and attending to the dead one. Antigone collapses these two functions into one and turns them into their opposite: she is said to "marry" Polyneices in death in order to interrupt the life of Oedipus's *atè*. In other words, because she could contingently hold the property as an *epikleros*, Antigone's marriage to death could bury Oedipus's reproductive futurity.⁵⁵

Unlike Antigone, who could temporarily hold the property as an *epikleros*, the nonpositionality of the socially dead to which black and indigenous peoples were first subjected under modern/colonial capitalism means that they were property that others could hold. Black and indigenous women in particular—hence the differential production of their gender—were also forced to become the sexual reproducers of that abject condition, as their negligible injury forced them to birth commodities for the master, rather than socially recognized persons for the *polis*. As Spillers claims, "The offspring of the female does not 'belong' to the mother, nor is s/he 'related' to the 'owner,' though the owner 'possesses' it, and in the African-American instance, often fathered it, *and, as often,* without whatever benefit of patrimony."⁵⁶

Here, Spillers touches on one of slavery's most shocking accomplishments: that in order to protect the color line of kinship's sociality, the white settler master was willing to sell the daughters and sons that he fathered in the marketplace. The consequence, as Spillers rightly concludes, is that under a system of slavery, the "customary aspects of sexuality, including 'reproduction,' 'motherhood,' 'pleasure,' and 'desire,' are all thrown in crisis."[57] What Spillers further complicates here, for both feminist and queer theory, is the racialized assumptions that go into the history of sexuality when sex and violence become entirely inseparable. Spillers thus wonders if to use the vocabulary of sexuality—"reproduction," "motherhood," "pleasure," "desire"—is not to use a set of signifiers whose semantic history already betrays a set of racialized assumptions, inadequate to understand what took place under chattel slavery and continues to take place in its aftermath.[58]

Sexual domination was central to the legal (re)production of slavery, and Spillers's analysis receives its most important development in Saidiya Hartman's account of how the normalization of sexual violence linked racial formation to sexual subjection in the United States. Hartman extends Spillers's insight on the inadequacy of the vocabulary of sexuality to name intimacy under slavery, criticizing the discourse of seduction that "mitigate[d] the avowedly necessary brutality of slave relations through the shared affections of owner and captive."[59] Through this discourse, the romance of affection shrouded the saturated violence that permeated the whole settler order of chattel slavery, whitewashing the

> anti-miscegenation statutes, rape laws that made the rape of white women by black men a capital offence, the sanctioning of sexual violence against slave women by virtue of the law's calculation of negligible injury, the negation of kinship, and the commercial vitiation of motherhood as a means for the reproduction and conveyance of property and black subordination. . . . How can rape be differentiated from sexuality when "consent" is intelligible only as submission?[60]

Hartman poses this question in reference to the case of *Alfred v. State* (37 Miss. 296, October 1859). In this case, the court sustained an objection to the testimony of a slave named Charlotte, on behalf of her husband, Alfred, explaining that her husband had killed his overseer, Coleman, only after learning that "Coleman 'had forced her to submit to sexual intercourse with him.'"[61] In the court's conviction of Alfred to death by hanging, Hartman reads the convergent repression of rape, negation of kinship, and invalidation of slave marriage that made up sexuality as a term of implied relatedness, here techno-politically constructed as the exclusive prerogative of white settlers. Yet Hartman refuses to interpret Spillers's "ungendering," as if suggesting that black women existed outside the economy of gender, an exteriority Hartman rightly decries for risking maintaining "the white normativity of the category 'woman.'"[62] Instead, Hartman claims, one should think about the differential ways in which gender was historically produced. But Hartman does retain from Spillers the fact that such violent gendering, rather than recognizing the individuality of black and indigenous women, coerced them farther through the simulacrum of their subjectivity (consent only intelligible as submission).[63]

Butler wanted to render this representational throwing-into-crisis politically generative in Antigone's impossibility to control the symbolic referentiality of her terms. Yet the scenario is more complicated in the case of the enslaved, for whom the inability to control language is just an extension of a series of radical dispossessions in which the captive body's entire existence, including the futurity of their kin, is under the control not only of their enslaver but of the settler class as a whole. The deconstructive inversion of the performative speech-act, by which poststructuralist critique drives our attention to how our attempts "to do things with language" turn into how "language does things with us," encounters a more radical limit to its assumptive *we* when it confronts the sociosymbolic speechlessness that historically subdues the enslaved. Antigone can try to do things with language, but her incestuous origins pluralize the positions she would like to fix in ways that she could not have anticipated, making it possible for language to do things with Antigone—and to render her available for the anti-heteronormative politics of contemporary U.S. feminist and queer theory. Charlotte also tries to do things with language, but language does not endow Charlotte with the transgressive power of Antigone's anti-Oedipal futurity. Language does not do things with Charlotte; more accurately, language extends the undoing of Charlotte to the undoing of Alfred and of all the other slaves and their kinship formations. Charlotte's claims are more radically silenced than those of Antigone, as her testimony is seen by the court as perpetually unacceptable. It is more important to silence her testimony in order to preserve the system that reduces her and Alfred to the status of captive bodies for the profit and enjoyment of white settlers. Antigone's claims, on the contrary, are eventually heard, and not only is Polyneices finally buried, Creon is eventually punished.

The coloniality of gender, in other words, does not confuse the subject-positionalities of the socially dead subject in the socially equivocal universe of kinship, as it does when Antigone forces the system to confront the heteronormative limits of the incest taboo. The coloniality of gender means that indigenous and black people are not to be heard, so as to be more fully confined into the socially dead universe of the commodity, where property undoes personhood. As Hartman reconstructs in her excellent analysis of the trans-Atlantic slave trade, "the slaves were called *kop,* or head, as in the head of cattle, and not *hoof'd,* as in human head."[64] Collectively, they were referred to as "*armazoen,* which meant living cargo, as distinct from other kinds of goods."[65] To confront the differential production of gender across that color line is to take the anti-heteronormative politics of feminist and queer theory toward confrontation with the coloniality of gender and the logics that sustain its most brutal forms of racialized sexual subjection. To confront that history is to amplify Charlotte's speech with the decolonial rumination of her negligible injury, not in order to assign her a gender but in order to politically address the differential production of her gender, as the site of an injury for which there is no redress.[66]

Whose Ethical Act of Sublimation?

What to make, then, of Lacan's controversial claim, in the seminar *Encore,* that "woman does not exist"? And what to make of the ethical act he champions in *Antigone* as the act that happens under the conditions of a "forced choice"?[67] What differential forms of gendering are further mystified through this otherwise incoherent universalization of *woman* as the nominal term to indicate an all-encompassing condition of ontological incompleteness? Furthermore, is ontology—that is to say, the belonging of the subject to the human order of Being—not already presupposed within Lacan's understanding of the ethical act in the form of a forced choice? Whose choice is considered "forced" when women are universalized against the background of a colonial history in which for black and indigenous women consent, as Hartman argues, was only intelligible as submission?

In this section I explore the more positive reception of Lacan's psychoanalytic interpretation of *Antigone* in the feminist theory of Copjec, which she develops in great part as a response to Butler's political challenge to psychoanalysis. In *Read My Desire,* Butler stands for historicism, which Copjec defines as "the indwelling network of relations of power and knowledge."[68] With this definition, Copjec stresses Butler's theoretical indebtedness to Michel Foucault's history of sexuality, who was perhaps the first to argue for such indwelling network. These relations of power and knowledge are historically discontinuous, which allows us to demonstrate that sexuality was actually invented at one point in history. To put it succinctly, the homoerotic love of Greek antiquity is not the homosexual love that Victorian modernity tried to regulate. The very discourse of sexuality that organizes the invention of the latter does not preexist a different arrangement of power-knowledge relations in history. This is the power that takes life, rather than death, as its primary object—that is, in Foucault's theory, modern biopolitics.[69] Sexuality is thus spoken, written, assigned and regulated, in short, discursively constructed at some point in history. The role of critique is, then, to analyze the relations of power that historically turn sexuality into a discourse, and into a discourse entrusted with the capacity to tell us the "truth" of the subject—psychoanalysis included. Against such historical analysis of sexuality, Copjec returns to Lacan and claims, against the historicists, that the innovative contribution of psychoanalysis is to have understood sexuality instead as that which cannot be written into discourse. Situating the universal drama of sexuality in language's other (the void in the structure, i.e., the Real), rather than in the contingent universe of discourse (history), Lacan allows us to confront that which escapes discourse and yet propels it as if from underneath.

The subject, for Lacan, is not just constituted by the power/knowledge of a specific historically localizable discourse, but by having to articulate a demand through language that cannot be rendered as such in any discourse. We are all sexual beings to the extent that we are all language-users, that is to say, cut by the signifier. This does not mean that discourses or power are irrelevant for psychoanalysis. Even if we are all cut by the signifier we are all cut differently; no experience of analysis is the same as another. Furthermore, we can only confront the cut, the severity of our repression, and the morphogenesis of the subject to which such symbolic cut gives form, by means of a certain interpretation of discourse. But the history of the subject is not exhausted by the relations of power that condition the subject's traffic in and through signs. There is a form of negation that, as Copjec puts it in a critique of Foucault's rejection of the transcendental, "while written in language, is nonetheless without content" and "cannot, by definition, be absorbed by the system it contests."[70] Copjec, too, thus fails to confront the cut that, as I just reconstructed, does not condition symbolic narration but extends to language, the material scene of subjection that holds the flesh captive to a political-economic structure.

The Ethics of Psychoanalysis

I consider Copjec's work, like that of Butler, to be of the greatest importance, yet it also fails to confront the coloniality of gender. In order to analyze this aspect in Copjec, let me begin by reconstructing a bit better Lacan's approach to *Antigone* in his 1959–60 seminar on the ethics of psychoanalysis. The first thing I would like to say is that psychoanalysis is ethical in a rather transgressive way. Psychoanalysis, at least of the Lacanian type, is not a moral technology by which to discipline the irrational desires of the analysand, helping them to distinguish the good object of their desires from the bad one and, like some versions of ego-psychology, help them to become better adapted to society. This, for Lacanian psychoanalysis, would be rather unethical. If anything, Lacanian psychoanalysis is ethical precisely because it situates desire beyond good and evil. Lacanian psychoanalysis, in fact, confronts the analysand with the choice whose performance not only renders the moralistic binary insufficient, but has the power to un/re-do them as subjects. Thus, unlike traditional philosophical ethics, the ethics of psychoanalysis takes place under what we might characterize as immoral conditions, under the nonideal conditions of a forced choice.

This also explains psychoanalysis's interest in tragedy, as it is in tragedy where we are faced with choices that are not simply either good or evil, but a little bit of both (i.e., forced or constrained). *Antigone* is a tragic and ethical text because the two main characters in dispute, Antigone and Creon, are both faced with forced choices. According to the moral structure of the *polis* for which the tragedy was staged, Creon cannot honor the body of the enemy in the same way in which he honors the body of the friend, as doing good to one's friends and harm to one's enemies pretty much defines the moral economy of the ancient Greek *polis*.[71] But he cannot leave the body unburied, either, as death represents a limit for mortal power. Creon could have given a differential burial to Polyneices. He could have made it secret and quick, while turning the burial of Eteocles into a festive scene for community bonding, in great Homeric style. Such a solution might have sidestepped the irreconcilability between two opposite choices. Rather than to bury or not to bury, Creon might have found an alternative third way, one that makes the nonburial that preserves enmity legible through the differential burial itself. Creon could have recreated the friend-enemy distinction that he wanted to preserve through the differential doing of the burials, rather than through the differential undoing of one of them. After all, Creon not only decides to bury Eteocles and not to bury Polyneices, his *kerugma* (edict) adds a punishment for whoever decides to bury Polyneices and forces citizens to watch the body ravished by dogs and birds. A forced choice is, thus, never just a choice between A or B; it is always also a choice about the ways in which one chooses A or B. "How shall I act?" here comes to define "who I am." Creon needs to choose, and it is through the *way* in which he chooses one of the forced choices with which he is confronted that he becomes Creon.

Antigone is also faced with a forced choice. Creon's *kerugma* prohibits the burial of Polyneices and punishes whoever buries him with death, and yet she is supposed to bury her brother. To bury Polyneices is one of her duties as a member of his family. If she does not bury her brother, she commits an injustice, an injustice to the gods, to her community, and to herself, but she also commits an injustice if she disobeys the law. She has to make a choice. Similarly, Antigone does not merely choose to bury her brother but also chooses how to choose. If we follow Honig's interpretation, and accept that Ismene performed the first burial, one notices the same variability between A and B that I just highlighted in the case of Creon. There are as many ways of choosing how not to bury as there are of choosing how to bury the body. Ismene decides to do it at night and in secrecy, Antigone decides to do it in broad daylight and to claim the disobedience publicly. Her own "how shall I act?" also gives us her "who I am." Through ethical action she becomes, to put it in Nietzsche's term, who she is.

But it is here that Lacan notices a crucial difference between Creon and Antigone, the one that in his view, Hegel most problematically occludes.[72] If tragedy is, as Aristotle defines it, "a means of accomplishing the purgation of the emotions by a pity and fear similar to this," Creon and Antigone confront us with two very different affective economies of purgation.[73] According to Lacan, Creon's purgation takes place at the level of *hamartia* (often translated as "error of judgment"), Antigone's take place at the level of *atè* (often translated as "misfortune"). *Hamartia* situates us within the living, and troubles the limits of what we can or cannot know. *Atè*, however, forces us to confront death and troubles our being rather than just the limits of our knowledge. Unlike Antigone, Creon's ethical choice does not confront him with death. In fact, it is precisely when he is faced with death, with the death that Tiresias prophesizes, that Creon is overcome by fear. And it is that fear that leads him not only to change the course of his action, but to err again in the way in which he undoes his actions. Creon decides to bury Polyneices's body first, disregarding Tiresias's suggested order of operations, thus giving enough time for Antigone to commit suicide (or be killed, which cannot be ruled out) and ignite the series of suicides that follow.⁷⁴ Again, in ethics one never just chooses between a forced choice that opposes the doing of A to the doing of B, one always chooses how one chooses either of them. And the same follows for the reversal, for the undoing of the deed. Fearing the death that haunts him, Creon rushes in judgment and errs a second time, making him pitiable in the eyes of the audience and the tragic hero in Aristotle's view.

Lacan's whole point is that Aristotle is simply wrong.⁷⁵ We only reach the ethical catharsis of tragedy when we go beyond the moral economy of fear and pity, that is to say, when the ethical hero confronts not an error in judgment (*hamartia*) but a more foundational error, let's say, an error in being (*atè*). Not only does Antigone show no fear, she acts already knowing that her actions will result in her death. Yet, in the way in which Antigones chooses A twice (unlike Creon), when she moves from the moral and universal law to the singular one, Lacan claims, she purifies her desire. Or, to put it differently, Antigone's second choice confronts us with the kind of form that desire takes in the raw, unsupported by the Symbolic order.

Morally flexible, Creon's own moral purgation is outshined by what Lacan calls Antigone's "splendor," her ethically inflexible act. And yet, her "splendor" is, precisely, the last subterfuge by which to ward off the death drive with which her desire otherwise confronts us. The death drive refers to that repetition that, as Freud claimed in *Beyond the Pleasure Principle* (1920), comes before the pleasure principle in order to then be subordinated to it.⁷⁶ *Beyond the Pleasure Principle* is, arguably, Freud's most important philosophical work, one in which he engages in what Gilles Deleuze adequately calls a "transcendental" investigation.⁷⁷ If the pleasure principle is what governs life, Freud asks himself, in virtue of what prior/higher principle is the field of life governed by this principle? To put it in Gilles Deleuze's terms, by "virtue of what higher connection—what 'binding' power—is pleasure a principle with the dominance that it has?"⁷⁸ It is at this level that Freud offers Eros as a grounding principle, as that which stirs life from its inanimate sleep, only to then have to confront Thanatos (the death drive), Eros's inescapable companion, as the one that "repeats what was before the instant of life."⁷⁹ Creon's purgation takes place at the level of morality, of the pleasure principle, of the exchangeable economy of fear and pity, of the calculation that measures a choice in relation to alternative goods and finite ends. Antigone's purgation, however, takes place at the level of ethics, of the death drive, of that unwritable binding power that precedes the pleasure principle and confronts us with the abyssal nature of our desires, the fact that nothing in the Symbolic order supports them and that it is toward that very nothingness, a return to the inanimate, that our desires are ultimately bound. This is what Lacan calls "the pure and simple desire of death as such," which Antigone "incarnates."[80]

How to understand that pure and simple desire of death as such, is what interests Copjec. This is the kind of death that is, arguably, only reachable when one sacrifices one's own place in the Symbolic order and thus moves from moral/mortal *hamartia* (error in judgment/pleasure principle) to ethical/immortal *atè* (error in being/death drive). Who we are, as we saw, is not independent of what we do. And yet, we are never equal to the sum of our acts, nor equal to the sum of our linguistically articulated representations of ourselves. Something always escapes the referential capacity of language to fully name us. That something, however, is not some transcendental Thing, a whole of being, an essential meta-Subject, but the symbolic byproduct of the structure itself, in Lacan's language, the "void of the Real." There must be a "not-all" of being for being to be able to be inexhaustibly articulated in language. In lieu of the transcendental place of Being, Lacan thus posits an immanent nonbeing, the inanimate Thanatos that accompanies the binding power of Eros.

In Lacan's framework, Antigone's act is ethical not because her actions can pass the test of the categorical imperative (Kant) and reach proper universality. It is ethical because the unique singularity that she attaches to Polyneices confronts us with a different kind of universality, the one that we reach precisely when all calculations of good and evil are surpassed. As we saw, there is no easy path to reach that universality, and the purification of one's desire probably requires a willingness to transgress the moral law, and to take that transgression to the extremity of sacrificing one's position in the Symbolic order, thus entering the space that Lacan defines as "the space in between two deaths."[81] This is the space from which the infinite, rather than the finite, can be measured (what Lacan refers to as the Last Judgment). And it is in relation to that ethical transgression that Copjec revisits Lacan's theory of the forced choice.

On Forced Choices

Here, Copjec productively invokes Lacan's reading of Søren Kierkegaard's analysis of the forced choice in order to discern the precise sense in which Antigone becomes a figure of the death drive, when she is confronted with the "either/or" structure of the ethical act. According to Copjec, Kierkegaard's formulation dramatizes the ethical act because the subject is forced to confront a choice that coincides with the elimination of its conditions of possibility, as the subject reaches the Real by sacrificing her position in the Symbolic order. But, as Copjec lucidly suggests, Kierkegaard's forced choice takes two formulations that are by no means equivalent, because one of them does not represent a lose/lose situation even if both of them confront us with choices between two options, one of which coincides with the conditions of possibility for the choice of the other.

The first formulation says, "your money or your life," the second, "freedom or death." If, in the first case, I choose money, I lose both money and life because life is not only a choice but the condition of possibility of the other's choice too. This means that life is the only real choice, but one that leaves me deprived of life's conditions of sustainability (although, Copjec fails to add, this holds only in a capitalist society, in which money can thus be generalized). The second case seems similar, as choosing freedom demonstrates the opposite, thus making death the only real choice that can prove the choice to be freely made. Once this decision is taken, Copjec adds, "you lose all freedom but the freedom to die. This is what Hegel called the 'freedom of the slave.'"[82] I will come back to this freedom of the slave shortly. "Freedom or death," however, does not correspond to the alienating structure of "your money or your life," Copjec argues, because psychoanalysis de-biologizes death at the point at which death intersects with freedom. In other words, while life is lost if one chooses money (choosing one automatically entails losing the other), freedom is, rather, gained by choosing death. Or, as Copjec puts it, at least "some of it" is won over.[83] Copjec's point is that the "death one opts for in the second example is not the same one that is avoided in the first," that it refers to a symbolic rather than biological death.[84] Antigone chooses that death. As she says, to Ismene, "Life was your choice, and death was mine" (A, 555 [183]), "you are alive, but my life died long ago, to serve the dead" (A, 559–60 [183]). In choosing death, knowingly violating the edict that prescribes death, Antigone resituates her action in a place where that action is no longer imaginarily prescribed by the Law. Rather, her act is made independent of external sanction.[85]

Lacan refers to this place as the "space in between two deaths," which the subject enters whenever she sacrifices her place in the Symbolic order and reaches her desire through her own laws, rather than through the laws by which the social order regulated her behavior. Antigone becomes autonomous and, in remaining faithful to her desire without the Symbolic support that otherwise regulates it, becomes a figure of the death drive. Antigone's autonomy is, then, more Sade than Kant, in that it takes place through a forced choice in which only by transgressing the moral law, rather than unconditionally obeying it, she can confront the abyssal foundation of her desire. Copjec is thus absolutely right when she claims that Lacan's ethical imperative, "do not give way on your desire," is not an uncritical insistence on the ethical priority of the individual's stubborn preferences but, as Lacan interprets *Antigone*, an insistence on the individual's ability to give themselves laws without validation from another authority. As Copjec lucidly puts it, "[I]t is not the otherness but the nonexistence of the Other on which Lacan's interpretation turns."[86] The ethics of psychoanalysis is not about going beyond ourselves through a certain alternative stylization of our subjectivity. The point of psychoanalysis is that we can only go beyond ourselves if we confront the radical abyss that is at the heart of who we are. The ethics of psychoanalysis is about confronting our extimate nonexistence, so to speak.

It is at this stage that Copjec brings back Freud's analysis of the death drive. As we saw, Freud understands the death drive (Thanatos) as "the restoration of an earlier state of things," the repetition of the inanimate that accompanies all of Eros's efforts to stir life from its dormant sleep. Thanatos is, then, unlike Eros, satisfied not through the achievement of its aim but through its inhibition. This means: first, that death is in the past rather than in the future; and second, that such death is always broken rather than continuous, that it refers not to a grand and original nothingness that precedes Being, but to small nothings instead. Both of these insights lead Copjec to underline a certain indifference, on the part of the drive, to the object through which it accomplishes its satisfaction, as indeed any object can serve as alibi. It is here that Copjec criticizes Lacan for conflating sublimation with idealization, when defining sublimation as "'the elevation of an ordinary object to the dignity of the Thing.'"[87] Copjec thus interprets Antigone's orientation to Polyneices, as the object of her desire, a bit differently. Not, let's say, as the raising of the ordinary object (Polyneices's corpse) into the dignity of the Thing, "the immortalization of her family's *atè*," but as a way of creating, ex nihilo, "an object, a thing in the very place where unified jouissance, *das Ding*, is absent."[88]

Butler insists, against Copjec and Lacan, that such creation is never ex nihilo. Antigone, Butler claims, gives a form to her way of not giving way on her desire and, thus, participates in politics, not just in ethics. For

Butler, the form that she gives to her desire makes it impossible for her to ever fully separate the Symbolic from the social.[89] Failing to confront the terms by which Antigone remains faithful to her desire, the many reasons that she offers as justifications for the burial of Polyneices, Copjec also fails to confront Antigone's claim to bury Polyneices because he was not Eteocles's slave. Copjec, thus, also turns away from the historical slave and engages in a similar abstraction, to the one that I questioned in the case of Butler. For in order to create an object, ex nihilo or not, one must not already be the object on whose violent de-animation the social order relies for the colonially circumscribed constitution and recognition of proper subjectivity.

The Unethical Enslaved Who Have Nothing to Lose

Copjec, thus, never contests the Hegelian equation of "all freedoms except the freedom to die" with the "freedom of the slave" that she then uses to analyze Antigone's forced choice. The problem with Hegel's analytic is that it presents us with a death that can presumably be chosen, as if uncomplicated by the history of chattel slavery and, as Hartman argues, its aftermath. The enslaved are, however, never confronted with a choice. The enslaver never says to the enslaved, either you give me your freedom or I take your life, choose. Rather, the enslavers take many lives and severely punish the ones that they do not take, in order to mark the displacement of the enslaved from the human order of being (who can choose) and into the inhuman order of the commodity (who cannot choose, or for whom "choice" is only intelligible as submission). Slavery kills the sociality of the enslaved, a sociality wherein choice, even forced choice, can be recognizable. In the Hegelian equation of "freedom or death" with the "freedom of the slave" resounds the problematic reciprocity of Hegel's master/slave dialectic. This is the reciprocity that Frantz Fanon criticizes, when he claims that the real master of the colonial situation, unlike the idealistic master of Hegel's *Phenomenology of the Spirit*, "scorns the consciousness of the slave," given that "what he wants from the slave is not recognition but work."[90]

What Antigone *gains* when she chooses death is simply not possible for the slave. Death is not an object of choice but the overwhelming reality that already disqualifies the slave from the consensual capacity to choose. To put it differently, Antigone does have a place in the social order of Greek antiquity. Hers is, undoubtedly, an extremely marginalized place, but Antigone was not a slave. She, then, has something that she can sacrifice. What she gives up, in order to remain faithful to her desire, is not exactly what she has but, as Alenka Zupančič so lucidly puts it, what she "could (perhaps) have had, had she continued to live."[91] The list includes marriage, the nurturing of children, friends, being mourned by others, and honor, among many other things.[92] The list is not unproblematically infinite, as Zupančič argues, rather it is quite circumscribed. But the list does convey the place that she could have had in the social order, had she been able to live. The modern enslaved, the natally alienated, by contrast, have no such list to give up. The enslaved are not moved from a socially marginalized place—the *oikos* to which "free" Athenian and *metic* women were partially confined—to a rocky cavern after transgressing the law. The enslaved are already confined, in life, to that rocky cavern as their mere existence is considered a kind of transgression to begin with. From the gallows to the slave ship to the plantation to the penal colony all the way to the prison industrial complex, the enslaved live under more or less violent rocky caverns. To put it differently, whereas Antigone can, by choosing death, *win* some freedom, the enslaved cannot. Not only because choice is unrecognizable under these conditions, but also because death itself is lost, as a category of being.

As Hartman asserts, citing a Dutch historian, the death rate of the slave trade reached "70% before the survivors were adjusted to life in the Western Hemisphere."[93] Laurent Dubois adds that social conditions never improved in the modern plantations because "it was cheaper to let slaves die and buy more from Africa."[94] Are not slaves, then, as Hartman claims, "for all intents and purposes dead, no less so than had [they] been killed in combat . . . no less so than had [they] never belonged to the world?"[95] And if they are already dead to the world, socially dead, how can we make sense of this "freedom to die" that Hegel associates with the "freedom of the slave"? Not only is some unclear list of freedoms problematically attributed to the slave, the very language of choice betrays the substitution of the social horrors of slavery with another reality, one which the enslaved are nonetheless called to help make intelligible. But when "consent," as Hartman claims, is only intelligible as submission, can force really be said to condition a "choice"? In other words, when all choices can be said to be forced, does it really make sense to speak of a "forced choice" as a distinctively ethical one? Or are, then, all "choices" within slavery ethical? If we attend to this difference, should we not consider the ethical "forced choice" as, in part, constituted through the exclusion of that other "forced choice" for which no proper grammar exists? I say "no grammar" not because its structure has not been grammatically articulated; it has, but it remains theoretically marginalized, as it does not inform the "forced choice" that qualifies an act as ethical in feminist psychoanalysis.

The grammatical articulation of this "choice" does not take the form of Hegel's "all freedoms except" but that of Assata Shakur's "nothing to lose but our chains," properly situating the words from Marx and Engels's *Communist Manifesto* under a thoroughly racialized labor regime of exploitation.[96] However, it is not Shakur's formulation but Hegel's that informs the "forced choice" of the ethical subject of psychoanalysis. To put it differently, it is not the real slave but the idealistic abstraction that offers psychoanalysis a framework through which to read the ethical act of the subject.

Who is the subject who can enter death, choose it, even if under duress? Moreover, if as an ordinary object in the Symbolic order, Polyneices's corpse can stand for the Thing, the moral good, in the ethical structure of Antigone's sublimation, what Thing does this extraordinary object, which Fred Moten characterizes as the "speaking/shrieking commodity," stand for in the brutal order of modern slavery?[97] Or are these, as Frank Wilderson calls them, "unspeakable ethics"?[98] Is this space in between two deaths—the space in which death can refer to something other than biological death, to death in life, to death as the contingent experience of a transgression that entails the death of the subject to the Symbolic order—not the space to which slaves were confined structurally, rather than one they could inhabit contingently through heroic transgression? Is not ethical sublimation, then, as the satisfaction of the drive through the inhibition of its aim, the everyday "life" of the slave, whose continuous "existence" cannot but be resistance to an already promulgated death, commuted on the condition of total submission? Is not the slave the one who must, every day and at every second, escape the overwhelming death that haunts them in order to extend an existence that expired long before it even started, in what could only be grotesquely called the "satisfaction" of a drive to *survive*? Does the ethical subject's contingent entering of the space in between two deaths, then, come to rest on the structural confinement of the unspeakably ethical enslaved to that most unlivable space?

According to the Lacanian psychoanalytic interpretation that informs Copjec's interpretation, Antigone becomes an ethical subject when she steps into the space between two deaths. Only then can she bind death together with freedom and reach an unintelligible form of desire that liberates her, since all the other ideologically false objects of her desire symbolically work to reconfirm her heteronomous place in the social order. She can follow her own law when she no longer seeks validation elsewhere. But she can do that, notwithstanding the constraints she faces, because she is not already regarded as socially dead to the Symbolic order. By sacrificing her own place in that order, thus splitting death in two (Symbolic and biological), she becomes autonomous and gives herself her own law, becoming an ethical subject. The very same act, for the enslaved, describes a subjective trajectory that ends not in ethical becoming but in political fugitivity, at best.

The enslaved, in other words, does not step into the space between two deaths when their ethical act is accomplished. In the best-case scenario, the enslaved step outside of that most unlivable condition, which they experience as the overwhelming brutality of their whole existence, when they perform an act that remains ethically unspeakable and morally criminalized from the get-go. The enslaved are forced to experience, as a structural form of total domination, what the ethical subject of feminist psychoanalysis experiences as the contingent occurrence of their transgressive and heroic autonomous act.

Copjec's otherwise critical understanding of women as the "not-all" of being reinscribes the coloniality of gender upon which her theory also draws but fails to fully interrogate. Consequently, the ontological opening of that "not-all" of being, the feminine act of sublimation performs against the Symbolic order of heteropatriarchy, comes to rest on the disavowed violence that differentially (re)produces black and indigenous women, who remain confined into the "all-not" of being. Antigone can, then, deny the existence of the Other, and force us to confront the abyss of the Symbolic order with the arbitrariness that confines her to a specific place, and become autonomous in the performative process by which she embraces death. But she can also reinscribe the otherness of slaves, through her otherwise ethical denial of the existence of the Other.

Tiresias's Gender Complementarity and the Fungibility-*cum*-Fugitivity of Black Transness

Antigone's fifth *epeisodion* (an interlude of the tragedy containing the main action) could be said to constitute a missed Hegelian moment of dialectical *aufhebung* (sublimation). In this *epeisodion,* Creon faces the third and final *agon* of the play. It is the blind prophet Tiresias who performs this *agon,* by which Creon is finally persuaded to bury Polyneices and unbury Antigone. Antigone performs the first *agon* against Creon, but he disregards her reasons on the basis of her gender. It does not matter if she has good reasons; gender politics regulate how subjects participate in the *logos* and already disqualify whatever she has to say. As Creon says to Haemon, "If we must accept defeat, let it be from a man; we must not let people say that a woman beat us" (A, 679–80 [187]). Haemon performs the second *agon*, and this time the speaker embodies the "proper" gender, but Creon disregards him on the basis of their kinship relation. Haemon lacks an *oikos* of his own, and thus stands in the subordinated position of a son to his father, rather than in the more politically enabling position of an equal *kyrios* (ruler) of another household that his marriage to Antigone would have afforded him. Differently subordinated to the *kyrios* of their *oikos*, Antigone and Haemon lack the equality that, from Creon's perspective, renders their speeches politically unpersuasive. With respect to them, Tiresias constitutes a sociosexual *aufhebung* (dialectical synthesis) of their positions. Tiresias's successful *agon* constitutes a dialectical third moment that both incorporates and overcomes the limitations of the two previous agonistic moments. This dialectical *aufhebung* is further supported by the dramatic architecture of ancient theater. According to the dramaturgical parameters of Greek tragedy, the same actor would have performed the roles of Antigone, Haemon, and Tiresias on the stage. In other words, the same actor who fails to persuade Creon as Antigone and fails a second time as Haemon finally succeeds as Tiresias. The hybrid son of a shepherd and a nymph, who was turned into a woman for seven years, Tiresias might indeed represent the missing *aufhebung* of what J. M. Bernstein's most generous interpretation of Hegel names "the social metaphysics of gender complementarity."[99] For Bernstein, it is the "presumptively natural complementarity between the sexes that sutures the competing political and religious regimes of law into a beautiful whole," which Hegel is claimed to endorse, that he actually criticizes.[100]

Despite Hegel's obsession with a triadic structure and the significance he assigns *Antigone* in his *Phenomenology of the Spirit*, Hegel misses this third moment of the play, as do all interpretations inspired by him, to the best of my knowledge. Tiresias's potential gender complementariness should not be underestimated, as feminist and queer theory have done in their failure to account for the success of his intervention. Nor should it be ahistorically characterized as a case of transgenderism, despite the fact that Tiresias was indeed, transformed into a woman for at least seven years. Not just because transgenderism, like queerness and homosexuality, has a history, but also because there is no transitioning, as a politically distinctive act, in the case of Tiresias. He is turned into another gender and then turned back, but he does not actively participate in that transition as a politically insurgent act of anti-heteronormative becoming. Yet, if Antigone can be said to generate a problematic that is of interest to queer theory, if not quite a queer heroine herself (as Butler rightly claims), Tiresias might help us to articulate a problematic that is of interest to trans theory, if not quite a trans figure himself.[101]

More like Haemon than Antigone, Tiresias's male-presenting body does not threaten the homosociality of the *polis*, and Creon cannot so readily disqualify his speech when Tiresias repeats what the sovereign does not want to hear. Tiresias is also not his kin but another member of the *polis*, so Creon cannot invoke his own position as *kyrios* of the *oikos* to disqualify him either. More like Antigone than like Haemon, however, Tiresias's knowledge refers to the unwritten domain of the divine that Hegel associates with Antigone. Furthermore, the arguments that Tiresias voices are not the exclusively civic ones advanced by Haemon, but the divine and civic ones originally advanced by Antigone (A, 450–60 [178]). If Antigone constitutes the impossible subject (structurally disavowed as a consequence of her gender) and Haemon constitutes the possible subject (since he is in the process of achieving autonomy, of ruling his own household and becoming relatively equal to Creon), Tiresias stands as an alternative who makes the impossible speak in the language of the possible. In other words, he has the credentials to speak that Haemon and Antigone lacked. And if Antigone's speech-acts demonstrate the social order's failure to restrict public agency to a specific gender, Tiresias's speech-acts can be said to demonstrate the powerful agency of a prefigurative transgender body in Greek antiquity—if only, arguably, in a male-presenting capacity.

By incorporating both principles, a trans-capable Tiresias *amplifies* the agential capabilities of "gender trouble" in this play, most notably in the divine punishment he conveys to Creon. By failing to bury Polyneices, and by burying Antigone alive in a cave, Tiresias claims, the sovereign will deliver a corpse from his "own loins" (A, 1065 [202]). Tiresias's prophecy holds the sovereign to democratic accountability: he will pay with one corpse from his own household (Eurydice and Haemon) for each of those he injured (Polyneices and Antigone). But such democratic equivalence passes through a kind of gender trouble, as Tiresias endows Creon with an artificial womb that births death rather than life. Creon becomes, in the curse of this *agon*, an organ without bodies, to riff again on Deleuze and Guattari's work. Tiresias—who can be characterized as a body without organs, given the blindness that endows him with greater sight—delivers the decisive blow in the third and final *agon* of this play.

Although it would be comforting if we could endorse Tiresias's moment as the dialectical *aufhebung* in the social metaphysics of gender complementarity that J. M. Bernstein claims Hegel's feminism criticizes in German Romanticism, the truth is that this narrative is equally insufficient. First, because Bernstein makes that point in relation to the nonincorporation of Antigone, not in relation to the dialectic synthesis of Tiresias's prefigurative transness. According to Bernstein, Antigone, whom Hegel infamously generalized as "the everlasting irony in the life of the community," represents a critique rather than an endorsement of Greek antiquity's ethical failure to properly and fully accommodate the spirit of individuality. But Antigone, and the womankind she is forced to represent, has an individuality recognizable neither by the Roman notion of personhood that supersedes the Greek *polis,* nor by Hegel's German state. Butler, too, is right when she argues against Hegel (and, by association, Bernstein) that there is no *aufhebung* in which Antigone ever gets recovered. Second, Tiresias's gender complementariness is also insufficient because its political efficacy depends not only on Tiresias's ability to dialectically subsume Antigone's and Haemon's spiritual moments only under a male-presenting body, but also on Tiresias's political status in the city, as a public servant who was, however, not a slave but a socially valued prophet.

Hence, Tiresias's successful *agon* against Creon includes neither a redress to citizenship's dependency on *metoikia* and slavery, nor a critique of the racialized production of gender and the interrelated gendered production of ethnic difference in antiquity. Tiresias' prefigurative transness is neutralized in the play, and actually has nothing to say about the spectacular circularity with which differences were co-constituted in antiquity. This is what happens, for instance, when Creon first claims that "if we must accept defeat, let it be from a man; we must not let people say that a woman beat us" (A, 679–80 [187]), only to then dismiss Haemon for having become a "women's slave" (A, 756 [191]. As Chanter argues, in Greek antiquity:

> Male barbarians are said to be effeminate, which helps to bolster up the argument that they are naturally slavish. Their ostensible effeminacy assumes the inequality of women to men, at the same time as it presupposes that women's inferiority allies women with slaves.[102]

Polyneices must be buried and Antigone unburied, Tiresias claims, not in order to break with the ethnic/gendered regulation of speaking bodies in the *polis*, but because Creon has violated a divine limit. Tiresias, like Antigone, fails to politically connect the plague that unattended corpses unleash in the *polis*, to the *polis*'s imperial war and its consequent anxious racialized regulation of sexuality and assignation of gender. Reading the flying patterns of the birds in the sky, which are unreadable because they are feeding on Polyneices's corpse, Tiresias fails to address the political dependency of the *polis* on slavery and the symbolic economies that slavery materially sustains. This is the slavery that, one could argue, Creon extended to the body of Polyneices, on whose slave-transmogrified body the birds are feeding. Tiresias fails to read all of this in the irregular flying patterns of the birds, and thus he misses the ethnic/gendered stratified division of membership that materially and symbolically constrains the future of the *polis*.

Fast-forward to modernity. C. Riley Snorton has offered, in my view, the best analysis of the trans-capable agency of slaves in colonial modernity, which is where I am situating the reception of *Antigone* in this chapter. According to Snorton, slaves were often able to use the colonial fungibility of their gender, which counted them not as gendered humans but as property (quantities), as Spillers argues, "as a contrivance for freedom."[103] Snorton thus crafts an alternative history of trans identity by focusing on the agency of the enslaved, as documented in their cross-gender and cross-dressing fugitive practices. *Fugitivity* differs from *freedom* in that it describes an experience of freedom within a structural condition of unfreedom. The fugitive is not granted a symbolically recognized place in the social order, nor afforded the legal protections that legal personhood bestows upon those whom the social order recognizes as equal members of the *polis*, as in fact those protections depend on the simultaneous production of the unprotected. The fugitive remains haunted by the policing forms of social subordination that can always result in recapture, even if they temporarily enjoy no longer being subjected to the brutal rule of their enslavers. *Fugitivity* refers to a "space of freedom that is at the same time a space of captivity," which Hartman characterizes as a "loophole of retreat," drawing from Harriet Jacobs.[104]

The fugitive "passing" that interests Snorton is not, however, the one on which most feminist and queer theorists focus, as in Butler's reading of Larsen's *Passing*. It is not, in other words, the passing whereby the black subject ascends into privilege by passing as white. Snorton focuses, rather, on Harriet Jacobs's use of charcoal in 1835 to darken her complexion after her enslaver, James Norcom, published a description of her that suggested she would be "seeking whiteness," thus making it possible for Jacobs to escape recapture by accentuating her blackness instead. As Snorton brilliantly puts it, in this case blackness "points to a place where being undone is simultaneously a space for new forms of becoming."[105] Accentuating blackness transforms, as he documents in various cases, the gender identity of the subject, whom the social order of slavery wanted to turn back into an object, by means of this inescapably racialized form of gender policing. The enslaved engaged in fugitivity, through the alternative mobilization of their "ungendered flesh" by maneuvering "from within the morass of slavery's identity politics."[106]

There is one case from Snorton's archive that politicizes even further the gap that separates the politically neutralized gender-complementariness of Tiresias' male-presenting prefigurative transness in Greek antiquity, from the politically more difficult to discern transness of blackness in colonial modernity. I close this section with an analysis of this case because it also orbits around the political supplement of disability, which is crucial to Tiresias's successful *agon* with Creon. As a socially recognized and valued prophet in a male-presenting body, Tiresias's disability endows him with greater political power in his agonistic confrontation with the sovereign. By contrast, the disabilities of the enslaved were only registered to the extent that they reinforced their objectification—that is to say, when disability marked them as damaged property. The enslaved were more often exposed to the loss of their limbs, and of their abilities more broadly, than citizens or *metics,* not only because of their inaccessibility to proper care, but also because of the gratuitous violence that sustained the brutality of their socially dead life. The enslaved, in other words, were both forced into various forms of disability that could reinforce their status as excluded labor (forced illiteracy included) and denied the recognition of those injuries as proper disabilities.[107]

In his analysis of Ellen and William Craft's escape, Snorton demonstrates that not only the color of their gender but also the racialized figuration of disability as the exclusive prerogative of whiteness, served them in turning their fungibility into fugitivity. The plan was for the light-skinned Ellen to dress herself in a man's clothing and pass as the master while her husband passed as the servant, in a performative rendering of William's social death that did not escape Snorton's attention. For Ellen to become a white master, it was crucial for her to render her disavowed disability socially recognizable. This she did by transforming the illiteracy to which she was structurally subjected into a socially recognizable sign of subjective impairment, wearing a "sling, poultice, and green spectacles."[108] The object, however, was not a sufficient condition, and William's performance reinforced the disability that secured their subversive imitation of the master-slave scene of subjection, under slavery's semiotics of subjectivity. The performance of disability, as Snorton claims—based on Ellen Samuels's analysis of the case and Jacques Derrida's theory—acted as the supplement by which the master-slave relationship accrued its symbolic credibility, allowing the Crafts to turn their fungibility into the "fertile ground [for] their flight."[109]

Fungible-*cum*-fugitive agency is what I tried to read in the ability of slaves to instrumentalize the symbolic mark by which they were signified as property and denied as persons, in order to reconstruct the otherwise violated universe of their kinship formations. It is that same fungibility-*cum*-fugitivity that one can read in Spillers's reclamation of "Sapphire," as an insurgent figure of empowerment. It is not, however, the kind of agency that one can distinguish in the trans-neutralized agency of the ancient Tiresias, who fails to connect the plague unleashed by Polyneices's slave-transmogrified corpse in the city to the material dependency of the *polis* on colonialism, stratified membership, and the gender policing of racialized sexuality.

Whose Future?

With Tiresias's figuration of Creon as the womb that births corpses, we are brought back to the future, to modern slavery as the ghost in the machine of North American kinship. Tiresias's language is figurative. By extending slavery to citizens, undoing the border that keeps life separate from death, death now contaminates the whole social order and Creon can be said to be responsible for the overwhelming reproduction of death in the whole city and the corpses in his own family. Modern racialized slavery in the United States turned what was only a dramatic figure in *Antigone* into the horrifying reality of chattel slavery. The decriminalization of rape made it possible for white masters (settler citizens) to rape black and indigenous women and reproduce, in the process, not a human being but a socially dead person. There is obviously a great deal of difference between the reproduction of a corpse, as a figure of speech by which to indict the ancient sovereign, and the legal institutionalization of sexual violence as negligible injury, in order to guarantee the reproduction of a socially dead person under the political arithmetic of modern chattel slavery.

The connection, however, allows us to understand the radical implications of Patterson's qualification of the slave as a natally alienated nonperson. The temporally endless condition of social death under modern slavery meant that death was in the past (slavery was inherited), in the present (slavery rested in the gratuitous violence of everyday brutality and general dishonor), and in the future (female slaves were forced to transfer their abject condition to their offspring). The consequence of such ubiquitous death, as David Marriott claims, was the loss of death itself as a category of being, as death "emerges as a transcendental fact of black existence but without transcendence. . . . This is no longer death but a deathliness that cannot be spiritualized or brought into meaning."[110] The de-spiritualization and demeaning of black death means that black corpses, too, continued to perform free labor for their masters.

Creon's instrumentalization of Polyneices's corpse Antigone adequately interprets as potentially forcing upon Polyneices the status of a slave, as some classics scholars have argued. Creon's violent act is rather exceptional, and other cities are willing to fight against it, including the people who, Haemon reports, praise Antigone's disobedient burial. The violation of slaves' corpses in modernity was, however, not exceptional at all. As Snorton claims—referring to the historical research of Harriet Washington—"the emphasis on anatomical instruction in nineteenth-century medical classrooms produced a demand for cadavers, which were frequently supplied through the theft of black flesh from cemeteries, mortuaries, and morgues," a supply system that extended well into the twentieth century (a study conducted in 1933 found that "southern medical schools . . . still used only black cadavers for teaching anatomy").[111] This theft of corpses extended slavery beyond the official date of its legal abolition. This is one of the many reasons Hartman's notion of the "aftermath of slavery," rather than freedom post-emancipation, is so important. To riff on Thomas Laqueur's monumental investigation in *The Work of the Dead* (2015), the work of the socially dead differs considerably from the (un)remarked work of the dead that, as Butler claims, constitutes the currency of normative whiteness, and to whom Laqueur devotes most of his book. The socially dead's dead continue to perform free labor for the settler order, since it is through the continuous violation and economic exploitation of their corpses, too, that the human becomes biologically dissected, anatomically identified, and even gender-assigned.[112]

But, enslaved corpses continue to fight back. The refusal of these bodies to be thus coerced in their afterlives outlives them too, and their bones carry on the subversive spirit of their multiple refusals. As Laqueur documents on one of those rare occasions in which he focuses on the deaths of slaves, when a 1794 slave burial ground was found in Lower Manhattan in October 1991, black people organized and forced the General Services Administration to radically alter the original $275 million federal office building to create "what became in 2006 the African Burial Ground National Monument."[113] I also want to draw attention to this example in order to articulate how the future of capital reinscribes the settler-colonial deathliness of the socially dead, but always fails to fully accomplish its intended de-spiritualization. In life as well as in death, the socially dead resist the horrifying conditions of their fungibility and continue to animate their undying fugitivity.

Social death was not inflicted exclusively upon black people; indigenous peoples were also subjected to modern slavery. The eventual assimilation of indigenous peoples to whiteness via reproductive policies in North America during the second modernity, however, did not grant them a futurity either. Like the antimiscegenation laws that made blackness unmodifiable against any amount of racial mixing, the biopolitical absorption of the native was a way of depriving indigenous peoples of their future *as* indigenous peoples. It was, in other words, a way to extend their social death, if not their biological one. One of the consequences of that logic of elimination was not only the violent taking of their lives but also the erasure of their deaths. Like the burial grounds of enslaved black people, indigenous peoples' burial sites were, and continue to be, expropriated, violated, and ultimately erased from history in order to legitimize the capitalist projects of the settler colony. One can go so far as to claim that the naturalization of the settler order ultimately depends on the continuous violent burying of the indigenous territories underground, where that violent burial constitutes the paradigmatic form of modern nonburial. The settler colony continues to occupy indigenous people's sacred burial sites and imposes an enforced colonial forgetting of their losses, as the sine qua non condition of social normalcy.

The aftermath of slavery subjects black and indigenous peoples to different albeit related forms of postmortem violence. In the case of black people, it is their labor rather than their land that interests the settler, so the master violates the corpses, not only the burial sites, and those corpses are forced to perform continuous free labor for the settler class. Since it is their land rather than their labor that the settler wants, indigenous peoples' burial sites are most often subjected to colonial erasure, and the memorialization of these sites is often criminalized. Even the recognition of enslaved burial sites can be instrumentalized for settlers' purposes, when that recognition fails to address the expropriation of native land and can help instead to solidify the settler's reappropriation of territorial indigeneity to itself.

The regulation of life and death converge in order to guarantee that only the white settlers get "properly" reproduced—recognized as subjects with legal personhood, with a beginning and an end, as Hannah Arendt would have put it.[114] Settlers become the exclusive enjoyers of natality, of proper chronological time, inheriting both the land and the labor that they expropriate. In short, the racial-*cum*-sexual politics of life and death in the settler colony makes reproductive futurism the exclusive prerogative of white settlers in North America.

Thus, I conclude this critique of feminist and queer theory by problematizing Lee Edelman's *No Future* (2004). Edelman turns to *Antigone* in order to radicalize the death drive that he heroically links to a racially unmarked queer subject. Edelman takes Antigone's death drive to represent not an alternative way of doing kinship (like Butler), opening democratic enfranchisement to the abject position of the queer, but, more radically, an undoing of kinship altogether. This is Edelman's antisocial thesis, which he raises against Butler's interpretation in *Antigone's Claim*. Butler's Antigone is more social than antisocial, since the equivocality of her terms exposes heteronormativity's failure to govern identity, particularly when the terms that the queer subject uses fail to identify the subjects they name, creating a politically generative misrecognition as a result. For Edelman, Butler's reclaiming of Antigone's aberrancy serves to widen the horizon of inclusiveness for queer couples, which he considers the dominant motto of liberalism's multicultural turn. Edelman criticizes Butler for repeating the fundamental tie to what he calls the ideology of reproductive futurism, which wants a different Symbolic order, a different future, rather than an end to this one: no future at all. The crisis that Antigone represents to the Symbolic limits of heteronormative kinship, Butler's theory posits as generative for alternative, that is, queer ways of doing kinship. Yet, Edelman argues, the entrance of the human into catachresis affirms the Symbolic order that this otherness would otherwise disrupt, by "affirming the identity of the future with the promise of meaning itself."[115] To put it in more political terms, by affirming the legitimacy of the institutions of legitimation, even if not that which they legitimize, Butler seeks to extend the Symbolic order beyond its current configuration of inclusion rather than to radically overthrow it.

In opposition to Butler, Edelman emphasizes the Antigone who dies not only unmarried but also childless, the child being the strongest fetishistic object in Edelman's critique of reproductive futurism. As a representative of what Edelman calls the "*sinthomo*sexual," the antisocial heroine of no future, Antigone "insists on the unintelligible's unintelligibility, on the internal limit to signification and the impossibility of turning Real loss to meaningful profit in the Symbolic without its persistent remainder."[116] It is this remainder, Edelman observes, that must always bear the burden of embodying the horror of Symbolic inclusiveness. And it is this horror that

> survives the fungible figures that flesh it out insofar as it responds to something in sex that's inherently unspeakable: the Real of sexual difference, the lack that launches the living being into the empty arms of futurity. . . . From that limit of intelligibility, from that lack in communication, there flows, like blood from an open wound, a steady stream of figures that mean to embody—and thus to fill—that lack, that would staunch intelligibility's wound, like the clotting factor in blood, by binding it to, encrusting it in, Imaginary form.[117]

In what sense, one might ask, does this "fungible figure" relate to the Fanonian "fungible object," connecting the antiblackness of colonial modernity to racialized slavery?[118] How does this "fleshing" relate to the body/flesh difference in Spillers's analytical distinction between captive and liberated positions, and their afterlives in the American grammar? Is this "something unspeakable in sex," highlighted by both Spillers and Edelman, equally relatable to the Real of sexual difference, or do we encounter here the historical limit that negligible injuries represent in the colonially differentiated production of gender? Does sexual difference encounter in the historical experience of black and indigenous enslaved women a limit that is, as Moten stresses, anti- and ante-originary to the sexual difference that the queer figure of the death drive represents?[119] Is there not a disavowed open wound that launches not a living being but a socially dead one, in this case, to the inhospitable antiblack and anti-indigenous world? Finally, into whose arms is this socially dead nonperson launched, if the arms that would (Imaginary) hold them are working in the plantation for the future of the master's progeny?

Like Butler and Copjec, Edelman also glosses over slavery. In an earlier reference to Lacan's engagement with Antigone in *No Future*, Edelman claims that, "perhaps . . . political self-destruction inheres in the only act that counts as one: the act of resisting enslavement to the future in the name of having a life."[120] Enslaved to the future, slavery's history also grants to the radical politics of queer antifuturism a grammar for the radical overthrowing of the Symbolic order, without ever entering the historical imaginary of its domain. Are we then not forced to confront the fact that, historically, the future is not kids' stuff but white kids' stuff, a place where Edelman is not willing to go, as "enslavement" figures only as a rhetorical way of naming the future that holds us captive to heteronormative, not as the reality of white supremacy in the racialized history of sexual difference?

Edelman's archive, more so than Butler's or Copjec's, includes only marginal references to racism's role in the construction of sexuality. Most notably, he performs that reading in an excellent chapter from his beautiful *Homographesis*, which he devotes to James Baldwin.[121] Like Butler's analysis of Larsen's *Passing*, however, Edelman's analysis of Baldwin's queerness does not pass *Homographesis*, and his racially unmarked *sinthomo*sexual also reproduces the currency of normative whiteness.[122] Edelman forgets that which resounds in Baldwin's reconstruction of his friendship with Norman Mailer, when Baldwin asserts that while Mailer "still imagines that he has something to save," Baldwin has "never had anything to lose."[123] We are back to the same distinction between the Hegelian misrecognition of the slave in the formulation "I lose all freedoms except the freedom to die" and the echo of Marx and Engel's revolutionary slogan in Assata Shakur's "we have nothing to lose but our chains." After all, is Hegel not liable to the same objection that Baldwin raises against Mailer, that "when trying to convey to a white man the reality of the Negro experience . . . he will face in your life only what he is willing to face in his"?[124] In Mailer's case that is the "something to save"; in the case of Hegel, "all freedoms except the freedom to die" in synthesis—the ultimate refusal to confront the "nothing to lose" of Baldwin and Shakur. And is not this "nothing to lose" not only illegible in the "something to save" that Edelman attributes to Butler's liberal inclusiveness, but also in the "no future" that he attributes to a racially unmarked *sinthomo*sexual subject?[125]

Like Baldwin, Wilderson also claims that when "the 'Negro' has been inviting whites, as well as civil society's junior partners [i.e., the queer], to the dance of social death for hundreds of years," "few have wanted to learn the steps," as they "have been, and remain today—even in the most antiracist movements, such as the prison abolition movement—invested elsewhere."[126] They have been invested, we could add, in the "all freedoms except . . ." of

Hegel, in the "something to save" of Mailer, and in the "having a life" of which Edelman is critical. Invested elsewhere, blackness and indigeneity are figuratively accumulated, if certainly not in the same ways they were consumed and appropriated when black and indigenous people were reduced to the status of fungible objects under the political arithmetic of chattel slavery.

Figuratively accumulated, however, the enslaved come and give Butler the key by which to problematize the historical impasse rendering the border between the Symbolic and the social more permeable, only to disappear again as the theory is ultimately invested elsewhere. Slaves come and give Copjec the structural constraints by which to qualify the choice that characterizes the feminine act of sublimation as ethical, only to disappear again, as this theory is also invested elsewhere. Slaves come and give Edelman the unintelligible wound of the Real against the reproductive futurism of the Symbolic order, only to never enter the *sinthomo*sexual frame of the death drive.

Fear of a Quare and Two-Spirit Planet

In this chapter, I have argued that the racially unmarked figure of the queer, as the embodiment of the "not-all" of sexual difference, experiences the space in between two deaths as a contingency rather than as a structure. It is time for me to clarify that I do not mean to suggest, by contingency, that homophobia, transphobia, patriarchy, and heteronormativity are not structural to white queers and white trans people. Here, we should remember that Butler's rereading of *Antigone* was not only influenced by alternative ways of doing kinship but also by the militant mourning of ACT UP (AIDS coalition to Unleash Power) against the politics of neglect with which the United States decided to let gay people die. These violences are structural to Eurocentric capitalism and affect us all, including white heterosexual cisgender people; the point is that they affect us all differently. By *contingency*, then, I only mean to suggest that such structural violence makes life unlivable for the white queer and trans subject, but does not displace that subject to the hellish condition of fungibility that characterizes social death. Hence, freedom can intersect with death, as Copjec argues, when the ethical subject is willing to sacrifice their otherwise precarious place in the Symbolic order to reach for that which cannot be symbolically mediated and upon whose abjection the normalization of the Symbolic order continues to rely for its future reproduction. The socially dead, as the embodiment of the colonial "all-not" of being, inhabits this most inhospitable space as a structural condition of total dispossession, not as a structure that can be contingently recast in heroic freedom under ethical action.

We can understand Calvin Warren's coinage of the term *onticide* to refer to such a condition. *Onticide* refers to the impossibility of the "black queer" as a social positionality, given the missing point at which queerness—that is, "an experience of unfreedom"—intersects with blackness, a "structural position of non-ontology."[127] Modern slavery was not inflicted exclusively on black people, however, as indigenous peoples were also subjected to it and continue to be denied futurity under slavery's aftermath. As I mention above, following a long trend of settler-colonial critique, settler policies codifying indigenous reproduction were actually oriented toward eliminating them rather than recognizing their existence. Ontologically killed, black and indigenous people lack a "proper" grammar in the machine of kinship. It is this gap between the subject that is not yet one (queer) and the object that refuses to be thus reduced (black and indigenous) that I have tried to understand as the colonial difference between the "not-all" of being and the "all-not" of being. The former can experience the negativity of the death drive as a liberatory act; the latter experiences the negativity of social death as a structural condition of ontological dispossession. The refusal of Symbolic intelligibility in the case of the former results in freedom, that is, autonomy; the refusal of the latter in fugitivity, that is, a loophole of retreat.

To understand the colonial history of racialized sexuality is to understand the radical politics of the black "quare" and the indigenous "two-spirit."[128] The social order definitely fears a queer planet, to echo Michael Warner.[129] "Homonationalism," as Puar argues, might have been one way by which the social order economizes that fear, in order to reinforce settler-colonial forms of imperial subjugation through the exclusive inclusion of entitled queer subjects.[130] There is, however, a considerably stronger fear when the social order confronts the prospect of a quare and two-spirit planet. *Quare* and *two-spirit* are ways of situating the liberatory politics of anti-heteronormative sexuality within the broader history of the coloniality of gender. These terms, rather than *queer*, trouble the disavowal of slavery by which the death of the subject in the social order is invoked to belabor some transgressive agency without the historical realities of that subjectivity, borne in abjection, ever becoming the foreground of that theory. Figuratively accumulated, the transgression of the racially unmarked queer risks reinscribing the subjugation of black and indigenous peoples, not unlike Antigone does when she justifies the burial of Polyneices on the basis that he was not a slave.

Importantly, as both Cathy Cohen and Roderick Ferguson have claimed, even straight bodies from these communities, although heterosexual, are not heteronormative, since the coloniality of gender denies them the performative features that would assign them to the subjective order of desire rather than to the objective side of labor.[131] This does not mean, as intersectional theory has criticized, that gender or sexuality are secondary to race.[132] It means, as Hartman and Snorton claim, that we must attend to the colonial history of gender's differential production and the conscripted agency that finds, within the morass of that condition, loopholes of retreat in cross-dressing and transgenderism, among other radical forms of gender trouble.[133] The project of black, indigenous, and queer of color critique, to which I hope this book contributes, is that of unpacking the differential constraints of these agencies, and amplifying their political contributions to a broader critique of racial/sexual capitalism.[134]

Not-all (Copjec), that is, not heteronormatively human, one could argue that the racially unmarked queer subject still clinches to the hyphen, though in the aberrant (Butler) form of political catachresis. A future awaits the "not-all" on the other side of this hyphen, a desire for inclusiveness in Symbolic intelligibility, a desire to be part of the "all," if the "all" could only be so radically deformed as to make room for the abject one. Those abject ones, Butler hopes, would no longer experience the horrors of living under the unlivable conditions of social negation—a form of negation that historically differs, nonetheless, from the "all-not" that characterizes the conditions of the socially dead. As Edelman rightly contends, the queer subject should refuse this future because it forever depends on the very horrors that it continues to displace into the other side of the hyphen. Yet those horrors remain equally uninterrogated in his theory, as he fails to confront the colonial history of reproductive futurism that makes social valuation rest on the brutally exacerbated conditions of racialized violence. All-not, that is, anti/ante-human, the socially dead have no hyphen to cling to, nothing to lose, and continue to be the first target of that very horror. Even the heroic survival of that horror can be claimed by others to inform their condition, and be figuratively accumulated in order to prioritize their own transformative agency instead.

Refusing to gloss over this difference is crucial in order for queerness to learn how to dance with death, to learn how to embrace and militate for the liberatory possibility of a quare and two-spirit planet, against the colonial history of Eurocentric capitalist heteronormativity. To continue to gloss over that colonial difference is to repeat the limited gesture of Antigone's claim when she problematizes Creon's friend/enemy distinction by reinscribing the citizen/slave one. As in her case and even in that of Tiresias, queer and trans social valuation come to rest on the devaluation of the racialized other, whose more radical exclusion they further conceal from political legibility. To properly historicize the coloniality of gender is to finally attend to the multiply subversive agencies of slavery's anti- and alter-sociality. Undoubtedly conscripted, these agencies reveal the future as the convergent outcome of the two settler-colonial logics of accumulation by which the elimination of the native and the exploitation of the alien result not only in the social reproduction of the settler but also in the reproduction of sociality, as invested in coloniality.

These agencies, however, also pluralize the signifying chains by which the settler future holds them captive to their future, as they modify these forms of signification in order to repair and reconstruct their damaged humanity. The quare and the two-spirit are the anti/ante-social heirs of these agencies, and of their most aberrant form of transmission, in fungibility-*cum*-fugitivity. Their agency produces not necessarily another future, but a loophole of retreat that denies the future as the sovereign time of the settler.

BLACK AND INDIGENOUS ANTIGONES IN NORTH AMERICA

Perhaps this is the kind of loophole of retreat that Antigone finally enacts in Dave Hunsaker's *Yup'ik Antigone* (1984) and Bryan Doerries's *Antigone in Ferguson* (2019).[135] The former was created in collaboration with the local Yu'pik community in Toksook Bay on the Bering Sea coast in Western Alaska, the latter with community members from Ferguson, Missouri, after Michael Brown was killed by police officer Darren Wilson and his body was left exposed and undignified for four hours in the street. In both of these plays, settler colonial violence takes hold of the corpse in order to extend the severity of its lethal capacities. The dangers of ignoring the Yup'ik elders and their traditions, which Hunsaker's play dramatizes, is not a one-time event, as Christian missionaries and corporations become more interested in the acculturation of the Yup'ik community and in the potential exploitation of their territories. In Ferguson, the possibility to publicly mourn the loss of Michael Brown is further denied, as not only did the police continue to destroy Brown's memorial, the state reacted to the public protest in Ferguson with the militarization of the city, de facto turning it into a war zone.

Both *Yu'pik Antigone* and *Antigone in Ferguson* keep Sophocles's structure almost intact, while taking more liberties with the choral songs. And it is in the chorus that settler colonial violence becomes clearer in both cases. In *Yu'pik Antigone*, the choral odes, unlike the rest of the play, are spoken in English. The language of the colonizer becomes the public language, when indigenous peoples are forced into the condition of *metics* in their territories of origin, forced to prioritize the learning of English at the expense of their own native languages. Elimination is a process, and the loss of the mother tongue, like the loss of the traditional burial practice, and confidence in the wisdom of the elders, calls attention to an ongoing colonial form of violence paradigmatically oriented toward their genocide. In *Antigone in Ferguson*, and against the desire of several members of the cast and of many more from the community, Theater of War Productions decided to include the participation of some of Ferguson's police officers in the chorus (only black police officers, to the best of my knowledge). Creon's exclusionary logic extends over the chorus, as the scene of captivity reflects a more structurally enduring subjection.

In *Yup'ik Antigone*, both Antigone and Creon are of Yup'ik origin, while in *Antigone in Ferguson*, Antigone is black, but Creon is white. I do not know if any of these versions translate Antigone's claim, that "[i]t was not Eteocles' slave, who died," as one of the reasons she offers to bury her brother and disobey the edict in Sophocles's original. If it was, I can only imagine that it would have had a much different connotation. On the one hand, the Yup'ik opposed any form of tyranny and, unlike the ancient Greeks, did not rely on slavery for its material production. On the other hand, a black Antigone in Ferguson would have been conscious of U.S. slavery, and the claim would have carried a different implication. Perhaps the line is absent from *Yup'ik Antigone*, as its presence there makes little sense. And perhaps its presence, in *Antigone in Ferguson*, refers to Antigone's way of saying to Creon that slavery was abolished, calling attention to Creon's way of giving it an aftermath, via his mistreatment of Michael Brown's corpse. Perhaps, in these two cases, the difference between the free and the unfree was, for once, mobilized not in order to reinscribe the abjection of black and indigenous peoples, but to refuse the oppressive longevity of slavery's aftermath.[136]

In the next chapter, I move from colonial modernity to colonial postmodernity, that is, to the contemporary conditions of neoliberalism that originated in Chile with the U.S.-backed dictatorship of Augusto Pinochet in the 1970s. From North to Latin America, I explore the ways in which Latin American *Antigones* contest the reactivation of the old settler colonial logics of elimination and exclusion under neoliberal conditions of accumulation that pluralize state violence. I move, finally, from the feminist and queer critique of sexuality and life, for which *Antigone* has become such an iconic figure, to the biopolitical critique of death, the third paradigm under which Sophocles's tragedy has been politically reinterpreted.

3

Antigone in Colonial Postmodernity
A Critique of Biopolitics in Latin America

> But what if slavery does not die, as it were, because it is immortal, but rather because it is non-mortal, because it has never lived, at least not in the psychic life of power? What if the source of slavery's longevity is not its resilience in the face of opposition, but the obscurity of its existence? Not the accumulation of its political capital, but the illegibility of its grammar?
>
> —Jared Sexton, "'The Curtain of the Sky': An Introduction"

Slavery, Metoikia, and Citizenship in Colonial Postmodernity

Slavery was officially abolished in the Americas during the nineteenth century. Haiti was the first country to abolish it, during the Haitian Revolution (1804), which was crucial for jumpstarting the hemispheric end of slavery. The Black Republic aided the anticolonial struggles of other independence campaigns—under the promise of abolishing slavery and institutionalizing racial equality—and the courageous defeat of the strongest empire at the time, under conditions of extreme military asymmetry, sent a powerful symbolic message that decolonization was possible. Many Latin American countries did abolish slavery after they achieved independence from Spain. Chile, for instance, which had passed the *libertad de vientres* law (often translated as the freedom of wombs) in 1811 when it was still under Spanish colonial rule, officially abolished slavery in 1823, after declaring independence from Spain on February 12, 1818. The process was more fragmentary in other places. In Nueva Granada, for example, slavery was first abolished in Cartagena in 1810, then in Antioquia in 1814, and in the whole of Nueva Granada—which included what are now Panama, Ecuador, Colombia, and Venezuela—in 1821, after the Congress of Cúcuta nationalized the *libertad de vientres* law. Something similar happened during the revolutionary government of Miguel Hidalgo in Mexico, which declared the abolition of slavery in all the territory in 1810, having not yet gained control over that vast territory. Other countries, such as the United States, abolished trans-Atlantic slavery (1808) but not their internal slave trade, which remained legal until the 1865 Civil War. Brazil was the last country in the Americas to abolish slavery, which it did in 1888.

Unlike slavery, *metoikia* and citizenship both increased their numbers in a world that no longer recognized the legal existence of slaves and gave to *metics* other names. The two most important changes, vis-à-vis citizenship, were the enfranchisement of those previously considered slaves and of women. The latter took place primarily during the first half of the twentieth century but excluded indigenous and black women, who continued to be disenfranchised for decades and are still struggling to be considered equal citizens in most places. Either explicitly or through loopholes, such as the literacy prerequisite that disenfranchised indigenous women in Peru and Ecuador (in 1930, the first Latin American country to grant suffrage to women), only white or light-skinned women were allowed to vote. Working-class women of color organized transnationally and forced Latin American states to recognize their rights in the 1940s and 1950s, but the loopholes that disenfranchised them persist today. Nor did the right of women to vote translate into their right to occupy public office and exercise power on equal terms, which no state in the Americas has ever achieved.

Metoikia changed, too. The shift of colonial power in the Americas from Europe to the United States translated into new forms of imperial intervention that produced more resident foreigners from the Global South. U.S. imperial interventions in Central and Latin America took the old colonial form of territorial annexation, as in the permanent occupation of practically half of Mexico's territory after the U.S.–Mexico War of 1846–48, and that of Hawaii and Puerto Rico, among other islands and indigenous territories that continue to be under U.S. colonial occupation.[1] Imperialism also took the form of more geographically extensive logics of exclusion, through which other alien labor forces, this time from Asia, were coerced to migrate, resulting in exclusionary regulations such as the Chinese Exclusion Act of 1882. Finally, imperialism also took the more postcolonial forms of forced bilateral agreements coercing other countries in the Americas and elsewhere to open their markets to U.S. transnational corporations, which proceeded to expropriate the land and exploit the labor in these territories without incurring in the additional costs of direct military occupation. This happened, for instance, with the United Fruit Company, said to have owned more than half of Guatemala's territory, among other territories in Central and South America. When the people resisted, the United States punished them with war, as happened and continues to happen in Guatemala, Cuba, El Salvador, Colombia, Nicaragua, Chile, Venezuela, and most, perhaps all, countries in the region. The consequence of these imperial policies, which intensified during the so-called Cold War and the counterinsurgency campaigns funded by the United States, was that more and more migrants found themselves trying to reach the empire. Millions of *metics* were either fleeing the ravaging violence and economic precariousness the empire and their local elites had normalized in their countries of origin or found themselves de facto occupied by the United States.

As a consequence of this process, the changes of *metoikia* have been remarkable. The old category of *metoikia* referred both to foreigners who decided to stay in the city and to freed slaves. Both were granted residency but not citizenship in the Athenian *polis*. Contemporary *metoikia* includes a considerably more compartmentalized and highly differentiated set of statuses. Stateless persons, refugees, and undocumented immigrants, for instance, are all differently marginalized from political recognition as equal members, even if they are considered to be "free," in that they are endowed with human rights considered to be inalienable. Green card holders like me, although U.S. *metics* in that we are not politically enfranchised, are not subjected to the same violence to which refugees, stateless persons, and undocumented immigrants are. The United States has thus subjected a larger pool of *metics* to a more compartmentalized, stratified, and highly bureaucratized form of violence that now includes detention centers, militarized borderlines, and a new apparatus of deportability.[2] Passports, checkpoints, biometrical scanners, background checks, among many other technologies of power are the new devices through which the *metic* is manufactured. These technologies are now exported to and implemented in other Latin American countries as a way for the United States to outsource the policing of labor migration, on which its economy still depends.[3]

The claim of this book, however, is that despite the increase in numbers of *metics* and citizens, the abolition of slavery did not end it. Legal enslavement might have ended, but political systems refurbished the racialized systems of labor subjugation that slave-trade systems in the Americas engendered, thus giving slavery an aftermath, as Saidiya Hartman has argued. In fact, slavery has, according to Kevin Bales, actually increased its numbers since its official abolition.[4] Here, we should remember that when black people officially replaced indigenous peoples as the main populations subjected to colonial enslavement, the enslavement of indigenous peoples did not end, either. Hence, slave contracts, although declared illegal by the Spanish monarchy in the first half of the sixteenth century, were still being signed in Peru in the late seventeenth century. What interests me the most, however, is the new forms that such violence takes and the ways in which these new modalities of violence are in fact connected to the old logics of settler-colonial capitalism that invented modern slavery, and thus continue to give it an aftermath.

The afterlives of slavery generate a paradox, as the distinctions between citizens, *metics,* and slaves simultaneously multiply and yet become increasingly blurred. On the one hand, nation-states no longer juridically recognize slaves, and further disaggregate among citizens and *metics*. Here, it is worth remembering that the abolition of slavery did not translate into equal citizenship, which took many decades and for most racialized populations still refers to a rather empty promise or purely abstract formality that affords them none of the protections that it affords white property-owning settlers. Modern nation-states in the Americas, also distinguish natural-born citizens from naturalized citizens, and although all are politically enfranchised they are not equally enfranchised in all the states in the Americas. *Metics* are also further disaggregated. Most nation-states in the Americas distinguish between those who migrate in order to reside with officially granted documents, from those who decide to reside while lacking proper documentation. They are all foreigner residents but depending on the papers that they have or do not have, the state subjects them to very different forms of violence. On the other hand, those distinctions have also become more permeable, as not only *metics* (in the more marginalized form of undocumented immigrants, for instance) but also officially recognized citizens, when racialized as black or brown, continue to be subjected to the social death of slavery. None of the protections ever afforded to citizens, and not even those granted to document-endowed *metics* of certain race and economic class, apply to them.

Even when these citizens and *metics* are de jure considered as such, they continue to be subjected to forms of violence invested in their social death. It is this aftermath of slavery, and the ways in which it continues to live in the neoliberal Global South, that interests me the most in this chapter.

Three factors are crucial when it comes to understanding the historical reconfiguration of the slave/*metic*/citizen triad in Latin America. First, the fact that old colonial logics of accumulation survive postcolonial independence. Take, for instance, the case of indigenous peoples in Chile's south, such as the Kawésqar, Selk'nam, Aónikenk, and Yámana. Indigenous peoples suffered mass genocide not only by the Spanish and British *conquistadores*, when they tried to take their land, but also by the new *criollo* elites who governed Chile post-independence.[5] The same is true in Colombia and in México, where indigenous peoples continue to be subjected to systematic lethal violence by state-sanctioned agents and the corporative capitalist interests that they protect.[6] The end of slavery, post-independence, does not translate into the undoing of colonialism and its racialized systems of labor subjugation and land expropriation. Second, the fact that most Latin American postcolonial states did not achieve the exclusive monopoly over legally sanctioned violence across the national territory—that infamous Weberian condition of the modern state—results in the pluralization of violence.[7] This means, for instance, that the eliminatory violence that European settlers first inflicted against indigenous populations has actually pluralized its agents in the postcolony. Gold seekers, landowners, international agribusiness corporations, Catholic missionaries, and the various repressive apparatuses of the state, the parastate, and the empire now inflict this violence with total impunity. The same happens with exclusionary violence: the carceral archipelago pluralizes its institutions and the punitive function is not only semi-privatized but becomes entangled with the new circuits of financial capital and the new global markets of punitive technologies. Finally, because slaves are no longer legally recognized but the systematic racialized violence that slavery engendered persists, there is a crucial change in the ways in which postmodern Latin American nation-states violate the bodies that they continue to subject to social death. Such state-sanctioned violence is now inflicted upon nominally recognized citizens and *metics* who are "free," and yet continue to be the target of technologies of power invested in the production and exploitation of their differentiated vulnerability to premature death.[8] The paradigmatic form that such violence takes, here I argue, is that of enforced disappearances.

My argument, in this chapter, is that enforced disappearances are the consequence of the ways in which these three changes reconfigure state violence under contemporary neoliberalism. Enforced disappearances are, in short, the solution to a political impasse that results when, having abolished slavery, the postcolonial regimes of the Americas nevertheless continue to reproduce the racialized forms of devaluation that engineered modern slavery for the purpose of greater accumulation of capital and the cultivation of settler life. Under these conditions, enforced disappearances allow the postcolonial states of Latin America: first, to disclaim the violence and thus continue to represent themselves as democratic in the international arena; second, to pluralize the violence by means of paramilitary and other policing forces whose structural connections the state can always disclaim while strengthening them; and third, to continue to activate the old settler colonial logics of elimination and exclusion, in order to expropriate people of their territories and extract more profit from the marginalization of their labor.

Enforced disappearances are, then, understandably, the main object of contestation of postmodern Latin American *Antigone*s. This explains the focus of this chapter on Ariel Dorfman's *Widows* (1981) in Chile, Sara Uribe's *Antígona González* (2012) in Mexico, and Patricia Nieto's *Los escogidos* (2012) in Colombia.[9] These are by no means the only *Antigone*s to have been rewritten in Latin America, which has accumulated dozens of *Antigone*s.[10] Nor are they the only ones to focus on enforced disappearances—starting with what is, arguably, the first Latin American *Antigone*: Juan Cruz Varela's *Argia*, written in the then-revolutionary port of Buenos Aires in 1824. My choice, however, is not arbitrary. I was motivated by the geopolitical extension of creating such an assemblage of *Antigone*s. Chile and Mexico constitute, so to speak, the geographical beginning and end of Latin America, with Colombia in the corner that connects Central and South America—thus allowing me to speak about the region in general, notwithstanding the specificity of neoliberal violence in each country and region. By drawing from them all, however, I try to show the systematic and geographically widespread aspect of this violence rather than focus on its local specificities.

In this chapter I am interested in the coloniality of postmodernity rather than in the coloniality of modernity. My use of *postmodernity* is indebted to Fredric Jameson's analysis of the postmodern as the cultural logic of late capitalism.[11] This usage includes Jameson's Giovanni Arrighi–influenced reconsideration of the "post" as the intensification of prior "cycles of accumulation," rather than as a temporal break.[12] I depart from Jameson in linking that "prior" to the convergence of the two settler colonial logics of capitalist accumulation that neoliberalism intensifies rather than to a "cycle of accumulation" more generally. Postmodernity, in short, does not refer to a third stage in a linear history that moves, progressively, from antiquity to modernity and then to postmodernity, as the structure of my chapters might otherwise deceivingly suggest. Postmodernity refers to the neoliberal intensification of the two settler-colonial logics of exclusion and elimination, which are no longer inflicted solely upon slaves, in a world that no longer recognizes their official existence but continues to subject millions to its aftermath.

I open with Dorfman's *Widows* because the U.S.-backed dictatorship in Chile historically inaugurated neoliberalism in the Americas, through what Naomi Klein has referred to as the "shock doctrine" of disaster capitalism.[13] I move from Chile to Colombia and Mexico to better understand the intensification of that neoliberal violence, when exclusion and elimination no longer take place under a dictatorship (Chile) but under self-characterized democracies (Mexico and Colombia), and when the primary agents perpetrating that violence are no longer the military (Chile) but the paramilitary (Colombia)—and their most radical indistinction, in what some adequately call today's narco-state (Mexico). The shock doctrine has become less shocking and more normalized as mass murder extends over time and massacres, torture, rape, human trafficking, forced displacement, organ trafficking, feminicide, and enforced disappearances, to name only a few of the many forms of violence that converge in the intensification of these logics, coexist with the otherwise apparent normality of democratic rule, the celebration of parliamentary elections, and the uninterrupted flow of international trade. The multiplication of these forms of violence justifies Sayak Valencia's coining of the term *gore capitalism* to refer to the hegemonic form that neoliberalism takes in the Global South.[14]

Finally, I focus on these *Antigones* because, in seeking to make visible that violence, they perform a critique that links contemporary violence to its colonial history, while at the same time articulating the limits of their own critique. These *Antigones* are not only critical of the violence they expose but also of themselves, as inescapably limited texts in their efforts to represent that violence. Hence, when searching for the voices of the disappeared, these Latin American *Antigones* resist the allure of speaking on their behalf, which is by no means the same as remaining silent. Rather, through aesthetic gestures that I consider more postmodern than modern, they teach us how to counterpolitically voice that silence while remaining within it.[15]

Ariel Dorfman's *Widows* (1981) is, to the best of my knowledge, the first Latin American *Antigone* to focus on the contemporary phenomenon of enforced disappearances. Sara Uribe's *Antígona González* (2012) and Patricia Nieto's *Los escogidos* (2012) are, if not the last, two of the most recent ones.[16] Dorfman historically contextualizes those disappearances during Pinochet's dictatorship in Chile, supported by the United States, and wrote the text while in exile for his opposition to the regime. Salvador Allende's government, it is worth remembering, was one of the first anticapitalist and anti-imperialist revolutionary governments to achieve power through democratic elections, suggesting an alternative to the Cuban model, and was also trying to return to indigenous peoples their land in Chile.[17] Uribe wrote her version of *Antigone* in 2012, in the aftermath of the discovery of seventy-two Central and South American migrants murdered by the criminal syndicate Los Zetas in a barn in San Fernando, Tamaulipas, in Northeastern Mexico in January 2010, in complicity with the police. These modern to-be *metics,* who were on their way north fleeing the disposability NAFTA had fueled in their territories of origin, were killed for refusing to work as *sicarios* (hitmen) in an economy whose violence is structurally connected to the United States' so-called War on Drugs.[18] Patricia Nieto also published her *Antigone* in 2012, seeking to give visibility to the practice of the working-class peasants of Puerto Berrío, Colombia, officially recognized as citizens, who started the funerary ritual of *escogidos* (adopted/chosen). In this political ritual, the people of Puerto Berrío adopt one of those the government buries as "NN" in the city's cemetery, in order to grant them a new identity, in contrast to the one they were robbed of when they were murdered.[19] Since the mid-1980s, paramilitary forces—primarily, although not exclusively—had thrown people into the Magdalena River in an effort to erase them from history. Such violence was institutionally supported through the U.S. counterinsurgency training that the Colombian military, among others, received in the *Escuela de las Americas* (School of the Americas), within the framework of the Cold War. Such violence was aggravated as a consequence of the U.S. criminalization of drug trafficking since the War on Drugs was declared, making the business more profitable and more lethal, with gendered and racialized repercussions.[20]

By reading all of these *Antigones* together as plays that help us understand the hegemonic consolidation of neoliberalism as the intensification of settler-colonial logics of capitalist accumulation, I do not mean to suggest that the postcolonial histories of all Latin American countries are interchangeable. The existence of an active revolutionary indigenous guerrilla such as the EZLN (the Zapatista National Liberation Army, according to its Spanish acronym) in Mexico, for example, contrasts with the decimated guerrillas of the Mapuche people in Chile, and with the demobilized indigenous guerrilla, Quintín Lame, in Colombia, during the peace process leading toward the Political Constitution of 1991. Similarly, the vibrant existence of politically active black communities in Colombia—from the *palenque* of San Basilio to the Communities of Peace in the Pacific Coast and the Black Women's Movement in La Toma, Cauca, to name only a few—contrast with the political forms that black organizing has taken in Mexico and Chile. These and many other differences are the result of unique colonial and postcolonial histories that scholars in comparative politics are better situated to analyze.[21] By tracing neoliberal violence to a common settler-colonial history, I am aware of the simplification that my theoretical abstraction exerts upon histories that are always irreducibly unique. Yet all postcolonial governments in Latin America have refused to return to indigenous peoples the land that Europeans first stole from them and to grant equal political membership to indigenous and black people who survived in their territories, both of which continue to be the main targets of postcolonial exclusion and elimination. More importantly, none of these postcolonial states have undone the technologies of power that continue to grant slavery an afterlife. Millions continue to be subjected to slavery's aftermath, in a world that misreads that aftermath, because, as Jared Sexton claims, we still lack a grammar by which to articulate its longevity. I seek this grammar in settler-colonial critique, which, I argue, is a better framework for understanding the (para)state violence that Latin American *Antigones* contest. This is the violence that makes the biopolitical cultivation of settler life rest on the necropolitical exposure of native and alien life to disposability, and thus continues to stratify political membership across the color line.

A Modern Biopolitical *Antigone* in Europe

If Sophocles's *Antigone* is the ancient tragic text par excellence, Jean Anouilh's *Antigone* could be considered its modern equivalent. Anouilh moves *Antigone* from ancient tragedy to modern melodrama, to echo Walter Benjamin's thesis, and historically recontextualizes *Antigone*'s drama in the violence that is at the heart of all biopolitical theories: the genocidal violence of Nazism.[22] Anouilh staged a rewritten *Antigone* in Nazi-occupied France in 1944, and the main modification that he introduces to the play reflects the significant change in the modalities of power that interests biopolitics. This change refers to a state that had become increasingly invested in the cultivation of the life of its citizens (modernity) yet was now subjecting millions of them to genocide. This is the puzzle that the theory of biopolitics tries to solve. The undoing/complication of the border between life and death is, obviously, a central theme of *Antigone*, perhaps *the* central theme of *Antigone*. Thus, it is only logical that *Antigone* has become such a crucial text for the theory of biopolitics.[23]

In the ancient tragedy, Tiresias tells the sovereign, Creon, that the gods are upset because he has left the one who should be underground aboveground (Polyneices) and has moved the one who should be aboveground underground (Antigone). Polyneices, who is dead, Creon can be said to keep artificially alive. The corpse is violently reanimated in the gore form of a state-punitive spectacle, as citizens are forced to watch it desecrated. Antigone, who is, rather, alive, Creon can be said to kill by confining her to the rockbound prison. In both cases, life and death do not merely exchange places but each can be said to exist in the form of its contrary. Polyneices's dead body is animated; Antigone's living body is buried. By doing so, Creon renders the border between life and death permeable and death contaminates the *polis* as a whole. The gods are furious because the birds are now distributing the rotten flesh of Polyneices in their sacred altars. So, they punish Creon with the multiplication of corpses from his own household.

This problematization/undoing of life and death changes considerably in modernity, when the gods can no longer play such a decisive role. Having killed the gods as an irrational foundation for political sovereignty in modernity, the problem of the untreated corpse—whose rotten flesh is being dispersed throughout the city—is less a question of divine justice than it is a problem of public health. We are, in other words, no longer in the ancient world, where the sovereign can kill the body in spectacular ways, but in the modern one, where the state becomes rather invested in cultivating the life of its citizens, in their longevity, their health, and even the individual capacities of their bodies. In modernity, we are in the territory of biopolitics. It is in relation to this individualized aspect of biopolitical power—the power that is not only invested in the population as a whole but in the individually disciplined laboring subject that modern capital needs for its reproduction—that Anouilh's version introduces its most important modification to the ancient tragedy of Sophocles.

In her wonderful turn to the democratic value of melodrama, Honig argues that if Anouilh successfully melodramatized Sophocles's tragedy, it was because he intensified "something already present in the play" that had become quite significant for modernity.[24] That "something," Honig clarifies, is Anouilh's arguably most innovative modification of the story: his introduction of greater ambiguity in the nonburial of Polyneices. In Anouilh's version, Creon is not sure if he buried Eteocles's body as Eteocles or if the dogs and birds are actually chewing on Eteocles's body in the place of Polyneices. As Honig says,

> [H]aving worked so hard to distinguish them in terms of friendship and enmity, it turns out [Creon] did not trouble himself to distinguish their actual bodies from each other. The fact that this revelation bothers us is one of the reasons the play continues to this day to grip us.[25]

Anouilh's Antigone is exposed to a different punitive economy than the one she contests in Sophocles's original. Having found both bodies physically unrecognizable in the field, Creon confesses to her, he assigned the "less damaged one" for his national funerals and "gave the order for the other one to rot where he was."[26] Not knowing which body belonged to the friend and which to the enemy, it was sufficient for the sovereign to know that there were two bodies to whom he could attach the respective identities to secure the code that, in Carl Schmitt's infamous definition, distinguishes the specificity of the political.[27]

Misidentifying the individual body, Anouilh thus touches on what many still conceive of as the foundational gesture of European modernity (from René Descartes's individualized *cogito* to Thomas Hobbes's individualized state of nature): the production of the willful abstract individual as the foundation of political sovereignty. This grounding of politics in individuals and their voluntary choices eventually became the sine qua non flag of political liberalism. Under such a model, citizenship was no longer the active public and collective government of the city but a statutory condition that entitled the subject to individual rights the sovereign had to protect in order to be considered legitimate. The sovereign could still punish the subject, but that subject was now entitled with individually recognized rights, so the sovereign was now under the obligation to produce the body. This is the modernity of *habeas corpus* (literally, "to have the body"), a legal figure often traced back to the charter of rights agreed to by King John of England at Runnymede, on June 15, 2015, known as the Magna Carta. The modern state had become invested in the cultivation of the individual body, in disciplining it, and in cultivating its capacities. This explains why the state's disregard for the body's identity, in Anouilh's *Antigone*, continues to grip us.

Anouilh, in fact, gives us an excellent phenomenological description of the transhistorical grip that Honig rightly attributes to his melodramatic version, when Antigone no longer knows if the brother she defiantly buried as Polyneices was actually Eteocles. It is worth going over that description if only because, unlike her classical counterpart, Creon's revelations succeed in neutralizing Antigone's rebellious "no!" with a transitory acquiescent "yes . . ." A long silence, the stage directions of Anouilh's play indicate, follows Creon's disclosure, which Antigone only breaks with the posing of a soft question: "Why are you telling me that?" "Would it have been better to let you die a victim to that insignificant story?" Creon replies. "Maybe," Antigone responds, and then she leaves with an unfinished "I believed . . ." standing in the air, heightening the sentimentality characteristic of melodrama.[28]

Antigone eventually regains her defiant tone, but for a few seconds—gripped, as Honig claims, by Creon's revelations—her resolute "no!" becomes deceptively "yes . . ." Creon asks her what she plans to do now, following a second and equally long silence. Antigone, now described as "standing up like a sleepwalker," claims that she is going to her room, back to the private sphere she had rebelliously transgressed. Creon tells her not to stay alone for too long, and to go and see Haemon in the morning in order to marry him quickly. Antigone replies "yes," while sighing. The state's disregard for the identity of the body is so powerful that it first silences Antigone, makes her docile, and finally—as if sleepwalking—pushes her to accede to Creon with a "yes," in contrast to what happens in the classical version. No wonder Lacan hated Anouilh's version.[29] Anouilh's Antigone will eventually reject that "yes" and claim that if Haemon "has to learn to say 'yes,' too," she will no longer love him.[30] But for a moment, in Anouilh's version, Antigone's rebelliousness is broken.

In order to more fully interrogate this surplus violence, we should revisit the past, the old *Antigone*, and explore the "something" that allows Anouilh to move Antigone from the classic genre of tragedy to the modern one of melodrama. Honig makes the link between Anouilh's Creon and Sophocles's by relating the controversial substitution of the body to Creon's democratic economy of exchangeability, emphasizing Creon's invocation of the phalanx formation of the hoplites as his good model of citizenship:

"When one fell, one from the next line would move in immediately to take his place."[31] The economic logic of substitution that seeks a replacement for the fallen hoplite, however, Creon extends beyond their heroic death in the battlefield. It is no longer the living hoplite who moves in, in order to take the place of the dead one. The fallen hoplite is moved, by living ones, in order to stand for (take the place) of another one. Violence no longer takes place at the level of the living, marking death as its limit. Violence extends beyond the endpoint of death. But if one form of exchange signals political equality on the battlefield, at the level of the living, the other does not. The first exchange refers to hoplites, to the equal replaceability of citizens, the second, as I have argued, refers rather to slaves.

What modern melodrama misses, however, in seeing tragedy as more democratic than aristocratic, is the colonial history of state-sanctioned violence, where enforced replaceability takes (social) death rather than life as its enabling condition of exchangeability. The dead body is thus killed a second time; denied individual identity; treated, as we have seen in previous chapters, like a slave, rather than like a (citizen) hoplite. Slaves were regarded as civically dead in antiquity, deprived of public personhood and doubly confined to the *polis* and the *oikos*. They could be replaced without that form of replacement indicating any kind of political equality, only equality in full devaluation. The enslaved were also treated as socially dead in modernity, where they were also denied individuality, starting with the violence of their naming. The enslaved were also not granted proper burials, rituals that would have marked their uniqueness, their significance for the community to which they belonged. The enslaved did transgress these prohibitions and subversively bury their own, giving names to themselves in defiance. Sometimes they even persuaded their enslavers to concede a plot of land to bury their own. But such deaths were never officially registered in the public records and, in the event of economic need, the master could always sell the land that they had granted, violating the burial resting site. Social death also haunts Anouilh's modern *Antigone* with something melodrama remains unable to confront. The de-individualization that Creon's edict enacts, under the kind of preposterous history that I am weaving to this play, extends the de-individualization that slavery's social death performs beyond slavery's formal end. It is not, in short, the democratic exchangeability of citizenship but the fungible exchangeability of slavery that melodrama fails to confront.

Anouilh's Antigone's silence is understandable: ruminating on the real identity of the body Creon subjected to desecration becomes a problem in itself. Antigone might be thinking, during the time lapse of that silence, that perhaps she did not bury Polyneices, whom she now suspects Creon buried with national honors as if he was Eteocles. Perhaps it does not really matter, or should not really matter, which one she buried as Polyneices, since they were both her brothers and what matters is that one of them was mistreated. But if it does matter whom she buried, would she have been willing to perform that burial if she knew that it was Eteocles's body that was mistreated in that way, rather than Polyneices's? And if she knew that it was not Eteocles but Polyneices who was thus mistreated, was burial the proper action for her to take, in order to expose sovereign violence to democratic accountability? Would the exhumation of Polyneices's body, violently forced to stand for the Theban nation that he sought to destroy, work instead?[32] Does her burial of Eteocles as Polyneices exposes one sovereign violence only to hide another, the one that would have required her to exhume the corpse instead? Might exhumation, rather than burial, better expose the sovereign instrumentalization of the dead body, as the state no longer exchanges living hoplites but socially dead ones to reinforce its forms of national security by subjecting citizens to a violence previously reserved only for slaves? And is Creon's funeral for Eteocles so unproblematically ethical that it merits no public opposition, if it was not for his mistreatment of Polyneices? Is not the instrumentalization of this funeral equally symptomatic of the perverse logic of sovereignty, which can continue to make claims upon its citizens after death, by instrumentalizing their corpses to fuel other forms of social control? Has this violence passed unnoticed, unchallenged?[33]

We can think of many other questions, and perhaps it is through that incessant questioning that Anouilh's Antigone finally regains her defiant tone as she questions the happiness Creon promises her. Although still speaking softly and referring to herself in the third person, Antigone asks: Who will this "little Antigone" have to "sell herself to" in order to snatch her "small shred of happiness?"[34] That sale evokes the problematic extension of economic exchange from the political transactions of the living to those of the dead, and locates the politics of burial under modern democratic rather than ancient tyrannical conditions. It is under these modern conditions that slavery's aftermath becomes more difficult to render legible.

FROM BIOPOLITICS TO NECROPOLITICS

Michel Foucault, arguably the foundational theorist of biopolitics, developed this term when seeking to explain how, under conditions in which the basic function of power is to improve life, to prolong its duration, to improve its chances,

> is it possible for a political power to kill, to call for deaths, to demand deaths, to give the order to kill, and to expose not only its enemies but its own citizens to the risk of death? How can the power of death, the function of death, be exercised in a political system centered upon biopower?[35]

Foucault's answer is that only racism offered a "biological-type caesura" so that the death of "the inferior race" could be turned into "something that will make life in general healthier."[36] Foucault knew that such racism "was not invented at this time," that it "had already been in existence for a very long time."[37] But then he disregarded the importance of analyzing that "elsewhere," thus missing the settler colonial history of these technologies of power. That is the history where settler colonial critique adequately resituates the convergence of a technology invested in the reproduction of (settler) life that turns into the mass production of (alien and native) death.

The historical and geographical misplacement of biopolitics in Europe thus leads Foucault to invert Clausewitz's proposition wrongly, when he claims that politics is "the continuation of war by other means."[38] Slavery, as I argued in the previous chapter, was the literal continuation of war by other means: as Patterson claims, it was not a pardon but the commutation of death for as long as the "slave acquiesced in [their] powerlessness."[39] This continuity could be interpreted neither under the repressive terms that Foucault rejects as interpretative lenses under which to understand power as confrontational and warlike, nor under the "political" characteristics he attributes to his more positive, relational, and conflictual understanding of biopolitical power. Slavery, once again, becomes the unthought of political modernity. Indistinguishable from the most negative notion of power, as hyper-repression, and the most positive notion of power, as the continuation of war by other means, slavery's grammar remains illegible in biopolitics.

In other words, although biopolitics effectively theorizes the paradoxical confluence of a modern technology of power oriented toward life that ends up reproducing mass death, it does not adequately explain the ways in which such violence relates to the modern/colonial history of racial/sexual capitalism. Biopolitics can, then, map the *bios/zoe* distinction, which is foundational in this theory, into the citizen/*metic* one, and all biopolitical interpretations of *Antigone* focus, predominantly, in one of today's variable figures of *metoikia*: the refugee, the stateless, or the undocumented immigrant.[40] What biopolitics fails to confront, when tracing the difference between *bios* and *zoe* into the modern crisis of political belonging, is the aftermath of slavery. This aftermath refers to the sale that takes (social) death, rather than life, as its enabling material condition. The enslaved were the first populations to have been subjected to convergent forms of exclusion and elimination, which work together in order to transmogrify uncommodified forms of life (*bios*) into commodified objects of exchange (*zoe*).[41]

Achille Mbembe's theory of necropolitics overcame several limitations of the theory of biopolitics.[42] Mbembe productively traces the first normalization of the state of exception, which the theory of biopolitics misplaced in the concentration camps of the Nazi, back to the conquest of the Americas, and all the way to the slave trade.[43] As he puts it in his landmark essay on "Necropolitics," any "historical account of the rise of modern terror needs to address slavery, which could be considered one of the first instances of biopolitical experimentation."[44] If slavery can be understood as the continuation of war by other means, the trans-Atlantic slave trade and the enslavement of indigenous peoples after the conquest of the Americas can be considered the ur-history of contemporary global warfare. All the characteristics of war that contemporary scholars attribute to modern warfare can be found in the warlike structure that is modern slavery.[45] Like modern wars, slavery was: global, in terms of its geographical territory; plural, in terms of the agents who were allowed to take lives with total impunity; everyday life, in terms of its privileged theater of its operations; and permanent, in terms of the endlessness that characterized an unsurpassable threat to the security of the living, which the enslaved were forced to embody. Unlike Foucault, Mbembe also understood the economic role that such normalization of violence represents for both early and contemporary global forms of capitalism. Thus, he claims that the entrepreneurial logic of colonial and postcolonial violence in fact "redistributed the means of terror within society."[46] Even prior to his landmark essay on "Necropolitics," Mbembe had already shown contemporary neoliberal policies—such as those the International Monetary Fund (IMF) and World Bank (WB) have enforced in Latin America, Africa, and Asia—to be necropolitical.[47] As meeting points between sovereign, disciplinary, and biopolitical technologies that discipline entire populations into austerity through debt-management programs, the IMF and WB can legally sanction entire populations in the third world to death: people lose access to food or health providers when the state is forced to privatize or cut their public services as the condition for acquiring international loans.

Mass death, through the destruction of the social infrastructure on which life depends for its social reproduction, is also the domain of necropolitics, and it is equally traceable to colonial epidemics and the life-threatening environmental conditions first imposed upon enslaved populations.

Necropolitics, in short, names the ways in which active colonial genocide made "war and race" into the new *nomos* of the earth.[48] We can thus understand Mbembe as arriving at a different formula from Foucault, proposing the "take life and let die" logic of necropower as the paradigmatic form of colonial capitalism. "Take life and let die" is the colonially enabling logic of the two technologies of power that Foucault historically and geographically misplaced in eighteenth-century Europe, when he distinguished between the right to "take life or let live" of classical sovereignty and the right to "make live and let die" of modern biopolitics.[49] "Take life and let die" describes, to riff on Walter Mignolo, the darker side of Western modernity.[50]

Notwithstanding the important extension of "Necropolitics" that Mbembe undertook in the book version of the article, *Necropolitics* (2019) nevertheless inherited some of the problems with the general theory of biopolitics. First, necropolitics misrepresents racial/sexual capitalism. Necropolitics cannot explain, for instance, why the biopolitical "make live" could be transformed into a certain way of taking that life, via the sexually regulated absorption of indigenous peoples into whiteness. Racialized sexuality, in short, remains undertheorized as the destruction of populations operates not only through their exclusion but also through their selective forms of inclusion. *Necropolitics* also participates in a reductive interpretation of Marxism. Here, Mbembe criticizes the communist figuration of an emancipated humanity for presumably eradicating the basic human condition of plurality. Thus, Mbembe claims that the subject of Marxian modernity is similar to Hegel, engaged in a narrative of mastery and emancipation whereby "terror and killing become the means of realizing the already known telos of history."[51] Finally, *Necropolitics'* understanding of "politics" as an idiom of war inherits biopolitics' undertheorization of the political. As Jacques Rancière and Wendy Brown rightly argue, biopolitics has actually very little to say about politics because it is actually interested in power, and governmental technologies of power more specifically, rather than in the public contestation over the distributions that such governmental regulations enforce, which is a better definition of politics.[52] Necropolitics, too, one could argue, refers not to politics but to regulatory violence, one that makes war the primary directive of Western sovereignty. This explains why

Rancière prefers to use the term *police,* instead of *biopolitics*—which he also borrows from Foucault—to speak about this general logic of governing a population by policing the differential location of the parts into which the community is divided, as antipolitical. And although it is tempting to propose *necropolicing* as an alternative term sensitive to Rancière's challenge—in that these theories analyze not politics but technologies of power—in order to supplement Rancière's theory with the much-needed decolonial revision that Mbembe inaugurated, that gesture is ultimately insufficient. What we need is not yet another term but a theory capable of explaining how the colonial production of racialized sexuality, and sexualized racism, which modern slavery helped to consolidate, made it possible for capitalism to link the production of settler life to the differential destruction of native and alien life. Settler-colonial critique, and the ways the logic of exclusion converges with the logic of elimination to cultivate settlers' lives, is just that theory, in my view.

NEOLIBERAL NECROPOLITICS

Under neoliberal conditions of accumulation, the violence that gives slavery an aftermath change significantly. First, the state-sanctioned exploitation of labor and expropriation of land privatizes those violences. Violence itself becomes its own industry and starts to follow its own economic logic. This means that killing, surveillance, punishment, and the trafficking of body parts and entire bodies (as in the case of sexual slavery or the instrumentalization of corpses for political-economic means) pluralize the commodity markets. Under conditions of extreme inequality, which are a direct consequence of neoliberal policies, the mutilated or dead bodies of those who are regarded as socially dead become more valuable than the exploitation of their labor-power.

Secondly, under conditions that turn entire populations into part of the socially dead disposable army, territories become more valuable than the populations that occupy them, and brutally forcing the removal of those populations is often cheaper than trying to legally negotiate with them the purchase or use of their lands (this is obviously not an argument for the promotion of legal coercion, but an interrogation of what its absence signifies in the intensification of neoliberal violence). Under these conditions, neoliberal forms of violence take hold not only of the living but also of the dead body. Rival armies competing for land turn once again to the spectacular instrumentalization of corpses for the purpose of territorial control. Under the gorier forms that such violence takes, as in the case of feminicides in México, the dead bodies of racialized, impoverished women are turned into textual surfaces in which the predominantly male agents of this violence can "write" their messages to each other and, as Rita Laura Segato argues, claim control over a territory.[53] Tortured bodies are once again exposed, and the brutal acts of violence inflicted on them are made to act as a text, in order to send a message to the rival power.

Finally, neoliberal disposability pairs direct forms of lethal violence with indirect structural violence that is no less lethal. In this context, legalized forms of tax evasion for the rich, the payment of salaries below the threshold of livability, and financial speculation can produce more death than the active massacres that the military and the paramilitary can inflict.[54] That is the case, too, with economic sanctions—such as those that the United States implemented in Cuba and currently imposes in Venezuela— which, Joy Gordon has argued, should be properly considered "weapons of mass destruction."[55] It is also the case with extractivism and waste, which corporations are more likely to dump in territories occupied by impoverished communities of color.[56] Free trade agreements like NAFTA and structural-adjustment programs such as those the IMF and the WB have imposed throughout the Global South should be included in the set of economic policies with the capacity to generate mass death and reinforce the production of socially dead disposable labor along these lines.[57]

As it is not socially living but socially dead labor that necropolitics regulates, this form of reproduction, expelled from the social, is managed today through the oversaturated violence that criminalizes survival economies. And it is under those economies, although by no means exclusively there, that enslavement, human trafficking, and other severely coercive forms of labor exploitation survive. In many cases, for the disposable army of slavery's aftermath the sole survival alternative is to participate in one of those criminalized economies, such as the drug-trafficking industry that, according to Olga Sánchez Cordero, has become the largest generator of employment in México since 2006.[58] Other economic opportunities are either nonexistent (mass unemployment and poverty), or are insufficient to sustain the reproduction of life, as the salaries that legal economies pay do not cover the basic costs of living. Criminalized economies are, however, saturated with death, and it is the enforcement of such criminalization that continues to enforce the cheapening function of reproducing socially dead, rather than living labor. Today's War on Drugs, which affects the entirety of the Americas, is capitalism's racial warfare by other means.

Postmodern Necropolitical Antigones in Latin America

From the classic *Antigone* of Sophocles—in which Eteocles is clearly buried with honors while Polyneices is left to be chewed by dogs and birds—to the modern *Antigone* of Anouilh, whereby the identity of the body being buried and the one left to rot is left in suspense, I will now move to what I call the postmodernity of Latin American *Antigones*. As I claimed earlier, my use of the prefix *post-* does not indicate a temporal sequence but an intensification of the settler-colonial logics of exclusion and elimination that converge in this violence under neoliberal conditions of accumulation. Postmodern Latin American *Antigones* add an additional complication to the story: it is not only the identity of the one being mis-buried that is at stake, but the location of the burial itself. Dorfman's, Uribe's, and Nieto's Antigones confront not a mistreated corpse, whose individual identity is at risk of being lost, but a disappeared member of their community, and Antigone cannot claim for sure whether they are dead or alive. There is, in short, no body to bury.

Dorfman's *Widows* initially presents us with Anouilh's modern scenario: the body by the shore of the river "was totally unrecognizable," the lieutenant says to the captain in order to dismiss the claim of Sofía Angelos (Dorfman's Antigone figure) that this body belongs to her family.[59] Neither fingerprints nor facial features can be distinguished, given its "prolonged stay in the water."[60] Unlike her French homologue, Angelos "hasn't even seen [the body]," "hasn't even been to the river," yet she has already claimed it.[61] Sofía unflinchingly claims the body that Anouilh's Antigone hesitates to claim, gripped by Creon's revelation. More importantly, it is not burial she claims. The body was buried by the soldiers, who she says "had no right to bury my father," so she demands exhumation.[62]

As we move from Chile to Mexico and Colombia, more and more bodies accumulate by the shores of the rivers. Uribe opens her *Antígona González* with Antígona González's new instructions on how to count the dead:

> *First, the dates, like the names, are the most important. The name above the caliber of the bullets.*
>
> Second, sit down in front of the monitor. Look for the crime reports in all online newspapers. Keep the memory of those who died.
>
> *Third, count the innocent and the guilty, hitmen, children,*

> *the armed, civilians, municipal presidents, migrants, victors, kidnapped ones, policemen.*
> Count them all.
> Name them all in order to say: this could be my body.
> The body of one of mine.
> In order not to forget that all nameless bodies are our lost bodies.
> My name is Antígona González, and I look for my brother's cadaver among the dead.[63]

Dates and names are signifiers with which to counteract national erasure, the erasure of bodies now dispersed/disappeared throughout a vaster territory. There are too many dates and too many names, requiring the technological prosthesis of the monitor to circumvent the spatial and temporal extension that pluralizes the sites and the agents who normalize this violence. Antígona González needs to count them all and to counteract what she already anticipates will happen if she is not vigilant: that she could also forget, because they are simply too many.

Like Antígona González, the Antigones of *Los escogidos* wonder "who lies in the first tomb of this shelter for the forgotten? From what lineage they came unstrung leaving no trace?"[64] when unidentified bodies are buried as NN in Puerto Berrío's cemetery. According to Francisco Luis Mesa Buriticá, owner of the San Judas Funerary, in twenty-four years he claims to have touched with his own hands the bodies of 786 unidentified bodies. He has found bodies in "ditches, swamps, wells, streams and in the Magdalena River" but, no matter where they are, he continues to look for them.[65] By his calculations, every single day twenty-five bodies are thrown into the river.[66] In Mexico and Colombia, Antigone has not yet claimed Polyneices, even if unable to fully identify him, when there are two additional Polyneices already accumulating by the river.

As we move from a dictatorship in Chile to democratically elected governments in Mexico and Colombia, something else happens: the misidentified body of modernity returns, if only in order to further intensify the postmodern disappearance of the body in what I call the *necro-dialectic* of enforced disappearances. This necro-dialectic refers to what in Colombia is known under the euphemism of *falsos positivos* (literally, "false positives"). *Falsos positivos* is the name given to the state-sanctioned violence by which the military forces the identity of guerilla member onto poor peasants, student activists, unionized workers, and social leaders, among other progressive actors, in order to report combat numbers and achieve indicators of military efficiency—which they can then transform into monetary remuneration.[67] This necro-dialectic violence is further radicalized in México, where the state no longer needs to legitimize the killings in such ways and can simply pass off the ones that it kills simply as "criminals." Necro-dialectic (para)state violence reactivates the fungibility of slavery and subjects those who are now officially recognized as *metics* and citizens to the violence of slavery's aftermath.

The Necrodialectic of Enforced Disappearances

Let's recapitulate. In antiquity, Creon wants to instrumentalize Polyneices's corpse in order to secure the friend/enemy distinction, if only by undoing the border that separates life from death. Hence, he keeps the one that should be below (Polyneices) above, and the one that should be above (Antigone) below. In modernity, Creon wants one of the fallen bodies to serve that same sovereign function, but he no longer cares which of the two bodies can serve that function as long as one of them can. And what grips us is this disregard for the real identity of the individualized body, instrumentalized to serve a sovereign function of control. The postmodern Creon wants the body disappeared, because it exercises this colonial form of violence upon *metics* and citizens, in a world that no longer recognizes slaves (this is obviously not an argument for the need to recognize slavery, but an interrogation of what its unrecognized afterlife implies for an interrogation of contemporary (para)state violence).

Antigone's mourning is thus not interrupted because Creon prohibits it (classic), nor just because Creon has made it impossible for her to identify the buried body as the enemy of the state (modern), but because the body is nowhere to be found. Here, it is worth recalling Jacques Derrida's definition of mourning as an attempt to "ontologize remains, to make them present, in the first place by *identifying* the bodily remains and by *localizing* the dead."[68] What postmodern *Antigones* represent, as a certain intensification of modernity, is adding the problem of (settler colonial dis-) location to the existing problem of individual identification.

Anouilh's *Antigone* is not postmodern to the extent that Antigone still knows that Eteocles, like Polyneices, can only be located in one of two places. The equivocal location of Polyneices forces the modern Antigone to think—silently, in Anouilh's version—about how her actions can address the supplementary violence. Postmodern Latin American *Antigones*, however, cannot keep the ambiguous location of the body so geographically contained, because the bodies they search for are nowhere to be found. The sovereign regime that violently claimed those bodies through abduction (taking the body out of the visual domain of the public space) now disclaims possession of them (refusing to give them back or to even recognize that it took them in the first place).

The different ways the sovereign instrumentalizes the slave to erase its violence are, thus, also performative. Visibility is what is at stake in antiquity. Citizens must watch the desecration of Polyneices, and Creon trusts the spectacle with the affective capacity to secure the futurity of the friend/enemy distinction he thinks Polyneices's revolt compromised. Invisibility, on the contrary, is at stake in modernity. Citizens must not know who exactly was unburied as Polyneices in a punitive economy that moves, as Foucault claimed, from the public spectacle of sovereign torture on the scaffold to the invisible apparatus of disciplinary power in the prison.[69] What is at stake in postmodernity is a certain interplay of visibility and invisibility—or, more precisely, hypervisibility and hyperinvisibility. Citizens must know that the body was forcibly taken but not exactly who took it or what was done to it. As Gordon claims, "Everyone must know just enough to be terrified, but not enough either to have a clear sense of what is going on or to acquire the proof that is usually required by legal tribunals or other governments for sanction."[70] Hyperinvisibility—the dislocation of the tortured body into what Banu Bargu has adequately identified as the "invisible penal archipelago"—paradoxically gives an afterlife to the cruel violence of the hypervisible.[71] Torture is also exercised in the prison-industrial complex (including the detention centers in which *metics* are now confined), but in the invisible penal archipelago (including concentration camps), it can take some of its most dehumanizing and spectacular forms. For enforced disappearances to perform their sovereign function, however, the secret must be partially known. The sovereign entity no longer monopolizes that function and perhaps never did, in Latin America. Many other actors seeking territorial control over vast regions can enact it. Others, like transnational corporations and big landowners, can purchase it.

The epitome of this necro-dialectic corresponds to what in Colombia is euphemized as *falsos positivos*, also massively practiced in Mexico. Unlike the French Creon, who might have buried Polyneices as Eteocles and mis-buried Eteocles as Polyneices, the Latin American Creons, in the plural, can now bury any poor working-class peasant *as* Polyneices. Colombia adds one twist to the horrifying story: the misidentified body of modernity can be made functional for the disappeared body of postmodernity. By passing off one disposable worker for a different one, you can now cash a bigger check in this necroeconomy of state violence. And when the state follows under scrutiny, because of its human rights violation record, the state can then organize a paramilitary apparatus (as has happened in Colombia since the 1980s). That apparatus allows the state to perform extreme forms of violence while having such violence attributed to a different repressive agency, in whose organization the state can disclaim active participation. Mexico adds yet one final twist: if the people resist, you can also produce the criminal they want to hold accountable, and exchangeability can work as efficiently to heroize the state and preserve its violence in its course. As Antígona González says, whenever the regime "brags when it announces the capture and dead of 'armed civilians,' I no longer know if those men, if those women who look at the camera with an unfathomable face from the wall of the accused, or who lay lifeless over the pavement, are real criminals or just cannon fodder."[72]

Enforced Disappearances as the Neoliberal Intensification of Settler Colonial Violence and the Figure of the Rebel

According to Lacqueur, the term *disappeared* is "a derivative of the Spanish *desaparecido,* when Amnesty International used it to refer to a class of people who, as a consequence of state action, had vanished without a trace."[73] Amnesty International first referred to enforced disappearances in Guatemala, whose indigenous populations continue to be subjected to genocide.[74] I, however, would like to trace this violence farther back in history: to the logics of elimination and exclusion, which first targeted all indigenous peoples in the Americas and enslaved black people coercively trafficked to the Americas, with genocide.

Here, I would like to expand on the persuasive thesis of Banu Bargu, who characterizes enforced disappearances as perhaps the sine qua non form of violence of Western sovereignty.[75] As the title of her essay "Sovereignty as Erasure" puts it, sovereignty is the name for the power of the state to erase its own violence, and "the ability to assert *erasibility*" is "the ultimate proof of power."[76] Bargu here touches on what settler colonial studies has tried to explain primarily through the logic of elimination, which links the settler-sovereign reclamation of indigeneity to the territory to the erasure of its original inhabitants from history. Erasure is not, then, an operation that exhausts itself in genocide, if genocide is the paradigmatic form that it takes. The legitimacy of the colonial power depends just as much on the symbolic erasure of the indigenous population, which explains why it can learn to coexist with their decimated numbers—if only insofar as they survive as new subjects of the state and not as legitimate prior claimants to the territory; in other words, by counting them no longer as indigenous peoples or *pueblos originarios,* but, for example, as Native Americans in the United States. This explains why elimination is an endless operation and why genocide, although paradigmatic of this logic, is not the sole form that it takes. The territory must also be renamed, referred to as the Americas and no longer as *Abya Yala*, and indigenous languages must be erased, forcing their speakers to learn Spanish, Portuguese, English, or French. Their culture and entire forms of life must be eliminated, too, and heteropatriarchy, Christianity, and gender dimorphism—among other forms of organizing social intelligibility—imposed upon them. Their languages, cultures, and forms of social and political organization must be eliminated as alternative forms of sociality. Elimination, in short, reorders the relationship between security, territory, and the population, which otherwise constitutes the biopolitical triad.[77] A proprietorial form of relationship is colonially imposed through the erasure of a prior relationship between peoples and their territories, which was predicated upon neither security nor appropriation.[78]

As a paradigmatic form of sovereign erasure, enforced disappearances are thus genealogically traceable to this logic of elimination, even if irreducible to it, since they represent the reactivation of elimination under very different conditions of accumulation. They constitute a way of asserting sovereign erasability in a historical context that, to start, had already abolished slavery and could no longer openly institutionalize the elimination of those it continued to target with social death. Thus, unlike the indiscriminate subjection of all indigenous peoples to elimination during colonial genocide, enforced disappearances were initially more selective. During the Latin American military dictatorships of the 1960s and 1970s, as Bargu argues, the most frequent targets of this violence were those labeled as "rebels."[79] Rebels were socialists, communists, anarchists, and other militant leftists whom the military dictatorships, through their counterinsurgency manuals, had redefined as enemies of the state. Rebellion, however, was never solely attributed to those who were politically active in this way. In fact, the agglutinative, concentric, and endless aspects Bargu distinguishes in enforced disappearances make that restriction impossible. As General Breno Borges Forte, then chief of staff of the Brazilian army, put it:

> The enemy is undefined . . . it adapts to any environment. . . . It disguises itself as a priest, a student or a campesino, as a defender of democracy or an advanced intellectual, as a pious soul or as an extremist protestor: it goes into the fields and the schools, the factories and the churches, the universities and the magistracy. . . . It will wear a uniform or civil garb . . . [and] it will . . . deceive.[80]

This paranoiac structure of sovereignty can also be traced back to settler-colonialism. Indigenous peoples were eliminated not only because they actively resisted the colonial occupation of their territories, but because their very existence rendered the European presence a colonial occupation and not the legitimate nation-state it needed to be in order to naturalize its rule. As the original inhabitants of the territory, their very existence rendered them enemies in perpetuity. This meant, however, that indigenous peoples were also neither "proper" enemies, nor simply "criminals," but complicated such distinctions and elicited extreme forms of violence previously reserved only for external enemies of war, to be redeployed internally as a way of policing the social order.

Through a compelling reinterpretation of Thomas Hobbes's theory of sovereignty as resting not on war but on the potential for war, Bargu uses the figure of the "rebel" to complicate Michel Foucault's way of distinguishing sovereignty from biopolitics. The enemy is to sovereign power, one could say, what the criminal is to biopolitical power. As Bargu argues, however, "The confluence of the criminal and the enemy in the rebel work as a justification for the deployment of unregulated, indiscriminate, and boundless violence in the name of security."[81] The rebel, in other words, is a kind of limit-figure that renders the distinction between sovereignty and biopolitics permeable and "acts as a remainder and reminder of the imperfect juridicalization of sovereignty."[82] What I would like to add to Bargu's excellent analysis is that the rebel of the '60s/'70s is less originary and more reiterative of a colonial history, where that violence had been previously inflicted upon slaves. Or, to put it differently, that indigenous and black enslaved peoples are the original (and ongoing) rebels of colonial modernity, those whose colonial construction first enabled such indistinction and the deployment of such unregulated violence in the name of security and on behalf of property. Taking them as internal/external enemies and stripping them of their rights, colonial powers criminalized their entire being; any expression of their freedom was to be regarded as a criminal offense.

The Preposterous History of Enforced Disappearances in the Americas, in the Ancient Tragedy of Antigone

What if settler colonial violence in the Americas allows us, then, to reinterpret Creon's violence in colonial antiquity, as a case study on sovereign erasure? What if the slavery that he could be said to have forced upon Polyneices, when he subjected his body to the indignity of exposure, calls attention to the ability of the sovereign to assert erasability? What does slavery do for sovereign erasability? One could argue that Creon's violence encounters a sovereign limit precisely because Polyneices was not a slave. As Antigone suggests, by instrumentalizing his corpse, however, Creon could be said to have de facto turned Polyneices into a slave. Such transmogrification allows Creon, if only temporarily, to extend his sovereign right beyond the endpoint of death, as a way of surveilling the living. Polyneices becomes a kind of ancient "rebel," a figure that allows external military war to recirculate internally, as a way of policing those living in the *polis* (biopolitics). Antigone understands what happens and thus claims that Polyneices was not Eteocles's slave, as a valid argument by which to oppose Creon's measures, if one that, as we have seen, nevertheless reinscribes slavery's abjection. Antigone's supporters, according to the rumors that Haemon reports to Creon, might also have understood what that extension meant. It meant that Creon could continue the war, although it had ended, in its absence. Slavery, as I cannot stress enough, was and is the continuation of war by other means. By keeping Polyneices's corpse alive, for that body to endure the performative function of sovereign erasability, Creon could be said to have turned Polyneices into a slave. *Like* a slave is significant, here, as the likeness entails an extension, a way of making the *demos* and the *doulos* (slave) potentially interchangeable, which in antiquity marked the ultimate threat of tyranny.

Perhaps partially conscious of the transgression that he was committing, Creon left Polyneices's corpse unburied at the city limits, at the seventh gate, abandoned just outside the city in order not to pollute it, but close enough for the citizens to behold its desecration. This strategic location dramatizes the liminal location of slaves as bodies that were neither only external enemies (spoils of war) nor only internal criminals, but both, with the potential for war resting not so much in their actions as in their living existence in the city. Treated like a slave for daring to violate the edict, Antigone is also put in a similarly ambiguous location when she is confined to the rockbound cave. Antigone is, in that sense, the paradigmatic rebel. As Gsoels-Lorensen argues, Antigone is not offered human food but "animal fodder" or "forage" (*phorbic*) as nourishment that would allow "her gods"—as Creon dismisses her claims—enough time to save her and avoid polluting the city. And Creon's reference to her as a horse to be subdued already engages in such dehumanizing transmogrification. As I articulated in chapter 1, Antigone's confinement and potential enslavement would also be the logical condition of losing the status of *metoikia*, which Creon claims to have revoked, when he calls for the guards to take her *metic* rights on earth away. The political dislocation of Polyneices and Antigone reveals both their transitory transformation into slavelike conditions but also, and paradoxically, Creon's awareness of what that extension represented for the *polis*. His edicts inaugurated a tyrannical world in which citizens could be subjected to the same kind of sovereign instrumentalization the *polis* reserved exclusively for slaves.

Instrumentalized as such, the sovereign redefines what is done to Polyneices and to his family not as violence, but as a legitimate way of caring for the good of the city: in modern vernacular, as a defense of society against its antisocial body (the antisociality that slaves represent, more precisely, as bodies that are already dead to the social order). Leaving Polyneices's corpse to rot while being eaten by dogs and birds, and legally forcing all Thebans to watch this horrifying spectacle, erases state violence. The legal codification of state violence as a way of "defending society," means that it is the burial of Polyneices's body, rather than its desecration, that is now to be considered as violent. The action that resists one violence is re-signified as a violation against the social order, for which the sovereign edict now stands as representative. In this double displacement of violence, sovereignty erases the real body that suffers its real violence and replaces it with the imaginary "body politic" the sovereign is called to defend, from the antisocial violence that it spectrally animates.

But this is not the sole function that the slavelike transmogrification of Polyneices offers Creon, when he can be said to extend slavery to dissident citizens/*metics*. By treating Polyneices as a slave, and thus taking hold not only of his life but also of his death, Creon also defers the temporality of sovereign violence. By inflicting violence upon a corpse rather than upon a living body, the sovereign overcomes the temporal boundaries that limited classical sovereignty. Here, it is worth recalling the limitations of the

French king's sovereign violence inflicted upon the publicly tortured body of Damiens, in the spectacle of the scaffold with which Foucault opens his genealogy of the modern prison as a biopolitical institution. Death, in other words, represents a limit to the exercise of sovereign violence—but only when death in fact marks such a limit. Slaves, as we know, were also robbed of their own deaths (deathliness); their corpses could thus be instrumentalized, extending the taking of their lives beyond the actual physical taking, if one that obviously entailed their vulnerability to that taking in the first place. Theban citizens faced a body for which death no longer constituted an endpoint in the performative struggle between the subject and the sovereign. Hence, they revolted. Postmortem violence represented a radical change in the status of Polyneices. Exercised upon a corpse, sovereignty would no longer be threatened by that body's endurance of its violence beyond the public's toleration of its horrors, reversing the popular perception of sovereign power that turned, as Foucault persuasively argued, legitimate rule into illegitimate despotism. Discharged upon a corpse, violence could become endless; war could be materially and not just imaginarily sustained by making some bodies bear the spectral re-apparition of the rebellious body and the materialization of war's potentiality beyond its actual end in the battlefield. By taking hold of the corpse, rather than of the living body, the potential of the war that had just ended was turned into the actuality of postwar forms of social control as the continuation of war by other means. War will take the form of looking for Polyneices's criminalized sympathizers, among all the other dissident voices in the city. War was now the *nomos* of the earth.

Bargu is thus right when she claims that Foucault's analysis of disciplinary power misses the fact that when punitive power moved from the scaffold to the prison, and from sovereignty to disciplinary institutions, torture did not disappear. Nor did, here I add, the instrumentalization of corpses to terrorize a population and extend sovereign violence as a way of policing the living. But in a world that no longer recognizes slaves, if one that keeps the colonial technologies of sovereignty as erasure intact, the instrumentalization of the dead body can no longer be as publicly exercised as it was in modernity.

FROM THE ROCKBOUND PRISON TO THE INVISIBLE PENAL ARCHIPELAGO

Torture did not disappear, nor did it merely morph into the disciplinary power of the prison system, which enacts its own kinds of torture. The cruelty of extreme forms of torture, such as the ones inflicted on Damiens, continues to exist, but is displaced into what Bargu names: the "*invisible penal archipelago*."[83] Legal sovereignty has since been exercised in the prison-industrial complex, where torture takes other forms, less visible if not less inhumane, such as today's widespread practice of solitary confinement in U.S. prisons. Torture's excesses, however, are displaced into a different apparatus, where the bodies are taken out of view in order not to fully compromise the self-representation of the state that takes these bodies as democratic, just, or humane. In a world that had abolished slavery and could no longer subject these bodies to such desecration, the state had to disclaim having taken them in the first place. The invisible penal archipelago, including the offshore concentration camp, was the institutional result of that political calculation.

As some have argued, the prison-industrial complex has its prehistory in the slave ship, thus giving us an alternative genealogy of punitive power that—unlike Michel Foucault's *The Birth of the Prison* (1976)—no longer brackets the colonial history of modern surveillance and disciplinary power and connects that disciplinary power to the racialized history of capitalist exploitation.[84] I here suggest that if we can trace the panopticon of the prison-industrial complex back to the slave ship, we should also trace the dispersed, mobile, and adaptable invisible penal archipelago, in which a plurality of actors can inflict enforced disappearances with total impunity today, back to the historical genocide of indigenous and black peoples.[85] The Atlantic Ocean constitutes one version of that invisible penal archipelago: in it, "slavers tossed out any among their load who were failing, [because] if one in three survived the journey, the trade still worked out as a cheap method of acquiring labor."[86] The invisible penal archipelago, however, also includes the jungles, rivers, and deserts that European settlers turned into mass graves to erase *Abya Yala*'s inhabitants and remake this territory into the Americas. If the prison-industrial complex reactivates, in neoliberal postmodernity, the logic of exclusion that one can trace back to the slave ship, the invisible penal archipelago reactivates the logic of elimination that one can trace back to the transformation of oceans and rivers into mass graves.

From enforced disappearances during a military dictatorship to enforced disappearances during a democratically elected government, the move from Dorfman's to Uribe's and Nieto's *Antigones* is also the move from the disappearances of mainly political dissidents and activists, labeled rebels by the authoritarian regime, to the indiscriminate disappearance of mostly racialized working-class peasants, in some cases irrespective of their political orientation. This move also marks a change in the number of agents capable of inflicting such violence—not only the military and the police but also the paramilitary, the drug cartel, the landowner, the repressive apparatuses of the empire, and the transnational corporation can inflict it, either through their own private armies or by purchasing those available. The pluralization of these agents, together with the normalization of violence that no longer requires suspending the law and can even tolerate the celebration of elections, explains the horrifying increase in its numbers.

Thus, unlike the 1,248 enforced disappearances, documented by the 1991 Rettig Report, under Pinochet's dictatorship in Chile, the Observatorio de Memoria Histórica (Observatory for Historical Memory) documents a total of 60,630 enforced disappearances in the ongoing Colombian armed conflict, from 1970 to 2015.[87] The situation in Mexico is considerably worse. Since then-president Felipe Calderón launched the War on Drugs in 2006, more than 37,485 enforced disappearances have been documented.[88] Unlike in Chile, the military and the police are no longer the main perpetrators in Colombia and Mexico. The main perpetrators now are paramilitaries in Colombia and drug cartels in Mexico, although they never act without the complicit participation of the state and have become increasingly indistinguishable from it (i.e., Colombia's *parapolítica* and Mexico's "poliZetas," to name but two of the forms that such indistinction has taken).

Such a multiplication of targets and agents of death, it should be clear, is in part a consequence of the neoliberal policies that Pinochet's dictatorship inaugurated in Chile, which rapidly extended throughout the whole region. War has become an industry, and under neoliberal conditions that displace more people to the "disposable" pool of the unemployable army, criminalized economies have flourished. This is the context in which the *endriago* subject emerges, which is Sayak Valencia's name for the gore version of the neoliberal *homo economicus*.[89] The *endriago* is one of the ways by which socially dead people resist their disposability—if only by becoming perpetrators of violence that functions as an economic force of accumulation, before they become one of its victims. *Endriagos,* however, do not work for a "productive" economy in the conventional understanding of that term. *Endriagos* work in a necroeconomy that, in neoliberal fashion, has made of death one of those human domains and endeavors that, "along human themselves," as Wendy Brown argues, neoliberalism "transmogrifies into a specific image of the economic."[90] Death is for sale, and like any other commodity, it has disaggregated that commodity in order to open new markets and new sources of profit. It is this commercialized death, and these intensified conditions of (para)state violence, that Latin American *Antigones* contest.

From Modern Melodrama to Postmodern Decolonial Cacophonies

Democratic theory, understandably, celebrates the move from classic tragedy to modern melodrama; artists no longer focus on the exceptional drama of the ruling aristocratic families but on the everyday life dramas of democratically exchangeable individuals. Unlike ancient tragedy, which conveyed democratic values by throwing the mythical aristocratic family into crisis, modern melodrama conveys the mundanity of human suffering through characters to whom any spectator in the audience can relate.[91] Melodrama proves limited, however, when artists confront the challenge of representing a form of suffering that lacks a grammar. This form of suffering is not so difficult to represent because many in the audience would refuse to relate to it. Rather, it is precisely because of the *ease* with which audiences, irrespective of their social positionality, can relate to it that it is so problematic. The pained body of the enslaved saturates the representational field and the system of chattel slavery facilitates the continuous appropriation of that body to work someone else's pain.[92] Melodrama thus proves limited when seeking to politicize this violence aesthetically, as it misrepresents the deathliness that structures the real and symbolic appropriability of the enslaved.

Instead of melodrama, I suggest that Latin American *Antigones* should be better understood as literary experiments in decolonial cacophony. *Cacophony* is the term used by Jodi Byrd and Aliyyah Abdur-Rahman to refer to a plurality of sounds and noises—shrieks, moans, wails—that inhabit language but are actually "in excess of legibility," as Hartman would put it.[93] Hartman's own method of "critical fabulation" is a form of decolonial cacophony in that it also recognizes failure as an inescapable condition of its critical practice.[94] Decolonial cacophonies thus recognize the plurality of sounds and their different registers, as colonialism makes some of them audible on the condition of silencing others. Decolonial cacophonies recognize that the condition of passing from noise to speech entails reinscribing an injury that can only be addressed if the critical artist is willing to remain within that noise.

Seeking to counteract the reinscription of the racialized injury through aesthetic distribution, decolonial cacophonies reject the full legibility of transitioning to representational signs—a transition that betrays the longevity of slavery. Thus, as the etymology of the word indicates, decolonial *cacophony* is particularly interested in "bad" or "ill" (*kakos*) sounds, those which this critical practice seeks not so much to represent but to reach for in their most radical unintelligibility. Decolonial cacophonies claim that the stories we have are broken and that we need to educate the ear, the eye, and our entire sensible apparatus to that brokenness, in order to publicly address it as ongoing, rather than betraying it by placing something far more legible in its place. It is important to stay with the noises and to hear them as noises first, but to do so not to repeat their exclusion but to fully understand the weight of their loss.

In their own unique ways, the three Latin American *Antigones* on which I have focused in this chapter engage in this type of decolonial cacophony. They all gesture toward the irrecoverable aspect of disappearances or the insufficiency and superfluity of language, while seeking to capture the lives of those who continue to be subjected to social death. Through gaps, brackets, and supplemental photographs, these *Antigones* trace the unsayable with neither pity nor voyeuristic consumption, allowing us to confront the social weight of these losses as irrecoverable. They do so under a critical lens in which the failure to recover them does not translate into their abandonment but, on the contrary, into a search that neither romanticizes the severe conditions of their inhuman exclusion nor replaces it with a romance of their own.

Dorfman does this first through the inclusion of a foreword written by the fictional author's son, Sirgud Lohmann, who tells us, during a section entitled only "{x}," that:

> [My father had indicated here the existence of a section in the original manuscript, coinciding with the above number. As there seems, in fact, to be a gap at this point in the text, it's preferable to advise the reader of this omission. There is no way of knowing what might have happened or what was planned for this section of the novel.][95]

In the following chapter, just after introducing the gap of {x}, Dorfman radicalizes *Widows*'s decolonial cacophony. Unlike the previous chapters, which are structured by fluctuating conversations among the main characters and the descriptive supplements of the omnipresent narrator, a voice conveyed in italics lets us into the otherwise unspeakable thoughts of a captive Alexis, who is about to be tortured by the captain and most likely disappeared as well. Knowing that Alexis's voice is ultimately irrecoverable, Dorfman decides for the first time to break the grammar of the text. The writing tilts and the italics visually thin the density of a voice that is about to be erased when Alexis is granted a short and silent visit by his grandmother, Sofía Angelos:

> *what's grandma whispering with her hand. what would be blowing into your ear, spilling into you, if her words could get to you through some secret tunnel, like sap through a tree trunk, like a stream through a hollow, what whispered advice? that you speak as little as possible, child, she'd start with that. that you keep to yourself half, more than half, of what you're thinking. and that's why she dared to talk to the captain? she wasn't afraid? because what she was thinking, child, was infinitely worse. you mustn't forget there are several things they can't do, many things, many: one of them is to read our minds.*
>   *and the fear?*[96]

{x} is the sign of the slave, the signature of the nameless, the "missing" ones Dorfman rightly describes as deprived not only of their homes, livelihoods, and families, but "also deprived of their graves," as if "they had never existed."[97] Alexis is about to become another missing chapter in the violent history of Latin American coloniality. The novel aesthetically registers the severity of his erasure by representing the ill voice in its illness, rather than by giving him a clear voice instead. Not a single word is capitalized, as if forcing the language to go underground. We are left with whispers, secret tunnels, and unreadable minds, in a code that resists full inclusion into the transparent legibility of the social sign.

In contrast to Dorfman's *Widows*, in Uribe's text, gaps multiply to such extent that they can no longer be considered as exceptional as they are in Dorfman's. This is a symptom that the violence has become even more normalized, as not even the suspension of the law is necessary for making extrajudicial killings routine. Uribe's whole text speaks from the brackets, the gaps, and the cacophonous discontinuity of voices forcing that which is unsaid to bear its political weight upon that which is actually said in the text. From inside the brackets Uribe poses the most difficult and compelling questions:

[
    : Who is Antigone in this scene, and what are we going to do with her words?
    : Who is Antígona González and what are we going to do with all the other Antígonas?
    : I did not want to be an Antígona
    but I was forced to become one
][98]

Like Dorfman and Uribe, Nieto feels the need to supplement the textual with what exceeds textuality. The novel, which is also a journalistic report, includes photographs from Érika Diettes's series *Rio Abajo*. Language is insufficient when faced with the challenge of reconstructing the Antigonian ritual of the people in Puerto Berrío, who have transformed the tombstones in which unidentified bodies were buried as NN by the state into a kaleidoscope of political artworks. This political-aesthetic transformation has been recorded in Juan Manuel Echavarría's beautiful artistic project, *Réquiem NN* (2006) (Figure 3.1).[99] As the forensic doctor of Puerto Berrío, Jorge Pareja claims that one day he woke up to, instead of the black, white, and gray tombstones of the cemetery's pavilion, "yellows, ochres, magentas, indigos, purples, turquoises, cyans, sapphires, corals, golds, emeralds, lavenders, ambers, oranges, salmons, and violets."[100] The district attorney's office reprimanded Pareja for allowing the people "to turn the NN's tombs into a circus," making it more difficult for state authorities to establish the identity of the one being buried as NN # {x}, because the people painted over the numbers assigned to each tomb, giving them a name of their choice. At first, Pareja tried to undo the people's will. In Creon's fashion, he ordered the destruction of the painted tombstones, but the people recommenced the ritual. By the end, he found that the only way to protect those identities was for him too to engage in the ritual himself. And it is to Pareja, Nieto claims, that we owe a beautiful litany of supplementary names: "Nelson Noel, Nevado Nevado, Nancy Navarro, Narciso Nanclares, Narana Navarro."[101]

Like any forensic doctor, Pareja knows that the bones of the dead speak. But unlike most forensic doctors, from the Antigonian actions of people such as Liliana, he has also learned that in order to properly understand them, one needs to decolonially attune one's ear to their cacophonous sounds.[102]

144   Antigone in the Americas

Figure 3.1. "Puerto Berrío's Mausoleum." Lenticular Photograph from Juan Manuel Echavarría's series Réquiem NN (2006–2013), reproduced with artist's permission.

Antigone's Decolonial Mourning

Latin American *Antigones* are not only aesthetic mediations of the gore forms that neoliberal violence takes today but political representations of how the people have tried to resist the (para)state violence to which they are subjected through public acts of dissident mourning. Yet when you confront not just one disappeared body but thousands, neither the performance of a public burial nor the public reclamation of the body might be enough. The existence of not just one but many Polyneices challenges the contestatory claims of Antigone in unique ways.

Take, for instance, the case of *Widows*, where Sofía Angelos is not the sole claimant of the body. Sarakis claims that the second body corresponds not to Sofía Angelos's husband, as she claims, but to his own brother, Theodoro. Theodoro, a friend of the Angeloses and a political opponent of the dictatorship, had also been disappeared. Yet by burying the unrecognizable second body as that of Theodoro, claimed by the protesters as Sofía Angelos's husband Michael Angelos, the dictatorial regime might succeed in disqualifying the political claim of these Antigonian protesters as unfounded, and the movement already built around their claim as illegitimate.

The protest, in other words, is never just about getting the bodies back—and perhaps not primarily about getting them back, if always also about that. The protest is about ending the structure of power that reproduces their disposability and legitimizes their taking in the first place. With each disappearance something else disappears, the space of the political that, as Fradinger claims, is "transformed into the militarization of politics."[103] It is that extinction of the political that decolonial mourning contests, not only by refusing the normalization of (para)state violence, but also by insurgently reconstructing an otherwise interdicted sociality.

DISMEMBERING VALUE AND THE AGENCY OF WOMEN IN THE COMMUNITY OF SLAVES

In the face of Sarakis's counterclaim, Fidelia, Sofía Angelos's granddaughter, asks Alexis, "What'll we do?" Alexis replies with the only possible solution: "Either he belongs to us all or he belongs to nobody. All the women have to claim him for burial, all the families."[104] Alexis's political response is one way of performing Barrett's political formula, when Barrett productively interpellates us to re-member the "other" by dis-membering value. Alexis knows that the revaluation of the Angelos's loss cannot come at the expense of devaluing Sarakis's claim, which Sofía disqualifies with the same patriarchal epithets the military regime uses to render her inaudible and invisible when she calls Sarakis a "whore" in justifiable anger. Such relational valuation only works to the benefit of the dictatorial regime, which can, in the future, play another disappearance against the one being challenged, in order to cancel the political conflict over who counts and who is uncounted.

In this case, dismembering value means turning the corpse into a political signifier that exceeds the political economy of modern kinship. The role of women in the slave community, I claim, is what gets animated in this case. As I argued in chapter 2, following Spillers, under slavery all claims to kin could be arbitrarily invaded by property relations. The enslaved were thus forced to replace blood ties with consensual forms of affiliation as an alternative way of doing kinship. As a consequence, motherhood was not only de-biologized but also, and uniquely, politicized. As Davis so lucidly argues, the patriarchal and white supremacist ideology that assigned to enslaved women responsibility for care in the living quarters of the enslaved nevertheless changed the political nature of those gendered obligations:

> [I]n the infinite anguish of ministering the needs of the men and children around her (who were not necessarily members of her immediate family), she was performing the *only* labor of the slave community which could not be directly and immediately claimed by the oppressor. . . . Precisely through performing the drudgery which has long been a central expression of the socially conditioned inferiority of women, the black woman in chains could help to lay the foundation for some degree of autonomy, both for herself and her men. Even as she was suffering under her unique oppression as female, she was thrust by the force of circumstances into the center of the slave community. She was, therefore, essential to the *survival* of the community.[105]

As Davis argues, unlike the domesticity to which white settler women were confined, the domestic tasks of the enslaved women, otherwise deprived of political life, uniquely politicized them. Performing the only form of labor that could not be directly appropriated by their enslavers, and becoming the essential support system for the survival of their community, their domestic labor in the slave quarters acquired an insurgent dimension. Not only were women made acutely conscious of the oppression suffered by their people but also "uniquely capable of weaving into the warp and woof of domestic life a profound consciousness of resistance."[106]

Under current neoliberal conditions, where the commercialization of life and death can, once again, invade kinship, if differently, protestors react once again with consensual affiliations. What they reanimate, in this case, is the political role that women played in the community of the enslaved. The law of value is, as Barrett puts it, dismembered, and thirty-seven widows can claim the same body to belong to each and all of them.[107] So, in Dorfman's political solution, the undecidable identity of the corpse, the very problem that modernity establishes as continuing to grip us all, becomes part of the political solution.

The same happens in Nieto's *Los escogidos*, which refers to the real practice of Puerto Berrío's inhabitants. In this practice, the adopters not only adopt an NN and give them a name, but also choose a form of kinship by which to relate to them under political, rather than biological terms.[108] Subjected to gore capitalism, when neoliberalism makes it possible, once again, for property in the form of commodified death to invade kinship, the inhabitants of Puerto Berrío also reanimate consensual affiliation.

Working-class peasants in Puerto Berrío adopt the dead, give them a new identity, and engage in a ritual of reciprocal obligation whereby they keep the tombstones clean, cared for, and decorated in exchange for favors that they ask from the dead. Some of those favors have economic connotations, like getting a job, but they are not reducible to such economic transaction. Something else, something more fundamental, is established through the reconstitution of an otherwise violated relation of social reciprocity with the dead. Furthermore, in some cases a dead person can have more than one foster family, and the different claimants mutually negotiate how to care for the one they each give a different name. In other cases, as with the tomb of an NN that was given the name of "Daniel/Daniela," gender ambiguity is performatively registered, refusing to assign the dead body a gender of the adopter's choice (Figures 3.2 and 3.3). Daniel/Daniela might also extend the transness that Snorton traces back to the fungibility of blackness, as a way of re-membering a gender-undecidable body and creating an alternative sociality not only for the cis-commons but also for the quare and two-spirit undercommons. Through these political gestures, the people of Puerto Berrío engage in what one might call an insurgent politics of care against neoliberal disposability and slow death.[109]

Finally, those who do the adopting often have family members of their own who have been disappeared. This might be what happened to Carmen Piedrahita, who no longer knows where her older brother Guillermo lies.[110] In fact, it is possible that the bodies that mourners like Piedrahita adopt are the bodies of the soldiers responsible for the disappearance of their own family members. The inhabitants of Puerto Berrío know that, yet they adopt them and grant them burial, reinscribing them into an otherwise broken community by an undeclared civil war.

If Creon wanted to extend the friend/enemy distinction beyond life and continue the war in its absence by taking hold of the enslaved corpse, the people of Puerto Berrío take the struggle for peace to the same postmortem level. By burying the dead irrespective of their identity in war, they contest the fiction of the state with a rival fiction of their own, and in so doing regenerate a political space that the state is most interested in militarizing. Fungibility, as Snorton argued, also becomes in this case a condition for a new becoming of the otherwise broken community. The unnamed are given names not to exclude them from social belonging—as when the enslavers named their enslaved—but to give them an alternative social belonging that can undo the war in whose continuity the state

Figure 3.2. "Daniel/Daniela 1." Lenticular Photograph from Juan Manuel Echavarría's series *Réquiem NN (2006–2013)*, reproduced with artist's permission.

Figure 3.3. "Daniel/Daniela 2." Lenticular Photograph from Juan Manuel Echavarría's series *Réquiem NN (2006–2013)*, reproduced with artist's permission.

is highly invested. The alternative names they give to the dead that they adopt seek not so much to connect "language and life" but, as Fradinger has argued, "language and political life."[111]

The Political Mourning of Maternal Activism under Conditions of Feminicide

Like all ancient and modern Antigones, postmodern Antigones are also disqualified on the basis of their gender. The captain in *Widows* disqualifies "this mania for burying men who have nothing to do with your families" as "a collective hysteria," not unlike Creon calling Antigone "mad."[112] This disqualification generates a paradox, when the contestatory claim over the disappeared body mobilizes a kin relation in which these regimes are invested and thus can be said to reinforce a problematic identity.

This paradox was well captured in Diana Taylor's excellent analysis of maternal activism as being trapped in what she called a "bad transcript," referring to the scripts available for women to stage their public dissidence against dictatorial regimes in Latin America.[113] After all, as Taylor argues, it is their performance of motherhood that otherwise shields the women from the most lethal forms of violence they would have encountered had they performed their protest under a different script. Taylor refers to the protest of the Madres de la Plaza de Mayo in Argentina, who have become the paradigm of political mourning *à la* Antigone in Latin America. Mothers were patriarchally valorized as such by the dictatorial regime, which in *Widows* (dis)qualifies them as "the sweetheart" and "the wife" that the "Supreme Government, like a benevolent father, knows how to punish and how to forgive."[114] Performing their mourning as "mothers," thus reconfirming their selective inclusion according to the terms imposed by the patriarchal/militarized order, proves limited. Hence, other feminist critics have questioned the limitations of the Mothers of the Plaza de Mayo's activism in particular, and maternal activism in general, as inevitably flawed and potentially antipolitical.[115]

But if traditional gender roles gave mothers some protection under the Chilean and Argentinian military dictatorship, which (de)valued them while claiming motherhood to be the essence of womanhood, those roles no longer protected them in the Colombian armed conflict and, most radically, in the case of Mexico, where 23,800 feminicides have been registered.[116] Of the 37,485 enforced disappearances documented in Mexico, 8,974 are disappeared women. This takes place in a country where 41.3 percent of women (more than 19 million) report having suffered sexual violence and 66.1 percent report being a victim of violence in general.[117]

In other words, it is no longer Polyneices but poor working-class women who serve as textual surfaces by which a plurality of armies can send messages to each other, as Segato argues, and reactivate in the present the old territorial logic of settler-colonial elimination. When that violence is normalized to such an extent that it can even cohabit with democracy, it is no longer even necessary to invisibilize the tortured body. Ravaged corpses are once again displayed in public to force populations out of their territories and the ones who remain into silence and acquiescence. In a context in which a public demand for the state to counteract that violence is more likely to result in the public protestor's death than in any kind of state redress or international sanction, the agents of this violence can disregard the additional costs of invisibility and profit instead from their investment in its gore publicity. The *Global Impunity Index México 2016* calculates that 95 percent of the 234,996 killings registered in Mexico since Calderón's "War on Drugs" have not been punished. This number does not include the rate of "unrecorded" crimes, leading Ariadna Estévez to claim that the impunity figure should be 99 percent.[118] Vulnerable to state, corporate, and parastate terror, the community not only knows that the body was taken, but also that its disappearance will elicit no state action of redress and no international intervention to stop the normalization of such violence—that, just like the bodies of the enslaved under colonial capitalism, these bodies can also be disposed of with total impunity.

Under such conditions, in which motherhood no longer offers any kind of shield, maternal activism changes considerably and, one could argue, acquires the more politically insurgent aspects it had under slavery. Women in Mexico are once again being forced into sexual slavery in what Estévez rightly renames a new necropolitical "war for the dispossession of women's bodies."[119] Under such conditions, as Elva Fabiola Orozco Mendoza has so brilliantly articulated, maternal activism exercises an additional "expressive" function whose political aspect cannot be denied. According to this function, by embodying the precariousness to which they are sanctioned, the mothers expose gender-based violence as "an effect of existing institutions, traditions, structures, and gender norms."[120]

From the Madres de la Plaza de Mayo to the Madres de Chihuahua, motherhood no longer protects women from violence inflicted by the military or the police or by the paramilitary, the parapolice, the transnational corporation, the maquiladora, or the drug cartel, with which that state has become often indistinguishable. And when that violence uses women's publicly ravaged bodies as a pedagogy of cruelty, Orozco-Mendoza claims, the public performance of motherhood constitutes what Segato calls "a counter-pedagogy of cruelty."[121] Cruelty, Segato argues, habituates and programs a population to turn forms of life into exchangeable objects. A counter-pedagogy of cruelty, Orozco-Mendoza expands, might be the mothers' way of undoing that transmogrification, of reversing its course, as they take on the restorative functions that the state is no longer willing to undertake, fully complicit as it is with the logics leading to the widespread reproduction of feminicides. The maternal is not essentialized because it is no longer a biologically determined relationship but most fully politicized, as those engaged in maternal activism engage in a public conflict over the official narrative vis-à-vis the quality of life and also of death in the *polis*. The maternal indexes an insurgent politics of care, against the accelerated slow death to which these communities are subjected by multiple sources of neoliberal violence.

Under neoliberal conditions of gore capitalism, the dissident staging of a public burial might also not be possible. The mothers recur to other theatrical and performative strategies, resulting in what Orozco-Mendoza calls "the funeralization of the city."[122] In contexts of feminicide and extreme gender violence, in which contestatory actions cannot be so readily embodied by human actors because their dissidence is likely to result in their own killing, and one equally subjected to impunity, objects such as pink crosses, graffiti, monuments, poems, and photographs of the victims give an afterlife to their voices. Objects give a material endurance to their dissident messages in their absence. As sexual enslavement, as Estévez argues, becomes once again normalized, this public "funeralization," Orozco-Mendoza concludes, makes the public "bear witness to the repeated episodes of sexual violence, enforced disappearance, and murder of women in northern Mexico with the purpose of denouncing the state politics of neglect that partakes in the production of poor Mexican women as disposable subjects."[123] In other words, it is not only the "maternal" but also the "activism" that changes, as humans and objects creatively come together to contest the structural conditions of their disposability and refuse the racialized logics of value that turn them into commodified objects of exchange, for the new necro-economies of death.

Resisting the Allure of Intelligibility

Colombian and Mexican Antigones face one additional challenge. Under the neoliberal intensification of this violence, they are also forced to bury the *endriagos,* members of rival armies, who are often responsible for the disappearance of their own family members. Here, we should remember that Polyneices's intentions were not noble. The war that he waged against his natal city was to enslave Thebes, not to free it from tyrannical rule. Yet subjecting Polyneices to the indignity of nonburial does not ameliorate the neoliberal logics of accumulation that criminalize him in the first place—it only exacerbates them.

How, then, to bury the many contemporary Polyneices while resisting the allure of intelligibility that forces one to establish their innocence first? What if the men and women who look at the camera with an unfathomable face from the wall of the accused, or who lie lifeless on the pavement—those of whom Antígona González cannot decide whether they are real criminals or just cannon fodder—are in fact both? Do we not encounter here the more difficult gesture of Antigone's decolonial mourning, in resisting the need to valorize Polyneices so as to disclaim the violence that he met, if only by reinscribing another form of devaluation?

I would like to end this chapter by revising Lisa Marie Cacho's extraordinary meditation on the difficulties involved in her own mourning of her cousin, Brandon Jesse Martínez, which I consider an exemplary case of decolonial mourning. Confronted with the temptation to explain Brandon's death as a result not of his own agency and choice to participate in "nonormative activities" but of the racialized international division of labor, Cacho realizes that "for racial exclusion to work as a sympathetic narrative, it needs to draw upon the neoliberal ideologies that legitimate global capitalism, naturalize inequality, and stigmatize nonnormativity."[124] In other words, in order for Brandon to be seen as a victim of the system, and not the culprit as neoliberal ideology represented him, Cacho "had to ignore [Brandon's] decision to not make decisions and erase his talent for choosing nonoptions."[125] Revalued as a victim of neoliberalism, Brandon was not re-membered, as his choices remained the "negative resource" for a relational system of value that could only celebrate Cacho's academic accomplishments, as the "good" *metic*-cum-citizen's successful narrative of assimilation, on the basis of not mourning Brandon's nonoptions, as the "bad" *metic*-cum-slave object of exclusion and elimination. Under such relational system, Brandon's death had problematically become "his most legible asset."[126]

We come to understand the value of analysis such as Valencia's and Cacho's which, instead of morally condemning those who participate in a necroeconomy of empowerment by participating in activities that the state criminalizes, theorize opting for nonnormative forms of life as a way of resisting neoliberal exclusion and elimination—becoming perpetrators instead of victims. From the either/or to the both/and, Antigone's decolonial mourning would refuse to valorize Polyneices by distinguishing him from others, for whom she would not perform the burial. She would no longer bury the Polyneices that neoliberalism produces by the hundreds of thousands, because, let's say, they were not criminals. She would include criminalization as one of the forms that colonial violence takes and suture a broader connection to those most radically displaced to the "disposable" pool, forced to survive within the confines of criminalized existence.

The criminalization of entire populations is a byproduct of racial/sexual capitalism, and Antigone's mourning should avoid fueling it by seeking to distinguish the victim of this violence as undeserving, by legitimizing the criminal as deserving of it. Here, it is worth recalling Davis's criticism of Frederick Douglass, whose focus on lynching and silence in regard to the convict lease system Davis questions as a "vision of black liberation [too] solidly anchored in the promise of legislated justice to permit him to ponder the possibility of the profound complicity of legal institutions in the continuation of this micro-cosmic slave system."[127] Perhaps the Colombian and Mexican cases make that complicity more difficult to sustain, given the radical impunity of state-sanctioned violence, and the flagrant violation of human rights documented in these prisons. But the risk of fighting the invisible penal archipelago by strengthening the prison-industrial complex, or the detention centers in which many *metics* are confined today, is real.

In Antígona González's inability to distinguish the "real criminals," who presumably deserve state repression, from those turned into cannon fodder, one can hear the desire for such a distinction to be possible—not unlike Antigone's desire to distinguish her brother from slaves, for whom she would not have opposed the edict. To mourn decolonially is to resist the allure of such a distinction: not in order to excuse the perpetrators or further guarantee the impunity of their crimes, but to redirect the political challenge toward the colonial system that reproduces criminality and abjection, as the real target of dissident action and mass mobilization.[128]

Davis's critical examination of Douglass's silence aimed to show how academic confidence in the Enlightenment and the bourgeois state to guarantee racial progress was crucial to Douglass's failure to understand the prison system. That prison system, like lynching and Jim Crow segregation, extended the racist structures of labor subjugation, giving slavery an aftermath in the United States. And just as the struggle against lynching might have shielded the convict lease system from revolutionary critique, the struggle against enforced disappearances might shield the prison-industrial complex and other institutionalized repressive apparatuses of the state from critique as well in Latin America. The challenge is to mourn decolonially otherwise, in a way that shows both systems as part of mutually reinforcing settler-colonial logics of accumulation that first subjected enslaved black and indigenous people to convergent forms of exclusion and elimination.

Neoliberal forms of violence continue to subject black and indigenous people to such violence, but it has also extended that violence to other working-class people of color whom postcolonial Latin American states officially recognize as either *metics* or citizens. Slavery has been given an aftermath, making it all the more crucial for us to draw, learn, and repoliticize the fugitive agency of the enslaved. This is the agency that democratic theory, feminist and queer theory, and the theory of biopolitics have failed to recognize as the liberatory and transformative agency that it was and continues to be.

In the next and last chapter of this book, I situate *Antigone*'s mourning against the discourse of the Anthropocene. Here I argue that the inability to confront and interrogate racial/sexual capitalism and the ways in which it regulates difference, resurfaces when we move from the human to the posthuman. That claim leads me to revisit Hegel's analysis of burials as border-events, privileged occasions in which the separation of the human from the nonhuman is sexually and racially engineered. Here, I also critique Jacques Derrida for failing to confront the material history of racial differences in his own critique of Hegel, thus limiting the ability of deconstruction to politicize differences in the present. Through Ian Baucom's and Avery Gordon's work on ghosts and specters, I then inscribe the deconstruction that *Antigone in the Americas* seeks to perform in a more decolonial spirit of Marxism. Thus, I conclude that chapter with an analysis of black and indigenous mo'nin (Fred Moten) and wake work (Christina Sharpe) that I consider crucial for the creation of a more political, rather than ethical, New International in the struggle against the racial Capitalocene.

4

Antigone in the Settler-Colonial Present of the Racial Capitalocene

A Critique of Deconstruction in the Americas

> Specters are still haunting, not only in Europe and not only of communism. Our contemporary society is still a "society that has conjured up such gigantic means of production and of exchange . . . like the sorcerer, who is no longer able to control the powers of the nether world whom he has called up by his spells" (Marx and Engels). The task then remains to follow the ghosts and spells of power in order to tame this sorcerer and conjure otherwise.
>
> —Avery Gordon, Ghostly Matters

Antigone in the Age of the Racial Capitalocene

The settler colonial present is a formulation I borrow from Lorenzo Veracini, who claims that neoliberalism's worldwide extension of warehousing technologies, which originally targeted indigenous peoples with elimination, today "'indigenize' us all."[1] They do not, of course, "indigenize" us all in the same ways, and I hope to have demonstrated how an attention to the capitalist regulation/reproduction of racial and gender differences remains politically crucial. In this chapter, however, I would like to situate the present of settler colonialism in a more difficult and, for some, even inscrutable spatial-temporal configuration: that of the racial Capitalocene.

Jason Moore uses the term *Capitalocene* to critique how the otherwise depoliticized phenomenon that scientists have named the *Anthropocene*—a term that understands humans as acting in the "natural" form of a geological force—conceals the "naturalized inequalities, alienation, and violence inscribed in modernity's strategic relations of power and production."[2] The term *racial Capitalocene*, however, was first coined, to the best of my knowledge, by Françoise Vergès.[3] While both Moore and Vergès critique as ideological the scientific attempt to blame climate change on uncontrollable forces rather than structures of power, Vergès also critiques the language of the Anthropocene for its depoliticization of racial capitalism. She does this by highlighting the historical role of structural racism in exposing (not all but) some people to environmentally horrifying conditions, which more often than not sentence them to premature death. Vergès traces this much-needed politicization, which situates the problem of climate change at a planetary level, back to the 1991 First National People of Color Environmental Leadership Summit Report, *Principles of Environmental Justice*. She acknowledges that indigenous peoples have been the leaders of global activism against the capitalist conditions leading to climate change as well as in linking today's extractive capitalism to its colonial history.[4]

Wondering about the methodology that would be needed in order "to write a history of the environment that includes slavery, colonialism, imperialism and racial capitalism, from the standpoint of those who were made into 'cheap' objects of commerce," Vergès enunciates the Antigonian challenge of the anti–settler-colonial present that I would like to confront in this chapter.[5] "We must," Vergès argues, "in our narrative of the racial Capitalocene, integrate this long memory of colonialism's impact and the fact that destruction in the colonial era becomes visible in the postcolonial era."[6] The integration of that memory faces one significant challenge, well formulated by Avery Gordon. Referring to the massive loss of life during the state-sponsored terror in Argentina, which Gordon links to the equally horrifying tossing of slaves into the Atlantic Ocean during the Middle Passage, Gordon claims that here we contemplate "ghosts and haunting at the level of the making and unmaking of world historical events."[7] But then, Gordon adds, "if there is one point to be learned from the investigation of ghostly matters, it is that you cannot encounter this kind of disappearance as a grand historical fact, as a mass of data adding up to an event, marking itself in straight empty time, settling the ground for a future cleansed of its spirit."[8] How, then, can we confront ghostly matters at the level of world-historical events? Do all confrontations of disappearances as a grand historical fact involve such an aggregative gesture? Does any confrontation of losses, in the plural, entail straightening empty time to cleanse the spirit? Can there be a form of mourning that, recognizing the singularity of each loss, nonetheless gestures toward mourning all these losses together and not just one at a time? Can mourning, then, be about not cleansing the spirit but confronting the pile of debris accumulated in its wake? What would it mean, in other words, for the anti–settler-colonial capitalist Antigone to seek Polyneices not in an individualized body but in de-individualized millions? What would it mean to seek for those millions in the otherwise neutralized *anthropos,* understood now as a geological force? What if by re-membering those millions, by integrating their memory into a critique of the present, we finally understand that climate change is not, and has never been, an all-inclusive problem for "all humans" in the future, but the past-present-and-imminent-future reality of those who have never been considered human in the first place?[9]

According to Vergès, in order "to unpack the different levels of racialized environment," precisely that which the discourse of the Anthropocene neutralizes, "we need to go back the long sixteenth century, the era of Western 'discoveries,' of the first colonial empires, of genocides, of the slave trade and slavery."[10] Where we go, in terms of time and space, is not inconsequential to the kind of political critique that we can offer of the plague that has been affecting the planet for centuries. Simon Lewis and Mark Maslin propose the year 1610 as the beginning of the Anthropocene and even try to integrate the colonial genocide into their framework. Their argument is based on the significant decline in atmospheric CO_2 between 1570 and 1620, documented in two high-resolution Antarctic ice-core records, which resulted from the genocidal consequences of the European colonization of the Americas. As they claim,

> The arrival of Europeans in the Caribbean in 1492, and subsequent annexing of the Americas, led to the largest human population replacement in the past 13,000 years. . . . Besides permanently and dramatically altering the diet of almost all of humanity, the arrival of Europeans in the Americas also led to a large decline in human numbers. Regional population estimates sum to a total of 54 million people in the Americas in 1492, with recent population modeling estimates of 61 million people. Numbers rapidly declined to a minimum of 6 million people by 1650 via exposure to diseases carried by Europeans, plus war,

enslavement, and famine. The accompanying near-cessation of farming and reduction in fire use resulted in the regeneration of over 50 million hectares of forest, woody savanna and grassland with a carbon uptake by vegetation and soils estimated at 5-4Pg within 100 years.[11]

The genocide of indigenous people and its environmental consequences are at the heart of the only identifiable "golden spike" to date the beginnings of the otherwise misnamed Anthropocene. A golden spike is the empirically registerable significant change in stratigraphic material, such as the accumulation of CO_2 in glacier ice, that allows scientists to date geological ages—to determine when we moved, so to speak, from the Holocene to the Anthropocene. The otherwise politically neutralized vocabulary of the Anthropocene is the racial Capitalocene, and the ice registers not only the massive, albeit differentiated, loss of life European colonialism inflicted, but the refusal of these socially dead ones to accept the reproductive futurity of *this* settler-colonial world in silence.[12] Although dead, those first subjected to the genocidal conditions of modern slavery continue to haunt this colonial order, to mark it as what it is: a world that massively reproduces death while making some forms of labor more vulnerable to its lethal conditions than others. But the traces of their existence, and the enormity of their yet unaddressed loss, are still de-colonially legible in the ice.

What if Antigone's gesture, within this context, is not so much that of burying the single body of Polyneices, so as to take the stage and voice her own individual message, but of exhuming a mass of bodies from historical oblivion? What if that colonially imposed forgetting, is precisely what has enabled the turning of racial/sexual capitalism into the apocalyptic racial Capitalocene, which white geology is only now awaking to?

There is, as I articulated in chapter 3, a historically forgotten political genealogy connecting the ghosts of today's enforced disappearances and the historical genocide of indigenous and black people. My preposterous history of *Antigone* in the Americas has tried to no longer treat those genocides as histories of the past, and to seek, instead, to treat their spectral reappearance as agents with the capacity to unhinge the present, to deconstruct "America" as an ongoing colonial laboratory of racial/sexual capitalism. To re-member these losses means, also, to complicate the exceptionality of contemporary violence and to recall that their history is still our history of the present and imminent future. To deconstruct the Americas is to understand that racial/sexual capitalism is the engine of the racial Capitalocene, that the impossibility of re-membering *Abya Yala* is what makes possible the ongoing naturalization of settler-colonial America.

As a deconstructive reading, however, *Antigone in the America* differs from Jacques Derrida's deconstructive foundational texts on *Antigone*, mourning, and the specter. My book differs from Derrida's project in that I focus on the politicization of intersectional differences I believe deconstruction insufficiently addresses, within its own crucial efforts at pluralizing differences beyond the constraints of the Hegelian dialectic. This explains my return, yet again, to Hegel's dialectic. Here, I show the ways in which the binary between the human and the nonhuman that is at the center of the discourse of the Anthropocene can be traced back to the ways in which Hegel constructs the burial as a kind of border-event of "the human." I then critique Derrida's deconstructive undoing of the dialectic. In my view, in seeking to free difference from the confines of the Hegelian system Derrida fails to grant to all differences the same capacity to metaphorize otherwise. This allows me to further complicate the specters to which critical theory recognizes a political, rather than an ethical indebtedness, and thus to read the carbon dioxide accumulating in the ice under more materialist senses. I conclude this chapter with a reflection on the differential mourning that is indigenous and black people's wakeful mo'nin. In the ability of this mo'nin to awake the past in the present, I seek a better foundation for a New International capable of confronting the apocalyptic racial Capitalocene of the present with decolonial mourning.

The Racialized Burial and the Human Border

Let me turn one last time to Hegel. Here, I argue that in his infamous interpretation of *Antigone*, Hegel actually conceptualized the burial as a privileged border-event, crucial in Western humanism's efforts at distinguishing the human (culture) from the mere animal (nature). This is the very distinction that, according to some interpretations, the Anthropocene is said to have also thrown into crisis. From Hegel, one could argue, the discourse of the Anthropocene not only inherits the highly linear notion of time and space that this discourse reproduces, but also the construction of humanity as a "collective" actor in the form of a geological force. The Anthropocene puts the Anthropos where Hegel had placed the Spirit, and thus inherits the racial/sexual marginalization of de-spiritualized differences. To deconstruct the material history of these differences is to move from the easy story that is the Anthropocene, and focus instead on "the relations of power, capital, and nature that rendered fossil capitalism so deadly in the first place."[13] As I will show shortly, all of this actually hinges on our ability to politicize a different burial.

According to Hegel, through the culturally mediated act of burying the body, humans were able to distinguish the endpoint of a human life from the cyclical endlessness of animal and vegetal life. Burial transforms death, which otherwise marks a natural condition, into a subjective act, invested, in Hegel's terms, with will and consciousness. Burial thus qualifies human finitude as distinct from the end of other sentient beings, who do not properly die but only cease to be. Through burial, the dead are re-membered, given a place in the Symbolic order of the community. Death mimics birth in the human condition's inescapable interdependence with others, a condition that, actually, characterizes the whole of life. To be in the world, to belong to it, is to be with others, and that interdependency characterizes the beginning as well as the end of human life. But it would be a mistake to conceive of a burial as the logical consequence of what follows after death, just as it would be wrong to conceive of death as a "natural" phenomenon. Rather, it is more precise to conceive of burial as the political act that retroactively produces the natural fact that grounds it, as deconstruction would put it. In other words, it is through the burial itself that the metaphysical division between a natural death and a culturally mediated act is artificially reproduced so as to carve the edges of the human. Nonburial is *made* into "nature," into a condition of subhuman animality, so as not to confront our own productive power. Burial, deconstructed, denaturalizes death by showing it as something that we do rather than as something that happens to us—a deed that is, quite significantly, decisive to the formation of that "we."

Who is buried, by whom, and under what conditions, makes burial inescapably political. As the border that separates "the human" from nature, and marks the distinctiveness of a life with a determinable end, burial is, like birth, the subject of great political anxiety. It becomes, as Hegel articulates it, an event in which other hierarchies must be established, and certain differences policed and confined:

> The duty of the family member is thus to augment this aspect so that his [sic] final *being*, this *universal* being, will also not belong solely to nature and remain something non-rational. It

is to make it so that it too may be *something done,* and that the right of consciousness would be asserted within that being.[14]

In Hegel's analysis of *Antigone* in the *Phenomenology*, the protection of the (rational) culture/(irrational) nature division, that is crucial for the self-definition of "the human," requires the supplement of heteronormative kinship. In other words, Hegel does not grant the same ethical power to raise the human family above the merely natural to all burials. It is the burial of the brother by the sister in particular that secures the border between "the human" and "mere nature," if only by fixing another border on its course, that of sexual difference. According to Hegel, unlike the ethically mixed relationships between husband and wife and parents and children—mixed, for Hegel, because they are differently affected by reproduction and desire—the more egalitarian relationship between the brother and the sister is ethically "unmixed," as they "neither desire each other, nor have they given or received this being-for-itself to each other."[15] The funeral ritual in which the sister buries the brother constitutes the paradigmatic case in which the natural is somehow allowed to participate in the universal. That participation threatens, however, the confinement of women into the depoliticized space of the *oikos,* and the consequence naturalization of "nature" for which they are forced to stand, as the community's everlasting irony. Their subordinated participation in the universal of the other is also the effect of a repression, as the prohibition of incest is replayed in the burial. Antigone's burial is, hence, doubly repressed, as not only her transgression of the domestic space but also her incest, and the ways in which both complicate the difference that she is supposed to play are glossed over. Otherwise haunted by incest and gender defiance, those transgressions play no role in Hegel's universalization of the brothers' funeral by the sister as the sole scene of ethical equilibrium. She must remain in the *oikos* (stand for the family and for the divine) and the incest taboo persists in death, when the burial of the brother by the sister secures human intelligibility from nature's grip, on the condition that desire is absent.

As feminist interpretations of Hegel's *Phenomenology* have demonstrated, however, Antigone never buries Polyneices in the form that Hegel expected.[16] She does not remain in the *oikos*—neither when she plots the burial with her sister nor when she performs and then publicly claims it. Actually, Antigone buries Polyneices conscious of the consequences of her act, despite Hegel's claims to the contrary.[17] And the language that she employs is not just filial but also erotic.[18] But, as Chanter has argued, her conscious refusal to serve as a token for the system of citizenship from which she and her sister Ismene are otherwise excluded reinscribes another exclusion, as Polyneices is also *not* her brother's slave. The feminist troubling of one cultural frame of intelligibility supports itself in the further renaturalization of the other. The ancient *oikos* is, after all, not only composed of parents, children, and siblings in the prepolitical exclusion of the family from the public sphere, but also of the enslaved.

It is this other, interrelated operation of power, that interests me. Not only women but the enslaved, too, are also produced as the "other" of the human, as the other of culture, and as that over which the human presumably dominates. But unlike the unassimilable difference that Antigone represents, as ethically partial, the difference that these racialized others represent is entirely excluded from the ethical. Settler colonial capitalist regimes of power thus subject racialized populations to various forms of nonburial. Nonburial, here, refers not only to the forced absence of a burial when the body is violently disappeared, but also to the negation of some funerary rites as recognizably human, or ethical, when they are actually performed. As a consequence, the sacred burial sites of indigenous people were subordinated to the needs of settler-colonial capital, as were the dead bodies of black people, which continued to be instrumentalized by the settler/master class to engage in their humanistic experimentation, long after the official abolition of slavery. Nonburial, improper burial, or unintelligible burial, as a structural rather than contingent phenomenon, reinforced the subhumanization of black and indigenous peoples that came to define, in opposition, the humanity of the settler as the sole ethical burial.

If burial is what finally marks a life as distinctively human, nonburial puts that humanity into question. Only the settler has a past and a future in a colonial context that, de facto if not also de jure, restricts citizenship through racial and sexual forms of structural exclusion and selective inclusion. For the citizen to enjoy the linear temporality of a form of life under settler-colonial conditions of capitalist accumulation, slaves were forced to bear the cyclical temporality of de-formed life, associated with nature. *Metics* were placed somewhere in between. It is thus crucial for the settler-colonial order not to bury the socially dead body so as to "naturalize" their exclusion. The colonial interdiction of this memory, which is to say, the necropolitical construction of these deaths as insignificant and nonuniversal, explains why not all deaths, nor all burials, suggest an ecological crisis of planetary proportions. As Kathryn Yusoff argues,

> If the Anthropocene proclaims a sudden concern with the exposures of environmental harm to white liberal communities, it does so in the wake of histories in which these harms have been knowingly exported to black and brown communities under the rubric of civilization, progress, modernization, and capitalism. . . . The Anthropocene as a politically infused geology and scientific/popular discourse is just now noticing the extinction it has chosen to continually overlook in the making of its modernity and freedom.[19]

What would it mean for the decolonial Antigone of the Americas to bury Polyneices, not in order to rescue him from his otherwise forceful displacement into mere nature, but in order to break with the colonial fold of "the human"? What would it mean for Antigone to perform that burial in order to trouble the coloniality of power/gender that, through burial, separates "the human" from "nature" and establishes the former as the dominator of the latter? Within the context of the racial Capitalocene, Antigone must exhume, rather than bury, these bodies from colonial oblivion. Antigone must learn how to integrate this memory, and the integration of this memory is the condition of understanding the current ecological crisis under a more political script. Climate change does not, as the discourse of the Anthropocene suggests, pose an undifferentiated threat to all of "humanity" in the future. Climate change, as the discourse of the racial Capitalocene argues, has been posing that threat for centuries, and continues to pose it in the present, for black and brown people.

Addressed not to the brother but also to the slave, Antigone's decolonial burial would show our current social conditions of life and death to be the geopolitical effect of our still colonially conditioned making, hence a potentially transformable effect of our decolonial unmaking. "I would only do it for my brother," Antigone claims at the end, citing the Persian story of Intaphrenes's wife. Her citation of the foreign story means that her burial no longer fulfills her filial duty with the unconscious immediacy of her ethical nature, as Hegel would like to have it, but with the conscious geopolitical mediation of the coloniality of power. Persia erupts into Thebes through the politics of her citations, and the foreign tyrant appears more pious than the presumably native democrat, revealing the democratic deficit of her city. The semantic dispersion of Antigone's citations, by which Butler politicizes the equivocality of her kinship, makes not only the *oikos* but also the *polis* more equivocal and perhaps elicits, as I have claimed, a misinterpellated appropriation of this figure to stage a different kind of *agon* against racial/sexual capitalism. This other Antigone, which renders kinship structurally equivocal in modernity, reveals (re-)membering as a political act of bordering and one that, perhaps, might be mobilized to destroy some walls in the way.

What would it mean, then, for Antigone to bury not Polyneices but his slaves, and to also perform those burials in broad daylight and in opposition to the sovereign? And what would it mean for her to perform that burial not only for one body, as the exceptional depositary of that violence, but for the millions lying at the bottom of the ocean and in unmarked graves across the territory renamed the Americas, where that violence first normalized itself as the very condition of entry into the liberal humanism of the settler?

WHICH INADMISSIBLE DIFFERENCES: THE LIMITS OF DECONSTRUCTION

Hegel's theorization of the burial was not only concerned with the natural reclamation of the body. Hegel was also concerned, and perhaps more so, with the irrational nature that inhabits the human and thus he can be said to have anticipated psychoanalysis, as many critical theorists have argued. As he claims, "The family keeps the dead away from the dishonoring acts of unconscious desire and abstract creatures, and in place of them, it puts their own acts."[20] Sexual difference emerges, in this case, as a foundational difference to the ways in which difference itself is theorized by Hegel and, one might argue, policed and confined in his text and that of Western philosophy. Thus, it is understandable that, in seeking to problematize the Western metaphysics of presence and its foundational dichotomies, Jacques Derrida also turns to Hegel and proceeds to deconstruct Hegel's reading of *Antigone* in his beautiful *Glas*.[21] As Rosalind Morris claims, "In Hegel's writing Derrida finds the philosophical scene in which that entry into difference is construed as an acquisition of the capacity to differentiate, with sexual difference providing not only the primary instance of difference itself, but also the material for its metaphorization."[22] But is sexual difference the sole primary instance of difference itself? Is there not another difference that Hegel's dialectic, and Derrida's deconstruction of it, fails to confront? And is not this difference the one that is at the heart of the problematic reproduction of humanism's constitutive exclusions in the posthumanistic discourse of the Anthropocene?

In this book I have been arguing for an alternative difference to the one that Antigone represents, a more inscrutable one that in my view Derrida only marginally touches on during his deconstruction of Hegel's text. It is possible that those unconscious desires do refer to her, to the sister, and to Antigone, problematically generalized as womankind's representative. Antigone, however, is not the sole figure forced to stand for an unconscious desire that the philosophical discourse of Western liberal humanism must repress in order to separate the human from mere nature. Those unconscious desires also refer to the racialized other, in Hegel's text, to "the Negro," or "the African," as I will show shortly. The proliferation of these racialized/gendered figures, and the ways in which they dispossess the brother-sister relationship of its ethical significance in the Global South, shows that the settler colonization of the Americas and European organization of a trans-Atlantic slave trade already speak through Hegel. But also, and this is the crucial point of this chapter, they speak through the limits of the deconstructive critique of Hegel and its philosophical legacy. Seeking to liberate difference from the confines of the dialectic, deconstruction does not grant to all differences the same capacity for metaphorization. There are differences, both racial and sexual (racialized sexuality and sexualized racism), whose political deconstruction allows us to move from the depoliticizing language of the Anthropocene to the more politically enabling language of the racial Capitalocene, in order to complicate the human/posthuman binary with what remains repressed in both.

Derrida does include an analysis of colonialism by the end of *Glas*. And yet, as I will show, Derrida also fails not only to grant to racial/sexual differences the same kind of power of metaphorization that he grants to racially unremarked sexual difference, he fails to interrogate the material history of their colonial co-constitution. Derrida, thus, reads the passage that I just quoted from Hegel a bit differently. According to Derrida if, on the one hand, burial spares the dead from being "destroyed-eaten-by matter nature, the spirit's being-outside-self," on the other hand burial also spares it from "the probably cannibal violence of the survivors' unconscious desires."[23] Derrida's reference to the violence of the cannibal is odd, as it is not included in Hegel's original citation in the *Phenomenology*. However, Hegel does connect burial and cannibalism, during his racist interpretation of African fetishism. And it is through that interpretation that Hegel actually constructs the racialized burial as entirely unethical, not only incapable of entry into "the human" but fully subsumed into nature, irrespective of the actual existence of culturally mediated funerary rites.

Having just gestured toward the racialized cannibalism of colonial modernity, in an engagement with Hegel's reflection on the funeral rite, Derrida turns away from the coloniality of sexual difference in order to focus almost exclusively on the kind of limit that the ancient Greek Antigone poses to the Hegelian dialectic. In what is arguably the most often quoted passage from *Glas*, Derrida claims Antigone to be

> [a] figure inadmissible in the system. Vertiginous insistence on an unclassable. And what if what cannot be assimilated, the absolute indigestible, played a fundamental role in the system, an abyssal role, the abyss playing an almost transcendental role and allowing to be formed above it, as a kind of effluvium, a dream of appeasement? Isn't there always an element excluded from the system that assures the system's space of possibility? The transcendental has always been, strictly, a transcategorical, what could be received, formed, terminated in none of the categories intrinsic to the system. The system's vomit. And what if the sister, the brother/sister relation represented here the transcendental position, ex-position?[24]

Derrida characterizes Antigone, the sister, as a figure whose difference cannot be accommodated within the dialectic system that she nonetheless helps to construct. That is the case because the brother-sister relationship stands at multiple and yet conflictive mediations. On the one hand, the brother-sister relationship differs from the husband-wife relationship and from the parents-children relationship, in that neither desire nor reproduction is constitutive of it. On the other hand, unlike all the other relations outside of the family, the struggle for recognition that is constitutive of the formation of an individual consciousness is also absent from it. This is the struggle that Hegel had previously analyzed through the master/slave dialectic. In the brother-sister ethical relationship, Hegel thus identifies a form of difference that is at odds with the dialectic difference that he confines to the relation of opposition and contradiction. The dialectic of difference, however, comes to rest on the disavowed labor of this specific difference, as it is the work of mourning by the sister that keep the final *being* of the brother from returning to mere nature and achieving proper and final universality. The system, as Derrida argues, should have come to a standstill and nothing should have been able to survive Antigone's death. This difference is characterized by equilibrium, a more stable notion of difference, which differs from the difference as a contradiction whose need for dialectic synthesis fuels the teleological mobility of the Spirit. And yet, the system does not come to a standstill. Antigone, as Derrida concludes, becomes the crypt "of the transcendental or the repressed, of the unthought or the excluded—that organizes the ground to which it does not belong."[25]

Antigone is and is not part of the system, as the system needs her, needs the difference that she is forced to embody and represent, yet cannot actually accommodate her. *Glas* is, to some extent, an alternative articulation of the difference that the unclassifiable Antigone represents. *Glas*, as an exemplary deconstructive text, both explores and voices this difference through the intertextual inclusion of another figure: the queer text of Jean Genet, which comes to undercut the cis-text of Hegel, its dialectic system, and its naturalization of sexual difference. Composed of two columns, the left one dedicated to Hegel, the right one to Jean Genet, *Glas* gestures to the big phalluses of ancient Greek comedy, and this book is not short of humor. But it is tragedy, rather than comedy, that occupies most of Derrida's commentary. In fact, Derrida defines *glas* at one point as the "work of mourning."[26] Thus, it is not farfetched to suggest a greater indebtedness of deconstruction to the tragic text that it uses, to liberate difference from the confines of the Hegelian dialectic. Perhaps we can rethink the columnar division of *Glas* as a sort of aesthetic reanimation of the tragic *agon* between Creon and Antigone. Hegel, the royal eagle (animal), the systemic philosopher, the champion of spiritual civility, confronts Genet, the queer flower (plant), the literary writer, the revolutionary anti-moralist thief who endorses a liberatory criminality. Creon and Antigone are to *Antigone* what Hegel and Genet are to *Glas*, remaking deconstruction into the rebirth of ancient tragedy in European postmodernity (to riff on Nietzsche).[27] Deconstruction's tragic spirit is a way of voicing—through the tracing of the rhetorical maneuvers a text disavows but fails to fully erase—the alternative meanings on whose repression a dominant form of signification relies. As an antirepressive discourse of difference, deconstruction is, thus, a crucial interlocutor of this project. After all, I have been arguing for a similar voicing of differences, otherwise repressed in the dominant discourse of critical theory, and in the discourse of the Anthropocene more precisely, in this chapter. But not all differences are that easy to voice. Deconstruction endows some differences with the liberatory power of the inadmissible/unclassifiable that it does not extend to others. Not all works of mourning, in other words, represent the same kind of crisis to the Hegelian confinement of difference to the aesthetic rhythms of the dialectic. Not all forms of mourning force us to confront the racial Capitalocene that is otherwise neutralized in the discourse of the Anthropocene.

Glas has received, in my view, two dominant interpretations. One turns to philosophy and focuses on the topic of the quasi-transcendental, that is to say, on the moments in which the difference between the empirical and the transcendental are troubled by a figure that is actually both: the condition of possibility and impossibility of that system of differences.[28] This is the difference that Antigone is forced to represent, as both dramatic role and philosophical character, literary figure and real sister. The second dominant interpretation focuses, rather, on psychoanalysis. In this case, it is Derrida's distinctive approach to fetishism that gets accentuated. Derrida, it is worth highlighting, no longer conceives fetishism in terms of an opposition between the real and the illusory. Rather, as Morris argues, Derrida considers fetishism as "the undecidability between two possibilities that do not appear as alternatives but as equally compulsive propositions, between which there is, at best, a vacillation."[29] Few texts have tried to simultaneously address both the philosophical and the psychoanalytic, and confront too the colonial history of the production of differences.[30] To this excellent list of interpretations, whose knowledge of Derrida and deconstruction far exceeds mine, I have little to add. What I would like to do, instead, is to insist on the problematic silencing of racial/sexual differences, as indicative of an economy of membership that links the valuation of the citizen to the differential devaluation of the *metic* and of the enslaved. That silence resurfaces in *Glas*, and is perhaps unintentionally repeated in *Glas*'s vast readership.

Sina Kramer's work represents a notable exception in this regard. Meditating on Derrida's way of introducing *Antigone* by means of a "stroke (*coup*)" to the "middle: passage" of the *Phenomenology of the Spirit*, Kramer includes the following reflection in a footnote:

> Without getting too speculative too quickly, I am forced to stop and wonder at the repercussions of this phrase in ears constituted to hear, in English, in the United States, something quite particular in this phrase: the middle passage. What lies buried there, what sets this ringing, this time not from below the earth or from within the rock, but from beneath the surface of the Atlantic Ocean? Or rather, how does the middle passage subtend the very idea of the United States itself?[31]

Hesitant to speculate too quickly, Kramer's analysis of the "middle passage" does not elicit a way of rereading Derrida's Antigone through the prisms of "the Negro," which Derrida does discuss in *Glas* and yet Kramer fails to address. To be fair, Kramer's text does turn to questions of racial/

sexual difference. She does this through her excellent analysis of the occlusion of Claudette Colvin from the dominant narrative of the civil rights movement that reifies instead the more socially acceptable Rosa Parks, and also through her equally powerful analysis of the 1992 Los Angeles riots and rebellion in the United States. Attending to those differences, Kramer shows how *multiple exclusions* means that "those who occupy the position of the 'outside' are, however, also multiple."³² This means that some radical actors, such as Antigone herself, can be rendered constitutively excluded in relation to one axis of exclusion, while participating in exclusions of their own, as Antigone does when she "positions her brother as belonging to the polity by reinscribing the exclusion of slaves."³³ The fact that constitutively excluded figures occupy multiple identities, Kramer concludes, means that "those who contest their exclusion can play one aspect of their identities off others in order to effectively translate their claims from politically unintelligible to politically intelligible claims," it means, in short, "that no one is purely excluded, or purely outside."³⁴ These are excellent points, crucial to any understanding of Antigone's differential politics of burial. But why is that intersectional attention to difference not addressed to Derrida's own reading of Hegel? Why is the problem of race and its constitutive forms of exclusion absent from the political analysis of Derrida's quasi-transcendental, when the European colonization of Africa is neither absent from Hegel nor absent from *Glas*'s commentary on Hegel?

Glas includes a reference to Hegel's racist ways of referring to African people and to their customs, precisely in relation to fetishism. Moreover, *Glas* includes a critique of Hegel's racist ways of referring to African burials, which appear to Hegel as entirely unintelligible. In a passage that expands on the ways in which the Hegelian philosophical system establishes a relationship between "the Negro" and "nature" that is, unlike that of Antigone, entirely unethical, Derrida criticizes the contradictory Hegelian characterization of "the Negro" as entirely subsumed by nature. In a brief commentary on *Reason in History*, Derrida goes over Hegel's racist characterization of African people as "savage," "barbarian," "improperly conscious," and ultimately "not human" and writes the following:

> The cult of the dead itself—elsewhere considered to be the inaugural stage [*stade*] of the ethical—is corrupted by fetishism: "They resort to them (the deceased) in the same way as to fetishes, offering them sacrifices and conjuring them up:

but where this proves unsuccessful, they punish the departed ancestor himself, casting his bones away and desecrating him. On the other hand, they believe that the dead avenge themselves if their needs are not satisfied. . . . The power of the dead over the living is indeed recognized, but held in no great respect; for the Negroes issue commands to their dead and cast spells upon them. In this way, the substance always remains in the power of the subject. Such is the religion of the Africans, and it does not extend any farther."[35]

The cannibal had just been introduced by Hegel prior to this passage, in order to disqualify the African from history, consciousness and humanity. And Derrida, who had already mentioned the cannibal as the real figure of the European unconscious, problematizes it again. So, it is not any burial, nor just the burial of the brother by the sister, that protects the human from the irrationality of nature, and from the irrational nature that persists in the human and thus renders the border between the human and nature porous and prone to subversive rearticulation. There is, already, another difference at work, the colonial difference that distinguishes the European funeral from "the African" one. Such difference, unlike sexual difference, even in the presence of the actual burial, continues to disqualify the ritual as unable to assert the right of consciousness to final being, which Hegel does grant to Antigone.

Hegel, who, as Robert Bernasconi has shown, not only repeats but actually exaggerates the colonial distortion of Ashanti social practices—inclusive of his way of indistinguishably grouping Dahomey with Ashanti practices under a fungible Negro—cannot restrain himself and adds that "the eating of the human flesh is quite compatible with the African principle."[36] From that compatibility, Hegel concludes, one could argue that "slavery has awakened more humanity among the Negroes" and thus recommend that it "should be eliminated gradually."[37] As Bernasconi argues, the conclusion of such theorizing implied "that the colonization of Africa would complete the process of introducing Africans to history, a process that had begun when the first slaves were transported to America."[38]

It is true that Derrida does include a critique rather than an endorsement of those passages, and yet the citation of Hegel's racist text receives nowhere the same philosophical analysis that Derrida affords to Hegel's reading of *Antigone*. And the same happens, with only a few exceptions, with regard to *Glas*'s readership. This is all the more surprising given Hegel's own claim that "in order to speak of the African all our 'categories' would have to be abandoned," a claim Derrida criticizes but does not grant the same quasi-transcendental productive troubling that he attributes to the limit that Antigone is said to represent.[39]

Would it be fair to claim that "the Negro," like Antigone, is yet another inadmissible figure in the system, another unclassifiable, another element excluded from the system that assures the system's space of possibility, another system's vomit, another ex-position? Is all that was said about Antigone equally valid to say about "the Negro," or "the African" in yet another problematic Hegelian generalization? But if that is the case, what do we make of Hegel's claim that slavery, in this case, is rather beneficial? What do we make of the fact that even if there is a culturally distinctive funeral rite, this burial is not endowed with the capacity to assert consciousness and will, and cannot recuperate final *being* from nature, rather, its difference is mobilized to further naturalize the subhumanity of "the African" for whom Hegel considered slavery beneficial? Why, in short, is there no further deconstruction of the ways in which the Hegelian text colors and not only genders the inclusive universality of the dialectic? If we can agree that Antigone represents a kind of crisis to the Hegelian dialectic system, a way of no longer subordinating difference to opposition and contradiction and demonstrating, instead, what Kramer has identified as a third—albeit repressed—notion of difference in Hegel as multiplicity, what kind of crisis does "the Negro" represent?

Perhaps it is unfair to raise this issue through Derrida's work, who did reflect on the whiteness of Western philosophy, unlike most European philosophers of his generation.[40] He even showed how colonialism affected his own thinking, as a Sephardic Jew who was born in French-occupied Algeria.[41] The enslaved, however, remain a repressed figure within the antirepressive discourse that is deconstruction. It is unclear to me if the deconstructive embrace of the difference that Antigone represents, as an indigestible figure for the metaphysical text of Western philosophy, includes other differences. One has to entertain the possibility that the colonial figuration of "the Negro" also disrupts the discursive economy of deconstruction with a difference that is in excess of its pluralization. To confront that difference is not to abandon deconstruction but to take deconstruction into a more radical destination: that of decolonization.

"The Negro," a figure constructed as entirely dominated by nature, is as illegible in the humanistic discourse of Hegel as it is in the posthumanistic discourse of the Anthropocene. The colonial construction of this figure haunts the deconstructive undoing of the human/nonhuman binary with an insufficiently problematized difference. This difference is the historical product of a colonial project that disqualified racialized/gendered "others" from equal membership in the *anthropos* and continues to misrecognize them within the posthuman orbit of the Anthropocene. Today, we are once again confronted with an *agon* over whose burials denote an ecological crisis of planetary proportions. Today, Creon interdicts the burial by displacing climate change's mass graves to the all-inclusive future of the Anthropocene. Antigone reacts by re-membering the millions who have lost their lives in the past, and continue to lose them in the present, to the racial Capitalocene.

A Specter Is Haunting the Americas

In this book I have been arguing for the need to deconstruct the Americas, to speak not only of the Americas, in the plural, but also of *Abya Yala*. Like deconstruction, I have found in the tragedy of *Antigone* a resource by which to contest settler colonialism's enforced forgetting. Like deconstruction, finally, I have also claimed for the need to conjure the specters that haunt our modernity otherwise. It makes sense that deconstruction would take hold of the specter to characterize the labor of its critical work. The specter is one of those undecidable figures by which deconstruction seeks to trouble what it characterizes as the metaphysics of presence, the dichotomous ordering of the modern world: essence versus appearance, spoken versus written, man versus woman, etc. The specter troubles this duality to the extent that it is neither just matter (only flesh) nor just spirit (only idea) but the paradoxical becoming-body of the spirit, to paraphrase Derrida. Deconstruction is, in that sense, the true animation of one of the spirits of Marx.[42]

Derrida defined the specter as the "something disappeared, departed in the apparition itself as reapparition of the departed."[43] This reapparition of the departed has two meanings in Derrida. The specter is both a *revenant*, the past that returns to haunt the present, but also an *arrivant*, the future yet to come. Both reappearances, whether of the past or of the future, call into question the unaddressed violence of the present that forces the ghost to linger. Yet, as I have been articulating, not all specters are endowed with the same capacity to unhinge our present. In *Specters of Marx*, Derrida's most important work on the specter, the most prominent specters are the ghosts of Hamlet's father, of Marx, and of communism. Yet, these are not the sole or even the most important specters that *Specters of Marx* conjures in order to reanimate Marxism after (neo)liberalism had proclaimed its funeral oration

Antigone in the Settler-Colonial Present of the Racial Capitalocene   173

post the Fall of the Berlin Wall. Derrida dedicates the book to the famous antiapartheid revolutionary Chris Hani, who was killed and is mourned in the first pages, only to disappear from the rest of the book as Derrida's reflection veers elsewhere. The South African struggle for liberation, and Hani's socialist alternative to Mandela's more liberal version of black liberation, never configures an alternative spirit of Marxism for Derrida.

Actually, the main specter of *Specters of Marx* is—quite problematically, in my view—a figure of the royal father with a unique interpellative agency. As Derrida claims, the ghost of the father interpellates Hamlet into blind submission to his secret. Given that the exclusion of the alien and the biopolitical elimination of the native in the Americas were significantly enforced through the regulation of the mother (*partus sequitur ventrum*), there is no interpellation that imposes a similar indebtedness to the one that deconstruction reclaims, via the figure of the father, in *Specters of Marx*. When we realize that the enslaved could not, like Hamlet's father, interpellate their children into justice, do we not encounter the limits of deconstruction's hauntology?[44] The socially dead lack the armor, the technical prothesis or performative "costume" that allows the father "to see and to speak" in *Hamlet*.[45] Actually, settler colonialism first tried to reduce the enslaved to a sort of technical prothesis for the self-representation of the master as sovereign speaker, as quasi-king-like. If the specter is "some 'thing,'" a "nonobject," which Derrida links to the King by means of that famous speech in which Hamlet claims the King to the be "the thing," what would it mean to situate the specter at the level of the enslaved, as the first ones reduced to the status of "things"? How can we make sense of these specters if hauntology, as the science of deconstruction, also invests in a social grammar (filial genealogy, indebtedness) that already betrays the ongoing unreality of slavery and its aftermath?[46] What kind of noncontemporaneity does this specter enact, if noncontemporaneity is already the prerogative of another specter's action? In my view, the spirits of Chris Hani and, by decolonial association, of black and indigenous liberation against racial/sexual capitalism, haunt *Specters of Marx* with another spirit of decolonial Marxism to which deconstruction fails to recognize a debt.[47] And it is to those spirits that I would like *Antigone in the Americas* to be indebted.

TOWARD THE HISTORY OF THE ICE

Although my critique of deconstruction differs from that of contemporary Marxist scholars, it nonetheless retains a crucial aspect of their materialist concerns. Fredric Jameson voiced the most radical form of this critique when he considered deconstruction as another form of idealism.[48] According to Jameson, deconstruction's otherwise correct demonstration that all history is haunted by that not registered as historical turns regressively against history and relapses into the most uncritical empiricism. This empiricism is most evident in Derrida's list of ten injustices, as haunting the celebratory end of history, in the form of Francis Fukuyama's praise for liberal capitalism, with its unaddressed debris. In a related way, Pierre Macherey laments that in critiquing capitalism's phantasmagoria (the superstructural ideality of the commodity-form), Derrida misses what could by no means be merely reduced to pure spectrality: the infrastructural materiality of living labor.[49] Finally, Antonio Negri celebrates deconstruction's ability to see that the law of value had been "thrown 'out of joint,'" mainly in those wonderful passages in which Derrida troubles the separation of use-value from exchange-value. But then he laments deconstruction's inability to take such disjointedness into politics, relapsing instead into the depoliticized horizon of ethics.[50]

Unable to confront history (Jameson), labor (Macherey), and politics (Negri), Derrida seems to have been more haunted by the specter of communism as the imaginary promise of society's self-reconciliation than by the very real specter of neoliberal capitalism, as the dominant condition of the present. The specter of the proletarian revolution as the realization of a society fully reconciled with itself—one wrongly conceived as lying beyond politics, if not beyond history—also haunts deconstruction with a spirit it refuses to claim. The problem, as Slavoj Žižek claims, is that the deconstructive warning against any positive identification with such an emancipatory reality, in its effort "to main the gap between the Void of the central impossibility and every positive content giving body to it," conservatively makes democracy "no longer into that which is to-come but into that which has already arrived."[51]

I do not think that all of these criticisms are entirely valid. I do not think, for instance, that Derrida's emphasis on textuality necessarily entails the dematerialization of labor. The point of Derrida's claim that nothing exists outside of the text is to call attention to the performative role that language and signification perform in producing the very material reality that texts otherwise innocently claim only to be referring to. There is, however, a notable weakness in the textuality through which Derrida inscribes deconstruction in one of the spirits of Marx, so as to celebrate a form of difference that is always yet-to-come. After all, liberal democracy could very much accept the noncontemporaneity of the living present with itself *as* the end of history, to the extent that it can commodify that perpetual differentiation of the present with itself. In other words, differences can be thought outside of the dichotomous confines of the dialectic, as multiplicities, without that antirepressive gesture resulting in a political undoing of capitalism's captivity. As Negri and the Italian *autonomista* tradition have articulated, neoliberal exploitation is based not so much on technologies of power oriented toward the reproduction of sameness (the Fordist reduction of every single worker into the same economically exchangeable unit of labor) as on the accelerated reproduction and coerced cultivation of labor differences (the post-Fordist injunction for workers to constantly reinvent themselves anew and become entrepreneurs of the self). So, the specter of Marx into which Derrida would like to inscribe deconstruction is, in that sense, also haunted by all those *other* specters to which perhaps he would not like deconstruction to be indebted. The otherwise productive undoing of the distinction between exchange-value and use-value, by means of which Derrida assails Marx's attempt to critique the phantasmagoria of capital from the perspective of an ontology of labor, altogether abandons the question of labor and the political internationalization of the class struggle.

Such an abandonment, in my view, does render deconstruction less able to criticize the racialized and gender-differentiated systems of labor exploitation and land expropriation, by which settler-colonial capitalism reproduces and naturalizes itself. I am, thus, sympathetic to the critique the Marxist theorists referenced above have raised against deconstruction, mostly on its turn away from politics, and I am equally skeptical of deconstruction's ethical turn to messianism. I am, however, less critical of Derrida's turn to Walter Benjamin and to the materialist work of mourning, as a crucial factor for materialist criticism and the liberation/pluralization of difference, if only because I consider the politicization of the present to be inescapably haunted by the past, in a more Benjaminian way.

Here I follow Susan Buck-Morss's claim, that Benjamin developed his past-awoken-in-the-present image of the dialectic in response to Marx's claim that "the social revolution of the nineteenth century cannot create its poetry out of the past, but only from the future."[52] As Buck-Morss argues, Marx left "unexplained just how this shedding of the past was to be achieved," a gap he filled with "an implicit faith in historical progress."[53] Martin Harries has demonstrated that Marx was by no means indifferent to this problem.[54] Knowing that he could not seize the postrevolutionary language of future poetry without contradicting his own reversal of Hegel's idealism, Marx could only "allude" to it via his own awakening of ghosts from the past. Hence, the otherwise contradictory citation of the New

Testament's "let the dead bury the dead" at the precise moment Marx calls for a poetry of the future, stripping off superstition as the precondition for the beginning of revolutionary language. By gesturing to the unlived past, to what has been forgotten or actively disavowed, Benjamin's historical materialism does not develop progressively by "burying the dead" but by awakening them and, in so doing, showing a present that is nonsynchronous with itself. That awakening, which happens through the materialist crafting of dialectical images capable of seizing thought, is what interrupts history's homogenous, empty time.[55]

Dialectical images *à la* Benjamin interrupt two modes of historical homogeneity: the teleological form of history as progress that denies the violence it reproduces by inscribing it into a superseding logic, and the safe displacement of the history of the oppressed to the neutralized past, rather than as something happening still. It is not difficult to see both of these views converging in the discourse of the Anthropocene, troubled with the Antigonian gesture of integrating the forbidden memory of colonialism's ongoing violence, which characterizes the alternative political grammar of the racial Capitalocene. It is also in the sense of "still happening" that settler colonial critique has argued that settler colonialism is a structure, not an event.[56] It is, finally, in the present plastic forms that such "still happening" takes, that slavery and *metoikia* continue to be the undersides of citizenship and political (non)membership in the Americas.

Benjamin's dialectical images are, however, limited when it comes to confronting specters that do not flash in a moment of danger but rather accumulate in the discarded archive of settler-colonial history. Édouard Glissant, in my view, offers us a much better image of the dialectic for the kind of political conjuring of the death that I am arguing for. As Ian Baucom claims, Glissant and Benjamin converge in their understanding of history as well as in their turn toward the awakening of the past, but differ in the image they use to articulate the critical labor of the materialist historian.[57] "To the extent that the time of the past survives, nonsynchronously, into the present, for Glissant (and this indeed is his fundamental point of departure from Benjamin) that time survives not as that which flashes up but, rather, as that which accumulates," says Baucom.[58] Closer to Glissant, on the enduring image of the past that accumulates, Baucom arrives at a poetic formulation inspired by Derek Walcott: "The sea is history." My own version of this materialist grounding of the specter that haunts modernity with its colonial history, in my own effort to resituate Antigone's mourning against the background of the racial Capitalocene, would be: "The ice is history."

I focus on the ice, rather than the sea, not to deny the importance of the trans-Atlantic slave trade, but to include indigenous people alongside the genocide of black people in the structural violence of racial/sexual capitalism that continues to accumulate in the settler-colonial present of the racial Capitalocene.[59]

Decolonial Mourning at the Level of World-Historical Events

The event that Baucom raises to an ur-event of modernity, the paradigmatic history of the sea, is the massacre of 132 slaves aboard the Liverpool-owned slave ship *Zong*, in November 1781. According to an unaddressed letter Granville Sharp sent to the Lords Commissioners of the Admiralty on July 2, 1783, requesting an investigation, ship captain Luke Collingwood threw the slaves from the deck, confident that he would not be destroying his employer's commodities but securing their monetary value. As Baucom argues, "Central to that form of value was a reversal of the protocols of value creation proper to commodity capital. For here, value does not follow but precedes exchange."[60] The 440 slaves aboard the *Zong* had been valued at 13,200 pounds (thirty pounds per head), and their loss had already been calculated as more profitable to the company than their survival in this settler-colonial politico-economic calculation.

What interests me the most about Bauman's formulation is that it situates finance, the leading form of late (postmodern) capitalism, as historically grounded in modern slavery. To put it in Baucom's words, "[T]he engine of that speculative regime of accumulation"—that is, contemporary neoliberalism—"was the trans-Atlantic slave trade."[61] Baucom's history gives the specter a more materialist foundation, as the ghosts that haunt speculative capitalism with its necroeconomic insistence that "the real test of something's value comes not at the moment it is made or exchanged but at the moment it is lost or destroyed," are the ghosts of slavery.[62] The ghosts of slavery are also, unlike other commodities, uniquely spectral, in that the enslaved were not transmogrified into any kind of commodity but into a kind of "interest-bearing money" that "functioned in this system simultaneously as commodities for sale and as the reserve deposits of a loosely organized, decentered, but vast trans-Atlantic banking system."[63]

Baucom turns to one specter but fails to attend to the other. My effort to situate Antigone's subversive mourning in the age of the racial

Capitalocene and supplant "the sea is history" with "the ice is history" is my own way of confronting not only the sixty million and more losses to which Toni Morrison dedicates her *Beloved* (1987) but also the sixty million and more losses to which Leslie Marmon Silko dedicates *Almanac of the Dead* (1991). These are not losses that belong to the past in a chronological order that neutralizes their persistence in the present. Their disavowal or historical neutralization strengthens the logics of exclusion and elimination by which neoliberalism makes racially marked disposable citizens and *metics* the targets of a violence previously reserved only for slaves, thus giving slavery an aftermath.

My theoretical deconstruction of the Americas as a global territory haunted by many specters might not be as rigorous as Baucom's dialectical synthesis of Arrighi's theory of "cycles of accumulation" and Benjamin's materialist reconstruction of Paris as the capital of the nineteenth century, in Baucom's effort to present Liverpool as the capital of the long twentieth century. I have tried, however, to give the Americas a similar world-historical significance to that which Baucom gives Liverpool, in making the Americas a kind of megacapital of the racial Capitalocene. Yet I offer no equivalent to the *Zong*, to the mourning of its losses, as a truth-event Baucom articulates based on Alain Badiou's theory of the event. My own decolonial ruminations around various *Antigone*s in the Americas do not constitute an event because I understand the risks involved in merely adding them up into one great gesture, as Gordon warns.

I understand the political gesture of turning the *Zong* into an event, recentering the critique of capitalism and its dominant speculative regime of accumulation, back into what the materialist critique of political economy has most often failed to address: slavery and its aftermath. However, I am worried that eventalizing the *Zong* misses the bleakest aspect of this genocidal violence: that it was recorded as uneventful, if recorded at all, and continues to be treated as such. Hence, it was not only 132 enslaved humans who died in the ships of William Gregson, one of the owners of the *Zong*. Gregson became a slave trader in 1744, and an estimated 9,914 enslaved humans died in his ships.[64] Baucom is absolutely aware of the normalized character of this violence and the problematic aspects of raising the *Zong* to the status of the symptomatic (this time influenced by Spivak's work).[65] This is something he expresses more vividly when, after recalling the repetitive nature of the massacre, the "one hundred thirty-two repetitions" of throwing slaves overboard, he then writes: "One hundred-thirty-two deaths.

One Event. One?"⁶⁶ In that question mark he registers the tension inherent in the political eventalizing of a genocide whose unaddressed repetition actually de-eventalizes genocide as the routine of colonial violence. This rightly moves Baucom to claim, without any sentimental innuendo, that "the number we need to find some way to comprehend is neither one hundred thirty-three nor one hundred thirty-two but one, one, one."⁶⁷

These ones and their accumulation still haunt the Anthropocene with the unaddressed violence of the racial Capitalocene. Arundhati Roy is right when she claims that the story of capitalism is a ghost story.⁶⁸ Ghosts are, so to speak, industrially produced in mass, as the profit-oriented system comes to rest on the greater vulnerability of the racialized working class to the acceleration of their slow death. These ghosts, as Gordon argues, haunt us. They represent the "animated state in which a repressed or unresolved social violence is making itself known, sometimes very directly, sometimes more obliquely."⁶⁹ I have linked this violence to the logics of exclusion and elimination by which settler-colonial critique explains the differential integration of various labor regimes into the lethal violence of racial/sexual capitalism. Polyneices's abandoned body haunted Antigone and moved her to action in ways the abandoned bodies of the enslaved would not have. Many other Antigones in the Americas have followed her, with a different kind of politics at stake, situating the agential capacity of that haunting against the background of a multiplicity of globally interconnected violences. Such violence takes nonhuman forms, as in global warming, desertification, acid rain, etc., but it is all part of the same reverberated violence of racial/sexual capitalism. This is the violence that exposes the "disposable" to the deadliest forms of environmental degradation, pandemics—like COVID-19—and premature death resulting from structural inequality.⁷⁰

Which ghosts we conjure in our critique of such violence is not inconsequential. Some violences are more repressed than others. Some memories are easier to integrate. I am not suggesting that we hierarchize these ghosts or the violences they continue to suffer, but that we interrogate the relationality of settler-colonial violence so as to learn how to conjure these ghosts otherwise. Haunting, Gordon adds, describes "those singular yet repetitive instances when home becomes unfamiliar, when your bearings on the world lose direction, when the over-and-done-with comes alive, when what's been in your blind spot comes into view."⁷¹ Gordon invokes the Freudian notion of the uncanny, the moment when what was repressed returns and, through its repetition, renders the familiar unfamiliar again. The uncanny is, in that sense, the signature of a haunting and is thus generalizable to all settler-colonial nation-states. These must repress the colonial origins of their history to appropriate the indigeneity of those under their yoke, who are then relegated to histories safely displaced and confined to the past. But these states remain haunted by that repression, and to conjure the ghost, to reanimate the dead, or to awaken the past still happening in the present, is to make the nation-state's founding politically revisable again.[72]

To situate Antigone's mourning in the context of these violences is also to confront how settler colonialism can, at times, instrumentalize violence to which it subjects the alien in order to reinforce violence against the native—like Antigone, contesting one violence by reinforcing another. After all, aliens not only perform a material function for the settler, when they replace the labor force of natives. Aliens perform an additional symbolic function, helping to repress the origin of the *polis* in colonial violence, removing it from political contestation and whitewashing the founding. The alien, in the form of the potential foreigner-*cum*-citizen, is the only one who can actualize the choiceworthiness of the nation-state. Only the foreigner can sign the social contract, a signature that replaces the violence of indigenous genocide with the politically neutralized myth of an elected national identity. By "voluntarily" choosing the *polis,* the alien—as *metic*—aids the settler colony in emerging as a nation-state, no longer appearing as the ongoing repetition of indigenous dispossession. That repressed history reemerges, like the other bodies covered up by Polyneices, whenever we re-member the real violence of the nation-state's origins. Capitalism and colonialism explain why not all aliens, only specific ones and under specific historical circumstances, are called to perform this function and allowed to become citizens (if often under a differential system). Antigone's mourning is all the more contestatory when it shows that violence to be less originary and more iterative—that is, less past-eventful and more present-structuring, less historically repressed and more cumulatively current.

It is not easy to live in a haunted house. It is scary and disorienting. Antigone's challenge in the Americas is to address several interrelated colonial hauntings. As Gordon articulates, living in a haunted house refers to "the sociality of living with ghosts, a sociality both tangible and tactile as well as ephemeral and imaginary."[73] Tangible and tactile as well as ephemeral and imaginary, like the losses whose traces are still legible in the carbon dioxide that accumulates in the ice—if we read the ice with the decolonial lens of a materialist historian such as Glissant.

Black and Indigenous Wakeful Mo'nin

In one of Derrida's best moments in *Specters of Marx*, he repeats the otherwise controversial claim that he first articulated in *Glas*, that the work of mourning "is not one kind of work among others," but "work itself, work in general, the trait by means of which one ought perhaps to reconsider the very concept of production—in what links it to trauma, to mourning, to the idealizing iterability of exappropriation, thus to the spectral spiritualization that is at work in any *tekhnê*."[74] To understand Derrida's claim, it is worth revisiting Freud's definition of mourning as the time that it takes for the subjects to sever themselves from the lost object when reality, as Freud puts it, starts "beckoning" and, having revealed that the beloved object no longer exists, "demands that the libido as a whole sever its bonds with that object" and reattach itself to a new one.[75] The time it takes for the libido to sever itself from that object is the time of mourning, in which, Freud claims, the lost object has to be killed a second time at the symbolic level, having been lost at the level of the real. Freud, in other words, makes the opposite claim to Derrida. Mourning is a form of labor that occupies itself specifically with death; it repeats death at the symbolic level to allow mourners to move on at the level of the real. Mourning's killing is not, however, a conventional murder. The mourner must go over each individual memory that still holds the libido captive, to finally let them all go. This happens, according to Freud, when the libido reattaches itself to an object that is no longer related to the lost one.

For Freud's model to work, those individual memories must have some kind of symbolically recognized space, a map that allows you to locate them, and gives the mourner sufficient to time to work through them. But settler-colonial racialization affects both of those conditions. It is precisely in relation to that colonial cartography that Derrida's claim, in contrast to Freud's, can be considered more radical. In what sense, then, is mourning not just a specific kind of work but work in general, as Derrida claims? In what sense does mourning link all production to trauma, specifically to the idealizing iterability of exappropriation, to use Derrida's terms? Exappropriation productively links expropriation and appropriation as perhaps two inseparable logics, the logics I have been emphasizing all along. Here, it is worth recalling that, according to Marx, capitalism begins with the original accumulation of capital via the conquest of the Americas, the trans-Atlantic slave trade, and the colonization of India. As Marx claims,

> The discovery of gold and silver in America, the extirpation, enslavement and entombment in mines of the indigenous population of that continent, the beginnings of the conquest and plunder of India, and the conversion of Africa into a preserve for the commercial hunting of blackskins, are all things which characterize the dawn of the era of capitalist production.[76]

It is in the potentially decolonial spirit of that Marxist claim, which connects four continents, that I have tried to also inscribe the deconstruction that *Antigone in the Americas* performs as equally indebted to one of the spirits of Marx. And it is on the basis of that specter that I want to explore anew Derrida's thesis on the differential work that decolonial mourning performs, when one focuses on settler colonial logics of accumulation instead.[77]

Following settler-colonial critique, the original accumulation of capital refers more precisely to the logics of elimination and exclusion that settler-colonial capitalism set in motion. These expropriate racialized workers from the social means of reproducing their own labor power, expropriate the land of indigenous peoples as the material condition of their social reproduction, but also expropriate them both of their entire symbolic realities through the denial of personhood and reduction to property. Expropriation is, then, at the basis of the accumulation of capital, in an origin that is never just an origin but a reiterative activity, as both settler-colonial critique and deconstruction show. Production and destruction converge, and expropriation (theft) turns into appropriation (property). As Robert Nichols has so excellently argued, the settler colonial formula of capitalism is "theft is property."

For capitalism to transmogrify colonial expropriation into legal property (exappropriation), there must be no integration of this most deeply upsetting memory in the settler colony. This interdiction is not enforced to avoid the second killing of the lost object at the symbolic level, but because the real loss of these lives must have no symbolic space at all for the necropolitical taking of their life to be normalized as the acceptable cost of social valuation. Settler colonial capitalism can only reproduce itself as the *nomos* of the land to the extent that its massive losses are symbolically repressed, and their memorialization interdicted. Ongoing genocide becomes routine, as the loss of life is not the differentiated consequence of capitalist accumulation but the rather "unfortunate" effect of, let's say, the politically neutralized agency that an undifferentiated Anthropocene poses to all of humanity in the future.

Faced with black and indigenous ongoing death, whose loss lacks a map, Antigone's mourning becomes more difficult to perform. To more fully understand such difficulty, I turn to Fred Moten's claim that "the (exchange-) value of the speaking commodity exists also, as it were, *before* exchange."[78] Moten makes that claim through an excellent critique of Marx's own way of ventriloquizing the speaking commodity, in Marx's own critique of liberalism and classical political economy. According to Marx, "If commodities could speak, they would say this: our use-values may interest men, but it does not belong to us as objects. Our own intercourse as commodities proves it. We relate to each other merely as exchange-values."[79] As the only commodity that does speak, the enslaved, whom Moten characterizes as "the trace of a subjectivity born in objection," lies outside the scope of Marx's counterfactual *if*.[80] The enslaved, Moten claims, engage in forms of exchange that are neither the social realization of use-values that may interest men, nor the exchange-values that are inherent to all other commodities as commodities. The enslaved are both, violently transmogrified into a mean of production for the enslaver and yet irreducible to the status of pure object, as they do and can speak. Or, more accurately, the enslaved can scream, as the phonographic event of the enslaved exists in excess of speech and beyond the assumptive humanism that excludes commodified humanity from its sonic repertoire. This is the meaning of identifying a trace of subjectivity (that can scream) who is born in objection (transmogrified into a commodified object of exchange). The form of exchange value *before* exchange, which Moten attributes to the enslaved, also relates to the retroactive function that, as an interest-bearing commodity, Baucom attributed to the historical production of slaves as the ur-commodity of speculative capitalism, which most critics of neoliberalism have also failed to interrogate.[81] Moten's "before," in other words, refers not to a temporally antecedent prior, but to the continuous (anti/ante)-originary form that makes expropriation the engine of capitalism and links the social reproduction of labor to the continuous reproduction of its racialized system of social (de)valuation. Unlike Baucom, however, for Moten that form of exchange also refers to "the capacity for a literary, performative, phonographic disruption of the protocols of exchange."[82] This phonographic disruption is the sonic matter that Moten then traces in and as the aesthetics of the black radical tradition, extending Cedric Robinson's project through Spillers's and Hartman's work. And it is that phonographic disruption that Moten reconceptualizes as black mo'nin, in a meditation on the militant mourning articulated around the open casket holding Emmett Till's dead body.

What Moten, grounded in Robinson's theory of racial capitalism, unpacks is the fact that the capitalist distinction between use-value and exchange-value comes to rest on a sort of prepolitical indistinction of an (exchange) value prior to exchange, which slaves are forced to endure. As exchange values *before* exchange, mourning slaves becomes considerably harder, as the individual memories that, according to Freud, mourners most go through in order to move on lack a symbolic space that can properly recognize them, let alone locate their individual imprint in the psyche's map. Racial/sexual capitalism gives slavery an aftermath, and thus continues to subject racially marked bodies to such violated cartography. As Moten and Stefano Harney put it during a meditation on the settler-colonial violence unleashed against Michael Brown, left desecrated for hours in the street by the Ferguson police:

> In the interest of imagining what exists, there is an image of Michael Brown we must refuse in favor of another image we don't have. One is a lie, the other unavailable. If we refuse to show the image of a lonely body, of the outline of the space that body simultaneously took and left, we do so in order to imagine jurisgenerative black social life walking down the middle of the street—for a minute, but only a minute, unpoliced, another city gathers, dancing. We know it's there, and here, and real; we know what we can't have happens all the time.[83]

The re-membering of Michael Brown faces yet another difficulty. As an exchange-value that exists *before* exchange, the instrumentalization to which he was subjected in life extends over his death as well (deathliness). His death can be made continuously useful, can be turned into a cypher "for our serially unachieved and constitutionally unachievable citizenship," which partakes "in the ghoulish, vampiric consumption of his body."[84] Re-membering Michael Brown, dismembered by settler colonial valuation, forces us to ponder the limitations of Freud's distinction and the need to articulate a different modality of grief. Sensitive to Harney and Moten's critique, I thus propose that if "the (exchange-)value of the speaking commodity exists also, as it were, *before* exchange," the mischaracterized melancholic attachment of black and indigenous people to their dead ones exists also, as it were, *before* melancholia.

Melancholia is replete with blackness—from the black bile of the individual body to the black sun of the cosmic body—without colonial antiblackness ever entering its symbolic space.[85] Freud distinguished melancholia from mourning in the withdrawal from consciousness of the lost object, but that withdrawal is redoubled when loss confronts a split consciousness, a process that W. E. B. Dubois famously characterized as "a sense of always looking at one's self through the eyes of others."[86] The demands of reality are successful under white settler mourning because loss belongs to an ontological sense of reality that is symbolically mediated to be thus real. In other words, because death is socially recognizable as the endpoint of a life (*bios*), mourning is possible, but it is impossible when confronted with the condition of what Marriott rightly refers to as "deathliness," when death is lost as a category of being, as I articulated in chapter 2.

Hence, the work of mourning that Freud understands as a sort of second "killing" of the lost object faces an impasse in the case of the enslaved, since "killing" oversaturates the absolute expulsion of the enslaved from the symbolic order of being that reproduces the unreality of their loss at the level of the real. Unlike the melancholic pathology of civil society, where the subject "positivizes the void of the Real" in order to possess the lost object through "an unconditional fixation on loss itself," the melancholic attachment of black and indigenous people to their dead constitutes an ultimate refusal of the continuous possession of the black and indigenous body as the law of the social.[87] This is the law by which the settler erases the horrifying conditions that restrict "civility" to their own forms of being. By this I do not meant to suggest that the solution lies simply in lifting the restriction. Nor do I want to romanticize mourning as the ultimate weapon in the struggle against racism and settler colonialism. What I am trying to articulate, by means of this analysis, is that for "civility" to work as a form of social valuation that renders mourning possible, the "uncivilized" are forced to bear the burden of an unmediatable loss.

Moten's *black mo'nin'* registers this in mourning, as this melancholic attachment seeks not to possess the black body but to refuse possession as the condition of modern subjectivity, and to pass on that refusal as the emancipatory inheritance of the slave's struggle for freedom (fugitivity).[88] This is the fugitive mo'nin that Moten traces from the subversive sound of Frederick Douglass's Aunt Hester's scream, all the way to the phonographic disruption to the protocols of exchange captured in the sonic photograph of Emmett Till's open casket funeral. Black, and here I add, indigenous mo'nin', are refusals of the possessive economy that the exchangeability of symbolic mourning extends. Black and indigenous mo'nin' refuse to turn real loss into symbolic profit, by reactivating, again and again, the resistance of the object to the modern/colonial order of being. As Harney and Moten conclude, during their own mo'nin' of Michael Brown:

> On August 9, like every day, like every other day, black life, in its irreducible sociality, having consented not to be single, got caught walking—with jurisgenerative fecundity—down the middle of the street. Michael Brown and his boys: black life breaking and making laws, against and underneath the state, surrounding it. They had foregone the melancholic appeal to which we now reduce them, for citizenship and subjectivity, and humanness. That they had done so is the source of Darren Wilson's genocidal instrumentalization in the state's defense. They were in a state of war and they knew it. Moreover, they were warriors in insurgent, if imperfect, beauty.[89]

Mo'nin' is further elaborated by Christina Sharpe, in *In the Wake* (2016).[90] The *wake*, like *glas*, is a polysemic word, a word that captures a variety of interrelated meanings able to link mourning to militancy (jurisgenerative fecundity) and extends the politics of aesthetics of the black radical tradition to the funeral event. Unlike *glas*, however, *wake*-work confronts not just the violence of a philosophical system, or of Western metaphysics, but of a settler-colonial system of dehumanized racialization. Sharpe gives us a definition of the wake only after having introduced the many deaths that twice, in her life, she had to confront in a very short span. Sharpe connects those deaths to the Middle Passage, and to the disavowed history that helps to make America into the "land of opportunity," that is: *ob* (toward) and *portum* (port). Sharpe thus claims that the wake is, first, "the trace left on water's surface by a ship; the disturbance caused by a body swimming or moved, in water; it is the air currents behind a body in flight; a region of disturbed flow."[91] Such definition of the wake is not unrelated to the one that links it to mourning, to the vigil held beside the body of someone who has died. Except the vigil is precisely what is problematized by the colonial de/re-configuration of both the dead being mourned and the work of mourning itself. Such de/re-configuration is well captured in the title of poet Claudia Rankine's 2015 op-ed piece for *The New York Times*, in the aftermath of the June 17, 2015, murders of six black women and three black men in the Emmanuel African Methodist Episcopalian Church in South Carolina: "The Condition of Black Life Is One of Mourning."[92] Here, it is important to read that title within the context of the "racial calculus and political arithmetic" that, Hartman rightly asserts, survives the end of slavery and gives it an afterlife via "skewed life chances, limited access to health and education, premature death, incarceration, and impoverishment."[93] Not all lives, in other words, are subjected to living in perpetual mourning. For some lives, mourning is no longer an extraordinary event but forced to be experienced as ordinary, through the severe devaluation of life and greater exposure of their community to lethal surveillance and political disposability. Sharpe's critical category of the wake, like Moten's black mo'nin', registers the fact that both the mourner and the one being mourned are subjected to such a racialized form of death *in/as* life. Under such conditions, *mourning* and *melancholia* become insufficient terms. Both the mourners and the ones being mourned, always irremediably in the plural, face the overwhelming normalization of exceptional death. Settler colonialism normalizes death, as the people acquiesce both to the frequent extrajudicial killing of black people, and the no less terrifying social acceptance of an imposed accelerated slow death, via environmentally degraded conditions, infrastructural abandonment, and imposed poverty.

But the wake, as Sharpe claims, also describes a condition of nonbeing that differs from simply being *as* subjected. This is a condition of refusal, of bodies in flight, of fugitivity, which Sharpe identifies in her own mother, and insurgently inherits from her. Thus, Sharpe claims, "[s]he was attuned not only to our individual circumstances but also to those circumstances as they were an indication of, and related to, the larger antiblack world that structured all of our lives. *Wake; the state of wakefulness; consciousness.*"[94] If, as we saw in chapter 3, the natal-creative work of black women in the community of the enslaved was the only activity that was not directly appropriable by the enslaver, wake-work reactivates that insurgent natality at the level of coloniality's deathliness, and against the background of slavery's aftermath.

In the face of deathliness, Sharpe argues, the work that is the wake insists on black existence. The wake is a material and aesthetic response to the immanence and imminence of black death. Living in the wake means: (1) "living the history and present of terror, from slavery to the present, as the ground of our everyday Black existence," (2) and living that terror while being forced to become the "terror's embodiment, and not the primary object of terror's multiple enactments."[95] Living in the wake also means (3) insisting on the "Black visualsonic resistance to that imposition of nonbeing" that makes antiblackness into the climate of the normal/normative/social order.[96]

In the Wake thus opens with the multiple meanings of wake-work and ends with an acknowledgment of antiblackness as the total climate of white supremacy. Antiblackness is most certainly a dominant part of that climate, I would only like to add that settler colonial capitalism makes anti-indigeneity and other forms of racialized violence also part of that climate. What Sharpe adds to our meditation on the racial Capitalocene and the limits of mourning and melancholia to confront its most disavowed forms of normalized death is an understanding of wake-work in relation to racialized atmospheric conditions. These conditions force mourners to confront the militant convergence of burial and exhumation, well captured in Sharpe's political conceptualization of aspiration. Sharpe understands aspiration not in its conventional association with opportunity, but in relation to the question of "how to keep breath in the black body" in the face of antiblackness as weather.[97] This is the weather that makes life unbreathable and, according to Frantz Fanon, leads to revolt, to a combat form of breathing.[98] Such unbreathable weather refers not only to a polluted air, although it is most definitely related to environmental racism as part of the overall logic of settler colonial violence. Other forms of structural asphyxiation, however, like the police chokeholds that killed Eric Garner and most recently George Floyd, are part of the colonially unbreathable atmosphere that encompasses "the totality of the environments in which we struggle, the machines in which we live."[99]

Seeking to navigate the weather, Sharpe recurs to NourbeSe Philip's *exaqua*. This is the poetic word Philip arrives at, when searching for one that could bring bodies back from water (exhumation), in her own meditation on the *Zong*. Searching for a more materialist map by which to navigate settler-colonial violence, we need to look more deeply into the ocean and into the land, rather than looking up to the stars. Sharpe then links *exaqua* to the poetic exclamation point by which Philip "transforms and breaks *Zong* from a proper name into *Zong!*" that is "song/moan/chant/shout/breath." Such wakeful gesture, in the sense of consciousness, Sharpe then traces in other aesthetic gestures that she reconceptualizes as black annotation and black redaction. To all of these gestures Sharpe extends the ability of the black radical tradition to contest power even in militant mourning, offering a dissentious wake for the racialized other of atmospheric white supremacy.

Wake-work is thus a way of insisting on black and indigenous insurgent life, in confrontational opposition to the atmospheric antiblackness and anti-indigeneity of the racial Capitalocene that pollutes the settler colony. Sharpe, like Moten, turn to the cries that break into songs. These oral *ruttiers* (a notion Sharpe takes from Dionne Brand), or phonographic disruptions (Moten), Sharpe understands as "our internalized maps in the long time of our displacement," maps that give some navigational possibility to a form of loss that has no cartography.[100] If, as Freud argues, the mourner must go over each individual memory that still holds the libido captive, to finally let them all go, wake-work is about the construction of an alternative map by which those subjected to slavery's aftermath can situate those memories in a symbolic order that offers them no map. Confinement, in this case, refers not to the relationship that exists between the mourner and the individual memory that holds the libido captive. Confinement is, rather, the social condition that renders it impossible for racially marked mourners to locate those individual memories, otherwise destroyed and de/re-formed by the colonial archive of racial/sexual capitalism. It is racialized captivity, as the settler-colonial condition of social (de)valuation, that holding to these memories seeks to destroy.

MILITANT MOURNING AND THE NEW INTERNATIONAL

Let us, then, as contemporary decolonial Marxists argue, consider the original accumulation of capital the transformative activity of capitalism. Let us understand the conquest of the Americas and the trans-Atlantic slave trade, in a more Benjamin/Glissant–inspired way, as the past that continues to accumulate in and as the present. Let us follow settler colonial critique and argue that settlement is never an accomplished fact but always an iterative labor of exappropriation. Let us relate the labor of settling the homeland (America) to the interrelated interdiction of misremembering the indigenous land (*Abya Yala*). With this alternative political framing, let us ask, yet again: What would it mean to situate Antigone's subversive mourning of Polyneices as the lost object of settler-colonial capitalism, at the world-historical scale of such incommensurable (non)events? Will this mourning take, perhaps, the more militant form of a symbolic jurisgenerative fecundation, rather than that of a symbolic killing? Would it need a supplemental Gordonian conjuring, a Benjaminian reawakening, a Sharpean wake-work?

Perhaps it was not Derrida but Marx and Engels who first argued for that redefinition of labor *as* mourning. Despite the otherwise teleological implications, we might read their claim that "what the bourgeoisie, therefore, produces, above all, is its own grave-diggers" in a more decolonially ruminated Antigonian sense, that suggests just more militant conjuring/awakening/waking.[101] We might read their claim not so much as expressing their teleological confidence in the inevitable arrival of communism, as the end of history and the logical consequence of capitalism's internal contradictions, but in the more historically undecidable sense that makes ending domination and exploitation contingent upon digging the grave of settler-colonial capitalism. As Moore claims, "Shut down a coal plant, and you can slow global warming for a day; shut down the relations that made the coal plant, and you can stop it for good."[102] Perhaps the activity of racialized mourning is not to repeat a symbolic killing, but to destroy the system that naturalizes some losses as symbolically insignificant, in order to create a symbolic space that is no longer contingent on its being only available to a few. Mourning is, then, neither only nor primarily about public memorials and recognition, but about the material transformation of our social reality and mode of social (re)production, for symbolic space to no longer be predicated on exposing its unaccounted majority to the normalized threat of uneventful loss.

If *Antigone in the Americas* teaches anything, it is that to dig such a grave, more than one burial needs to take place—and for certain burials to take place, some exhumations are necessary. In many cases, as in the case of Emmett Till, the difference between burial and exhumation becomes all the more unstable, as both acts coexist in the same gesture (as in Philip's *exaqua*). That is the case, because the militant burial needs not only to contest the lethal violence of racism, but also the additional violence of its disavowal. By this I do not suggest that all exhumations will be emancipatory, just as not all burials are liberatory. Some bodies are buried to conceal the violence of the social order. Public acts of recognition have been shown to not only whitewash but refuel colonialism.[103] Likewise, exhuming the body and returning that body to the family who searches for it might be the last ideological subterfuge by which that social order seeks to remain in place, as we saw in chapter 3.

Decolonial Antigones, to echo the title of Holland's book, need to learn how to "raise the dead" differently, a difficult task, since it is

> the relationship of enslaved peoples to their legion of unnamed and unrecognized ancestors—the same ancestors who are designated as the "Sixty Million and more" lost to the middle passage in Toni Morrison's dedication of *Beloved* and the unnamed "Sixty

million Native Americans [who] died between 1500–1600" in the frontispiece to Leslie Marmon Silko's *Almanac of the Dead* that has been and continues to be historically broken.[104]

To attend to these legions and to the differential logics of accumulation that organize such historical brokenness, is to expand on the commons and include the differential losses of the undercommons. Communism is one emancipatory strategy in a struggle that would need to include, among the historically variable versions of the commune, equally plural versions of the indigenous *cabildo* (independent communities created by indigenous peoples) and the black *palenque* or *marronage* (independent communities created by people who escaped slavery) in its emancipatory repertoire. Such is the New International for our settler-colonial present, one in which, as Gordon argues, "specters are still haunting, not only in Europe and not only of communism." These ghosts, as Gordon interpellates, need to be conjured otherwise to reorient the liberatory energies of the multiracial commune, the indigenous *cabildo,* and the black marronage toward their convergent emancipation(s) from settler-colonial capitalism in a New International that is more political than ethical.[105]

"The ghost," Gordon claims, "is not other or alterity as such, ever. It is (like Beloved) pregnant with unfulfilled possibility, with the something to be done that the wavering present is demanding."[106] But ghosts are also, as Esther Peeren argues, "figures of a compromised agency."[107] Thus, we need a reframing of spectrality in order to rework our own political camaraderie to the dead. Mourning can be taken to be not one kind of work but work in general (Derrida). The work of mourning can be reoriented in the more revolutionary direction of digging a grave to bury *this* exploitative and expropriative settler-colonial order (Marx and Engels). Under such a political frame, perhaps it is not any "reality" beckoning the libido of the grieving militant to let the lost object go and reattach to another, but the "ghost" haunting the present of the socially dead militant with the unfulfilled possibility of a decolonial liberation in which various emancipations can converge (Moten and Sharpe), that is at stake.

"This something to be done," Gordon rightly qualifies, "is not a return to the past but a reckoning with its repression in the present, a reckoning with that which we have lost, but never had."[108] I conclude this chapter by calling for a reckoning with the ghost in the ice that we have lost but never had. I have tried to situate Antigone's subversive mourning against the more-difficult-to-confront reality of the racial Capitalocene. But I have done so neither to freeze the present by saturating it with the otherwise wrongly conceived of as crimes of the past, nor to replace a Hegelian philosophy of history as progress with a misconceived Benjaminian philosophy of history as catastrophe. I have done so to situate the Leninist-sounding political question "What is to be done?" in the subversive act of decolonial mourning, as attuned to black and indigenous mo'nin' and in the spirit of forming a wakeful New International.

Because Polyneices was not properly buried, his body decomposed, and the birds distributed his rotten flesh all over the city. A plague followed, and Thebes was destroyed because it failed to properly understand the political nature of the violence leading to the plague. Today, as COVID-19 spreads, corpses are once again left unburied in the streets, primarily affecting black and brown people. How we confront these unburied bodies, that is to say, under what kind of politics, will make all the difference. State agents and policing authorities have already engaged in one necropolitical interpretation. They have underplayed the pandemic, racialized its source—calling COVID-19 "the Chinese virus"—and blamed alien labor forces in order to fuel the war apparatus of the U.S. empire and its settler-colonial forms of social policing. They have done all of this while redesigning public relief bills in order to generate an even greater transfer of wealth, from the most vulnerable to the rich. As a consequence, the atmospheric antiblackness unleashed against Emmett Till, Eric Garner, Michael Brown, and Sandra Bland continues to be enforced against Ahmaud Arbery, Breonna Taylor, and George Floyd, to name only a few. Similarly, the atmospheric anti-indigeneity once unleashed upon the Cherokee, Choctaw, Chickasaw, Seminole, and Creek nations—3,500 of 10,000 Creeks died of "bilious fevers" upon arrival in present-day Oklahoma, as a result of the 1830 Indian Removal Act—has been most recently enforced against the Standing Rock Sioux Tribe and the Navajo Nation, among others.[109]

Reflecting on the interrelated nature of these violences, Saidiya Hartman turns to W. E. B. Dubois's apocalyptic story, "The Comet." As Hartman argues, "The influenza pandemic of 1918 does not appear" in Dubois's apocalyptic story, because "for every year between 1906 and 1920, black folks in cities experienced a rate of death that equaled the white rate of death at the peak of the pandemic."[110] Black people had been enduring another kind of pandemic over a decade, but "had been allowed to die in great numbers without a crisis ever being declared."[111] Failing to understand the ways in which both of these pandemics are the differential products of the racial Capitalocene, will prove as devastating today as it was for ancient

Thebes. The challenge remains to militantly mourn otherwise and, like the mass protests in the street, honor these deaths through the active political interruption and public undoing of racial/sexual capitalism.

Conclusion

What Is There Instead of Being Born?

Somewhere, Aristotle claims that thinking begins beside the corpse.[1] In this book, I have argued that not all corpses, in fact, elicit the same kind of critical thinking. The corpses of the enslaved, for instance, did not generate the same thoughtful meditation on "the human" for Aristotle who, a *metic* in Athens, crafted the most influential rationale for the naturalization of slavery in Greek antiquity—turned into one of the canonical arguments by which slavery was biologically constructed as inheritable in modernity.[2] The enslaved also did not generate the same politically thoughtful action by which Antigone opposed the state-sanctioned desecration of Polyneices. Thoughtlessness, instead, overwhelms the structural violence that makes the loss of enslaved lives ordinary and uneventful.

As I have argued, the unburied corpse is perhaps not just *a* symptom but *the* symptom of the political. The structurally unburied corpse is the flesh that, refusing to be placed outside of the body politic's dominant forms of social belonging, returns to it with a destructive capacity and unleashes a rightful plague. These are corpses that are systematically, rather than accidentally, unburied and are unburied even when they are actually buried, as often happens with those who are forcefully disappeared in order to erase (para)state violence. There is a politics in deciding *whether* to bury or not the body the state marks as abject. This politics distinguishes the position of Creon, who wants to instrumentalize the corpse in order to extend the violence of the state beyond the spatial-temporal limits of the living, from the position of Antigone, who wants to interrupt this violence. *How* to bury that body involves another set of politics. This set distinguishes the politics of Ismene, who wants to perform the burial at night and in secrecy, from those of Antigone, who wants to do it in broad daylight and in public. *What* reasons we offer to bury that body, finally, adds yet another set of politics. This set distinguishes multiple versions of Antigone, as she does it first because the god of death demands it, and last because her brother is uniquely irreplaceable, but also because Polyneices was not Eteocles's slave.

Antigone is, thus, a play about the multiple ways in which the bio/necropolitical reproduction of life and death intersect with the democratic regulation of political membership. Because she was not enslaved, Antigone's political influence extended to the beginning and end of life. She was supposed to procreate citizens for the *polis* and attend to the burial of her family members. As many have argued, the democratic regulation of funeral lamentation contextualizes the politics of her burial. Death is as political as life, and her prioritization of the natal over the conjugal family, when she decides to risk her life by performing the forbidden burial, links both obligations in one subversive act. Antigone chooses death and dies, unlike all other heroines from the ancient tragic corpus, the sole suicidal virgin.[3] But Antigone's choices are also framed by Athenian exceptionalism. Enslaved women did not have the same political influence that citizen or *metic* women had. In this book, I have tried to analyze the ways in which the political stratification of membership persists and complicates our understandings of different agencies and the constrains that they face. I have also tried to understand the aftermath of that stratification in the ways in which settler colonialism affects modern democracy, racialized sexuality, and necropolitical death in the Americas. I have, finally, tried to decolonially ruminate on the political meaning of this play, in order to show how some burials are more difficult to perform than others, and some reasons, more difficult to politicize than others.

As Martel argues, in an excellent short book on the unburied corpse, dead bodies present a particular challenge to the state's biopolitical power. This is the challenge that he summarizes as the confrontation between the vertical authority of archism—whose funerals seek to recuperate the dead within a nonthreatening narrative of subjection to the state—and the anarchist authority of the dead—where corpses refuse that narrative not so much "by telling us but by *untelling*" us something about the *polis*.[4] In this book, I have tried to do three things in relation to the racialized logic of that confrontation and the political modalities of that *untelling*. First, I have tried to relate such archist violence, more specifically, to the two settler-colonial logics of capitalist accumulation by which political membership was vertically organized among citizens, *metics,* and slaves in order to distinguish settlers from natives and aliens in the Americas. Secondly, I have tried to identify the ways in which archist violence can be reproduced in our own anarchist efforts at contesting it. This is what happens when we fail to address capitalism's relational modes of social (de)valuation, whereby mourning invests some dead with authority by deauthorizing others. Finally, I have shown how this structure affects our theoretical efforts at interpreting the meaning of Antigone's militant mourning. I have, thus, tried to confront archism, as it is reproduced in radical democratic theory, feminist and queer theory, the theory of biopolitics, and the theory of deconstruction. Archism is reproduced whenever these theories fail to attend to the racialized scene of subjection that takes hold not of the dead but of the socially dead corpse instead.

As I argued, following the political guidelines of the black feminist radical tradition and settler colonial critique, neither the elimination of the native nor the exclusion of the alien ever ends with the death of those who are targeted with state-sanctioned lethal violence. Nor was slavery, as a certain way of turning death into a condition coextensive with living (social death), merely abolished when slavery was declared illegal. Slavery, as Saidiya Hartman argues, was given an aftermath, and the racialized system of labor subjugation and land expropriation that racial/sexual capitalism engendered remain intact. Some bodies are, thus, not only more frequently exposed to frequent death and improper burial (when buried at all); the communities that publicly mourn them are equally targeted with state-sanctioned lethal violence. This investigation led me to entertain the misinterpellated possibility of a *metic* Antigone and an enslaved Polyneices and to speculate on the political meanings of this tragedy, if read through those lenses, for our present. This book, in short, has been a call to modify Aristotle's claim and resituate critical thinking beside the socially dead corpse instead.

The audibility of Antigone's humanistic and antihumanistic claims has come to rest, I thus argued, on the silencing of the enslaved and the *metic* as alternative positionalities for the imagination of political agency. But the positionality of the socially valued citizen can no longer be taken for granted. As I demonstrated in this book, this has important political ramifications for the ways in which we do democratic theory (chapter 1), approach feminist and queer theory (chapter 2), theorize bio- and necropolitics (chapter 3), and engage in deconstruction (chapter 4). In short, I have tried to extend the politics of burial back to the distinction between modes of burying slaves, *metics,* and citizens in order to relocate the political around the question of membership, of deciding who counts and who does not count for the community.

The democracy of the ancients was by no means the same as the democracy of the moderns. Nor was, for that matter, any other political category that we use. Freedom, slavery, sexuality, death, and tragedy—all of these categories have changed. I registered the significance of those changes in order to unpack the different dynamics of state violence as I moved from colonialism in ancient Athens, to settler colonialism in modern North America, and to the pluralization and intensification of its logics in postmodern neoliberal Latin America. The point of my use of the citizen/*metic*/slave triad across different historical times was not to suggest that those categories have remained the same throughout history. The point was to stress that something about the relationality between these positions persists, and that such persistence is indebted to changing dynamics of colonialism. The most important change I insist upon in this book was the result of the European conquest of the Americas and the trans-Atlantic slave trade, in other words, the transformation of racial/sexual capitalism into a world-system that integrated four continents through the articulation of two logics: exclusion and elimination. This historical transformation made that stratification of political membership thoroughly racialized and gave form to the apocalyptic racial Capitalocene of our present.

I use this ancient-indebted triad because critical theory continues to be indebted to a certain reading of the tragic ancients. Every time we rethink these terms—democracy, sexuality, and death—we turn to their original articulation in Greek tragedy. Yet, as Simon Critchley has argued, "the ancients need a little of our true blood in order to speak to us," and when they do speak to us they "do not merely tell us about themselves [but] about us."[5] Whose blood, however, have we been giving them? Whose blood is the "true blood," since the whole problem of blood-based membership is what is at stake in this play, and yet continues to be glossed over in the dominant political interpretations of this tragedy? This book has been an effort to inject a different kind of alien blood into the ancients, so as to take a journey through the disavowed afterlives of slavery and *metoikia* in/ and through theory, and in/and through the Americas.

I would like to conclude this book with a tentative answer to the question with which Anne Carson opens her meditation on Antigone's name, in the preface to what is arguably the most ambitious translation/rewriting of Sophocles's *Antigone* to date: *AntigoNick* (2012). In a letter addressed to

Antigone ("dear Antigone," she says), Carson writes, "your name in Greek means something like 'against birth' or 'instead of being born.' What is there instead of being born?"[6] Carson leaves this question open, but suggests, as resources to help us answer it: Brecht, Hegel, Lacan, Butler, George Eliot, Slavoj Žižek, Jean Anouilh, John Ashbery, Samuel Beckett, John Cage, and Ingeborg Bachman. Reading *Antigone* under the misinterpellated lenses of modern slavery and *metoikia*, I have crafted a different constellation of theoretical and literary mediations, this time from black radical feminism, settler colonial critique, women of color feminism, and queer and trans of color critique. There, instead of being born, is having been born black and/or indigenous under settler colonial conditions of political membership, whereby natives and aliens are born natally alienated, enslaved for the biopolitical cultivation of settlers. Iyko Day, Tina Chanter, Moira Fradinger, Hortense Spillers, Angela Davis, Saidiya Hartman, María Lugones, C. Riley Snorton, Sara Uribe, Patricia Nieto, Ariel Dorfman, Jodi Byrd, Lisa Marie Cacho, Elva Orozco-Mendoza, Sayak Valencia, Ian Baucom, Avery Gordon, Fred Moten, and Christina Sharpe, among others, make my list of alternative mediations. Through them, I have tried to reconsider the meaning of this play anew and confront other limits of social intelligibility, insufficiently analyzed in this tragedy: above all, the limits of our political imagination.

Seeking to re-member the enslaved and the *metic,* upon whose differential exclusion the citizen is socially valued, I have tried to remain in the break, and with the most broken body: the desecrated corpse. I have thus tried to hear, and decolonially ruminate on, the silenced sounds that one can still hear from millions of dead bodies, if one learns how to conjure them otherwise. The effort of this book has been to hear in the breaking of the *demos* the cacophonous sounds of the *doulos* and the *metic* (chapter 1); and in the breaking-up of the death drive the anti-heteronormative sounds of the socially dead quare and two-spirit (chapter 2); and in the refusal of the sovereign disappearance of the body, the political sounds of maternal activism in the Global South (chapter 3); and in the crack of the ice, the militant sounds of black and indigenous mo'nin' against the racial Capitalocene (chapter 4).

In those breaks, I have tried to unpack the sedimented history of settler-colonial racialization and the refusal of the dead to grant futurity to *this* world. I consider this refusal best activated through the insurgent activity of black and indigenous wakeful mo'nin'. This world must end. There must be a burial, one that will inevitably be many burials, and several exhumations as well. That burial will first have to dig out the what-have-beens accumulated in the settler-colonial present and exhume millions of bodies from colonial oblivion. Only, then, it would not be Polyneices but the logics of accumulation themselves that militant Antigones will bury instead.

Perhaps it is time to give a new interpretation to the riddle of the Sphinx. The riddle asks about the creature that has four legs in the morning, two in the evening and three at night. Oedipus famously answers, "men," presumably solving the riddle. But what if these legs refer to another creature, to the triangulated stratification of political membership that I have been tracing in this book? What if the colonial erasure of this political triangulation is what universalizes "man" as the sign of "the human"? What if the four-legged creature of the morning refers to the enslaved, the two-legged creature of the evening to the citizen, and the three-legged creature of the night to the *metic*? After all, Tina Chanter has already demonstrated that *tetrapoda* (four-footed thing), a Greek word for cattle, inspired the analogous use of the term *andrapodon* to designate slaves and she suggests just such a connection to the riddle in her own book. Oedipus's legs were, arguably, tied in the morning when he was newly born, like the legs of animals about to be sacrificed. And slaves were compared with animals, in antiquity and in modernity. Through the servants' insurgent actions, (two servants, arguably slaves, whose added legs equal four) Oedipus's legs are untied. His body crosses the border, by means of this dissident agency, and he is given an alternative life (*bios*) as the son and heir of Polybus and Merope, the sovereigns of Corinth, a known slave center. Oedipus becomes the two-legged creature of the evening, a sovereign citizen-in-the-making. Citizenship comes to materially rest on the labor of slavery. But Oedipus would not stay in Corinth. Untied, his legs are rather restless. Fearing the prophecy that turns him abject, he leaves Corinth, killing his birth father at the crossroads. Then, believing himself to have solved the riddle of the sphinx that has turned Thebes infertile, he becomes the monstrosity that he defeats. It is his marriage to Jocasta that marks the new pollution of the city and becomes the new source of infertility. It is at Thebes, too, as its *metic* sovereign, that he tortures the slave who first saved his life in order to know the truth about his origins. Anxious to prove that he was not a slave, he discovers the truth and is thus forced to leave Thebes yet again, as a punishment for the heinous crimes that he committed unknowingly. Needing another body to support himself in old age, he takes Antigone with him and starts a long and nomadic journey through foreign lands. Antigone, acting as a sort of prosthetic cane, becomes Oedipus's third leg. By the end of his life, that is to say, allegorically at night, he finally arrives at Colonus where he is granted *metoikia*. Antigone, almost a *metic* at Colonus, is then forced to return to her native city, where filicide awaits her. There she would have been considered a citizen, known to be a native of Thebes. And it is there, upon her return, that she reclaims *metoikia* for herself and claims to bury her brother because it was not Eteocles's slave who died. The four-legged creature of the morning that becomes a two-legged creature in the evening only to die a third-legged one at night is not "men," as Oedipus believes. Rather, this creature refers to the tripartite colonial stratification of political membership by which the state socially values the humanity of those it recognizes as full citizens, on the condition that others are differentially deprived of political power. The point of this alternative solution is not just to offer yet another interpretation of the play, but to suggest an interpretation that can take the rebelliousness of Antigone's mourning in the militant direction of decolonial re-membering. The point of this reading is, as Barrett suggests, to redefine the anarchist politics of the tragic as the confrontation between two modes of re-membering: one that members the lives it values through the settler colonial devaluation of those that it "others," versus one that values those devalued "others" by decolonially dismembering the subtending racialized logic of social valuation.

Notes

Introduction

1. I use *Antigone* when referring to the play, and Antigone when referring to the character in the play. Unless otherwise indicated, all citations from Sophocles are from David Grene's translation; see Sophocles, *Sophocles I*, trans. David Grene (Chicago: The University of Chicago Press, 1991). A is for *Antigone*, OT for *Oedipus Tyrannos*, and OC for *Oedipus at Colonus*. The first numbers refer to the lines in the Greek original, the ones in brackets to the numbers in the page.

2. On incest as a figure of aristocratic endogamy and political enclosure, see Edith Hall, "Antigone and the Internationalization of Theater in Greek Antiquity," in *Antigone on the Contemporary World Stage*, ed. Erin B. Mee and Helene Foley (Oxford: Oxford Classics, 2011); and Tina Chanter, *Whose Antigone? The Tragic Marginalization of Slavery* (New York: State University of New York Press, 2011), 137.

3. Lisa Lowe, *The Intimacies of Four Continents* (Durham: Duke University Press, 2015).

4. Mieke Bal defines "preposterous history" as a certain reversal of time that "puts what came chronologically first ('pre-') as an aftereffect behind ('post')"; Mieke Bal, *Quoting Caravaggio: Contemporary Art, Preposterous History* (Chicago: The University of Chicago Press, 1999), 7. Bal develops such an approach on a modality of quotation that troubles the view of art history as "having a foundational influence on everything that follows in its wake." The preposterous quotation of the historical text means, to put it in Derrida's terms, that one never returns to the quoted text "without the burden of the excursion through the quotation" (11). I do not want to overlook the differences between the baroque and ancient Greek tragedy, and yet, quoting Caravaggio is not that different from quoting *Antigone*, when it comes to the burden of that excursion. My book is about that burden, about unpacking the disavowed history of colonial racialization, as constitutive of that burden. I thank one of the anonymous reviewers of this manuscript for suggesting Bal's work to me, as a methodological interlocutor.

5. See Chanter, *Whose Antigone?* esp. introduction and chapter 2.

6. Translation modified by Rebecca Futo Kennedy, *Immigrant Women in Athens: Gender, Ethnicity, and Citizenship in the Classical City* (New York: Routledge, 2014), 40. Kennedy criticizes most translators of *Antigone*, for translating *metoikos* with the sense of "one who dwells with" in all of these instances, rather than with an explicit reference to the "resident foreigner," for eliding crucial aspects of Antigone's metaphorical use. It elides, first and foremost, her way of characterizing her situation in the *polis* as one that resembles that of a *metic*, "a state of limbo, an in-between status that gains neither the commemoration due the dead nor the freedoms of movement, speech and human interaction of the living" (Kennedy, *Immigrant Women in Athens*, 40).

7. To give one example, based on official reports from medical examiners, county sheriffs, and border patrols, Humane Borders—a U.S.-based organization founded in 2000—has created maps indicating that 2,269 migrants died in the Sonora Desert between October 1, 1999, and March 28, 2012. See http://www.humaneborders.org and maps at https://dabrownstein.files.wordpress.com/2013/08/migrant-deaths-and-water-stations-1999–2012.jpg; accessed July 20, 2016. This is obviously not a condition exclusive to the United States, as the main place of destination for migrants around the world, under the current geopolitical regulation of labor movement. Think about the bodies of migrants, predominantly if not exclusively from Africa, whose lives are "lost" in the Mediterranean when trying to migrate to Europe. Drowned in the Mediterranean, the bodies cannot be properly buried. I put "lost" in scare quotes in order to problematize the assignation of innocence, when of course the militarization of the border, and criminalization of the aiding vessel, are among the forces responsible for the killing. And yet, by simply calling it a killing, which it is, one misses the most horrific aspect of this violence, its way of criminalizing both the crossing and the agency of those who try to save these lives.

8. See Kelly Lytle Hernández, *Migra: A History of the US Border Patrol* (Berkeley: University of California Press, 2010); and Justin Akers Chacón, "Opening the Border through Class Struggle and Solidarity," *Punto Rojo*, January 13, 2020.

9. Virtually all interpretations that I have read, with the exceptions of Cecilia Sjöholm, "Naked Life: Arendt and the Exile at Colonus," in *Interrogating Antigone in Postmodern Philosophy and Criticism*, ed. S. E. Wilmer and Audronė Žukauskaite (Oxford: Oxford University Press, 1992); Tina Chanter, *Whose Antigone?*; and Jutta Gsoels-Lorensen, "Antigone, Deportee," *Arethusa* 47, no. 2 (2014): 111–44, tend to assume the position of the citizen as the subjective lens by which to interpret the play. See, for instance, Warren Lane and Ann M. Lane, "The Politics of Antigone," in *Greek Tragedy and Political Theory*, ed. Peter Euben (Berkeley: University of California Press, 1986); Jean Bethke Elshtain, "Antigone's Daughters," *Democracy* 2, no. 2 (1982): 39–45; Christiane Sourvinou-Inwood, "Sophocles's Antigone as a 'Bad Womam,'" in *Writing Women into History*, ed. F. Dieteren and E. Kloek (Amsterdam: Amsterdamse historische reeks, 1990); Larry Bennett and Tyrrell Blake,

"Sophocles' *Antigone* and Funeral Oratory," *AJP* 111, no. 1 (1990): 441–56; Gail Holst-Warhaft, *Dangerous Voices: Women's Laments and Greek Literature* (London: Routledge, 1992); Helene Foley, "Tragedy and Democratic Ideology: The Case of Sophocles' Antigone," in *History, Tragedy, Theory: Dialogues on Athenian Drama*, ed. Barbara Goff (Austin: University of Texas Press, 1995); Costas Douzinas, "Law's Birth and Antigone's Death," *Cardozo Law Review* 16, no. 4 (1995): 1325–55; Seyla Benhabib, "On Hegel, Women and Irony," in *Feminist Interpretations of G. W. F. Hegel*, ed. Patricia Jagentowicz Mills (University Park: Pennsylvania State University Press, 1996); Seth Benardete, *Sacred Transgressions: A Reading of Sophocles' Antigone* (South Bend: St. Augustine's Press, 1999); Patchen Markell, *Bound by Recognition* (New Jersey: Princeton University Press, 2003); Samuel Weber, "Antigone's *Nomos*," in *Theatricality as Medium* (New York: Fordham University Press, 2004); Erika Fischer-Licthe, "Politicizing Antigone," in *Interrogating Antigone in Postmodern Philosophy and Criticism*, ed. S. E. Wilmer and Audronė Žukauskaite (Oxford: Oxford University Press, 2010); Judith Fletcher, "Sophocles' *Antigone* and the Democratic Voice," in *Interrogating Antigone in Postmodern Philosophy and Criticism*, ed. S. E. Wilmer and Audronė Žukauskaite (Oxford: Oxford University Press, 2010); Bonnie Honig, *Antigone, Interrupted* (Cambridge: Cambridge University Press, 2013); and Larissa Atkison, "*Antigone*'s Reminders: Choral Ruminations and Political Judgment," *Political Theory* 44, no. 2 (2015): 219–39.

10. On the social stratification of Athenian tragedy, see Simon Goldhill, "The Great Dionysia and Civic Ideology," in *Nothing to Do with Dionysus? Athenian Drama in Its Social Context*, ed. John Winkler and Froma Zeitlin (Princeton: Princeton University Press, 1986); and "The Language of Tragedy: Rhetoric and Communication," in *The Cambridge Companion to Greek Tragedy*, ed. P. E. Easterling (Cambridge: Cambridge University Press, 1997).

11. James Martel, *The Misinterpellated Subject* (Durham: Duke University Press, 2017), 25.

12. Ibid., 124.

13. I use this triad to call attention to a crucial theoretical silencing, vis-à-vis blood-based differential membership status, in the political interpretation of this play. However, all of these categories could be further disaggregated, as even in the case of slaves, for instance, one could distinguish *andrapoda misthophorounta*, which refers to the most debased form of chattel slavery in Greek antiquity, from *apophora*-bearing slaves, a different subcategory of slaves "who worked, and sometimes lived, apart from their masters, conducted their own businesses, and handed over some fraction of their earnings, called the *apophora*, to their masters"; Deborah Kamen, *Status in Classical Athens* (Princeton: Princeton University Press, 2013), 19. Likewise, *metics* and citizens should also be differentiated. Kamen distinguishes, for instance, *isoteleis* from *proxenoi* and others, that is, *metics* who were granted more rights than the average *metic*. She also distinguishes naturalized citizens from natural-born citizens, and bastards (*nothoi*), disenfranchised citizens (*atimoi*), and

female citizens, all of whom were subjected to different forms of dispossession and regulation. Full citizens, as we know from Solon's reforms, were equally divided across four property classes. In short, the triad, though useful, should alert us to the ways in which it also glosses over other significant differences. For a broader analysis of these differences, see G. E. M. de Ste. Croix, *The Class Struggle in the Ancient Greek World: From the Archaic Age to the Arab Conquests* (Ithaca: Cornell University Press, 1981).

14. Denise Eileen McCoskey, *Race: Antiquity and Its Legacy* (Oxford: Oxford University Press, 2012), 23.

15. Ibid., 54. For a broader discussion of race versus ethnicity, in the analysis of Greek antiquity, see Paul Cartledge, *The Greeks: A Portrait of Self and Others* (Oxford: Oxford University Press, 1993); Benjamin Isaac, *The Invention of Racism in Classical Antiquity* (Princeton: Princeton University Press, 2004); and Jonathan Hall, *Ethnic Identity in Greek Antiquity* (Cambridge: Cambridge University Press, 1997).

16. Modern capitalism was invented in what the literature now refers to as the "long sixteenth century" (1450 to 1650). See, for instance, Fernand Braudel, *The Perspective of the World. Civilization & Capitalism 15th–18th Century* (Berkeley: University of California Press, 1992), Eric Mielants, *The Origins of Capitalism and the Rise of the West* (Philadelphia: Temple University Press, 2008), and Jason Moore, *Capitalism in the Web of Life: Ecology and the Accumulation of Capital* (London: Verso, 2015).

17. In fact, much like modern racism, ancient hierarchies revealed a spectacular circularity in which devalued differences fed on each other. As Chanter claims: "The fact that male barbarians are thought incapable of controlling what are construed as 'their' women is taken to be a sign of their political incompetence, their weakness as rulers, while their ostensible effeminacy (and therefore alleged similarity to women) already functions as grounds for suspicion of their allegedly inherently slavish natures" (*Whose Antigone?*, xxvii). Here, Chanter complements Paul Cartledge's way of understanding how different binaries (Greek/barbarian, men/women, citizen/alien, free/slave, god/mortal) intersect in Greek antiquity, by showing how such binaries do not merely overlap but "are constructed in terms of one another, fabricated with the help of one another. They blend into one another, feed off one another, do metaphorical work for one another, borrowing from one another, helping to constitute one another, and bolstering one another up" (*Whose Antigone?*, xxv; see Cartledge, *The Greeks*).

18. Susan Lape, *Race and Citizen Identity in Classical Antiquity* (Princeton: Princeton University Press, 2010), 186–239.

19. Ibid., 3.

20. See Edith Hall, *Inventing the Barbarian: Greek Self-Definition Through Tragedy* (Oxford: Clarendon Press, 1991).

21. Iyko Day, *Alien Capital: Asian Racialization and the Logic of Settler Colonial Capitalism* (Durham: Duke University Press, 2016), 19.

22. Ibid., 30.
23. Ibid., 28. I will expand on this in ch. 3.
24. Kamen, *Status in Classical Athens*, 43.
25. Saidiya Hartman, *Lose Your Mother: A Journey along the Atlantic Slaver Route* (New York: Farrar, Straus and Giroux, 2007), 6.
26. Kennedy, *Immigrant Women in Athens*, 16.
27. Ibid., 22.
28. Ibid., 101 and 103.
29. See Jacques Rancière, *Dis-agreement. Politics and Philosophy*, trans. Julie Rose (Minneapolis: University of Minnesota Press, 1999).
30. Ibid., 18.
31. Racial/sexual capitalism is a feminist way of honoring, and yet expanding, on Cedric Robinson's call to refer to capitalism as "racial capitalism," in recognition that the "development, organization, and expansion of capitalist society pursued essentially racial directions," See Cedric Robinson, *Black Marxism: The Making of the Black Radical Tradition* (Chapel Hill: The University of North Carolina Press, 1983), 2. Robinson coins "racial capitalism" not in order to distinguish a racialized form of capitalism from one that is not racial, but in order to call attention to the often invisibilized history of racialized labor subjugation that capitalism inherited from feudalism, and that continues to inform its subsequent structure. Racial/sexual capitalism calls attention to a more intersectional understanding of capitalism, which addresses and confronts the co-constitution of class, race, gender, and sexuality. For an excellent articulation of such an understanding, see Ashley Bohrer, *Marxism and Intersectionality: Race, Gender, Class, and Sexuality under Contemporary Capitalism* (Bielefeld: Transcript, 2019).
32. According to Joan O'Brien, via his debasement of the corpse Creon does end up treating "Polyneices' body as if he were a slave-thing"; *Guide to Sophocles' Antigone* (Carbondale and Edwardsville: Southern Illinois University Press, 1978), 40.
33. Kennedy, *Immigrant Women in Athens*, 40.
34. Lindon Barrett, *Blackness and Value: Seeing Double* (Cambridge; Cambridge University Press, 1999).
35. *Abya Yala* is one of the names by which several indigenous communities, primarily the Kuna people, continue to refer to the vast territory that colonizers renamed as the Americas, after the conquest.
36. Martin Bernal, *Black Athena* (New Brunswick, NJ: Rutgers University Press, 2006).
37. Chanter, *Whose Antigone?*, 33–55.
38. See Phiroze Vasunia, *The Gift of the Nile: Hellenizing Egypt from Aeschylus to Alexander* (Berkeley: University of California Press, 2001).
39. See Lorna Hardwick and Carol Gillespie, eds., *Classics in Post-Colonial Worlds* (Oxford: Oxford University Press, 2007); and Barbara Goff and Michael

Simpson, eds., *Crossroads in the Black Aegean: Oedipus, Antigone, and Dramas of the African Diaspora* (Oxford: Oxford University Press, 2007).

40. Aníbal Quijano, "Colonialidad del Poder y Clasificación Social. In Festschrift for Immanuel Wallerstein," *Journal of World Systems Research* 5, no. 2 (2000): 346. On decolonial theory, and its understanding of capitalist modernity, see Sylvia Wynter, "Unsettling the Coloniality of Being/Power/Truth/Freedom: Towards the Human, After Man, Its Overrepresentation—An Argument," *The New Centennial Review* 3 (2003): 257–337, Santiago Castro-Gómez, *La Hybris del Punto Cero: Ciencia, Raza e Ilustración en la Nueva Granada (1750–1816)* (Bogotá: Pontificia Universidad Javeriana, 2005), Enrique Dussel, "Alterity and Modernity (Las Casas, Vitoria, and Suárez: 1514–1617)," in *Postcolonialism and Political Theory*, ed. Nailini Persram (New York: Lexington Books, 2007), and George Ciccariello-Maher, *Decolonizing Dialectics* (Durham: Duke University Press, 2017).

41. For some of the literature that informs my understanding of race as a power structure that seeks to naturalize inferiority via an appeal to biological differences that disavow their contingent historicity, see David Theo Goldberg, *The Racial State* (London: Blackwell, 1993); Michael Omi and Howard Winant, *Racial Formation in the United States: From the 1960s to the 1990s* (New York: Routledge, 1994); Charles Mills, *The Racial Contract* (Ithaca: Cornell University Press, 1997); Gayatri Spivak, "Race Before Racism: The Disappearance of the American." *boundary 2* 25, no. 2 (1998): 35–53; Eduardo Bonilla-Silva, "Race in the World System," *DuBois Review: Social Science Research on Race* 1, no. 1 (2001): 189–94; Hortense Spillers, *Black, White, and In Color: Essays on American Literature and Culture* (Chicago: University of Chicago Press, 2003); Patrick Wolfe, "Settler Colonialism and the Elimination of the Native," *Journal of Genocide Research* 8, no. 4 (2006): 387–409; and Denise Ferreira da Silva, *Toward a Global Idea of Race* (Minneapolis: University of Minnesota Press, 2007).

42. Chanter, *Whose Antigone?*, xiii.

43. See George Steiner, *Antigones* (Oxford: Oxford University Press, 1984).

44. Ariel Dorfman, *Widows* (New York: Seven Stories Press, 2002 [1981]), 6.

45. See James Porter, "Feeling Classical: Classicism and Ancient Literary Criticism," in *Classical Pasts: The Classical Traditions of Greece and Rome*, ed. James Porter (Princeton: Princeton University Press, 2006).

46. Honig, *Antigone, Interrupted*, 32.

47. Ibid.

48. See Pierre Macherey, *A Theory of Literary Production* (New York: Routledge, 2006).

49. Ibid., 97. See also Gayatri Spivak, "Can the Subaltern Speak?," in *Marxism and the Interpretation of Culture*, ed. C. Nelson and L. Grossberg (Chicago: University of Illinois Press, 1988), 81–82.

50. Rajeswari Sunder Rajan. "From Antagonism to Agonism: Shifting Paradigms of Women's Opposition to the State," *Comparative Studies of South Asia, Africa and the Middle East* 30, no. 2 (2010), cited in Honig, *Antigone, Interrupted*, 222n70.

51. Moira Fradinger, "Nomadic Antigone," in *Feminist Readings of Antigone*, ed. Fanny Söderbäck (Albany: State University of New York Press, 2010).

52. Moira Fradinger, "Demanding the Political: *Widows*, or Ariel Dorfman's Antigones," *Hispanic Issues on Line. Special Issue: Whose Voice Is This? Iberian and Latin American Antigones* 13 (2013): 63–64.

53. This is a term I borrow from Françoise Vèrges, "Racial Capitalocene," in *Futures of Black Radicalism*, ed. Gaye Theresa Johnson and Alex Lubin (London: Verso, 2017), 72.

54. My invitation, obviously, echoes the long historical development of critical race theory since its formulation by Kimberlé Crenshaw, Derrieck Bell, Richard Delgado, Mari Matsuda, and Patricia Williams, among other critical legal scholars in the United States. See Kimberlé Crenshaw et al., *Critical Race Theory: The Key Writings that Formed the Movement* (New York: The New Press, 1995). But just as critical theory no longer refers exclusively to the history of the Frankfurt School with which it is historically associated, critical race theory no longer refers exclusively to its otherwise proliferous development in critical legal studies. I understand my injunction to locate the intellectual labor of "critique" in a broader contestation of the coloniality of power, as one that connects queer of color critique, settler colonial critique, decolonial critique, and the black radical tradition, among others, in the same critical space "critical race theory" sought to open in the '80s, and beyond the exclusive study of the law.

Chapter 1

1. I am modifying Robert Fagles's translation here, who translates *metoikos* in this line as: "I am a stranger!" Sophocles, *The Three Theban Plays*, trans. Robert Fagles (New York: Penguin Books, 1984). The first pages in the brackets correspond to Fagles's translation, the second ones to Grene's. Grene captures the positionality of the *metic* within the poetic figure itself. Thus, he has Antigone claim not a specific position but a sort of no-position, in the form of having a home neither with the living nor with the dead.

2. See Jacques Rancière, *Proletarian Nights: The Worker's Dream in Nineteenth Century France*, trans. John Drury (London: Verso, 2012 [1981]); *The Politics of Aesthetics: The Distribution of the Sensible*, trans. Gabriel Rockhill (London: Continuum, 2004); and *The Hatred of Democracy*, trans. Steven Corcoran (London: Verso, 2013).

3. On those debates, see the essays edited by Seyla Benhabib, ed., *Democracy and Difference: Contesting the Boundaries of the Political* (Princeton: Princeton University Press, 1996). On democratic theory's multiple turn to ancient tragedy, see Peter Euben, *The Tragedy of Political Theory: The Road Not Taken* (Princeton: Princeton University Press, 1990), Robert Pirro, *The Politics of Tragedy and Democratic Citizenship* (New York: Continuum, 2011), Steven Johnston, *American Dionysia:*

Violence, Tragedy, and Democratic Politics (Cambridge: Cambridge University Press, 2015), and Demetra Kasimis, *The Perpetual Immigrant and the Limits of Athenian Democracy* (Cambridge: Cambridge University Press, 2018), to name only a few.

4. Walter Benjamin, "The Work of Art in the Age of Mechanical Reproduction," in *Illuminations*, trans. Harry Zohn (New York: Schocken, 1969); Rancière, *Dis-agreement*, 58.

5. Rancière, *Dis-Agreement*, 30.

6. Ibid., 101.

7. Thus, Rancière defines the people (*demos*) that comprise the subject of democracy as "the supplementary part in relation to every count of the parts of the population, making it possible to identify 'the count of the uncounted' with the whole of the community"; Jacques Rancière, *Dissensus: On Politics and Aesthetics*, trans. Steven Corcoran (London: Bloomsbury, 2010), 3.

8. Rancière, *Dis-Agreement*, 12–14.

9. Ibid., 13.

10. Although Rancière is careful to distinguish the *demos* as a theoretical concept from its historical origins in fifth-century Athens, his reference to the lottery system as the institutional arrangement by which the "unqualified" were able to rule, and his citation of *seisachtheia*, among others, make the historical reference less indeterminate. In other words, when Rancière moves from a theory of democracy as subversive *praxis* to a theory of democracy as the institutionalized exercise of power, the theoretical *demos* slips into the historical one. Here, it is important to note that Solon's *seisachtheia*, according to Kurt Raaflaub, paradoxically "prevented the emergence of a political concept of freedom," as his valuation of freedom actually inscribed it within a hierarchy of values that prioritized order and disorder, and justice and injustice. See *The Discovery of Freedom in Ancient Greece* (Chicago: The University of Chicago Press, 2004), 56. Raaflaub claims that the properly political concept of freedom only emerged during the Persian Wars, when the threat of war made the problem of communal independence a political concern.

11. This reflection is taken from Andrés Fabián Henao Castro, "Oedipus at the Border," *Public Books*, November 11, 2017. https://www.publicbooks.org/oedipus-at-the-border/.

12. Kasimis, *The Perpetual Immigrant*, 137.

13. Ibid., 139.

14. Ibid., 20.

15. Ibid., 181.

16. Ibid., 12.

17. Ibid., 183.

18. Here I am inspired by Neil Roberts, *Freedom as Marronage* (Chicago: The University of Chicago Press, 2015), who rightly claims that most Western political theories of freedom acknowledge slavery as the enabling site of freedom's imaginary, only to disavow it and make "freedom" rest elsewhere but in the collective agency

of slaves. Roberts targets Hannah Arendt's and Philip Petit's theories; I extend that critique to Rancière, who offers in my view a more radical theory of democracy than the one inspired by Arendt or Petit.

19. Animalization, it is worth noting, was one of the ways through which Aristotle also tried to naturalize slavery, see Book I of Aristotle's *Politics*, trans. C. D. C. Reeve (Indianapolis: Hackett, 1998), 5–14.

20. Literariry (*littérarité*) is the name given by Rancière to the disorder peculiar to writing in its ability to "introduce dissonance into the communal symphony" to "confuse the destination of living speech"; Jacques Rancière, *The Flesh of Words: The Politics of Writing*, trans. Charlotte Mendell (Stanford: Stanford University Press, 2004), 103. For an excellent analysis of that concept, see Samuel Chambers, *The Lesson of Rancière* (Oxford: Oxford University Press, 2013), 88–122.

21. Edith Hall, "The Sociology of Athenian Tragedy," in *The Cambridge Companion to Greek Tragedy*, ed. P. E. Easterling (Cambridge: Cambridge University Press, 1997), 118.

22. Despite their differences, all four occupied a similar space of speechlessness in Athenian democracy, and their constructed differences feed off each other in spectacular, circular ways, as Chanter demonstrates, *Whose Antigone?*, xxvii.

23. Martel, *The Misinterpellated Subject*, 4.

24. Goldhill, "The Great Dionysia and Civic Ideology."

25. According to Hall, "in the tragic theater individuals whose ethnicity, gender, or status would absolutely debar them from public debate in democratic Athens can address the massed Athenian citizenry" (Hall, *Inventing the Barbarian*, 123). By emphasizing such rhetorical transgressions I do not want to overlook how the Dionysia confirmed ethnic boundaries and worked toward the political hegemony of Athens. What interests me, however, is how the tragic theater operated as a conflictive stage upon which the ideological conception of barbarians as naturally inferior to Greeks clashed with the imagined agencies, speeches, and plots that troubled such inferiority in the Greeks' effort to reproduce it.

26. See Hannah Arendt, *On Revolution* (New York: Penguin, 2006).

27. Richard Halpern is right in highlighting that this theatrical link between politics and aesthetics represents a major difference between Hannah Arendt and Rancière. The former uses the theater to distinguish the political as a realm into itself, separate from the *oikos,* while the latter considers that "theater visibly contaminates [this realm] with precisely the private space of economic production"; Richard Halpern, "Theater and Democratic Thought: Arendt to Rancière," *Critical Inquiry* 37, no. 3 (2011): 567.

28. Rancière, *Dissensus*, 192–211.

29. See Sourvinou-Inwood, "Sophocles' Antigone as a 'Bad Womam,'" and Bennet and Tyrrell, "Sophocles' *Antigone* and Funeral Oratory."

30. See Nicole Loraux, *The Invention of Athens: The Funeral Oration in the Classical City*, trans. Alan Sheridan (New York: Zone Books, 2006 [1986]); and

Jean-Pierre Vernant and Pierre Vidal-Naquet, eds., *Myth and Tragedy in Ancient Greece* (New York: Zone Books, 1988).

31. For this conference, the organizers situated tragedy in a dual setting: first in history, seeking to interpret the text through its context, and second in theory, which had advanced, primarily through the work of deconstruction, a notion of "textuality" that defied the very historical contextualization as the guarantor of its meaning. As Barabara Goff puts it in her account of the theoretical challenge posed to history: "Deconstruction, if pursued, therefore renders difficult any relation with history; it jeopardizes the very notion of historical inquiry into 'documents' or 'evidence' by its insistence both on the metaphoricity of all texts and on the impossibility of there being any 'reality' or 'referent' that is not also constituted by relations of textuality"; Barbara Goff, "Introduction. History, Tragedy, Theory," in *History, Tragedy, Theory: Dialogues on Athenian Drama*, ed. Barbara Goff (Austin: University of Texas Press, 1995), 4. Foley takes up the challenge of confronting historically contextualized interpretations of the play, like Sourvinou-Inwood's and Bennett and Tyrrell's, with deconstructive insight on the metaphoricity of language.

32. Foley, "Tragedy and Democratic Ideology," 132.

33. Ibid., 133, 144.

34. Ibid., 144.

35. Ibid., 145.

36. Nicole Loraux, *The Mourning Voice: An Essay on Greek Tragedy*, trans. Elizabeth Trapnell Rawlings (Ithaca: Cornell University Press, 2002), 19.

37. Bonnie Honig, "Antigone's Laments, Creon's Grief. Mourning, Membership and the Politics of Exception," *Political Theory* 37, no. 1 (2009): 5–7.

38. See Honig, "Antigone's Laments, Creon's Grief," and "Antigone's Two Laws: Greek Tragedy and The Politics of Humanism," *New Literary History* 41, no. 1 (2010): 1–33.

39. Honig, *Antigone, Interrupted*, 142–47.

40. To the best of my knowledge, the other notable exception is Jennet Kirkpatrick, "The Safeguard of Silence: Un-Heroic Resistance in Sophocles' *Antigone*," SSRN eLibrary (2010).

41. Honig, *Antigone, Interrupted*, 165.

42. Martel is right when he claims that Honig's *Antigone Interrupted* performs a misinterpellated reading of *Antigone*, where Antigone is no longer "the tragic heroine that she usually is considered to be" but becomes a subversive conspirator "with her sister, the much-overlooked Ismene," Martel, *The Misinterpellated Subject*, 178n44. For a broader analysis of the many merits of *Antigone Interrupted*, see my review of Honig's book, "Antigone and Democratic Theory—(B.) Antigone, Interrupted," *The Classical Review* 64, no. 2 (2014): 606–608.

43. David Whitehead, *The Ideology of the Athenian Metic* (Cambridge: Cambridge University Press, 1977), 7.

44. Alberto Maffi, "Family and Property Law," in *The Cambridge Companion to Ancient Greek Law*, ed. Michael Gagarin and David Cohen (Cambridge: Cambridge University Press, 2005), 259.

45. Idelber Avelar, *The Letter of Violence. Essays on Narrative, Ethics, and Politics* (New York: Palgrave, 2004), 35.

46. On the broader implications of that representational mediation, see Froma Zeitlin, *Playing the Other: Gender and Society in Classical Greek Literature* (Chicago: University of Chicago Press, 1996).

47. Gsoels-Lorensen, "Antigone, Deportee," 124.

48. Deborah Roberts uses Gérard Genette's concept of the paratext to show how a reader interprets Antigone even before engaging the text. She refers not only to the title, preface, and introduction that accompany the publication of the play, all of which are paratextual to Antigone's script, but also, for example, to the inscription of *Antigone* into a cycle that Sophocles never envisioned as such. Although critical of this gesture, here I follow what Roberts otherwise considers a mistake, taking the "publication [of *Antigone*] with the other Sophoclean plays that tell the story of Oedipus and his family" as contextualizing "the story of Antigone as part of a continuing story and [insisting] on a relationship of one sort or another to the other two plays about the family"; Deborah Roberts, "Reading *Antigone* in Translation: Text, Paratext, Intertext," in *Interrogating Antigone in Postmodern Philosophy and Criticism*, ed. Wilmer and Audronė Žukauskaite (Oxford: Oxford University Press, 2010), 290.

49. See Freddie Rokem, "Antigone Remembers: Dramaturgical Analysis and *Oedipus Tyrannos*," *Theater Research International* 31 (2009): 260–69. My reading follows Stinnerbom's and Rokem's interpretative strategy, yet it differs from them in trying to assess the riddle of the play not by emphasizing Antigone's remembrance—the temporal gap by which the character gets even more inscribed in the Oedipal model of the return of the repressed from which they were trying to separate her—but in the political effects of migration on Antigone's temporally split subjectivity.

50. Mary C. Rawlinson, "Beyond Antigone: Ismene, Gender, and the Right to Life," in *The Returns of Antigone*, ed. Tina Chanter and Sean Kirkland (Albany: State University of New York Press, 2010), 121.

51. Ibid.

52. For a different interpretation of Ismene that I am happy to accept and endorse, even if it contradicts the one that I offer here, as a way to dramatize their historical differences between these two characters, see Rawlinson, "Beyond Antigone."

53. Kennedy, *Immigrant Women in Athens*, 68–87.

54. Cited in ibid., 46.

55. As Kasimis demonstrates in a reading of Euripides's *Ion*, Ion knows he would also be considered a *metic* in Kreousa's house if coming to it as Xouthos's son, and despite Xouthos's status as the sovereign. Such would have also been the

case of Antigone under Jocasta's roof, if we take this mythical Thebes as allegorizing historical Athens. See Demetra Kasimis, "The Tragedy of Blood-Based Membership: Secrecy and the Politics of Immigration in Euripides' *Ion*," *Political Theory* 41, no. 2 (2013): 231–56.

56. Pierre Vidal-Naquet, "Oedipus between Two Cities: An Essay on *Oedipus at Colonus*," in *Myth and Tragedy in Ancient Greece*, ed. Jean-Pierre Vernant and Pierre Vidal-Naquet (New York: Zone Books, 1988).

57. Ibid., 353.

58. Sue Blundell, *Women in Ancient Greece* (London: British Museum Press, 1995), 146.

59. For a broader analysis of *metic* women's multiple social and economic roles, which debunks the myth that they were only or predominantly employed in prostitution, see Kennedy, *Immigrant Women in Athens*, 123–53.

60. Ibid., 40.

61. Chanter, *Whose Antigone?*, 157n55.

62. Cartledge, *The Greeks*, 151.

63. Stefani Engelstein, "Sibling Logic, or Antigone Again," *PMLA* 126, no. 1 (2011): 48. On the contradictory Athenian myth of autochthony, see Nicole Loraux, *Born of the Earth: Myth and Politics in Athens*, trans. Selina Stewart (Ithaca: Cornell University Press, 2000).

64. As Hall claims in her own contextualized reading of *Antigone*, Athenian democracy linked the ruling aristocracy of Thebes with "barbarian" Persia, with whom Thebes sided during the battle of Plataea in 479 BCE. Later, they came to loathe Thebes when hostilities shifted from Persia to Sparta and Thebes "proved to be a crucial site of resistance when Athens succeeded in occupying Boeotia in the 450s and 440s—that is, in the years leading up to the traditional date of the first production of *Antigone*"; Edith Hall, "Antigone and the Internationalization of Theater in Greek Antiquity," in *Antigone on the Contemporary World Stage*, ed. Erin B. Mee and Helene Foley (Oxford: Oxford Classics, 2011), 53. The reference to Persia, and to this story in particular, is all the more relevant if one recontextualizes Antigone's insistence on the burial of her brother by means of this story with the Persian practice "of exposing corpses precisely in order that they can be consumed as carrion by vultures" (Chanter, *Whose Antigone?*, x). Chanter bases this claim on the research of Dietrich Huff, Robert Habenstein, William Lamers, and Shakrokh Razmjou on funeral customs in the ancient world, especially on the Zoroastrian ritual observed by some Iranians. According to Shakrokh Razmjou, "Religion and Burial Customs," in *Forgotten Empire: The World of Ancient* Persia, ed. John Curtis and Nigel Tallis (Berkeley: University of California Press, 2005), 154, Athenians associated the exposure of dead bodies with Persians.

65. There is, significantly, an important metric change when Antigone invokes the story of Intaphrenes's wife, found in the passage where she emphasizes the uniqueness of her brother as the reason she acted. This metric change made

Goethe suspicious of the passage's authenticity. He wrote a letter to Eckermann in 1827 expressing his doubts. The metric change, in my alternative interpretation, calls attention to the fact of her speaking Greek with an accent: she has been wandering around, and her political skills are a product of her foreignness, not of her indigeneity.

66. Honig, *Antigone, Interrupted*, 56.

67. See Judith Butler, *Antigone's Claim: Kinship between Life and Death* (New York: Columbia University Press, 2000); *Precarious Life: The Powers of Mourning and Violence* (New York: Verso, 2004), and chapter 2 of Honig, *Antigone Interrupted*.

68. See Page Dubois, *Torture and Truth* (New York: Routledge, 1991); Cartledge, *The Greeks*; and Isaac, *The Invention of Racism*.

69. Chanter, *Whose Tragedy?*, 91.

70. Ibid., 144.

71. This reflection is taken from Andrés Fabián Henao Castro, "Can the Subaltern Smile? *Oedipus* Without Oedipus," *Contemporary Political Theory* 14, no. 4 (2015): 315–34. The Greek word used to describe the Theban servant in *Oedipus Tyrannos* is *therapon*, which refers to whoever provides "free service" to a master and which the classic Greek language distinguishes from the *doulos,* as the slave proper. Having said that, Oedipus does invoke anxiously the category of the *doulos* when he manifests his own concerns in relation to his potentially ignoble origins in the play. This is what happens when he begins to doubt that Polybus and Merope are his parents by blood. When Oedipus asks the Corinthian messenger, "Was I a child you bought or found when I was given to him?" (OT, 1025 [54]), he is clearly referring to slavery. Moreover, Oedipus explicitly invokes the term *doulos* and even *tridoulos* to frame his concerns about his origins in front of Jocasta. As he claims, "Though I'm proved a slave, thrice slave, and though my mother is thrice slave, you'll not be shown to be of lowly lineage" (OT, 1063 [57]). Furthermore, classical scholars such as Pierre Vernant, Pierre Vidal-Naquet, and Page Dubois, and political philosophers like Michel Foucault, among others, refer to the *therapon* in this play as a slave rather than just a servant in their respective interpretations of *Oedipus Tyrannos*. This use is justifiable not only because the mythical Thebes was a hierarchical regime where the subjects of the king were not considered citizens, but also because in the connections of the play to its democratic audience, the torture inflicted by the sovereign on the servant reflected the juridical procedure to produce truth when democracy dealt with slaves in the Greek *polis*. In following their use, I am not claiming that theirs is the correct translation, but that it is one that has already been used and has acquired an important theoretical force that allows us to interrogate and read other agencies in this play. Highlighting slavery, rather than servitude, my claim is that such translation might be helpful in allowing us to unpack the stratified system of political membership that distinguishes citizens from *metics* and slaves and yet allows us, too, to redistribute the agency in the play in unexpected ways.

72. This reading was inspired by Bonnie Honig's own analysis of the sororal conspiracy that she interpreted in the *agon* between Ismene and Antigone. See Henao Castro, "Can the Subaltern Smile?," 328.

73. Michel Foucault, "Truth and Juridical Forms," in *Power: Essential Works of Foucault 1954–1984*, ed. James Faubion (New York: The New Press, 1994 [1974]).

74. See David Cohen, "Theories of Punishment," in *The Cambridge Companion to Ancient Greek Law*, ed. Michael Gagarin and David Cohen (Cambridge: Cambridge University Press, 2005), 170.

75. Page Dubois, *Torture and Truth*.

76. Honig first offered that analysis in *Democracy and the Foreigner* (Princeton: Princeton University Press, 2001), 53, she returns to it in *Antigone, Interrupted*, 22.

77. According to Pierre Vidal-Naquet and M. M. Austin, the exchange between the two shepherds at the border exemplifies the political transition from the Homeric social structure, based on shepherds pasturing in the distant corners of the city, where foreigners encounter each other, to the Athenian democracy, based on the citizen-farmer. Such transition speaks about the plural positions such servants had within the Homeric structure, given that their physical spaces were not subjected to the same kind of surveillance as happened, for example, with domestic slaves in democracy. See Pierre Vidal-Naquet and M. M. Austin, *Economic & Social History of Ancient Greece: An Introduction* (Berkeley: University of California Press, 1984), 287.

78. Isaac, *The Invention of Racism*, 81.

79. Blundell, *Women in Ancient Greece*, 74.

80. Ibid.

81. Ibid., 96.

82. Cohen, "Theories of Punishment," 259; Kennedy, *Immigrant Women in Athens*, 104.

83. Chanter, *Whose Antigone?*, xx.

84. Mark Griffith, *Sophocles Antigone* (Cambridge: Cambridge University Press, 2010), 308.

Chapter 2

1. Decolonial theory's emphasis on coloniality, understood as an ongoing structure whose lasting effects survive the postcolonial break, is also a response to the challenges that Anne McClintock, in "The Angel of Progress: Pitfalls of the Term 'Postcolonialism,'" *Social Text* 31/32 (1992): 86, and Gayatri Spivak, in *Critique of Postcolonial Reason: Towards a History of the Vanishing Present* (Cambridge: Cambridge University Press, 1999), raise against postcolonial theory's problematic recentering of global history around European colonialism, conferring upon it the siting of proper history (the rest being pre- or post-). Of great importance to this

body of literature is the work of Quijano, who first conceptualized the "coloniality of power" as the imposition of a racial/ethnic system of social classification that permeates what Quijano divides into different areas of social existence: labor, sex, knowledge, authority, (inter)subjectivity, and nature. Absent from Quijano's "coloniality of power" is a more critical interrogation of what María Lugones refers to, as the "colonial/modern gender system," based on patriarchy, heteronormativity, and gender dimorphism yet irreducible to sex (against Quijano's exclusive location of gender in one of his areas of human existence) and equally co-constitutive of all areas of human existence. See María Lugones, "Heterosexualism and the Colonial/Modern Gender System," *Hypatia* 22, no. 1 (2007): 186–209.

2. See Paula Gunn Allen, *The Sacred Hoop: Recovering the Feminine in American Indian Traditions* (Boston: Beacon Press, 1992), Oyèrónkẹ́ Oyěwùmí, *The Invention of Women: Making an African Sense of Western Gender Discourses* (Minneapolis: University of Minnesota Press, 1997), and Lugones, "Heterosexualism."

3. Lugones, "Heterosexualism," 196. Eurocentered capitalism should be understood, then, as the racial-ethnic system of social classification that, in conjunction with the modern/colonial gender system, explains the global distribution of the different labor regimes that capitalism combines under the global hegemony of wage labor. One should not, however, understand coerced labor regimes as "precapitalist" when wrongly collapsing wage labor and capitalism in the geography of eighteenth-century Europe. See for instance, Immanuel Wallerstein, *The Modern World-System: Capitalist Agriculture and the Origins of the European World-Economy in the Sixteenth Century* (New York: Academic Press, 1974). Such a collapse erases forms of unwaged labor exploitation that cannot be considered epiphenomenal to the consolidation of Eurocentered capitalism, as is the case, for instance, with the unwaged exploitation of domestic labor, which is absolutely crucial for the accumulation of capital. See Silvia Federici, *Caliban and the Witch: Women, the Body, and Primitive Accumulation* (New York: Autonomedia, 2004), and Wilma Dunaway, "Commodity-Chains and Gendered Exploitation: Rescuing Women from the Periphery of World-Systems Thought," in *The Modern/Colonial/Capitalist World-System: Global Processes, Antisystemic Movements, and the Geopolitics of Knowledge*, ed. Ramón Grosfoguel and Ana Margarita Cervantes-Rodriguez (Westport: Greenwood Press, 2002). In addition, this conceptualization wrongly displaces, temporally and geographically, the relations between waged forms of labor and other labor regimes capitalism generated in the colonies. As Robinson, *Black Marxism*, 177–205, and Dale Tomich, *Slavery in the Circuit of Sugar* (Albany: State University of New York Press, 2015), have demonstrated, plantation slavery in the so-called New World was a product of merchant capitalism, not a precondition. This means that slavery, not just citizenship and *metoikia*, changed with the hegemonic consolidation of Eurocentered capitalism during the long sixteenth century (1450–1650).

4. See Enrique Dussel, *The Invention of the Americas* (New York: Continuum, 1995).

5. According to Kennedy, *Immigrant Women in Athens*, 7, "the terminology of *metoikia* disappears from the historical record by 300BCE and seems to have been fading in importance even by the 320s."

6. The first ship that carried slaves to North America landed in the English settlement of Jamestown in the colony of Virginia in 1619.

7. For an analysis of slavery in antiquity I recommend Milton Meltzer, *Slavery I: From the Rise of Western Civilization to the Renaissance* (Chicago: Cowles, 1972); Cartledge, *The Greeks*, and Benjamin Isaac, *The Invention of Racism in Classical Antiquity* (Princeton: Princeton University Press, 2004); and Page Dubois, *Slavery: Antiquity and Its Legacy* (Oxford: Oxford University Press, 2009). For approaches that focus more on modernity, I recommend Orlando Patterson, *Slavery and Social Death: A Comparative Study* (Cambridge: Harvard University Press, 1982); Jennifer Morgan, *Laboring Women: Reproduction and Gender in New World Slavery* (Philadelphia: University of Pennsylvania Press, 2004); and Alys Eve Weinbaum, *The Afterlife of Reproductive Slavery: Biocapitalism and Black Feminism's Philosophy of History* (Durham: Duke University Press, 2019).

8. Wynter, "Unsettling the Coloniality," 283–303. The first modernity corresponds, broadly, to the long sixteenth century.

9. According to Alison Games, *Witchcraft in Early North America* (New York: Rowman and Littlefield, 2010), 23–24, smallpox was the worst, but influenza, measles, diphtheria, mumps, and chicken pox also contributed to the devastating genocide. To name one example, it reduced the Huron population from thirty-five thousand in the early seventeenth century to ten thousand by 1640.

10. Robinson, *Black Marxism*, 81.

11. Wolfe, "Settler Colonialism," 388.

12. Indigenous peoples, however, continued to be enslaved in Canada. Still under the British Empire, Canada officially abolished slavery in August 1834, when the Slavery Abolition Act came into effect. The United States officially abolished slavery with the Thirteenth Amendment to its Constitution in 1865. In neither of these cases, however, did the abolition of slavery represent the abolition of the racialized system of valuation that slavery helped to sediment. On Canada, see Robert Davis and Mark Zannis, *The Genocide Machine in Canada: The Pacification of the North* (Montreal: Black Rose Books, 1973); Alfred Taiaiake, *Wasáse: Indigenous Pathways of Actions and Freedom* (Peterborough: Broadview Press, 2005); and Glen Sean Coulthard, *Red Skin, White Masks: Rejecting the Colonial Politics of Recognition* (Minneapolis: University of Minnesota Press, 2014).

13. Although both Orlando Patterson and Hortense Spillers refer to the enslavement of indigenous peoples in their respectively most influential texts, their theories are often taken to be exclusively about the antiblackness that modern slavery engendered. Notwithstanding the fact that black people were enslaved for longer and under a very different logic, it is important not to erase the fact that indigenous peoples were also enslaved under modern conditions of capitalist accumulation. See

Andrés Reséndez, *The Other Slavery: The Uncovered Story of Indian Enslavement in America* (New York: Houghton Mifflin Harcourt, 2016). I thus include them, not in order to erase the historical differences between these two logics, but in order to stress a shared expulsion from the order of the human that comes to overdetermine their colonial immobilization across the slave/*metic*/citizen triad.

14. Patterson, *Slavery and Social Death*, 5.

15. For a genealogy of contemporary forms of confinement targeting people of color that extends back to modern slavery and colonial forms of racialization, see Simone Browne, *Dark Matters: On the Surveillance of Blackness* (Durham: Duke University Press, 2015).

16. To unpack this subhumanized form of commodification, and the ways in which it includes the "humanization" of the slave, as one of the ways through which it operates, I recommend the work of Zakiyyah Jackson, "Losing Manhood: Animality and Plasticity in the (Neo)Slave Narrative," *Qui Parle* 25, no. 1–2 (2016): 95–136.

17. See Fanny Söderbäck, ed., *Feminist Readings of Antigone* (Albany: State University of New York Press, 2010).

18. On the roles of ancient Athenian women, see Blundell, *Women in Ancient Greece*, 95–169; and Sarah Pomeroy, *Goddesses, Whores, Wives, and Slaves: Women in Classical Antiquity* (New York: Schocken Books, 1995), 79–127.

19. Butler, *Antigone's Claim*, 77.

20. Ibid.

21. Lacan claims that it is "precisely because [this passage] carries with it the suggestion of a scandal, [that] this passage is of interest to us"; Jacques Lacan, *Book VII. The Ethics of Psychoanalysis 1959–1960*, trans. Dennis Porter (New York: Norton, 1997), 255. One way of rearticulating the main concern of this book, is to say that precisely because Antigone's claim to have buried Polyneices on the basis that he was not Eteocles's slave, suggests no scandal at all, that such passage is, by contrast, of interest to me.

22. G. W. F. Hegel, *Phenomenology of Spirit*, trans. Terry Pinkard (Cambridge: Cambridge University Press, 2018), 263. I will return to this claim in chapter 4.

23. Jacques, Lacan, *The Ethics of Psychoanalysis*, 279.

24. Luce Irigaray, *Speculum of the Other Women*, trans. Gillian Gill. (Ithaca: Cornell University Press, 1985), 216.

25. Butler, *Antigone's Claim*, 2; emphasis in original.

26. Ibid., 53.

27. Hortense Spillers, "Mama's Baby, Papa's Maybe: An American Grammar Book," *Diacritics* 17 no. 1 (1987): 74.

28. On the relationship of slavery to the proprietorial conception of individual freedom, characteristic of capitalist modernity, see Robert Cover, *Justice Accused: Antislavery and the Judicial Process* (New Haven: Yale University Press, 1975); Orlando Patterson, *Freedom, Slavery, and the Modern Construction of Rights* (Johannesburg: University of Witwatersrand, 1994); Sora Han, "Slavery as Contract: Betty's Case

and the Question of Freedom," *Law and Literature* 27, no. 3 (2015): 395–416; and Christina Sharpe, *Monstrous Intimacies: Making Post-Slavery Subjects* (Durham: Duke University Press, 2010).

29. Holland, *The Erotic Life of Racism*, 62.

30. Ibid., 5.

31. Butler, *Antigone's Claim*, 73.

32. As Hartman claims, "The law's selective recognition of slavery personhood failed to acknowledge the matter of sexual violation, specifically rape, and thereby defined the identity of the slave female by the negation of sentience, and invulnerability to sexual violation, and the negligibility of her injuries"; Saidiya Hartman, *Scenes of Subjection: Terror, Slavery, and the Self-Making of Nineteenth-Century America* (Oxford: Oxford University Press, 1997), 97.

33. Patricia Williams, *The Alchemy of Race and Rights* (Cambridge: Harvard University Press, 1991), 217. Along the same lines, see Grace Hong's excellent critique of Patterson, in *Death beyond Disavowal: The Impossible Politics of Difference* (Minneapolis: The University of Minnesota Press, 2015), 101–104.

34. Judith Butler, *Bodies that Matter: On the Discursive Limits of Sex* (New York: Routledge, 1993), 123.

35. Ibid. Here it is worth remembering that the term *miscegenation*—from the Latin *miscere* (to mix) and *genus* (kind)—was first popularized in pro-slavery and pro-segregationist Civil War propaganda pamphlets.

36. Judith Butler, *Undoing Gender* (New York: Routledge, 2004), 122.

37. Cited in ibid., 103.

38. For a more historically nuanced analysis of racialized sexuality and the antiblack violent forms that it takes, see Aliyyah Abdur-Rahman, *Against the Closet: Black Political Longing and the Erotics of Race* (Durham: Duke University Press, 2012); Patrice Douglass, "Black Feminist Theory for the Dead and Dying," *Theory & Event* 21, no. 1 (2018): 106–23; and Weinbaum, *The Afterlife of Reproductive Slavery*. On the interrelated racialized sexual violence that is specific to indigeneity, see Andrea Smith, *Conquest: Sexual Violence and American Indian Genocide* (Durham: Duke University Press, 2015); and Sarah Deer, *The Beginning and End of Rape: Confronting Sexual Violence in Native America* (Minneapolis: University of Minnesota Press, 2015).

39. Hartman, *Scenes of Subjection*, 97.

40. Spillers, "Mama's Baby, Papa's Maybe," 66.

41. See Angela Davis, *Women, Race, and Class* (New York: Vintage, 1981), 222–44; Hortense Spillers, *Black, White, and in Color*, 206, and Lugones, "Heterosexualism," 188–99.

42. I am, obviously, oversimplifying here. Lacan's theory of the subject has been more fully analyzed by others: I recommend Slavoj Žižek, *The Sublime Object of Ideology* (London: Verso, 1989), Jean Copjec, *Read My Desire: Lacan Against the Historicists* (Cambridge: MIT Press, 1994), and Alenka Zupančič, *Ethics of the Real: Kant, Lacan* (London: Verso, 2000). What the more Foucauldian-inspired performative

theory of gender adds, to such understanding, is the fact that subjectivity precedes language-use. Actually, the sociosymbolic construction of gender precedes conception, as it already organizes a whole set of desires and aversions that are constructed even prior to the pregnancy. Those regulations continue to work throughout the pregnancy itself, and the subject-to-be is already the receptor of social interpellations. This is what happens during the gender-ritual of the ultrasound to which Butler, in *Bodies That Matter*, 8, famously referred as the "girling of the girl." This and many more interpellations sediment a form of gender identity that exists prior to the articulation of the infant's first words.

43. Spillers, "Mama's Baby, Papa's Maybe," 67.

44. As a queer nonblack Latino, I am here honoring black people's demand for those of us who are not black to refuse the use of this word.

45. Angela Davis, *An Autobiography* (New York: International Publishers, 1988), 96.

46. Toni Morrison, *Beloved* (New York: Vintage Books, 2007 [1987]), 72.

47. Spillers, "Mama's Baby, Papa's Maybe," 80.

48. Butler, *Bodies that Matter*, 125.

49. Butler, *Antigone's Claim*, 55.

50. Elsewhere, I offer a reading of Butler's return to *Antigone* in *Precarious Life* (2004), where I claim that Butler does succeed in situating *Antigone* within a settler-colonial context, making ethics and politics inseparable. See Andrés Fabián Henao Castro, "Can the Palestinian Antigone Grieve? A Political Reinterpretation of Judith Butler's Ethical Turn," *Settler Colonial Studies* 10, no. 1 (2020): 94–109.

51. Roger Just, *Women in Athenian Law and Life* (New York: Routledge, 1989), 95.

52. Ibid., 98.

53. Helene Foley, *Female Acts in Greek Tragedy* (Princeton: Princeton University Press, 2001), 33.

54. Gilles Deleuze and Félix Guattari, *Anti-Oedipus: Capitalism and Schizophrenia*, trans. Robert Hurley, Mark Seem, and Helene R. Lane (New York: Continuum, 2004).

55. Based on passages from Demosthenes and Aristotle, Evangélos Karabélias, *L'épiclerat attique* (Athens: Académie d'Athènes, 2002), 84 concludes that unlike *metics*, for whom the institution of the *epikleros* still operated—despite the barriers separating the *politai* from the *metoikoi* and even if the regulations were not identical to those governing the Athenian *oikos*—slaves were entirely excluded, constituting another opposition between the free and the enslaved. As Kennedy, *Immigrant Women in Athens*, 2 argues, "An independent metic woman was recognized in law as being 'her own master' (*autê autês kuria*), and she was assumed to have been unmarried or widowed and without a male relative to stand as her representative."

56. Spillers, "Mama's Baby, Papa's Maybe," 74.

57. Ibid., 76.

58. Thus, Spillers, claims, "We could go so far as to entertain the very real possibility that sexuality, as a term of implied relatedness, is dubiously appropriate, manageable, or accurate to *any* of the familiar arrangements under a system of enslavement, from the master's family to the captive enclave"; "Mama's Baby, Papa's Maybe," 76. Holland claims that we should revise Spillers's thesis, as it might be true that sexuality as a term of implied relatedness is dubiously appropriate for the master's family but not so for the captive enclave; see *Erotic Life of Racism*, 88.

59. Hartman, *Scenes of Subjection*, 88.

60. Ibid., 84.

61. Cited in ibid., 85.

62. Ibid., 97. Hartman is here problematizing a certain interpretation of Spillers's claim, that the "Middle Passage" constituted a sort of historical materialization of Sigmund Freud's otherwise figurative notion of the "oceanic," in which the enslaved was "neither female, nor male, as both subjects are taken into 'account' as *quantities*. The female in 'Middle Passage,' as the apparently smaller physical mass, occupies 'less room' in a directly translatable money economy. But she is, nevertheless, quantifiable by the same rules of accounting as her male counterpart"; Spillers, "Mama's Baby, Papa's Maybe," 72.

63. As Hartman, *Scene of Subjection*, 95, claims, sexual violence "did not decrease productivity or diminish value—on the contrary, it might actually increase the captive's magnitude of value—nor did it, apparently, offend the principles of Christian enlightenment." Jared Sexton has since taken Spillers's and Hartman's insights a step further, when he categorically claims that "there is no interracial sexual relationship." Here, Sexton's claim both mirrors and yet radicalizes Lacan's famous claim, that "there is no sexual relationship." This is, first, because according to Sexton the interracial reifies the schemes of racial categorization that it seeks to displace; second, because within this frame the sexual is morally displaced and sanitized through a disciplinary emphasis on reproduction; and third, because there is actually no relationship when multiracialism "refuses to countenance the fissure between the intermingling of racialized bodies and the social-symbolic effort to mediate racial antagonism at the levels of sexual practice and identity formation"; Jared Sexton, *Amalgamation Schemes: Antiblackness and the Critique of Multiracialism* (Minneapolis: University of Minnesota Press, 2008), 154.

64. Hartman, *Lose Your Mother*, 78.

65. Ibid.

66. Notice here how other excellent pluralizations of *Antigone*, such as Stefani Engelstein's analysis of the play through the undertheorized lenses of sibling logic, inclusive of her own engagement with Bracha Ettinger's "matrixial borderspace," fails also to confront the differential violence visited upon captive wombs. Like Ettinger, whose interpretation is also radically influenced by feminist theory's engagement with *Antigone*, Engelstein takes for granted the differences between citizens, *metics,* and slaves, and fails to confront the undoing of siblinghood under

what Joy James adequately refers to, as the captive maternal. See Bracha Ettinger, *The Matrixial Borderspace* (Minneapolis: University of Minnesota Press, 2006); and Joy James, "The Captive Maternal and Abolitionism: A Tribute to Erica Garner," in *Carceral Cultures Conference*, a conversation with Robyn Maynard at Simon Fraser University, March 3, 2018. https://www.thesocialjusticecentre.org/blog/2018/3/11/the-captive-maternal-and-abolitionism-a-tribute-to-erica-garner.

67. Jean Copjec, *Imagine There's No Women* (Cambridge: MIT Press, 2004), 5.

68. Jean Copjec, *Read My Desire: Lacan Against the Historicists* (Cambridge: MIT Press, 1994), 6.

69. See Michel Foucault, *History of Sexuality: An Introduction* (New York: Vintage, 1976 [1990]). I will expand on this in chapter 3.

70. Copjec, *Read My Desire*, 8.

71. When Polemarchus voiced this argument in Book I of Plato's *Republic* he was voicing the standard definition of justice for the *polis*. See Plato, *Republic*, trans. C. D. C. Reeve (Indianapolis: Hackett, 2004), and Mary Whitlock Blundell, *Helping Friends and Harming Enemies: A Study in Sophocles and Greek Ethics* (Cambridge: Cambridge University Press, 1991).

72. Actually, Lacan thought very little of Hegel's interpretation of *Antigone*, claiming that nowhere does Hegel appear to be as "weak" as in his own reading of the play, see Lacan, *Ethics of Psychoanalysis*, 249.

73. Ibid., 244.

74. Tiresias orders Creon to unbury Antigone first and then to bury Polyneices, to show that he has learned to privilege the living over the dead. He succeeds in persuading Creon. But Creon inverts the temporality of the order and attends to Polyneices first. Perhaps he does not know that Antigone is at risk of dying and is more worried about the fact that Polyneices is at risk of physically disappearing. Perhaps, as Honig claims against Patchen Markell's interpretation, Creon is still plotting, choosing "not only to try (and fail) to undo his deed, as Markell suggests, but also or instead to *permit* the deed to continue to outrace his efforts to undo it—Antigone dies in the time it takes Creon to get there, having stopped first to bury Polyneices." Markell reads the failure of Creon's acts to get the temporal order of the reparations right as tragedy's ultimate commitment to the contingency and finitude of human agency, in which the consequences of our acts always exceed our human efforts to control them. See Markell, *Bound by Recognition*. Honig takes that insight in a more conspiratorial route. But perhaps, via the interpretative path that I am following, Creon fears the powerful figuration of slave agency that he just forced Polyneices's flesh to bear. What if there is not only more agency in Creon's decision to temporally rearrange the order of the reparations, as Honig suggests, but also more agency in the slavery that, one could said, he forced Polyneices to endure after death? What if what Creon realizes, and fears the most—even more than the continuity of Antigone's *atè*, her marriage to Haemon represents—is for the audience to notice that the social life of the citizens of the *polis* depends on

the social death of slaves, a structural form of dependency that endows them with the capacity to destroy it?

75. Lacan, *Ethics of Psychoanalysis*, 277.

76. Sigmund Freud, *Beyond the Pleasure Principle and Other Writings*, trans. John Reddick (New York: Penguin, 2003 [1920]).

77. Gilles Deleuze, "Coldness and Cruelty," in *Masochism*, trans. Jean McNeil and Aude Willm (New York: Zone Books, 1991), 111.

78. Ibid., 113.

79. Ibid., 114.

80. Lacan, *Ethics of Psychoanalysis*, 282.

81. Ibid., 280.

82. Copjec, *Imagine There's No Women*, 18.

83. Ibid.

84. Ibid.

85. In *Ethics of the Real*, 217–20, Alenka Zupančič argues that classical ethics cannot be understood under the more properly modern "freedom or death" structure of the ethical forced choice, only under the structure of "your money or your life." Contra Copjec, Zupančič considers Antigone a classical, rather than modern figure, because of the ways in which she realizes her own desire. Antigone thus "gives (away) everything in order to preserve some final 'having.' In the end, she realizes herself in this final 'having;' she merges with it, she becomes herself the signifier of the desire which runs through her, she incarnates this desire" (258–59). By contrast to Antigone, Sygne de Coûfontaine takes the realization of her desire to the extreme of having to give up "on this final 'having'" as the very condition through which she does not give up on her desire (259).

86. Copjec, *Imagine There's No Women*, 42.

87. Ibid., 38.

88. Ibid., 39.

89. Unlike Copjec, *Imagine There's No Women*, 42, who claims that "Antigone does not give reasons for her love," Butler focuses on the reasons that she does give, on Antigone's citation of Intaphrenes's wife's speech, where she claims to have done it on the basis of her brother's irreplaceable singularity. As I claimed before, in that citation Antigone cannot but fail to secure the singularity of her desire, as the incestuous history of her family disperses her desire. Honig unpacks even more politically salient functions in the form that Antigone gives to her refusal to give way on her desire, by more fully interrogating the politics of that citational scene. According to Honig's argument, Antigone's dirge mimics Pericles's Funeral Oration when she suggests that Polyneices's irreplaceability rests in her parent's death. In this foundational democratic text of Athens, Pericles urged parents "if still of childbearing age not to mourn too long over their lost sons but to have more children to replace them" (Honig, *Antigone, Interrupted*, 129). The comic element of this parody rests in equalizing death (in the case of Antigone) with

old age (in the case of Pericles), therefore appropriating the democratic motto of replaceability—equality—for the purpose of advancing an aristocratic emphasis on irreplaceability—the uniqueness of her brother. She also mimicked Creon, appropriating for herself the prerogative Creon "reserved for his son and perhaps for all sons": the fact that, like Haemon, of whom Creon coldly claimed, "there are other fields for him to plow" (A, 569 [184]), Antigone has "also other fields for *her* plow" (Honig, *Antigone Interrupted*, 130; emphasis in the original). Finally, Antigone also cites Herodotus's story, a citation that Lacan, *Ethics of Psychoanalysis*, 255, symptomatically dismisses as insignificant. This is the story of a woman, referred to only as Intaphrenes's wife, who invoked the same reasons Antigone used to justify her privilege of the natal (Polyneices) over the conjugal (Haemon) family. By quoting Intaphrenes's story, Honig argues, Antigone puts "Creon on trial" by highlighting the difference between the responses given by the two sovereigns: Darius and Creon, the first one responding with piety to Intaphrenes's wife's reasoning, granting her the life of her brother and that of her eldest son, while Creon resolved it in violence (Honig, *Antigone, Interrupted*, 137). All of this gets lost when we move from the social to the Symbolic, and the purity of the ethical is only achieved on the condition that the political is repressed.

90. Frantz Fanon, *Black Skin, White Masks*, trans. Richard Philcox (New York: Grove Press, 2008), 195n.10.

91. Zupančič, *Ethics of the Real*, 257.

92. Although the list of her anticipated losses is sometimes portrayed as endless, as is her lament itself (first of all by Creon), her list is actually quite concrete and rather limited to all those things through which she is socially valued in Greek antiquity. In other words, she lists what she could have had, not what she would not have been allowed to have had she continued living. Hence, although I agree with Zupančič, *Ethics of the Real*, 257, in that her listing of losses "realizes this virtual remainder through its loss, by establishing it as lost," and thus "puts an end to the metonymy of desire," I disagree with her, when she adds that she puts an end to that metonymy "by realizing, in one go, the infinite potential of this metonymy." The metonymy of Antigone's desire is not infinite, it is, rather, quite circumscribed, and although one can still establish some modality of infinity within that circumscription, politics is pretty much at stake in the production of a very different series of infinites.

93. Hartman, *Lose Your Mother*, 79.

94. Laurent Dubois, *Haiti: The Aftershocks of History* (New York: Picador, 2012), 21.

95. Hartman, *Lose Your Mother*, 68.

96. Assata Shakur, *Assata Shakur: An Autobiography* (Chicago: Lawrence Hill Books, 1987), 52; Karl Marx and Friedrich Engels, "Manifesto of the Communist Party," in *The Marx-Engels Reader*, ed. Robert C. Tucker (New York: W. W. Norton, 1978).

97. Fred Moten, *In the Break: The Aesthetics of the Black Radical Tradition* (Minnesota: University of Minnesota Press, 2003), 3.

98. Frank Wilderson, *Red, White & Black: Cinema and the Structure of U.S. Antagonisms* (Durham: Duke University Press, 2010), 1.

99. J. M. Bernstein, "'The Celestial Antigone the Most Resplendent Figure Ever to Have Appeared on Earth:' Hegel's Feminism," in *Feminist Readings of Antigone*, ed. Fanny Söderbäck (Albany: State University of New York Press, 2010), 112. On Tiresias, see Nicole Loraux, *The Experiences of Tiresias: The Feminine and the Greek Man*, trans. Paula Wissig (Princeton: Princeton University Press, 1995). Bernstein, it is worth clarifying, also misses Tiresias's moment.

100. Bernstein, "'The Celestial Antigone," 115.

101. Since Michel Foucault's *History of Sexuality*, queer theory has turned to ancient Greece in order to denaturalize heteronormativity, historicize homosexuality/queerness, and de-pathologize the eroticization of life, notably in the work of David Halperin, "Is There a History of Sexuality?" *History and Theory* 28, no. 3 (1989): 257–74. The history of sexuality and the consequent identification of the historical processes by which homo- and heterosexuality were invented in modernity, are a good warning against the reclamation of ancient Tiresias as a trans figure. Tiresias is not a transgender figure, to the extent that it is the gods who turn him into a woman. He is assigned a different gender and has to live under the force of that assignation. Transgender and gender nonbinary people, by contrast, choose their gender identity and engage in an alternative political process of subjectification through the process of that (dis)identification. And yet, social orders constantly refuse to recognize transgender and gender nonbinary people's choices, de facto assigning them a gender that they did not choose. It is with regard to this problematic assignation, among others, that Tiresias can be said to contribute to the gender trouble of this play and be of relevance, to trans theory.

102. Chanter, *Whose Antigone?*, xxvii.

103. C. Riley Snorton, *Black on Both Sides: A Racial History of Trans Identity* (Minneapolis: University of Minnesota Press, 2017), 57.

104. Hartman, *Scenes of Subjection*, 9. See also Harriet Jacobs, *Incidents in the Life of a Slave Girl* (Cambridge: Harvard University Press, 1987), 277n1, who takes the phrase "loophole of retreat" from William Cowper's "The Task," which appeared as an epigraph to "The Curtain," a column in *Freedom's Journal*.

105. Snorton, *Black on Both Sides*, 70.

106. Ibid., 69.

107. On the ways in which race affects our political analysis of disability, and hence on the political significance of the additional terminology of "debility," see Jasbir Puar, *The Right to Maim: Debility, Capacity, Disability* (Durham: Duke University Press, 2017).

108. Ellen Samuels, cited in Snorton, *Black on Both Sides*, 84.

109. Snorton, *Black on Both Sides*, 84.

110. David Marriott, *Haunted Life: Visual Culture and Black Modernity* (New Brunswick, NJ: Rutgers University Press, 2007), 231.

111. Harriet Washington, *Medical Apartheid: The Dark History of Medical Experimentation on Black Americans from Colonial Times to the Present* (New York: Doubleday, 2006); Snorton, *Black on Both Sides*, 48.

112. On slavery's role in the development of the modern technologies of gender assignment, see the excellent first chapter of Snorton, *Black on Both Sides*; and Washington, *Medical Apartheid*.

113. Thomas Laqueur, *The Work of the Dead* (Princeton: Princeton University Press, 2015), 133.

114. Hannah Arendt, *The Human Condition* (Chicago: University of Chicago Press, 1998), 97.

115. Lee Edelman, *No Future. Queer Theory and the Death Drive* (Durham: Duke University Press, 2004), 105.

116. Ibid., 106.

117. Ibid., 108.

118. Fanon, *Black Skin, White Masks*, 92.

119. Moten, *In the Break*, 14.

120. Edelman, *No Future*, 30.

121. Lee Edelman, "The Part for the (W)hole: Baldwin, Homophobia, and the Fantasmatics of 'Race,'" in *Homographesis: Essays in Gay Literary and Cultural Theory* (New York: Routledge, 1994).

122. For a critique of Edelman's interpretation of James Baldwin, see Moten, *In the Break*, 185–92.

123. James Baldwin, "The Black Boy Looks at the White Boy," in *Nobody Knows My Name: More Notes of a Native Son* (New York: Dell, 1961), 172.

124. Ibid.

125. José Esteban Muñoz, *Cruising Utopia: The Then and There of Queer Futurity* (New York: New York University Press, 2009) raises a different, albeit related, critique of Edelman's whiteness. For an alternative political interpretation of Edelman's antisocial thesis, which mobilizes the radical queerness of his antifuturism against the imperial geopolitics of settler colonialism, see Heike Schotten, *Queer Terror: Life, Death and Desire in the Settler Colony* (New York: Columbia University Press, 2018).

126. Frank Wilderson, "The Prison Slave as Hegemony's (Silent) Scandal," in *Warfare in the American Homeland: Policing and Prison in a Penal Democracy*, ed. Joy James (Durham: Duke University Press, 2007), 32.

127. Calvin Warren, *Onticide: Afropessimism, Queer Theory, & Ethics* (Ill Will Editions, 2015), 6. Warren's initial thesis has been further developed in Calvin Warren, *Ontological Terror: Blackness, Nihilism, and Emancipation* (Durham: Duke University Press, 2018), in which the racialized dimension of antiblackness remains problematically prioritized in Warren's quarrel with black feminist intersectionality.

128. See Patrick Johnson, "'Quare' Studies, or (Almost) Everything I know about Queer Studies I Learned from My Grandmother," in *Black Queer Studies: A Critical Anthology*, ed. Patrick Johnson and Mae Henderson (Durham: Duke University Press, 2005), 125–28; Sabine Lang, "Various Kinds of Two-Spirit People: Gender Variance and Homosexuality in Native American Communities," in *Two-Spirit People: Native American Gender Identity, Sexuality, and Spirituality*, ed. Sue-Ellen Jacobs, Wesley Thomas, and Sabine Lang (Chicago: University of Illinois, 1997); and Qwo-Li Driskill, "(*Aseti Ayetl*): Cherokee Two Spirit People Reimagining Nation," in *Queer Indigenous Studies: Critical Interventions in Theory, Politics, and Literature*, ed. Qwo-Li Driskill, Chris Finley, Brian Joseph Gilley, and Scott Laurie Morgensen (Tucson: The University of Arizona Press, 2011).

129. Michael Warren, ed., *Fear of a Queer Planet* (Minneapolis: University of Minnesota Press, 1993).

130. Jasbir Puar, *Terrorist Assemblages: Homonationalism in Queer Times* (Durham: Duke University Press, 2007).

131. Cathy Cohen, "Punks, Bulldaggers, and Welfare Queens: The Radical Potential of Queer Politics," *GLQ* 3, no. 4 (1997): 437–65; and Roderick Ferguson, *Aberrations in Black: Towards a Queer of Color Critique* (Minneapolis: University of Minnesota Press, 2003).

132. See Combahee River Collective, "A Statement," in *Words of Fire: An Anthology of African-American Feminist Thought*, ed. Beverly Guy-Sheftall (New York: The New York Press, 1995 [1977]); Gloria Hull, Patricia Bell-Scott, and Barbara Smith, *All the Women Are White, All the Blacks Are Men, But Some of Us Are Brave: Black Women's Studies* (New York: Feminist Press, 1982); and Patricia Hill Collins, *Black Feminist Thought: Knowledge, Consciousness, and the Politics of Empowerment* (New York: Routledge, 1990).

133. Hartman, *Scenes of Subjection*, 84; Snorton, *Black on Both Sides*, 69.

134. See José Esteban Muñoz, *Disidentifications: Queers of Color and the Performance of Politics* (Minneapolis: University of Minnesota Press, 1999); Siobhan B. Somerville, *Queering the Color Line: Race and the Invention of Homosexuality in American Culture* (Durham: Duke University Press, 2000); Patrick Johnson and Mae Henderson, eds., *Black Queer Studies: A Critical Anthology* (Durham: Duke University Press, 2005); Scott Laurie Morgensen, *Spaces Between Us: Queer Settler Colonialism and Indigenous Decolonization* (Minneapolis: University of Minnesota Press, 2011); and Qwo-Li Driskill et al., *Queer Indigenous Studies: Critical Interventions in Theory, Politics, and Literature* (Tucson: The University of Arizona Press, 2011).

135. See Dave Hunsaker, "To Mock the Spirits: Yup'ik Antigone in the Arctic," in *Antigone on the Contemporary World Stage*, ed. Erin B. Mee and Helene Foley (Oxford: Oxford Classics, 2011); Bryan Doerries, *Antigone in Ferguson*, Theater of War Productions, Ferguson, 2019. https://theaterofwar.com/projects/antigone-in-ferguson.

136. *Yup'ik Antigone* and *Antigone in Ferguson* are not the sole *Antigones* to represent Antigone as either black or indigenous in the Americas. An indigenous

Antigone was also imagined by the cultural group Yuyachkani in Peru, when José Watanabe translated and readapted the play in 2000. In Peru, an indigenous Antigone addresses multiple violences, as the subversive burial of the unburied corpse confronts the dirty war between the Peruvian state and Shining Path. A black Antigone in the Americas was probably first performed in Haiti, when Félix Morisseau-Leroy produced *Antigòn an Kreyòl* (1953). In Morisseau-Leroy's play Antigone is a Vodou goddess who speaks in Creole, not in order to reject modernity but in order to assert an alternative popular modernity to the aristocratic French-educated model imposed by the Haitian elite.

Chapter 3

1. Here, I should recall Janusz Glowacki's *Antigone in New York* (New York: Samuel French, 1997 [1993]) who represents Antigone as the Puerto Rican homeless, Anita, who buries her lover Paulie, a U.S. citizen, in a co-opted park in New York with the aid of Sasha, another homeless migrant of Russian origin. Glowacki here connects neoliberal gentrification and the criminalization of homelessness, with the many forms in which public space is lost to capital. Capitalism's enclosures, inclusive of the settler colonization of indigenous territories, are historically related to the United States' continuous occupation of Puerto Rico, and replayed in the racialized violence of gentrification.

2. See Nicholas De Genova and Nathalie Peutz, *The Deportation Regime: Sovereignty, Space, and the Freedom of Movement* (Durham: Duke University Press, 2010); and Hagar Kotef, *Movement and the Ordering of Freedom: On Liberal Governances of Mobility* (Durham: Duke University Press, 2015).

3. See Todd Miller, *Empire of Borders: The Expansion of the US Border around the World* (London: Verso, 2019).

4. Kevin Bales, *Disposable People: New Slavery in the Global Economy* (Berkeley: University of California Press, 1999).

5. Thus, by the end of the nineteenth century, the so-called *cazadores de indios* (Indian hunters) in Chile could sell indigenous men's testicles and indigenous women's breasts for one pound each and indigenous children's ears for half a pound, in total impunity, in a necro-economy of body parts that has its neoliberal variation in today's transnational traffic of organs. See Patricio Guzmán, *The Pearl Button* (film, 2015). Here, I should also recall César Rengifo, *La fiesta de los moribundos* (Caracas: Asociación de Escritores Venezolanos, 1970 [1966]), who represents Antigone as an "eighty-year-old Venezuelan woman in search for her sister Ismene's corpse, which has been stolen by a multinational corporation that sells bodies on the international market"; Fradinger, "Nomadic Antigone," 17.

6. Take, for instance, the most recent case of Colombia, where the ONIC (National Indigenous Organization of Colombia according to the Spanish acronym)

reports that until today every three days a member of an indigenous community is killed with total impunity. See Unidad Investigativa, "En Colombia asesinan a un indígena cada 3 días; 120 este año," *El Tiempo*, October 30, 2019.

7. Max Weber, *Economy and Society*, trans. Ephraim Fischoff et al. (Berkeley: University of California Press, 1978), 54. On Latin America, see Fernando López-Alves, *La Formación del estado y la democracia en América Latina* (Bogotá: Norma, 2003).

8. I am here echoing Ruth Wilson Gilmore's well-known definition of racism as "the state-sanctioned or extralegal production and exploitation of group-differentiated vulnerability to premature death"; *Golden Gulag: Prisons, Surplus, Crisis, and Opposition in Globalizing California* (Berkeley: University of California Press, 2007), 28.

9. Dorfman, *Widows*; Sara Uribe, *Antígona González* (Oaxaca: Surplus, 2012); and Patricia Nieto, *Los Escogidos* (Medellín: Editorial Universidad de Antioquia, 2012).

10. See Fradinger, "Nomadic Antigone."

11. Fredric Jameson, *Postmodernism, or, The Cultural Logic of Late Capitalism* (Durham: Duke University Press, 1991).

12. Fredric Jameson, "Culture and Finance Capital," *Critical Inquiry* 24, no. 1 (1997): 246–65.

13. Naomi Klein, *Shock Doctrine: The Rise of Disaster Capitalism* (New York: Penguin Books, 2014).

14. Sayak Valencia, *Gore Capitalism*, trans. John Pluecker (Cambridge: MIT Press, 2018), 19. Valencia takes the term *gore* from a genre of films "characterized by extreme, brutal violence," in order to name the "undisguised and unjustified bloodshed that is the price the Third World pays for adhering to the increasingly demanding logic of capitalism." Although applicable to the third world in general, the capacities of "gore capitalism" to turn "brutal kinds of violence [into] tools of *necroempowerment*," Valencia declares more evident in border cities, such as Tijuana, places in which death itself becomes the most profitable activity (20; emphasis in the original).

15. On the postmodern, see Jean-François Lyotard, *The Postmodern Condition: A Report on Knowledge*, trans. Geoff Bennington and Brian Massumi (Minneapolis: University of Minnesota Press, 1984); and Hall Foster, ed., *Postmodern Culture* (London: Pluto Press, 1985).

16. On *Widows*, see Fradinger, "Demanding the Political," 63–81. On *Antígona González*, see Luz Elena Zamudio Rodríguez, "El amor vivificante de 'Antígona González,' de Sara Uribe," *Romance Notes* 54 (2014): 35–43, and Lara Schoorl, "Will You Join Me in Taking Up the Body?: On Sara Uribe's 'Antígona González,'" *Los Angeles Review of Books*, July 11, 2017. On other Colombian *Antígone*s that also address this violence, see Moira Fradinger, "Making Women Visible: Multiple Antigones on the Colombian Twenty-First Century Stage," in *The Oxford Handbook of Greek Drama in the Americas*, ed. Kathryn Boshner et al. (Oxford: Oxford University Press, 2015).

17. See Régis Debray, *Conversations with Allende: Socialism in Chile* (London: Verso, 1972).

18. John Gibler, *To Die in Mexico: Dispatches From Inside the Drug War* (San Francisco: City Lights, 2011). See also Gibler's reconstruction of the interrelated violence inflicted on the forty-three students that the Mexican state disappeared on September, 24, 2014, in Ayotzinapa, with the support of the drug cartels, *I Couldn't Even Imagine That They Would Kill Us: An Oral History of the Attacks Against the Students of Ayotzinapa* (San Francisco: City Lights, 2016).

19. "NN" is the abbreviation of the Latin *nomen nescio*, which literally means "unknown name" but is often mistranslated in English as "no name." This unknowability also has a colonial history in modern slavery. See, for example, Leon Litwack, *Been in the Storm So Long: The Aftermath of Slavery* (New York: Knopf, 1979), 247–52, and Ralph Ellison, *Shadow and Act* (New York: Vintage, 1995), 147–48, both referenced by Lacqueur, who claims, "It is through our names that we place ourselves in the world, our names being the gift of others must be made our own" (Laqueur, *The Work of the Dead*, 394). Lacqueur refers to the fact that slaves were not given names; insofar as they had one, it was given by their enslavers. I only mention this because something of slavery and of its enforced anonymity, during life and after death, survives slavery's end, and repeats itself through the production of the NN by means of enforced disappearances.

20. Dawn Paley, *Drug War Capitalism* (Oakland: AK Press, 2014); and Kojo Koram, ed., *The War on Drugs and the Global Colour Line* (London: Pluto Press, 2019).

21. To give but one example, the eighteenth-century *cuadros de castas* in Nueva Granada differs considerably from the "one-drop rule" that governed the relationship between whites and blacks in the United States. Nueva Granada classified sixteen *tipos de sangre* (blood types) in a hierarchy that distinguished pure Spanish blood from mixed blood across a hierarchy that moved downward, from "Spanish" to *castizo, mestizo, mulato, morisco, chino,* and so on, until it ended with *torna atrás*. This last category, as Angel Rosenblat argues, meant that there was no possible social mobility across the racial hierarchy, as the individual thus classified had regressed to the bottom of the whitening process. See Angel Rosenblat, *La población indígena y el mestizaje en América* (Buenos Aires: Nova, 1954), 174. After independence, the governing *criollos* tried, as Castro-Gómez argues, to erase their miscegenated origins and remake themselves into the atemporal inhabitants of what he calls the *hybris del punto cero*, relegating indigenous, black, and all other working-class mestizos to the past that the new nation had to overcome in order to reach "proper" modernity. See Santiago Castro-Gómez, *La Hybris del Punto Cero: Ciencia, Raza e Ilustración en la Nueva Granada (1750–1816)* (Bogotá: Pontificia Universidad Javeriana, 2005). For a more detailed historical analysis of colonialism and racial constructions in Colombia, see Alfonso Múnera, *Fronteras imaginadas: la construcción de las razas y la geografía en el siglo xix colombiano* (Bogotá: Planeta, 2005); in Mexico, see Dorothy Tanck Estrada, *Independencia y educación: Cultura*

cívica, educación indígena y literature infantil (México: El Colegio de México, 2013); and in Chile, see Florencia Mallon, *Courage Tastes of Blood: The Mapuche Community of Nicolás Ailío and the Chilean State, 1906–2001* (Durham: Duke University Press, 2005), and Leslie Ray, *Language of the Land: The Mapuche in Argentina and Chile* (Denmark: IWGIA, 2007).

22. See Walter Benjamin, *Trauerspiel: The Origin of German Tragic Drama*, trans. John Osbourne (London: Verso, 2003).

23. See Sjöholm, "Naked Life," Audronė Žukauskaite, "Biopolitics: Antigone's Claim," in *Interrogating Antigone in Postmodern Philosophy and Criticism*, ed. S. E. Wilmer and Audronė Žukauskaite (Oxford: Oxford University Press, 2010), Gsoels-Lorensen, "Antigone, Deportee," and Andrés Fabián Henao Castro, "Antigone Claimed: 'I am a Stranger!' Political Theory and the Figure of the Stranger," *Hypatia: Special Issue "Crossing Borders"* 28, no. 2 (2013): 307–22.

24. Honig, *Antigone, Interrupted*, 233 n. 35.

25. Ibid., 247 n. 45.

26. Jean Anouilh, *Antigone* (Paris: La Table Ronde, 1947), 89; all translations are mine. For an alternative translation, see Jean Anouilh, *Antigone*, trans. Barbara Bay (London: Methuen Drama, 2005).

27. Carl Schmitt, *The Concept of the Political*, trans. George Schwab (Chicago: The University of Chicago Press, 1996).

28. Anouilh, *Antigone*, 90.

29. Lacan, *Ethics of Psychoanalysis*, 250.

30. Anouilh, *Antigone*, 93.

31. Honig, *Antigone, Interrupted*, 106.

32. Exhumation, rather than burial, represents a Latin American trope, which can be traced back to Rolando Steiner's version of Antigone in Nicaragua, *Antígona en el infierno* (1958), where Antigone demands the exhumation of her brother, who was improperly buried in a mass grave.

33. Incidentally, in a wonderful critique of the posthumous extension of U.S. citizenship to *metics,* Cacho (2012, 109) argues that the state considers noncitizens soldiers more valuable in death than in life since, following Sharon Holland, she rightly claims that it is "their 'desires' *not* their 'bodies' " that "are exhumed for use by the state," Lisa Marie Cacho, *Social Death: Racialized Rightlessness and the Criminalization of the Unprotected* (New York: New York University Press, 2012), 109; emphasis in original.

34. Anouilh, *Antigone*, 92.

35. Michel Foucault, *Society Must Be Defended: Lectures at the Collège de France 1975–1976*, trans. David Macey (New York: Picador, 2003), 254.

36. Ibid., 255.

37. Ibid. For an excellent critique of the theory of biopolitics see Weheliye, *Habeas Viscus*.

38. Foucault, *Society Must Be Defended*, 15.

39. Patterson, *Slavery and Social Death*, 5.

40. All texts from footnote 23 focus no longer on the citizen but on variations of what I am calling the *metic* in this book.

41. As Castro-Gómez argues, biopolitical technologies of government should be better understood as the technology "that 'makes live' those populations that are better adapted to the productive profile required by the capitalist state and, instead, 'lets die' those which do not contribute to productive labor, economic development and modernization"; Santiago Castro-Gómez, "Michel Foucault y la colonialidad del poder," *Tabula Rasa* 6 (2007): 157. See also Ariadna Estévez, *Administración de la vida y la muerte en América del Norte: Guerras Necropolíticas y Biopolítica de Asilo* (México: UACM-CISAN, 2018).

42. This reflection is taken from Andrés Fabián Henao Castro, "From the "Bio" to the "Necro": The Human at the Border," in *Resisting Biopolitics: Philosophical, Political and Performative Strategies*, ed. Stephen Wilmer and Audronė Žukauskaitė (New York: Routledge, 2015).

43. Achille Mbembe, *Necropolitics*, trans. Steve Corcoran (Durham: Duke University Press, 2019), 10 and 74.

44. Achille Mbembe, "Necropolitics," *Public Culture*, trans. Libby Meintjes 15 (2003): 21, reprinted in *Necropolitics*, 74.

45. On modern warfare see Mary Kaldor, *New and Old Wars: Organized Violence in a Global Era* (Stanford: Stanford University Press, 1999); Manuel Castells and Narcís Serra, eds., *Guerra y paz en el siglo XXI: Una perspectiva Europea* (Madrid: Tusquets, 2003); Mbembe, *Necropolitics*.

46. Mbembe, *Necropolitics*, 34–35.

47. Achille Mbembe, *On the Postcolony*, trans. A. M. Berrett (Berkeley: University of California Press, 2001).

48. Mbembe, *Necropolitics*, 6.

49. Foucault, *Society Must Be Defended*, 240–41.

50. Walter Mignolo, *The Darker Side of Western Modernity: Global Futures, Decolonial Options* (Durham: Duke University Press, 2011).

51. Mbembe, *Necropolitics*, 74.

52. Jacques Rancière, *Aesthetics and its Discontents*, trans. Steven Corcoran (New York: Polity Press, 2009); Wendy Brown, *Undoing the Demos: Neoliberalism's Stealth Revolution* (New York: Zone Books, 2015).

53. Rita Laura Segato, "Las nuevas fomas de la guerra y el cuerpo de las mujeres," *Sociedad e Estado* 29, no. 2 (2014): 344.

54. See David Graeber, *Debt: The First 5,000 Years* (Brooklyn: Melville House, 2014).

55. Joy Gordon, "Cool War: Economic Sanctions as Weapons of Mass Destruction," *Harper's Magazine* (2002), 43–44.

56. See Macarena Gómez-Barris, *The Extractive Zone: Social Ecologies and Decolonial Perspectives* (Durham: Duke University Press, 2017).

57. Saskia Sassen, *Expulsions: Brutality and Complexity in the Global Economy* (Cambridge: The Belknap Press of Harvard University Press, 2014).

58. Olga Sánchez Cordero, "Sebastiana, Andrés Manuel y la Ley de Amnistía/1," *Milenio*, 24 April 2018.

59. Dorfman, *Widows*, 25.

60. Ibid.

61. Ibid.

62. Ibid., 23.

63. Uribe, *Antígona González*; 13, emphasis in the text, all translations are mine. For an alternative translation, see Sarah Uribe, *Antígona González*, trans. John Pluecker (Los Angeles: Les Figues Press, 2016).

64. Nieto, *Los escogidos*, 3.

65. Ibid., 26.

66. Ibid., 32.

67. See CNMH (Centro Nacional de Memoria Histórica), *Hasta encontrarlos. El drama de la desaparación forzada en Colombia* (Bogotá: CNMH, 2016); Nicholas Casey, "Las órdenes de letalidad del ejército colombiano ponen en riesgo a los civiles, según oficiales," in *The New York Times*, May 18, 2019; and Gloria Castrillón, "El pueblo que desbordó su cementerio con falsos positivos," *El Espectador*, July 13, 2012.

68. Jacques Derrida, *Specters of Marx: The State of the Debt, the Work of Mourning, and the New International*, trans. Peggy Kamuf (New York: Routledge, 1994), 9.

69. Michel Foucault, *Discipline and Punish: The Birth of the Prison*, trans. Alan Sheridan (New York: Vintage Books, 1995).

70. Avery Gordon, *Ghostly Matters: Haunting and the Sociological Imagination* (Minneapolis: University of Minnesota Press, 2008), 110.

71. Banu Bargu, "Sovereignty as Erasure: Rethinking Enforced Disappearances," *Qui Parle* 23, no. 1 (2014): 45.

72. Uribe, *Antígona González*, 35.

73. Laqueur, *The Work of the Dead*, 431.

74. Amnesty International, *"Disappearances": A Workbook* (New York: Amnesty International Publications, 1981).

75. Bargu, "Sovereignty as Erasure," 43–44.

76. Ibid., 61; underlined in the text. For additional literature on enforced disappearances which focus on the more-often-studied Argentinian case, see Thomas C. Wright, *State Terrorism in Latin America: Chile, Argentina, and International Human Rights* (Lanham, MD: Rowman and Littlefield, 2007); Gabriel Gatti, *El detenido-desaparecido: Narrativas posibles para una catástrofe de la identidad* (Montevideo: Trilce, 2008); Pilar Calveiro, *Poder y desaparición: Los campos de concentración en Argentina* (Buenos Aires: Colihue, 2018). I focus on Bargu's work because of her long-lasting reflection on the political agency that is articulated through death itself, as happens in her analysis of the Death Fasters in Turkey. The complex agency of this group of prisoners, who used their own bodies in order to resist

state violence, Bargu reconceptualized as *necroresistance,* that is to say, "a form of *refusal* against simultaneously individualizing and totalizing domination that acts by wrenching the power of life and death away from the apparatuses of the modern state in which this power is conventionally vested"; Banu Bargu, *Starve and Immolate: The Politics of Human Weapons* (New York: Columbia University Press, 2014), 27. In clear conversation, expansion, and critical modification of Mbembe's work, Bargu then published "Another Necropolitics," *Theory & Event* 19, no. 1 (2016), to refer specifically to the kind of counterpolitics that take place through the uses and counter-uses of corpses for political purposes. For an excellent reading of Bargu's work on necropolitics and necroresistance, which links the hunger strike to the general strike as ways of opposing what he calls archist hegemony, see James Martel, *Unburied Bodies: Subversive Corpses and the Authority of the Dead* (Amherst: Amherst College Press, 2018).

77. Michel Foucault, *Security, Territory, Population: Lectures at the Collège de France 1977–1978,* trans. Graham Burchell (New York: Picador, 2009).

78. See Aileen Moreton-Robinson, *The White Possessive: Property, Power, and Indigenous Sovereignty* (Minneapolis: University of Minnesota Press, 2015); Robert Nichols, *Theft as Property: Dispossession and Critical Theory* (Durham: Duke University Press, 2019).

79. Bargu, "Sovereignty as Erasure," 47.

80. Cited in Gordon, *Ghostly Matters,* 125.

81. Bargu, "Sovereignty as Erasure," 56.

82. Ibid., 62.

83. Ibid., 45; emphasis in the original.

84. For such alternative genealogy see Dylan Rodríguez, "Forced Passages," in *Warfare in the American Homeland: Policing and Prison in a Penal Democracy,* ed. Joy James (Durham: Duke University Press, 2007); and Browne, *Dark Matters.* On the racial/sexual capitalist history of the modern prison, see Gilmore, *Golden Gulag.*

85. I am not the first to link the enforced disappearances of the twentieth century to the genocide of indigenous and black people since the European conquest of the Americas and the establishment of the trans-Atlantic slave trade. Gordon, *Ghostly Matters,* and Jean Franco, *Cruel Modernity* (Durham: Duke University Press, 2013), to mention only two, also make that link.

86. Marina Warner, *Indigo* (New York: Simon and Schuster, 1992), 97.

87. CNMH (Centro Nacional de Memoria Histórica), *Hasta encontrarlos. El drama de la desaparación forzada en Colombia* (Bogotá: CNMH, 2016), 74.

88. All of these numbers are contested, and all the institutions in charge of documenting the disappearances have recognized the under-registry of the cases. The differences are sometimes staggering. Hence, during the last exhibit of Jesús Abad Colorado's photographs of the Colombian armed conflict at the Claustro de San Agustín in Bogotá (from October 2018 to April 2019), the number of enforced disappearances was reported as 80,472. If we take this number, instead of the one

reported by the OMH, it means that for every 100,000 habitants in democratically recognized Colombia there are ninety-three enforced disappearances, versus the thirty enforced disappearances reported for the same range under Chile's dictatorship. The situation in Mexico is considerably worse. Alejandro Encinas, Undersecretary for Human Rights, Migration and Population in México, claimed that there were 40,000 disappeared people in México in addition to 26,000 unidentified bodies in the custody of Forensic Services Office, since the beginning of the "War on Drugs." Given that the Mexican "War on Drugs" has only officially existed for twelve years, the numbers reveal a considerably more saturated violent context in a country that is also still considered a democracy.

89. The *endriago* is a mythical creature—part man, part hydra, part dragon—who inhabits an infernal land and inflicts terror on his enemies, taken from a Spanish medieval text, *Amadis de Gaul.*

90. Brown, *Undoing the Demos*, 10.

91. On melodrama see Peter Brooks, *The Melodramatic Imagination* (New Haven: Yale University Press, 1976), and Elizabeth Anker, *Orgies of Feeling: Melodrama and the Politics of Freedom* (Durham: Duke University Press, 2014).

92. See Hartman, *Scenes of Subjection.*

93. Byrd, *Transit of Empire*, 65–66; Aliyyah Abdur-Rahman, "Black Cacophony: The Effect of the Scream," *Adventures in Ethics Lecture*, Emerson College, December 3, 2015; and Saidiya Hartman, "Venus in Two Acts," *Small Axe* 12, no. 2 (2008): 12.

94. Hartman, "Venus in Two Acts," 14.

95. Dorfman, *Widows*, 139.

96. Ibid., 144.

97. Ibid., 5.

98. Uribe, *Antígona González*, 15.

99. Juan Manuel Echavarría's work can be seen in: https://jmechavarria.com/en/work/requiem-nn/; last accessed July 11, 2019. For an excellent analysis of Echavarría's work, among other political artists in Colombia working against the Colombian state's imposed forms of forgetting, see Maria del Rosario Acosta López, ed., *Resistencias al olvido: Memoria y arte en Colombia* (Bogotá: Ediciones Uniandes, 2016).

100. Nieto, *Los escogidos*, 20.

101. Ibid., 21.

102. Ibid., 86. As Fradinger claims, other Colombian *Antígones*, such as Carlos Satizábal's *Antígona y actriz* (2005) and Patricia Ariza's *Antígona* (2006) reach for this cacophony of voices through other aesthetic strategies, like repetition and multiplication, see Fradinger, "Making Women Visible."

103. Fradinger, "Demanding the Political," 67.

104. Dorfman, *Widows*, 66.

105. Angela Davis, "Reflections on the Black Women's Role in the Community of Slaves," in *The Angela Y Davis Reader*, ed. Joy James (Malden: Blackwell, 1998), 115–16; emphasis in the original.

106. Ibid., 118.

107. Dorfman, *Widows*, 80.

108. Nieto, *Los escogidos*, 173.

109. Thanks to Ashley Bohrer for this insight.

110. Nieto, *Los escogidos*, 66–67.

111. Fradinger, "Demanding the Political," 71.

112. Dorfman, *Widows*, 86.

113. Diana Taylor, *Disappearing Acts: Spectacles of Gender and Nationalism in Argentina's "Dirty War."* (Durham: Duke University Press, 1997).

114. Dorfman, *Widows*, 88.

115. See Mary G. Dietz, "Citizenship with a Feminist Face: The Problem with Maternal Thinking," *Political Theory* 13, no. 1 (1985): 19–37.

116. Ariadna Estévez, "Necropolitical Wars," in *The War on Drugs and the Global Colour Line*, ed. Kojo Koram (London: Pluto Press, 2019), 101.

117. Ibid. Here, I should recall the significant pluralization of *Antigones* in México, and refer to Perla de la Rosa, *Antígona: las voces que incendian el desierto*, in *Cinco Dramaturgos Chihuahuenses*, ed. Guadalupe de la Mora (Juárez: Fondo Municipal Editorial Revolvente-Municipio de Juárez, 2005 [2004]), perhaps the first playwright to have contextualized Antigone within the struggle against feminicide in Ciudad Juárez.

118. Estévez, "Necropolitical Wars," 117.

119. Ibid., 204.

120. Elva Fabiola Orozco Mendoza, "*Las Madres de Chihuahua:* Maternal Activism, Public Disclosure, and the Politics of Visibility," *New Political Science* 41, no. 2 (2019): 232.

121. Rita Laura Segato, "Crueldad: Pedagogías y Contra-Pedagogías," *Lobo Suelto (Anarquía Coronada)*, March 26, 2018. http://lobosuelto.com/tag/contra-pedagogias/; Orozco Mendoza, "*Las Madres de Chihuahua*," 4.

122. Elva Fabiola Orozco Mendoza, "Feminicide and the Funeralization of the City," *Theory & Event* 20, no. 2 (2017): 353.

123. Ibid., 358.

124. Cacho, *Social Death*, 160.

125. Ibid.

126. Ibid., 148.

127. Angela Davis, "From the Prison of Slavery to the Slavery of Prison: Frederick Douglass and the Convict Lease System," in *The Angela Y Davis Reader*, ed. Joy James (Malden: Blackwell, 1998), 84.

128. Here, it is equally important to remember that resistance against capitalist exploitation and expropriation has always been criminalized. Thus, slaves

seeking to escape their captors were considered as "stealing" themselves away, and those helping them, as in the case of the Underground Railroad, as aiding and abetting fugitives. And the same happens today with those helping undocumented immigrants or unwanted refugees to cross the border. On the racialized history of the discourse of criminalization, see Hartman, *Scenes of Subjection*; Browne, *Dark Matters*; Cacho, *Social Death*.

Chapter 4

1. Lorenzo Veracini, *The Settler Colonial Present* (New York: Palgrave Macmillian, 2015), 95.

2. Moore, *Capitalism in the Web of Life*, 170. On the discourse on the Anthropocene, see Paul Crutzen and Eugene F. Stoermer, "Have We Entered the 'Anthropocene'?" *IGBP [International Geosphere-Biosphere Programme] Global Change Magazine Newsletter* 41, no. 17 (2000).

3. Françoise Vergès, "Racial Capitalocene." in *Futures of Black Radicalism*, ed. Gaye Theresa Johnson and Alex Lubin (London: Verso, 2017), 73.

4. I have since become familiar with the excellent work of Kathryn Yusoff, *A Billion Black Anthropocenes or None* (Minneapolis: University of Minnesota Press, 2018). Yusoff's alternative grammar to the racial Capitalocene is to speak instead of "a billion black anthropocenes," which Yusoff defines as "the proximity of black and brown bodies to harm in this intimacy with the inhuman" (xii). Even though I consider *the racial Capitalocene* to be a more inclusive terminology, ultimately all of these projects share the same decolonial politics.

5. Vergès, "Racial Capitalocene," 73, 75.

6. Ibid.

7. Gordon, *Ghostly Matters*, 63.

8. Ibid.

9. On the problematic universality of the Anthropocene, which even postcolonial theorists such as Dipesh Chakrabarty, "Postcolonial Studies and the Challenge of Climate Change," *New Literary History* 43, no. 1 (2012): 1–18, reproduce, see my article with Henrik Ernstson, "'Hic Rhodus, Hic Salta!' The Politics of the Anthropo(bs)cene," in *Urban Political Ecology in the Anthropo-Obscene: Interruptions and Possibilities*, ed. Henrik Ernstson and Erik Swyngedouw (Oxford: Routledge, 2019).

10. Vergès, "Racial Capitalocene," 80.

11. Simon Lewis and Mark Maslin, "Defining the Anthropocene," *Nature* 519, no. 7542 (2015): 174–75.

12. For an excellent critique of Lewis and Maslin, which recognizes their way of linking the Anthropocene to colonialism and yet shows its limitations, see Yusoff, *A Billion Black Anthropocenes*, 30–33.

13. Moore, *Capitalism in the Web of Life*, 172.

14. G. W. F. Hegel, *Phenomenology of Spirit*, trans. Terry Pinkard (Cambridge: Cambridge University Press, 2018), 260 [451]. The first numbers correspond to the numbers on the page, the ones in brackets to the original sections into which the book is divided.

15. Ibid., 263 [456].

16. For a detailed analysis see Patricia Jagentowicz Mills, "Hegel's *Antigone*," in *Feminist Interpretations of G. W. F. Hegel*, ed. Patricia Jagentowicz Mills (University Park: Pennsylvania State University Press, 1996).

17. Hegel, *Phenomenology of Spirit*, 263–64 [456].

18. Mark Griffith, "Psychoanalyzing *Antigone*," in *Interrogating Antigone in Postmodern Philosophy and Criticism*, ed. S. E. Wilmer and Audronė Žukauskaite (Oxford: Oxford University Press, 2010).

19. Yusoff, *A Billion Black Anthropocenes*, xiii.

20. Hegel, *Phenomenology of Spirit*, 261 [451]. Going over that passage, Luce Irigaray suggests that those unconscious desires refer not just to anyone's but to hers, she whom Hegel forced to stand as the eternal irony of the community. Irigaray, *Speculum of the Other Women*, 215.

21. Jacques Derrida, *Glas*, trans. John Leavy and Richard Rand (Lincoln: University of Nebraska Press, 1986 [1974]). I follow the convention to cite *Glas* by column, either left (L) or right (R).

22. Rosalind C. Morris, "After de Brosses: Fetishism, Translation, Comparativism, Critique," in *The Returns of Fetishism: Charles de Brosses and the Afterlives of an Idea*, ed. Daniel H. Leonard and Rosalind Morris (Chicago: The University of Chicago Press, 2017), 280.

23. Derrida, *Glas*, 145–46L.

24. The citation is stylistically broken through the insertion of Hegel's correspondence with his own sister. By means of that break, Derrida makes the empirical disrupt the transcendental, a gesture well captured in the figure of Antigonanette, which mixes Antigone with Nanette and brings Hegel's sister(s) into the picture. For an excellent analysis of that disruption, and the composite figure of Antigonanette, see Sina Kramer, "Derrida's 'Antigonanette': On the Quasi-Transcendental," *Southern Journal of Philosophy* 52, no. 4 (2014): 521–51.

25. Derrida, *Glas*, 166L.

26. Ibid., 86R–97R.

27. The final reference of *Glas* to Dionysus supports this interpretation.

28. See Kevin Thompson, "Hegelian Dialectic and the Quasi-Transcendental in *Glas*," in *Hegel After Derrida*, ed. Stuart Barnett (New York: Routledge, 1998), 250–51, and Sina Kramer, *Excluded Within: The (Un)Intelligibility of Radical Political Actors* (Oxford: Oxford University Press, 2017), 68–71.

29. Morris, "After de Brosses," 271. Sarah Kofman first captured such oscillation through the figure of "*ça cloche*," a rather difficult term to translate that,

like *glas*, gestures toward the oscillation of the pendulum that moves from Hegel to Genet and back, see "Ça Cloche," in *Selected Writings*, ed. Thomas Albrecht, Georgia Albrecht, and Elizabeth Rottenberg (Stanford: Stanford University Press, 2007 [1981]), 71–98. For a critique of the psychoanalytic emphasis on fetishism, which turns instead to the more general notion of repression, as *Glas*'s main focus, see Suzanne Gearhart, "The Remnants of Philosophy: Psychoanalysis After *Glas*," in *Hegel After Derrida*, ed. Stuart Barnett (New York: Routledge, 1998).

30. Most notably, Gayatri Spivak, "Glas-Piece: A Compte-Rendu," *Diacritics* 7, no. 3 (1977): 22–43; and Ranjana Khanna, "Frames, Contexts, Community, Justice," *Diacritics* 33, no. 2 (2003): 10–41.

31. Kramer, *Excluded Within*, 201n.7.

32. Ibid., 84.

33. Ibid.

34. Ibid., 84–85.

35. Derrida, *Glas*, 208L.

36. Cited in ibid. As Roberto Bernasconi argues, "There was no shortage of gruesome tales of Africa available to Hegel, but he seems to have been unwilling to confine himself to these," Robert Bernasconi, "Hegel at the Court of the Ashanti," in *Hegel After Derrida*, ed. Stuart Barnett (New York: Routledge, 1998), 51.

37. Cited in Derrida, *Glas*, 208L.

38. Bernasconi, "Hegel at the Court of the Ashanti," 59. The best criticism of Hegel's marginalization of slavery, in relation to *Antigone*, remains Chanter, *Whose Tragedy?*

39. Cited in Derrida, *Glas*, 207L.

40. On the critique of whiteness see Jacques Derrida, "White Mythology: Metaphor in the Text of Philosophy," in *Margins of Philosophy*, trans. Alan Bass (Chicago: The University of Chicago Press, 1982).

41. See Jacques Derrida, *Monolingualism of the Other; or, The Prothesis of Origin*, trans. Patrick Mensah (Stanford: Stanford University Press, 1998). On the positive reception of deconstruction in postcolonial studies, see Robert J. C. Young, "Deconstruction and the Postcolonial," in *Deconstructions: A User's Guide*, ed. Nicholas Royle (New York: Palgrave, 2000).

42. The opposition between spirit and specter, ontology and hauntology, not only has a history in Marxism but, as Ernesto Laclau, *Emancipation(s)* (London: Verso, 2000), 70, has claimed, "*is* the history of Marxism in its various oppositions: economic reductionism v. politics, scientific v. ideological."

43. Derrida, *Specters of Marx*, 5.

44. I do not want to underplay Derrida's crucial deconstruction of ethical interpellation, one that shows inheritance to be both unavoidable and yet heterogenous. That is the case, not only because the ancestor cannot control what will become of their injunction, but also because, as Esther Peeren rightly argues, "No single descendant can claim ownership of a unified 'true' legacy, for no one could

ever completely comprehend it"; Esther Peeren, *The Spectral Metaphor: Living Ghosts and the Agency of Invisibility* (London: Palgrave, 2014), 18.

45. Derrida, *Specters of Marx*, 7.

46. Concerned with reproductive futurism, Lee Edelman raises a similar critique to Derrida and on the basis of the same text, *Specters of Marx*; see "Against Survival: Queerness in a Time that That's out of Joint," *Shakespeare Quarterly* 62, no. 2 (2011): 148–69. Edelman, however, again misses; as I articulated most fully in chapter 2, the coloniality that I am highlighting is inseparable from the ideology of reproductive futurism.

47. Why, finally, to situate Marx—or his ghost—in the position of Hamlet's father? Marx was obviously obsessed with Shakespeare, quoted him in excess, and even performed his plays with his family in their living room, but is not Marxism's disjointing of history problematically domesticated when the spirit of Marx is confined to the feudalist drama of a royal family? Does Derrida's intertextual gesture not engage in the problematic quasi-oedipalization of critical theory here? Why, for instance, does Derrida refer to contemporary Marxists, who are critical of deconstruction, as Marx's sons in his own reply to them? Why not comrades, instead? See Jacques Derrida, "Marx & Sons," in *Ghostly Demarcations: A Symposium on Jacques Derrida's* Specters of Marx, ed. Michael Sprinker (London: Verso, 1999), 213–69.

48. Fredric Jameson, "Marx's Purloined Letter," in *Ghostly Demarcations: A Symposium on Jacques Derrida's* Specters of Marx, ed. Michael Sprinker (London: Verso, 1999), 37.

49. Pierre Macherey, "Marx Dematerialized, or the Spirit of Derrida," in *Ghostly Demarcations: A Symposium on Jacques Derrida's* Specters of Marx, ed. Michael Sprinker (London: Verso, 1999), 24.

50. Antonio Negri, "The Specter's Smile," in *Ghostly Demarcations: A Symposium on Jacques Derrida's* Specters of Marx, ed. Michael Sprinker (London: Verso, 1999), 8.

51. Slavoj Žižek, *The Tickling Subject: The Absent Center of Political Ontology* (London: Verso, 2000), 133.

52. Karl Marx, *The Eighteenth Brumaire of Louis Bonaparte* (New York: International Publishers, 2004), 17.

53. Susan Buck-Morss, *The Dialectics of Seeing: Walter Benjamin and the Arcades Project* (Cambridge: MIT Press, 1991), 123.

54. Martin Harries, *Scare Quotes from Shakespeare: Marx, Keynes, and the Language of Reenchantment* (Stanford: Stanford University Press, 2000), 86–89.

55. Walter Benjamin, *The Arcades Project*, ed. Rolf Tiedemann (Cambridge: The Belknap Press of Harvard University Press, 1999).

56. Wolfe, "Settler Colonialism," 388.

57. Édouard Glissant, *Poetics of Relation*, trans. Betsy Wing (Ann Arbor: University of Michigan Press, 1997), 33; Ian Baucom, *Specters of the Atlantic: Finance Capital, Slavery, and the Philosophy of History* (Durham: Duke University Press, 2005).

58. Ibid., 318–39.

59. For a similar argument, which uses the shoal instead of the ice as an offshore geological formation that serves metaphorically to bring Black and Native studies together, see Tiffany Lethabo King, *Black Shoals: Offshore Formations of Black and Native Studies* (Durham: Duke University Press, 2019).

60. Ian Baucom, *Specters of the Atlantic*, 17.

61. Ibid., 95.

62. Ibid.

63. Ibid., 61.

64. Ibid., 49. Consider, too, what Nicholas Robbins, in *Mercury, Mining, and Empire: The Human and Ecological Cost of Silver Mining in the Andes* (Bloomington: Indiana University Press, 2011), calls the double genocide, that is to say, the second wave of genocide that followed indigenous people's genocide, when "the afterlives of mercury pollution into the soil, ecologies, and bodies of local communities," (cited in Yusoff, *A Billion Black Anthropocenes*, 49) reduced the average "working" life of a miner to six to eight years in the mines of Potosi, and to eight to ten years in the southern sugar plantations.

65. Here, I should refer to another problematic exemplarity, all the more important to me, when Ranjana Khanna criticizes the use of Sophocles's Theban trilogy as the paradigm of exemplarity in critical theory. Hegel, Lacan, Steiner, Loraux, Irigaray, Patocka, Derrida, Butler, among others, all turn to Sophocles's tragedies and deny exemplarity to "non-Western, nonhuman, and *foreign* canons of origin," see Khanna, "Frames, Contexts, Community, Justice," 27, especially her discussion of parergons two (example) and three (foreigner).

66. Baucom, *Specters of the Atlantic*, 130.

67. Ibid.

68. Arundhati Roy, *Capitalism: A Ghost Story* (Chicago: Haymarket Books, 2014).

69. Gordon, *Ghostly Matters*, xvi.

70. Following Rob Wallace's argument "that agribusiness 'has entered a strategic alliance with influenza,'" Tithi Bhattacharya and Dale Gareth argue that "we can see how factory livestock farming sets up ideal environments for pathogens to spread"; "Covid Capitalism: General Tendencies, Possible 'Leaps.'" *Spectre*, April 13, 2020. https://spectrejournal.com/covid-capitalism/?fbclid=IwAR2w0nn6AeKf53ftNFRs-fYlnP2-BNASDdcJQGAMS_CuIn7UDtqalZ3pZGSw. Under neoliberal conditions of accumulation, where practically all the earth has been subjected to capitalism's enclosures and not only agrobusiness but also big pharma and healthcare systems too, among many others, enter into these kinds of deadly strategic alliances, the capacity of pathogens to leap from animals to humans dramatically increases, as does the lethal power of these viruses to take the life of the most vulnerable. To put it differently, from the Swine Flu to Ebola and Zika, COVID-19 is yet another symptom of the crisis of the racial Capitalocene.

71. Gordon, *Ghostly Matters*, xvi.

72. On the violence of foundings and the politics of re-foundings, see the excellent works of Honig, *Democracy and the Foreigner*; Moira Fradinger, *Binding Violence: Literary Visions of Political Origins* (Stanford: Stanford University Press, 2010); and Angélica Bernal, *Beyond Origins: Rethinking Founding in a Time of Constitutional Democracy* (Oxford: Oxford University Press, 2017).

73. Gordon, *Ghostly Matters*, 201.

74. Derrida, *Specters of Marx*, 121.

75. Sigmund Freud, *On Murder, Mourning, and Melancholia*, trans. Shaun Whiteside (New York: Penguin, 2004), 204.

76. Karl Marx, *Capital Vol. I* (New York: Penguin, 1976), 915.

77. I would like to think of this reflection on the differential agencies of the specter in affinity with Esther Peeren's excellent book on the spectral metaphor. Spectrality refers as much to the haunting agency of ghosts as it refers to the construction of racialized people as phantasmatic, forced to never fully materialize. Perhaps my reflection remains too attached to the perspective of the haunted that Peeren's emphasis on *spectral agency* seeks to displace. What brings us together, however, is what I believe is our mutual refusal to generalize the specter in a gesture that assumes all ghosts to be alike. Peeren also raises this criticism to Derrida and turns it into a nuanced interpretation of how undocumented migrants, domestic workers, mediums, and missing persons manifest in novels, films, and television series as living ghosts, subjected to different forms of dispossession and able to enact different forms of agency. I, instead, turn to settler-colonial capitalism and to its differential subjection of racialized populations to a forced spectrality, whose agencies I argue remain insufficiently conjured in critical theory's spectral turn. Thus, Peeren wants to focalize the ghost, to show "how the living ghosts of the present can manipulate their ghostly status to develop a form of spectral agency capable of challenging the mechanisms that produced them as ghosted" (*The Spectral Metaphor*, 24). I am also invested in those challenging mechanisms, but want to contextualize them instead in the settler colonial history of the racial Capitalocene.

78. Moten, *In the Break*, 10; emphasis in original.

79. Marx, *Capital* Vol. I, 176.

80. Moten, *In the Break*, 13.

81. See, for instance, David Harvey, *A Brief History of Neoliberalism* (Oxford: Oxford University Press, 2007); Brown, *Undoing the Demos*; and Michel Fehrer, *Rated Agency: Investee Politics in a Speculative Age* (New York: Zone Books, 2018). For another analysis of neoliberalism, which both focuses on race and gender and traces a connection between financial speculation and racial capitalism, see Hong, *Beyond Disavowal*, 63–94.

82. Moten, *In the Break*, 10.

83. Stefano Harney and Fred Moten, "Michael Brown," *boundary 2* 42, no. 4 (2015): 81.

84. Ibid., 85. As Martel claims, Harney and Moten's meditation not only succeeds in not instrumentalizing Brown for their own ends but also in the more difficult yet more politically generative task of "allowing him to deinstrumentalize them, altering the concepts of life and death, permitting other forms of life and politics to become visible in the process" (Martel, *Unburied Corpse*, 205).

85. See for instance, Julia Kristeva, *Black Sun: Depression and Melancholia* (New York: Columbia University Press, 1989). I am by no means suggesting that questions of race have not intersected with the problem of melancholia; a quick survey on the literature in this subject proves the opposite. From Anne Cheng, *The Melancholy of Race: Psychoanalysis, Assimilation, and Hidden Grief* (Oxford: Oxford University Press, 2000), to Paul Gilroy, *Postcolonial Melancholia* (New York: Columbia University Press, 2005), and David Eng and Shinhee Han, *Racial Melancholia, Racial Dissociation: On the Social and Psychic Lives of Asian Americans* (Durham: Duke University Press, 2019), the question of melancholia is rather prevalent in the political analysis of race and colonialism. The claim that I am making, based on Moten's distinctions, is that melancholia itself has to be problematized, rather than merely understood as one of those extraordinary conditions that colonialism renders normal for racialized populations.

86. W. E. B. Dubois, *The Souls of Black Folks* (New York: Grove Press, 1969), 45.

87. Slavoj Žižek, *Did Somebody Say Totalitarianism: Five Interventions in the (Mis)use of a Notion* (London: Verso, 2002), 143.

88. Moten, *In the Break*, 192–211.

89. Harney and Moten, "Michael Brown," 85–86.

90. Christina Sharpe, *In the Wake: On Blackness and Being* (Durham: Duke University Press, 2016).

91. Ibid., 2.

92. Claudia Rankine, "The Condition of Black Life is One of Mourning," *The New York Times*, June 22, 2015.

93. Hartman, *Lose Your Mother*, 6.

94. Sharpe, *In the Wake*, 3.

95. Ibid., 10.

96. Ibid., 16.

97. Ibid., 69.

98. Frantz Fanon, *A Dying Colonialism*, trans. Haakon Chevalier (New York: Grove Press, 1994), 65.

99. Sharpe, *In the Wake*, 71.

100. Ibid., 81.

101. Marx and Engels, "The Communist Manifesto," 483.

102. Moore, *Capitalism in the Web of Life*, 172.

103. See Coulthard, *Red Skin, White Masks*.

104. Sharon Patricia Holland, *Raising the Death: Readings of Death and (Black) Subjectivity* (Durham: Duke University Press, 2000), 14.

105. On the political convergence between global communism and indigenous decolonization, see Nichols, *Theft as Property*, and Lou Cornum, "Desiring the Tribe," *Pinko*, October 15, 2019. https://pinko.online/pinko-1/desiring-the-tribe.

106. Gordon, *Ghostly Matters*, 184.

107. Peeren, *The Spectral Metaphor*, 3.

108. Gordon, *Ghostly Matters*, 184.

109. Dan Stone, *Concentration Camps: A Short History* (Oxford: Oxford University Press, 2017), 13.

110. Saidiya Hartman, "The End of White Supremacy, An American Romance," *Bomb*, June 5, 2020.

111. Ibid.

Conclusion

1. Thanks to Ranji Khanna for this reference.

2. See Cartledge, *The Greeks*, and Isaac, *The Invention of Racism*.

3. Because in the world of tragedy, virgins have less autonomy than wives, Nicole Loraux argues; they do not kill themselves, but are killed instead. Antigone is the sole exception to that rule; see Nicole Loraux, *Tragic Ways of Killing a Woman*, trans. Anthony Forster (Cambridge: Harvard University Press, 1991), 31.

4. Martel, *Unburied Bodies*, 24; emphasis in the text.

5. Simon Critchley, *Tragedy, the Greeks, and Us* (New York: Pantheon Books, 2019), 7.

6. Anne Carson, *AntigoNick* (New York: New Directions, 2012), i.

Bibliography

Abdur-Rahman, Aliyyah. *Against the Closet: Black Political Longing and the Erotics of Race*. Durham: Duke University Press, 2012.

———. "Black Cacophony: The Effect of the Scream." *Adventures in Ethics Lecture*, Emerson College, December 3, 2015.

Acosta López, María del Rosario, ed. *Resistencias al olvido: Memoria y arte en Colombia*. Bogotá: Ediciones Uniandes, 2016.

Allen, Paula Gunn. *The Sacred Hoop: Recovering the Feminine in American Indian Traditions*. Boston: Beacon Press, 1992.

Amnesty International. *"Disappearances": A Workbook*. New York: Amnesty International Publications, 1981.

Anker, Elisabeth. *Orgies of Feeling: Melodrama and the Politics of Freedom*. Durham: Duke University Press, 2014.

Anouilh, Jean. *Antigone*. Paris: La Table Ronde, 1947.

———. *Antigone*. Translated by Barbara Bay. London: Methuen Drama, 2005.

Arendt, Hannah. *The Human Condition*. Chicago: University of Chicago Press, 1998.

———. *On Revolution*. New York: Penguin, 2006.

Aristotle. *Politics*. Translated by C. D. C. Reeve. Indianapolis: Hackett, 1998.

Atkison, Larissa. "*Antigone*'s Reminders: Choral Ruminations and Political Judgment." *Political Theory* 44, no. 2 (2015): 219–39.

Avelar, Idelber. *The Letter of Violence. Essays on Narrative, Ethics, and Politics*. New York: Palgrave, 2004.

Bal, Mieke. *Quoting Caravaggio: Contemporary Art, Preposterous History*. Chicago: The University of Chicago Press, 1999.

Baldwin, James. "The Black Boy Looks at the White Boy." In *Nobody Knows My Name: More Notes of a Native Son*. New York: Dell, 1961.

Bales, Kevin. *Disposable People: New Slavery in the Global Economy*. Berkeley: University of California Press, 1999.

Bargu, Banu. "Sovereignty as Erasure: Rethinking Enforced Disappearances." *Qui Parle* 23, no. 1 (2014): 35–75.

———. *Starve and Immolate: The Politics of Human Weapons*. New York: Columbia University Press, 2014.

———. "Another Necropolitics." *Theory & Event* 19, no. 1 (2016).

Barrett, Lindon. *Blackness and Value: Seeing Double*. Cambridge; Cambridge University Press, 1999.

Baucom, Ian. *Specters of the Atlantic: Finance Capital, Slavery, and the Philosophy of History*. Durham: Duke University Press, 2005.

Benardete, Seth. *Sacred Transgressions: A Reading of Sophocles' Antigone*. South Bend: St. Augustine's Press, 1999.

Benhabib, Seyla. "On Hegel, Women and Irony." In *Feminist Interpretations of G. W. F. Hegel*, edited by Patricia Jagentowicz Mills, 25–44. University Park: Pennsylvania State University Press, 1996.

———, ed. *Democracy and Difference: Contesting the Boundaries of the Political*. Princeton: Princeton University Press, 1996.

Benjamin, Walter. "The Work of Art in the Age of Mechanical Reproduction." In *Illuminations*, translated by Harry Zohn, 217–52. New York: Schocken, 1969.

———. *The Arcades Project*. Edited by Rolf Tiedemann. Cambridge: The Belknap Press of Harvard University Press, 1999.

———. *Trauerspiel: The Origin of German Tragic Drama*. Translated by John Osbourne. London: Verso, 2003.

Bennett, Larry, and Tyrrell Blake. "Sophocles' *Antigone* and Funeral Oratory." *AJP* 111, no. 1 (1990): 441–56.

Bernal, Angélica. *Beyond Origins: Rethinking Founding in a Time of Constitutional Democracy*. Oxford: Oxford University Press, 2017.

Bernal, Martin. *Black Athena*. New Brunswick, NJ: Rutgers University Press, 2006.

Bernasconi, Robert. "Hegel at the Court of the Ashanti." In *Hegel after Derrida*, edited by Stuart Barnett, 41–62. New York: Routledge, 1998.

Bernstein, J. M. "'The Celestial Antigone the Most Resplendent Figure Ever to Have Appeared on Earth:' Hegel's Feminism." In *Feminist Readings of Antigone*, edited by Fanny Söderbäck, 111–32. Albany: State University of New York Press, 2010.

Bhattacharya, Tithi, and Gareth Dale. "Covid Capitalism: General Tendencies, Possible 'Leaps.'" *Spectre*, April 13, 2020. https://spectrejournal.com/covid-capitalism/?fbclid=IwAR2w0nn6AeKf53ftNFRsfYlnP2-BNASDdcJQGAMS_CuIn7UDtqalZ3pZGSw.

Blundell, Mary Whitlock. *Helping Friends and Harming Enemies: A Study in Sophocles and Greek Ethics*. Cambridge: Cambridge University Press, 1991.

Blundell, Sue. *Women in Ancient Greece*. London: British Museum Press, 1995.

Bonilla-Silva, Eduardo. "Race in the World System." *DuBois Review: Social Science Research on Race* 1, no. 1 (2001): 189–94.

Bohrer, Ashley. *Marxism and Intersectionality: Race, Gender, Class, and Sexuality under Contemporary Capitalism*. Bielefeld: Transcript, 2019.

Braudel, Fernand. *The Perspective of the World. Civilization & Capitalism 15th–18th Century*. Berkeley: University of California Press, 1992.

Brooks, Peter. *The Melodramatic Imagination*. New Haven: Yale University Press, 1976.

Brown, Wendy. *Undoing the Demos: Neoliberalism's Stealth Revolution*. New York: Zone Books, 2015.

Browne, Simone. *Dark Matters: On the Surveillance of Blackness*. Durham: Duke University Press, 2015.

Buck-Morss, Susan. *The Dialectics of Seeing: Walter Benjamin and the Arcades Project*. Cambridge: MIT Press, 1991.

Butler, Judith. *Bodies that Matter: On the Discursive Limits of Sex*. New York: Routledge, 1993.

———. *Antigone's Claim: Kinship between Life and Death*. New York: Columbia University Press, 2000.

———. *Precarious Life: The Powers of Mourning and Violence*. New York: Verso, 2004.

———. *Undoing Gender*. New York: Routledge, 2004.

Byrd, Jodi. *The Transit of Empire: Indigenous Critiques of Colonialism*. Minneapolis: University of Minnesota Press, 2011.

Cacho, Lisa Marie. *Social Death: Racialized Rightlessness and the Criminalization of the Unprotected*. New York: New York University Press, 2012.

Calveiro, Pilar. *Poder y desaparición: Los campos de concentratción en Argentina*. Buenos Aires: Colihue, 2018.

Carson, Anne. *AntigoNick*. New York: New Directions, 2012.

Cartledge, Paul. *The Greeks: A Portrait of Self and Others*. Oxford: Oxford University Press, 1993.

Casey, Nicholas. "Las órdenes de letalidad del ejército colombiano ponen en riesgo a los civiles, según oficiales." *The New York Times*, May 18, 2019.

Castells, Manuel and Serra Narcís, eds. *Guerra y paz en el siglo XXI: Una perspectiva Europea*. Madrid: Tusquets, 2003.

Castrillón, Gloria. "El pueblo que desbordó su cementerio con falsos positivos." *El Espectador*, July 13, 2012.

Castro-Gómez, Santiago. *La Hybris del Punto Cero: Ciencia, Raza e Ilustración en la Nueva Granada (1750–1816)*. Bogotá: Pontificia Universidad Javeriana, 2005.

———. "Michel Foucault y la colonialidad del poder." *Tabula Rasa* 6 (2007): 153–72.

Chacón, Justin Akers. "Opening the Border through Class Struggle and Solidarity." *Punto Rojo*, January 13, 2020.

Chakrabarty, Dipesh. "Postcolonial Studies and the Challenge of Climate Change." *New Literary History* 43, no. 1 (2012): 1–18.

Chambers, Samuel. *The Lesson of Rancière*. Oxford: Oxford University Press, 2013.

Chanter, Tina. "Antigone's Political Legacies: Abjection in Defiance of Mourning." In *Interrogating Antigone in Postmodern Philosophy and Criticism*, edited by S. E. Wilmer and Audronė Žukauskaite, 1–30. Oxford: Oxford University Press, 2010.

———. *Whose Antigone? The Tragic Marginalization of Slavery*. Albany: State University of New York Press, 2011.
Cheng, Anne. *The Melancholy of Race: Psychoanalysis, Assimilation, and Hidden Grief*. Oxford: Oxford University Press, 2000.
Ciccariello-Maher, George. *Decolonizing Dialectics*. Durham: Duke University Press, 2017.
Cohen, Cathy. "Punks, Bulldaggers, and Welfare Queens: The Radical Potential of Queer Politics." *GLQ* 3, no. 4 (1997): 437–65.
Cohen, David. "Theories of Punishment." In *The Cambridge Companion to Ancient Greek Law*, edited by Michael Gagarin and David Cohen, 170–90. Cambridge: Cambridge University Press, 2005.
Collins, Patricia Hill. *Black Feminist Thought: Knowledge, Consciousness, and the Politics of Empowerment*. New York: Routledge, 1990.
Combahee River Collective. "A Statement." In *Words of Fire: An Anthology of African-American Feminist Thought*, edited by Beverly Guy-Sheftall, 213–40. New York: The New York Press, 1995 [1977].
Copjec, Joan. *Read My Desire: Lacan Against the Historicists*. Cambridge: MIT Press, 1994.
———. *Imagine There's No Women*. Cambridge: MIT Press, 2004.
Cornum, Lou. "Desiring the Tribe." *Pinko*, October 15, 2019. https://pinko.online/pinko-1/desiring-the-tribe.
Coulthard, Glen Sean. *Red Skin, White Masks: Rejecting the Colonial Politics of Recognition*. Minneapolis: University of Minnesota Press, 2014.
Cover, Robert. *Justice Accused: Antislavery and the Judicial Process*. New Haven: Yale University Press, 1975.
CNMH (Centro Nacional de Memoria Histórica). *Hasta encontrarlos. El drama de la desaparación forzada en Colombia*. Bogotá: CNMH, 2016.
Crenshaw, Kimberlé, Neil Gotanda, Gary Peller, and Kendall Thomas. *Critical Race Theory: The Key Writings that Formed the Movement*. New York: The New Press, 1995.
Critchley, Simon. *Tragedy, the Greeks, and Us*. New York: Pantheon Books, 2019.
Crutzen, Paul J., and Eugene F. Stoermer. "Have We Entered the 'Anthropocene'?" *IGBP [International Geosphere-Biosphere Programme] Global Change Magazine Newsletter* 41, no. 17 (2000).
Davis, Angela. *Women, Race, and Class*. New York: Vintage, 1981.
———. *An Autobiography*. New York: International Publishers, 1988.
———. "From the Prison of Slavery to the Slavery of Prison: Frederick Douglass and the Convict Lease System." In *The Angela Y Davis Reader*, edited by Joy James, 74–95. Malden: Blackwell, 1998.
———. "Reflections on the Black Women's Role in the Community of Slaves." In *The Angela Y Davis Reader*, edited by Joy James, 111–28. Malden: Blackwell, 1998.

Davis, Robert, and Mark Zannis. *The Genocide Machine in Canada: The Pacification of the North*. Montreal: Black Rose Books, 1973.
Day, Iyko. *Alien Capital: Asian Racialization and the Logic of Settler Colonial Capitalism*. Durham: Duke University Press, 2016.
Deer, Sarah. *The Beginning and End of Rape: Confronting Sexual Violence in Native America*. Minneapolis: University of Minnesota Press, 2015.
De Genova, Nicholas, and Nathalie Peutz. *The Deportation Regime: Sovereignty, Space, and the Freedom of Movement*. Durham: Duke University Press, 2010.
De Ste. Croix, G. E. M. *The Class Struggle in the Ancient Greek World: From the Archaic Age to the Arab Conquests*. Ithaca: Cornell University Press, 1981.
de la Rosa, Perla. *Antígona: las voces que incendian el desierto*. In *Cinco Dramaturgos Chihuahuenses*. Edited by Guadalupe de la Mora. Juárez: Fondo Municipal Editorial Revolvente-Municipio de Juárez, 2005 [2004].
Deleuze, Gilles. "Coldness and Cruelty." In *Masochism*, translated by Jean McNeil and Aude Willm, 9–138. New York: Zone Books, 1991.
———, and Félix Guattari. *Anti-Oedipus: Capitalism and Schizophrenia*. Translated by Robert Hurley, Mark Seem, and Helene R. Lane. New York: Continuum, 2004.
Derrida, Jacques. *Glas*. Translated by John Leavy and Richard Rand. Lincoln: University of Nebraska Press, 1986 [1974].
———. "White Mythology: Metaphor in the Text of Philosophy." In *Margins of Philosophy*, translated by Alan Bass, 207–72. Chicago: The University of Chicago Press, 1982.
———. *Specters of Marx: The State of the Debt, the Work of Mourning, and the New International*. Translated by Peggy Kamuf. New York: Routledge, 1994.
———. "The Time is Out of Joint." In *Deconstruction is/in America*, edited by Anselm Haverkampf, 14–40. New York: New York University Press, 1995.
———. *Monolingualism of the Other; or, The Prothesis of Origin*. Translated by Patrick Mensah. Stanford: Stanford University Press, 1998.
———. "Marx & Sons," In *Ghostly Demarcations: A Symposium on Jacques Derrida's Specters of Marx*, edited by Michael Sprinker, 213–69. London: Verso, 1999.
Dietz, Mary G. "Citizenship with a Feminist Face: The Problem with Maternal Thinking." *Political Theory* 13, no. 1 (1985): 19–37.
Doerries, Bryan. *Antigone in Ferguson*. Theater of War Productions. Ferguson, 2019. https://theaterofwar.com/projects/antigone-in-ferguson.
Dorfman, Ariel. *Widows*. New York: Seven Stories Press, 2002 [1981].
Douglass, Patrice. "Black Feminist Theory for the Dead and Dying." *Theory & Event* 21, no. 1 (2018): 106–23.
Douzinas, Costas. "Law's Birth and Antigone's Death." *Cardozo Law Review* 16, no. 4 (1995): 1325–55.
Driskill, Qwo-Li. "(*Aseti Ayetl*): Cherokee Two Spirit People Reimagining Nation." In *Queer Indigenous Studies: Critical Interventions in Theory, Politics, and Liter-*

ature, edited by Qwo-Li Driskill, Chris Finley, Brian Joseph Gilley, and Scott Laurie Morgensen, 97–112. Tucson: The University of Arizona Press, 2011.

———, Chris Finley, Brian Joseph Gilley, and Scott Morgensen, eds. *Queer Indigenous Studies: Critical Interventions in Theory, Politics, and Literature*. Tucson: The University of Arizona Press, 2011.

Dubois, Laurent. *Haiti: The Aftershocks of History*. New York: Picador, 2012.

Dubois, Page. *Torture and Truth*. New York: Routledge, 1991.

———. *Slavery: Antiquity and Its Legacy*. Oxford: Oxford University Press, 2009.

Dubois, W. E. B. *The Souls of Black Folks*. New York: Grove Press, 1969.

Dunaway, Wilma. "Commodity-Chains and Gendered Exploitation: Rescuing Women from the Periphery of World-Systems Thought." In *The Modern/Colonial/Capitalist World-System: Global Processes, Antisystemic Movements, and the Geopolitics of Knowledge*, edited by Ramón Grosfoguel and Ana Margarita Cervantes-Rodriguez, 127–46. Westport: Greenwood, 2002.

Dussel, Enrique. *The Invention of the Americas*. New York: Continuum, 1995.

———. "Alterity and Modernity (Las Casas, Vitoria, and Suárez: 1514–1617)." In *Postcolonialism and Political Theory*, edited by Nailini Persram, 3–35. New York: Lexington Books, 2007.

Echavarría, Juan Manuel. *Réquiem NN* (art installation), 2006–2013. https://jmechavarria.com/en/work/requiem-nn/.

Edelman, Lee. "The Part for the (W)hole: Baldwin, Homophobia, and the Fantasmatics of 'Race.'" In *Homographesis: Essays in Gay Literary and Cultural Theory*. New York: Routledge, 1994.

———. *No Future. Queer Theory and the Death Drive*. Durham: Duke University Press, 2004.

———. "Against Survival: Queerness in a Time That's Out of Joint." *Shakespeare Quarterly* 62, no. 2 (2011): 148–69.

Ellison, Ralph. *Shadow and Act*. New York: Vintage, 1995.

Elshtain, Jean Bethke. "Antigone's Daughters." *Democracy* 2, no. 2 (1982): 39–45.

Eng, David, and Shinhee Han. *Racial Melancholia, Racial Dissociation: On the Social and Psychic Lives of Asian Americans*. Durham: Duke University Press, 2019.

Engelstein, Stefani. "Sibling Logic, or Antigone Again." *PMLA* 126, no. 1 (2011): 38–54.

Estévez, Ariadna. *Administración de la vida y la muerte en América del Norte: Guerras Necropolíticas y Biopolítica de Asilo*. México: UACM-CISAN, 2018.

———. "Necropolitical Wars." In *The War on Drugs and the Global Colour Line*, edited by Kojo Koram, 103–27. London: Pluto Press, 2019.

Ettinger, Bracha. *The Matrixial Borderspace*. Minneapolis: University of Minnesota Press, 2006.

Euben, Peter. *The Tragedy of Political Theory: The Road Not Taken*. Princeton: Princeton University Press, 1990.

Fanon, Frantz. *A Dying Colonialism*. Translated by Haakon Chevalier. New York: Grove Press, 1994.

———. *Black Skin, White Masks*. Translated by Richard Philcox. New York: Grove Press, 2008.

Federici, Silvia. *Caliban and the Witch: Women, the Body, and Primitive Accumulation*. New York: Autonomedia, 2004.

Fehrer, Michel. *Rated Agency: Investee Politics in a Speculative Age*. New York: Zone Books, 2018.

Ferguson, Roderick. *Aberrations in Black: Towards a Queer of Color Critique*. Minneapolis: University of Minnesota Press, 2003.

Fischer-Licthe, Erika. "Politicizing Antigone." In *Interrogating Antigone in Postmodern Philosophy and Criticism*, edited by S. E. Wilmer and Audronė Žukauskaite, 329–52. Oxford: Oxford University Press, 2010.

Fletcher, Judith. "Sophocles' *Antigone* and the Democratic Voice." In *Interrogating Antigone in Postmodern Philosophy and Criticism*, edited by S. E. Wilmer and Audronė Žukauskaite, 168–84. Oxford: Oxford University Press, 2010.

Foley, Helene. "Tragedy and Democratic Ideology: The Case of Sophocles' Antigone." In *History, Tragedy, Theory: Dialogues on Athenian Drama*, edited by Barbara Goff, 131–50. Austin: University of Texas Press, 1995.

———. *Female Acts in Greek Tragedy*. Princeton: Princeton University Press, 2001.

Foucault, Michel. *History of Sexuality: An Introduction*. New York: Vintage, 1976 [1990].

———. "Truth and Juridical Forms." In *Power: Essential Works of Foucault 1954–1984*, edited by James Faubion, 1–89. New York: The New Press, 1994.

———. *Discipline and Punish: The Birth of the Prison*. Translated by Alan Sheridan. New York: Vintage Books, 1995.

———. *Society Must Be Defended: Lectures at the Collège de France 1975–1976*. Translated by David Macey. New York: Picador, 2003.

———. *Security, Territory, Population: Lectures at the Collège de France 1977–1978*. Translated by Graham Burchell. New York: Picador, 2009.

Fradinger, Moira. "Nomadic Antigone." In *Feminist Readings of Antigone*, edited by Fanny Söderbäck, 15–23. Albany: State University of New York Press, 2010.

———. *Binding Violence: Literary Visions of Political Origins*. Stanford: Stanford University Press, 2010.

———. "Demanding the Political: *Widows*, or Ariel Dorfman's Antigones." *Hispanic Issues on Line. Special Issue: Whose Voice is This? Iberian and Latin American Antigones* 13 (2013): 63–81.

———. "Making Women Visible: Multiple Antigones on the Colombian Twenty-First Century Stage." In *The Oxford Handbook of Greek Drama in the Americas*, edited by Kathryn Boshner, Fiona Macintosh, Justine McConnell, and Patrice Rankine, 556–75. Oxford: Oxford University Press, 2015.

Franco, Jean. *Cruel Modernity*. Durham: Duke University Press, 2013.

Freud, Sigmund. *Beyond the Pleasure Principle and Other Writings*. Translated by John Reddick. New York: Penguin, 2003 [1920].
———. *On Murder, Mourning and Melancholia*. Translated by Shaun Whiteside. New York: Penguin, 2004.
Games, Alison. *Witchcraft in Early North America*. New York: Rowman and Littlefield, 2010.
Garzón, Baltasar. *Operación Cóndor. 40 años despues*. New York: Unesco, 2015.
Gatti, Gabriel. *El detenido-desaparecido: Narrativas posibles para una catástrofe de la identidad*. Montevideo: Trilce, 2008.
Gearhart, Suzanne. "The Remnants of Philosophy: Psychoanalysis after *Glas*." In *Hegel after Derrida*, edited by Stuart Barnett, 147–70. New York: Routledge, 1998.
Gibler, John. *To Die in Mexico: Dispatches from Inside the Drug War*. San Francisco: City Lights, 2011.
———. *I Couldn't Even Imagine That They Would Kill Us*. San Francisco: City Lights, 2015.
Gilmore, Ruth Wilson. *Golden Gulag: Prisons, Surplus, Crisis, and Opposition in Globalizing California*. Berkeley: University of California Press, 2007.
Gilroy, Paul. *Postcolonial Melancholia*. New York: Columbia University Press, 2005.
Glissant, Édouard, *Poetics of Relation*. Translated by Betsy Wing. Ann Arbor: University of Michigan Press, 1997.
Glowacki, Janusz. *Antigone in New York*. New York: Samuel French, 1997.
Goff, Barbara. "Introduction. History, Tragedy, Theory." In *History, Tragedy, Theory: Dialogues on Athenian Drama*, edited by Barbara Goff, 1–37. Austin: University of Texas Press, 1995.
———, and Michael Simpson, eds. *Crossroads in the Black Aegean: Oedipus, Antigone, and Dramas of the African Diaspora*. Oxford: Oxford University Press, 2007.
Goldberg, David Theo. *The Racial State*. London: Blackwell, 1993.
Goldhill, Simon. "The Great Dionysia and Civic Ideology." In *Nothing to Do with Dionysus? Athenian Drama in Its Social Context*, edited by John Winkler and Froma Zeitlin, 97–129. Princeton: Princeton University Press, 1986.
———. "The Language of Tragedy: Rhetoric and Communication." In *The Cambridge Companion to Greek Tragedy*, edited by P. E. Easterling, 127–150. Cambridge: Cambridge University Press, 1997.
Gómez-Barris, Macarena. *The Extractive Zone: Social Ecologies and Decolonial Perspectives*. Durham: Duke University Press, 2017.
Gordon, Avery. *Ghostly Matters: Haunting and the Sociological Imagination*. Minneapolis: University of Minnesota Press, 2008.
Gordon, Joy. "Cool War: Economic Sanctions as Weapons of Mass Destruction." *Harper's Magazine* (2002), 43–44.
Graeber, David. *Debt: The First 5,000 Years*. Brooklyn: Melville House, 2014.
Griffith, Mark. *Sophocles Antigone*. Cambridge: Cambridge University Press, 2010.

———. "Psychoanalyzing *Antigone*." In *Interrogating Antigone in Postmodern Philosophy and Criticism*, edited by S. E. Wilmer and Audronė Žukauskaite, 110–34. Oxford: Oxford University Press, 2010.
Grosfoguel, Ramón. "The Epistemic Decolonial Turn." *Cultural Studies* 21, no. 2–3 (2007): 211–23.
Gsoels-Lorensen, Jutta. "Antigone, Deportee." *Arethusa* 47, no. 2 (2014): 111–44.
Guzmán, Patricio. *The Pearl Button* (film), 2015.
Hall, Edith. *Inventing the Barbarian: Greek Self-Definition through Tragedy*. Oxford: Clarendon Press, 1991.
———. "The Sociology of Athenian Tragedy." In *The Cambridge Companion to Greek Tragedy*, edited by P. E. Easterling, 93–126. Cambridge: Cambridge University Press, 1997.
———. "Antigone and the Internalization of Theater in Greek Antiquity." In *Antigone on the Contemporary World Stage*, edited by Erin B. Mee and Helene Foley, 51–65. Oxford: Oxford Classics, 2011.
Hall, Jonathan. *Ethnic Identity in Greek Antiquity*. Cambridge: Cambridge University Press, 1997.
Halperin, David. "Is There a History of Sexuality?" *History and Theory* 28, no. 3 (1989): 257–74.
Halpern, Richard. "Theater and Democratic Thought: Arendt to Rancière." *Critical Inquiry* 37, no. 3 (2011): 545–72.
Han, Sora. "Slavery as Contract: Betty's Case and the Question of Freedom." *Law and Literature* 27, no. 3 (2015): 395–416.
Hardwick, Lorna, and Carol Gillespie, eds. *Classics in Post-Colonial Worlds*. Oxford: Oxford University Press, 2007.
Harney, Stefano, and Fred Moten. "Michael Brown." *boundary 2* 42, no. 4 (2015): 81–87.
Harries, Martin. *Scare Quotes from Shakespeare: Marx, Keynes, and the Language of Reenchantment*. Stanford: Stanford University Press, 2000.
Hartman, Saidiya. *Scenes of Subjection: Terror, Slavery, and the Self-Making of Nineteenth-Century America*. Oxford: Oxford University Press, 1997.
———. *Lose Your Mother: A Journey Along the Atlantic Slaver Route*. New York: Farrar, Straus and Giroux, 2007.
———. "Venus in Two Acts." *Small Axe* 12, no. 2 (2008): 1–14.
———. "The End of White Supremacy, An American Romance," *Bomb*, June 5, 2020; https://bombmagazine.org/articles/the-end-of-white-supremacy-an-american-romance/?fbclid=IwAR1JpWZm6uS1twq8oFplHgccLaFXIXgJA3LO_o5HazDqhqZJJVK6iMhJDwA.
Harvey, David. *A Brief History of Neoliberalism*. Oxford: Oxford University Press, 2007.
Hegel, G. W. F. *Phenomenology of Spirit*. Translated by Terry Pinkard. Cambridge: Cambridge University Press, 2018.

Henao Castro, Andrés Fabián. "Antigone Claimed: 'I Am a Stranger!' Political Theory and the Figure of the Stranger." *Hypatia: Special Issue 'Crossing Borders.'* 28, no. 2 (2013): 307–22.

———. "Antigone and Democratic Theory—(B.) Antigone, Interrupted." *The Classical Review* 64, no. 2 (2014): 606–608.

———. "Can the Subaltern Smile? *Oedipus* without Oedipus." *Contemporary Political Theory* 14, no. 4 (2015): 315–34.

———. "From the "Bio" to the "Necro": The Human at the Border." In *Resisting Biopolitics: Philosophical, Political, and Performative Strategies*, edited by Stephen Wilmer and Audronė Žukauskaitė, 237–53. New York: Routledge, 2015.

———. "Oedipus at the Border." *Public Books*, November 11, 2019. https://www.publicbooks.org/oedipus-at-the-border/.

———. "Can the Palestinian Antigone Grieve? A Political Reinterpretation of Judith Butler's Ethical Turn." *Settler Colonial Studies* 10, no. 1 (2020): 94–109.

———, and Henrik Ernstson. "'Hic Rhodus, Hic Salta!' The Politics of the Anthropo(bs)cene." In *Urban Political Ecology in the Anthropo-Obscene: Interruptions and Possibilities*, edited by Henrik Ernstson and Erik Swyngedouw, 69–87. Oxford: Routledge, 2019.

Hernández, Kelly Lytle. *Migra: A History of the US Border Patrol*. Berkeley: University of California Press, 2010.

Holland, Sharon Patricia. *Raising the Death: Readings of Death and (Black) Subjectivity*. Durham: Duke University Press, 2000.

———. *The Erotic Life of Racism*. Durham: Duke University Press, 2012.

Holst-Warhaft, Gail. *Dangerous Voices: Women's Laments and Greek Literature*. London: Routledge, 1992.

Hong, Grace Kyungwon. *Death beyond Disavowal: The Impossible Politics of Difference*. Minneapolis: The University of Minnesota Press, 2015.

Honig, Bonnie. *Democracy and the Foreigner*. Princeton: Princeton University Press, 2001.

———. "Antigone's Laments, Creon's Grief. Mourning, Membership, and the Politics of Exception." *Political Theory* 37, no. 1 (2009): 5–43.

———. "Antigone's Two Laws: Greek Tragedy and The Politics of Humanism." *New Literary History* 41, no. 1 (2010): 1–33.

———. *Antigone, Interrupted*. Cambridge: Cambridge University Press, 2013.

Hull, Gloria, Patricia Bell-Scott, and Barbara Smith. *All the Women Are White, All the Blacks Are Men, but Some of Us Are Brave: Black Women's Studies*. New York: Feminist Press, 1982.

Hunsaker, Dave. "To Mock the Spirits: Yup'ik Antigone in the Arctic." In *Antigone on the Contemporary World Stage*, edited by Erin B. Mee and Helene Foley. 184–201. Oxford: Oxford Classics, 2011.

Irigaray, Luce. *Speculum of the Other Women*. Translated by Gillian Gill. Ithaca: Cornell University Press, 1985.

Isaac, Benjamin. *The Invention of Racism in Classical Antiquity*. Princeton: Princeton University Press, 2004.
Jackson, Zakiyyah. "Losing Manhood: Animality and Plasticity in the (Neo)Slave Narrative." *Qui Parle* 25, no. 1–2 (2016): 95–136.
Jacobs, Harriet. *Incidents in the Life of a Slave Girl*. Cambridge: Harvard University Press, 1987.
James, Joy. "The Captive Maternal and Abolitionism: A Tribute to Erica Garner." In *Carceral Cultures Conference*, a conversation with Robyn Maynard, Simon Fraser University, March 3, 2018. https://www.thesocialjusticecentre.org/blog/2018/3/11/the-captive-maternal-and-abolitionism-a-tribute-to-erica-garner.
Jameson, Fredric. *Postmodernism, or, The Cultural Logic of Late Capitalism*. Durham: Duke University Press, 1991.
———. "Culture and Finance Capital." *Critical Inquiry* 24, no. 1 (1997): 246–65.
———. "Marx's Purloined Letter." In *Ghostly Demarcations: A Symposium on Jacques Derrida's Specters of Marx*, edited by Michael Sprinker, 26–67. London: Verso, 1999.
Johnson, Patrick. "'Quare' Studies, or (Almost) Everything I know about Queer Studies I Learned from My Grandmother." In *Black Queer Studies: A Critical Anthology*, edited by Patrick Johnson and Mae Henderson, 124–57. Durham: Duke University Press, 2005.
Johnston, Steven. *American Dionysia: Violence, Tragedy, and Democratic Politics*. Cambridge: Cambridge University Press, 2015.
Just, Roger. *Women in Athenian Law and Life*. New York: Routledge, 1989.
Kaldor, Mary. *New and Old Wars: Organized Violence in a Global Era*. Stanford: Stanford University Press, 1999.
Kamen, Deborah. *Status in Classical Athens*. Princeton: Princeton University Press, 2013.
Karabélias, Evangélos. *L'épiclerat attique*. Athens: Académie d'Athènes, 2002.
Kasimis, Demetra. "The Tragedy of Blood-Based Membership: Secrecy and the Politics of Immigration in Euripides' *Ion*." *Political Theory* 41, no. 2 (2013): 231–56.
———. *The Perpetual Immigrant and the Limits of Athenian Democracy*. Cambridge: Cambridge University Press, 2018.
Kennedy, Rebecca Futo. *Immigrant Women in Athens: Gender, Ethnicity, and Citizenship in the Classical City*. New York: Routledge, 2014.
Khanna, Ranjana. "Frames, Contexts, Community, Justice." *Diacritics* 33, no. 2 (2003): 10–41.
King, Tiffany Lethabo. *Black Shoals: Offshore Formations of Black and Native Studies*. Durham: Duke University Press, 2019.
Kirkpatrick, Jennet. "The Safeguard of Silence: Un-Heroic Resistance in Sophocles' *Antigone*." SSRN eLibrary (2010).
Klein, Naomi. *Shock Doctrine: The Rise of Disaster Capitalism*. New York: Penguin, 2014.

Kofman, Sarah. "Ça Cloche." In *Selected Writings*, edited by Thomas Albrecht, Georgia Albrecht, and Elizabeth Rottenberg, 71–98. Stanford: Stanford University Press, 2007 [1981].
Koram, Kojo, ed. *The War on Drugs and the Global Colour Line*. London: Pluto Press, 2019.
Kotef, Hagar. *Movement and the Ordering of Freedom: On Liberal Governances of Mobility*. Durham: Duke University Press, 2015.
Kramer, Sina. "Derrida's 'Antigonanette': On the Quasi-Transcendental." *Southern Journal of Philosophy* 52, no. 4 (2014): 521–51.
———. *Excluded Within: The (Un)Intelligibility of Radical Political Actors*. Oxford: Oxford University Press, 2017.
Kristeva, Julia. *Black Sun: Depression and Melancholia*. New York: Columbia University Press, 1989.
Lacan, Jacques. *Book VII. The Ethics of Psychoanalysis 1959–1960*. Translated by Dennis Porter. New York: W. W. Norton, 1997.
Laqueur, Thomas. *The Work of the Dead*. Princeton: Princeton University Press, 2015.
Laclau, Ernesto. *Emancipation(s)*. London: Verso, 2000.
Lane, Warren, and Ann M. Lane. "The Politics of Antigone." In *Greek Tragedy and Political Theory*, edited by Peter Euben, 162–82. Berkeley: University of California Press, 1986.
Lang, Sabine. "Various Kinds of Two-Spirit People: Gender Variance and Homosexuality in Native American Communities." In *Two-Spirit People: Native American Gender Identity, Sexuality, and Spirituality*, edited by Sue-Ellen Jacobs, Wesley Thomas, and Sabine Lang, 100–18. Chicago: University of Illinois, 1997.
Lape, Susan. *Race and Citizen Identity in Classical Antiquity*. Princeton: Princeton University Press, 2010.
Lewis, Simon, and Mark Maslin. "Defining the Anthropocene." *Nature* 519, no. 7542 (2015): 171–80.
Litwack, Leon. *Been in the Storm So Long: The Aftermath of Slavery*. New York: Knopf, 1979.
López-Alves, Fernando. *La Formación del estado y la democracia en América Latina*. Bogotá: Norma, 2003.
Loraux, Nicole. *The Invention of Athens: The Funeral Oration in the Classical City*. Translated by Alan Sheridan. New York: Zone Books, 2006 [1986].
———. *Tragic Ways of Killing a Woman*. Translated by Anthony Forster. Cambridge: Harvard University Press, 1991.
———. *The Experiences of Tiresias: The Feminine and the Greek Man*. Translated by Paula Wissig. Princeton: Princeton University Press, 1995.
———. *Born of the Earth: Myth and Politics in Athens*. Translated by Selina Stewart. Ithaca: Cornell University Press, 2000.
———. *The Mourning Voice: An Essay on Greek Tragedy*. Translated by Elizabeth Trapnell Rawlings. Ithaca: Cornell University Press, 2002.

Lowe, Lisa. *The Intimacies of Four Continents*. Durham: Duke University Press, 2015.
Lugones, María. "Heterosexualism and the Colonial/Modern Gender System." *Hypatia* 22, no. 1 (2007): 186–209.
———. "Toward a Decolonial Feminism." *Hypatia* 25, no. 4 (2010): 742–59.
Macherey, Pierre. "Marx Dematerialized, or the Spirit of Derrida." In *Ghostly Demarcations: A Symposium on Jacques Derrida's Specters of Marx*, edited by Michael Sprinker, 17–25. London: Verso, 1999.
———. *A Theory of Literary Production*. New York: Routledge, 2006.
Maffi, Alberto. "Family and Property Law." In *The Cambridge Companion to Ancient Greek Law*, edited by Michael Gagarin and David Cohen, 254–66. Cambridge: Cambridge University Press, 2005.
Maldonado-Torres, Nelson. "On the Coloniality of Being: Contributions to the Development of a Concept." *Cultural Studies* 21, no. 2–3 (2007): 240–79.
Mallon, Florencia. *Courage Tastes of Blood: The Mapuche Community of Nicolás Ailío and the Chilean State, 1906–2001*. Durham: Duke University Press, 2005.
Markell, Patchen. *Bound by Recognition*. Princeton: Princeton University Press, 2003.
Marriott, David. *Haunted Life: Visual Culture and Black Modernity*. New Brunswick, NJ: Rutgers University Press, 2007.
Martel, James. *The Misinterpellated Subject*. Durham: Duke University Press, 2017.
———. *Unburied Bodies: Subversive Corpses and the Authority of the Dead*. Amherst: Amherst College Press, 2018.
Marx, Karl. *Capital Vol. I*. New York: Penguin, 1976.
———. *The Eighteenth Brumaire of Louis Bonaparte*. New York: International Publishers, 2004.
Marx, Karl, and Friedrich Engels. "Manifesto of the Communist Party." In *The Marx-Engels Reader*, edited by Robert C. Tucker, 469–500. New York: W. W. Norton, 1978.
Mbembe, Achille. *On the Postcolony*. Translated by A. M. Berrett. Berkeley: University of California Press, 2001.
———. "Necropolitics." *Public Culture* 15 (2003): 11–40.
———. *Necropolitics*. Translated by Steve Corcoran. Durham: Duke University Press, 2019.
McClintock, Anne. "The Angel of Progress: Pitfalls of the Term 'Postcolonialism.'" *Social Text* 31/32 (1992): 84–98.
McCoskey, Denise Eileen. *Race: Antiquity and Its Legacy*. Oxford: Oxford University Press, 2012.
Meltzer, Milton. *Slavery I: From the Rise of Western Civilization to the Renaissance*. Chicago: Cowles, 1972.
Mielants, Eric H. *The Origins of Capitalism and the Rise of the West*. Philadelphia: Temple University Press, 2008.
Mignolo, Walter. *The Darker Side of Western Modernity: Global Futures, Decolonial Options*. Durham: Duke University Press, 2011.

Miller, Todd. *Empire of Borders: The Expansion of the US Border Around the World.* London: Verso, 2019.
Mills, Charles. *The Racial Contract.* Ithaca: Cornell University Press, 1997.
Mills, Patricia Jagentowicz. "Hegel's *Antigone.*" In *Feminist Interpretations of G. W. F. Hegel,* edited by Patricia Jagentowicz Mills, 59–88. University Park: Pennsylvania State University Press, 1996.
Moore, Jason. *Capitalism in the Web of Life: Ecology and the Accumulation of Capital.* London: Verso, 2015.
Moreton-Robinson, Aileen. *The White Possessive: Property, Power, and Indigenous Sovereignty.* Minneapolis: University of Minnesota Press, 2015.
Morgan, Jennifer. *Laboring Women: Reproduction and Gender in New World Slavery.* Philadelphia: University of Pennsylvania Press, 2004.
Morgensen, Scott Laurie. *Spaces between Us: Queer Settler Colonialism and Indigenous Decolonization.* Minneapolis: University of Minnesota Press, 2011.
Morris, Rosalind C. "After de Brosses: Fetishism, Translation, Comparativism, Critique." In *The Returns of Fetishism: Charles de Brosses and the Afterlives of an Idea,* edited by Daniel H. Leonard and Rosalind Morris, 133–320. Chicago: The University of Chicago Press, 2017.
Morrison, Toni. *Beloved.* New York: Vintage Books, 2007 [1987].
Moten, Fred. *In the Break: The Aesthetics of the Black Radical Tradition.* Minnesota: University of Minnesota Press, 2003.
Múnera, Alfonso. *Fronteras imaginadas: la construcción de las razas y la geografía en el siglo xix colombiano.* Bogotá: Planeta, 2005.
Muñoz, José Esteban. *Disidentifications: Queers of Color and the Performance of Politics.* Minneapolis: University of Minnesota Press, 1999.
———. *Cruising Utopia: The Then and There of Queer Futurity.* New York: New York University Press, 2009.
Negri, Antonio. "The Specter's Smile." In *Ghostly Demarcations: A Symposium on Jacques Derrida's Specters of Marx,* edited by Michael Sprinker, 5–17. London: Verso, 1999.
Nichols, Robert. *Theft as Property: Dispossession and Critical Theory.* Durham: Duke University Press, 2019.
Nieto, Patricia. *Los Escogidos.* Medellín: Editorial Universidad de Antioquia, 2012.
O'Brien, Joan. *Guide to Sophocles' Antigone.* Carbondale and Edwardsville: Southern Illinois University Press, 1978.
Omi, Michael, and Howard Winant. *Racial Formation in the United States: From the 1960s to the 1990s.* New York: Routledge, 1994.
Orozco Mendoza, Elva Fabiola. "Feminicide and the Funeralization of the City." *Theory & Event* 20, no. 2 (2017): 351–80.
———. "*Las Madres de Chihuahua:* Maternal Activism, Public Disclosure, and the Politics of Visibility." *New Political Science* 41, no. 2 (2019): 211–33.

Oyěwùmí, Oyèrónkẹ́. *The Invention of Women: Making an African Sense of Western Gender Discourses.* Minneapolis: University of Minnesota Press, 1997.
Paley, Dawn. *Drug War Capitalism.* Oakland: AK Press, 2014.
Patterson, Orlando. *Slavery and Social Death: A Comparative Study.* Cambridge: Harvard University Press, 1982.
———. *Freedom, Slavery, and the Modern Construction of Rights.* Johannesburg, South Africa: University of Witwatersrand, 1994.
Peeren, Esther. *The Spectral Metaphor: Living Ghosts and the Agency of Invisibility.* London: Palgrave, 2014.
Philip, M. NourbeSe. *Zong!* Middletown: Wesleyan University Press, 2008.
Pirro, Robert. *The Politics of Tragedy and Democratic Citizenship.* New York: Continuum, 2011.
Plato. *Republic.* Translated by C. D. C. Reeve. Indianapolis: Hackett, 2004.
Pomeroy, Sarah. *Goddesses, Whores, Wives, and Slaves: Women in Classical Antiquity.* New York: Schocken Books, 1995.
Porter, James. "Feeling Classical: Classicism and Ancient Literary Criticism." In *Classical Pasts: The Classical Traditions of Greece and Rome*, edited by James Porter, 301–52. Princeton: Princeton University Press, 2006.
Puar, Jasbir. *Terrorist Assemblages: Homonationalism in Queer Times.* Durham: Duke University Press, 2007.
———. *The Right to Maim: Debility, Capacity, Disability.* Durham: Duke University Press, 2017.
Quijano, Aníbal. "Colonialidad del Poder y Clasificación Social." In Festschrift for Immanuel Wallerstein. *Journal of World Systems Research* 5, no. 2 (2000): 345–86.
Raaflaub, Kurt. *The Discovery of Freedom in Ancient Greece.* Chicago: The University of Chicago Press, 2004.
Rajan. Rajeswari Sunder. "From Antagonism to Agonism: Shifting Paradigms of Women's Opposition to the State." *Comparative Studies of South Asia, Africa and the Middle East* 30, no. 2 (2010): 164–78.
Rancière, Jacques. *Proletarian Nights: The Worker's Dream in Nineteenth Century France.* Translated by John Drury. London: Verso, 2012 [1981].
———. *Dis-agreement. Politics and Philosophy.* Translated by Julie Rose. Minneapolis: University of Minnesota Press, 1999.
———. *The Flesh of Words: The Politics of Writing.* Translated by Charlotte Mendell. Stanford: Stanford University Press, 2004.
———. *The Politics of Aesthetics: The Distribution of the Sensible.* Translated by Gabriel Rockhill. London: Continuum, 2004.
———. *Aesthetics and Its Discontents.* Translated by Steven Corcoran. New York: Polity Press, 2009.
———. *Dissensus: On Politics and Aesthetics.* Translated by Steven Corcoran. London and New York: Bloomsbury, 2010.

———. *The Emancipated Spectator*. Translated by Gregory Elliott. London: Verso, 2011.
———. *The Hatred of Democracy*. Translated by Steven Corcoran. London: Verso, 2013.
Rankine, Claudia. "The Condition of Black Life is One of Mourning." *The New York Times*, June 22, 2015.
Rawlinson, Mary. "Beyond Antigone: Ismene, Gender, and the Right to Life." In *The Returns of Antigone*, edited by Tina Chanter and Sean Kirkland. 101–23. Albany: State University of New York Press, 2010.
Ray, Leslie. *Language of the Land: The Mapuche in Argentina and Chile*. Denmark: IWGIA, 2007.
Razmjou, Shakrokh. "Religion and Burial Customs." In *Forgotten Empire: The World of Ancient Persia*, edited by John Curtis and Nigel Tallis, 150–56. Berkeley: University of California Press, 2005.
Rengifo, César. *La fiesta de los moribundos*. Caracas: Asociación de Escritores Venezolanos, 1970 [1966].
Reséndez, Andrés. *The Other Slavery: The Uncovered Story of Indian Enslavement in America*. New York: Houghton Mifflin Harcourt, 2016.
Robbins, Nicholas. *Mercury, Mining, and Empire: The Human and Ecological Cost of Silver Mining in the Andes*. Bloomington: Indiana University Press, 2011.
Roberts, Deborah. "Reading *Antigone* in Translation: Text, Paratext, Intertext." In *Interrogating Antigone in Postmodern Philosophy and Criticism*, edited by S. E. Wilmer and Audronė Žukauskaite, 283–312. Oxford: Oxford University Press, 2010.
Roberts, Neil. *Freedom as Marronage*. Chicago: The University of Chicago Press, 2015.
Robinson, Cedric. *Black Marxism: The Making of the Black Radical Tradition*. Chapel Hill: The University of North Carolina Press, 1983.
Rodríguez, Dylan. "Forced Passages." In *Warfare in the American Homeland: Policing and Prison in a Penal Democracy*, edited by Joy James, 35–57. Durham: Duke University Press, 2007.
Rokem, Freddie. "Antigone Remembers: Dramaturgical Analysis and *Oedipus Tyrannos*." *Theater Research International* 31 (2009): 260–69.
Rosenblat, Angel. *La población indígena y el mestizaje en América*. Buenos Aires: Nova, 1954.
Roy, Arundhati. *Capitalism: A Ghost Story*. Chicago: Haymarket Books, 2014.
Sánchez Cordero, Olga. "Sebastiana, Andrés Manuel y la Ley de Amnistía/1." *Milenio* 24 April 2018.
Sassen, Saskia. *Expulsions: Brutality and Complexity in the Global Economy*. Cambridge: The Belknap Press of Harvard University Press, 2014.
Schmitt, Carl. *The Concept of the Political*. Translated by George Schwab. Chicago: The University of Chicago Press, 1996.
Schoorl, Lara. "Will You Join Me in Taking Up the Body?: On Sara Uribe's 'Antígona González.'" *Los Angeles Review of Books*, July 11, 2017.

Schotten, Heike. *Queer Terror: Life, Death, and Desire in the Settler Colony*. New York: Columbia University Press, 2018.
Segato, Rita Laura. "Las nuevas fomas de la guerra y el cuerpo de las mujeres." *Sociedad e Estado* 29, no. 2 (2014): 341–71.
———. "Crueldad: Pedagogías y Contra-Pedagogías." *Lobo Suelto (Anarquía Coronada)*, March 26, 2018. http://lobosuelto.com/tag/contra-pedagogias/.
Sexton, Jared. *Amalgamation Schemes: Antiblackness and the Critique of Multiracialism*. Minneapolis: University of Minnesota Press, 2008.
———. " 'The Curtain of the Sky': An Introduction." *Critical Sociology* 36, no. 1 (2010): 11–24.
Shakur, Assata. *Assata Shakur: An Autobiography*. Chicago: Lawrence Hill Books, 1987.
Sharpe, Christina. *Monstrous Intimacies: Making Post-Slavery Subjects*. Durham: Duke University Press, 2010.
———. *In the Wake: On Blackness and Being*. Durham: Duke University Press, 2016.
Silko, Leslie Marmon. *Almanac of the Dead*. New York: Penguin, 1991.
Silva, Denise Ferreira da. *Toward a Global Idea of Race*. Minneapolis: University of Minnesota Press, 2007.
Silverman, Kaja. "The Lacanian Phallus." *differences: A Journal of Feminist Cultural Studies* 4, no. 1 (1992): 84–115.
Sjöholm, Cecilia. "Naked Life: Arendt and the Exile at Colonus." In *Interrogating Antigone in Postmodern Philosophy and Criticism*, edited by S. E. Wilmer and Audronė Žukauskaite, 48–66. Oxford: Oxford University Press, 1992.
Smith, Andrea. *Conquest: Sexual Violence and American Indian Genocide*. Durham: Duke University Press, 2015.
Snorton, C. Riley. *Black on Both Sides: A Racial History of Trans Identity*. Minneapolis: University of Minnesota Press, 2017.
Söderbäck, Fanny, ed. *Feminist Readings of Antigone*. Albany: State University of New York Press, 2010.
Somerville, Siobhan B. "Scientific Racism and the Emergence of the Homosexual Body." *Journal of the History of Sexuality* 5, no. 2 (1994): 243–66.
———. *Queering the Color Line: Race and the Invention of Homosexuality in American Culture*. Durham: Duke University Press, 2000.
Sophocles. *The Three Theban Plays*. Translated by Robert Fagles. New York: Penguin Books, 1984.
———. *Sophocles I*. Translated by David Grene. Chicago: The University of Chicago Press, 1991.
Sourvinou-Inwood, Christiane. "Sophocles's Antigone as a 'Bad Woman.' " In *Writing Women into History*, edited by F. Dieteren and E. Kloek, 11–38. Amsterdam: Amsterdamse historische reeks, 1990.
Spillers, Hortense. "Mama's Baby, Papa's Maybe: An American Grammar Book." *Diacritics* 17, no. 1 (1987): 64–81.
———. *Black, White and In Color: Essays on American Literature and Culture*. Chicago: University of Chicago Press, 2003.

Spivak, Gayatri. "Glas-Piece: A Compte-Rendu." *Diacritics* 7, no. 3 (1977): 22–43.

———. "Can the Subaltern Speak?" In *Marxism and the Interpretation of Culture*, edited by C. Nelson and L. Grossberg, 271–315. Chicago: University of Illinois Press, 1988.

———. "Race Before Racism: The Disappearance of the American." *boundary 2* 25, no. 2 (1998): 35–53.

———. *Critique of Postcolonial Reason: Towards a History of the Vanishing Present*. Cambridge: Cambridge University Press, 1999.

———. "At the *Planchette* of Deconstruction is/in America." In *Jacques Derrida: A Critical Assessments of Leading Philosophers*, edited by Zeynap Direk and Len Lawlor, 340–49. New York: Routledge, 2002.

Steiner, George. *Antigones*. Oxford: Oxford University Press, 1984.

Stone, Dan. *Concentration Camps: A Short History*. Oxford: Oxford University Press, 2017.

Taiaiake, Alfred. *Wasáse: Indigenous Pathways of Actions and Freedom*. Peterborough: Broadview Press, 2005.

Tanck Estrada, Dorothy. *Independencia y educación: Cultura cívica, educación indígena y literatura infantil*. México: El Colegio de México, 2013.

Taylor, Diana. *Disappearing Acts: Spectacles of Gender and Nationalism in Argentina's "Dirty War."* Durham: Duke University Press, 1997.

Thompson, Kevin. "Hegelian Dialectic and the Quasi-Transcendental in *Glas*." In *Hegel after Derrida*, edited by Stuart Barnett, 239–59. New York: Routledge, 1998.

Tomich, Dale. *Slavery in the Circuit of Sugar*. Albany: State University of New York Press, 2015.

Unidad Investigativa. "En Colombia asesinan a un indígena cada 3 días; 120 este año." *El Tiempo*, October 30, 2019.

Uribe, Sara. *Antígona González*. Oaxaca: Surplus, 2012.

———. *Antígona González*. Translated by John Pluecker. Los Angeles: Les Figues Press, 2016.

Valencia, Sayak. *Gore Capitalism*. Translated by John Pluecker. Cambridge: MIT Press, 2018.

Vasunia, Phiroze. *The Gift of the Nile: Hellenizing Egypt from Aeschylus to Alexander*. Berkeley: University of California Press, 2001.

Veracini, Lorenzo. *The Settler Colonial Present*. New York: Palgrave Macmillan, 2015.

Vergès, Françoise. "Racial Capitalocene." In *Futures of Black Radicalism*, edited by Gaye Theresa Johnson and Alex Lubin, 72–82. London: Verso, 2017.

Vernant, Jean-Pierre, and Pierre Vidal-Naquet, eds. *Myth and Tragedy in Ancient Greece*. New York: Zone Books, 1988.

Vidal-Naquet, Pierre. "Oedipus between Two Cities: An Essay on *Oedipus at Colonus*." In *Myth and Tragedy in Ancient Greece*, edited by Jean-Pierre Vernant and Pierre Vidal-Naquet. 329–60. New York: Zone Books, 1988.

———, and M. M. Austin. *Economic & Social History of Ancient Greece: An Introduction*. Berkeley: University of California Press, 1984.

Wallerstein, Immanuel. *The Modern World-System: Capitalist Agriculture and the Origins of the European World-Economy in the Sixteenth Century*. New York: Academic Press, 1974.

Warner, Marina. *Indigo*. New York: Simon and Schuster, 1992.

Warren, Calvin. *Onticide: Afropessimism, Queer Theory & Ethics*. Ill Will Editions, 2015.

———. "Afro-Pessimism, ~~Gay~~ Nigger # 1, and Surplus Violence." *GLQ* 23, no. 3 (2017): 391–418.

———. *Ontological Terror: Blackness, Nihilism, and Emancipation*. Durham: Duke University Press, 2018.

Warren, Michael, ed. *Fear of a Queer Planet*. Minneapolis: University of Minnesota Press, 1993.

Washington, Harriet. *Medical Apartheid: The Dark History of Medical Experimentation on Black Americans from Colonial Times to the Present*. New York: Doubleday, 2006.

Weber, Max. *Economy and Society*. Translated by Ephraim Fischoff et al. Berkeley: University of California Press, 1978.

Weber, Samuel. "Antigone's *Nomos*." In *Theatricality as Medium*, 121–40. New York: Fordham University Press, 2004.

Weheliye, Alexander G. *Habeas Viscus: Racializing Assemblages, Biopolitics, and Black Feminist Theories of the Human*. Durham: Duke University Press, 2014.

Weinbaum, Alys Eve. *The Afterlife of Reproductive Slavery: Biocapitalism and Black Feminism's Philosophy of History*. Durham: Duke University Press, 2019.

Whitehead, David. *The Ideology of the Athenian Metic*. Cambridge: Cambridge University Press, 1977.

Wilderson, Frank. "The Prison Slave as Hegemony's (Silent) Scandal." In *Warfare in the American Homeland: Policing and Prison in a Penal Democracy*, edited by Joy James, 23–34. Durham: Duke University Press, 2007.

———. *Red, White & Black: Cinema and the Structure of U.S. Antagonisms*. Durham: Duke University Press, 2010.

Williams, Patricia. *The Alchemy of Race and Rights*. Cambridge: Harvard University Press, 1991.

Wolfe, Patrick. "Settler Colonialism and the Elimination of the Native." *Journal of Genocide Research* 8, no. 4 (2006): 387–409.

Wright, Thomas C. *State Terrorism in Latin America: Chile, Argentina, and International Human Rights*. Lanham, MD: Rowman and Littlefield, 2007.

Wynter, Sylvia. "Unsettling the Coloniality of Being/Power/Truth/Freedom: Towards the Human, After Man, Its Overrepresentation—An Argument." *The New Centennial Review* 3 (2003): 257–337.

Young, Robert J. C. "Deconstruction and the Postcolonial." In *Deconstructions: A User's Guide*, edited by Nicholas Royle, 187–210. New York: Palgrave, 2000.

Yusoff, Kathryn. *A Billion Black Anthropocenes or None*. Minneapolis: University of Minnesota Press, 2018.

Zamudio Rodríguez, Luz Elena. "El amor vivificante de 'Antígona González,' de Sara Uribe." *Romance Notes* 54 (2014): 35–43.

Zeitlin, Froma. "Thebes: Theater of Self and Society in Athenian Drama." In *Nothing to Do with Dionysus? Athenian Drama in Its Social Context*, edited by John Winkler and Froma Zeitlin, 130–67. Princeton: Princeton University Press, 1990.

———. *Playing the Other: Gender and Society in Classical Greek Literature*. Chicago: Chicago University Press, 1996.

Žižek, Slavoj. *The Sublime Object of Ideology*. London: Verso, 1989.

———. *The Tickling Subject: The Absent Center of Political Ontology*. London: Verso, 2000.

———. *Did Somebody Say Totalitarianism: Five Interventions in the (Mis)use of a Notion*. London: Verso, 2002.

Žukauskaite, Audronė. "Biopolitics: Antigone's Claim." In *Interrogating Antigone in Postmodern Philosophy and Criticism*, edited by S. E. Wilmer and Audronė Žukauskaite, 67–88. Oxford: Oxford University Press, 2010.

Zupančič, Alenka. *Ethics of the Real: Kant, Lacan*. London: Verso, 2000.

Name Index

Arendt, Hannah, 35, 99, 211, 227
Aristotle, 9, 82, 83, 195, 197, 211, 221

Bal, Mieke, 5, 203
Baldwin, James, 101, 227
Bargu, Banu, 131–134, 137–138, 234, 235
Barrett, Lindon, 16, 27, 145, 146, 201, 207
Baucom, Ian, 26, 154, 176–179, 183, 199, 241, 242
Benjamin, Walter, 29, 117, 175, 176, 178, 189, 192, 210, 230, 241
Bernal, Martin, 17–18, 207
Bernstein, J. M., 91–93, 226
Blundell, Sue, 48, 55, 214, 216, 219
Buck-Morss, Susan, 175
Butler, Judith, 5, 24, 25, 50, 51, 64–70, 71, 73, 74–76, 78, 79, 81, 86–87, 92–94, 97, 99, 100, 101, 102, 104, 163, 199, 215, 219, 220, 221, 224, 242
Byrd, Jodi, 140, 199, 236

Cacho, Lisa Marie, 152, 199, 232, 237, 238
Carson, Anne, 198–199, 245
Cartledge, Paul, 206, 214, 215, 218, 245

Chanter, Tina, 1, 6, 18, 19, 27, 49, 51, 55, 57, 93, 162, 199, 200, 203, 204, 206, 207, 208, 211, 213, 214, 215, 216, 226, 240
Copjec, Joan, 25, 79, 80–81, 84–87, 89–90, 100, 102, 104, 220, 223, 224
Critchley, Simon, 198, 245

Davis, Angela, 68, 71, 73, 145–146, 153, 199, 220, 221, 237
Day, Iyko, 10–12, 199, 206
Deleuze, Gilles, 83, 224
 and Félix Guattari, 8, 76, 92, 221
Derrida, Jacques, 5, 26, 27, 96, 130, 154, 159, 164–175, 181, 182, 189, 191, 203, 234, 239, 240, 241, 242, 243
Driskill, Qwo-Li, 228
Dubois, Page, 53, 215, 216, 218

Echavarría, Juan Manuel, 143, 144, 148, 236
Edelman, Lee, 25, 99–102, 104, 227, 241
Engelstein, Stefani, 50, 214, 222

Fanon, Frantz, 87, 100, 188, 225, 227, 244

Foley, Helene, 24, 36–38, 39–40, 57, 75–76, 205, 212, 221
Foucault, Michel, 53, 79, 80, 122–126, 131, 134, 137, 138, 215, 216, 223, 226, 232, 233, 234, 235
Fradinger, Moira, 22–23, 145, 149, 199, 209, 229, 230, 236, 237, 243
Freud, Sigmund, 71, 83, 86, 181, 184–185, 189, 222, 224, 243

Glissant, Édouard, 176, 180, 189, 241
Goldhill, Simon, 35, 205, 211
Gordon, Avery, 27, 131, 154, 155–156, 178, 179–180, 191, 199, 234, 235, 238, 242, 243, 245
Gsoels-Lorensen, Jutta, 43, 136

Hall, Edith, 9, 34, 35, 203, 206, 211, 214
Hartman, Saidiya, 12, 25, 68–70, 77–79, 87, 88, 94, 97, 104, 112, 140, 183, 187, 192, 197, 199, 207, 220, 222, 225, 226, 228, 236, 238, 244, 245
Hegel, G. W. F., 4, 5, 6, 17, 18, 51, 64–66, 82, 85, 87, 89, 90, 91, 92, 93, 101, 102, 125, 154, 159–161, 163, 164–167, 169–171, 175, 192, 199, 219, 223, 226, 239, 240, 242
Holland, Sharon Patricia, 59, 67, 190, 220, 222, 232, 245
Honig, Bonnie, 5, 20, 22, 24, 37–40, 50, 51, 52, 54, 57, 82, 118, 119, 120, 205, 208, 212, 215, 216, 223, 224–225, 232, 243

Irigaray, Luce, 5, 51, 64, 65, 66, 219, 239, 242
Isaac, Benjamin, 55, 206, 218

Jameson, Fredric, 114, 173–174, 230, 241
Johnson, Patrick, 25, 228
Just, Roger, 75, 221

Kamen, Deborah, 205, 207
Kasimis, Demetra, 32–33, 57, 210, 213–214
Kennedy, Rebecca Futo, 13, 15, 46, 48, 204, 207, 213, 214, 216, 218, 221
Kramer, Sina, 168–169, 171, 239, 240

Lacan, Jacques, 4, 5, 51, 64–66, 71, 71, 79, 80–86, 89, 100, 120, 199, 219, 220, 222, 223, 224, 225, 232, 242
Laqueur, Thomas, 97, 132, 231, 234
Lape, Susan, 9, 206
Lewis, Simon, and Mark Maslin, 157–158, 238
Loraux, Nicole, 37–39, 40, 211, 212, 214, 226, 242, 245
Lugones, María, 60, 71, 199, 217, 220

Macherey, Pierre, 21, 174, 208, 241
Marriott, David, 97, 185, 227
Martel, James, 8, 28, 34, 44, 196, 205, 211, 212, 235, 244, 245
Marx, Karl, 69, 172, 174, 175, 176, 181, 182, 183, 241, 243
  and Friedrich Engels, 89, 101, 155, 189, 191, 244
Mbembe, Achille, 124–126, 233, 235
McCoskey, Denise Eileen, 9, 206
Moore, Jason, 156, 190, 206, 238, 239, 244
Morrison, Toni, 73–74, 178, 190, 221
Moten, Fred, 89, 100, 154, 183–186, 187, 189, 191, 199, 226, 227, 243, 244
  and Stefano Harney, 186, 243, 244

Negri, Antonio, 174–175, 241
Nietzsche, Friedrich, 114, 173–174, 230, 241

Orozco Mendoza, Elva Fabiola, 150–151, 237

Patterson, Orlando, 62, 67, 68, 75, 97, 123, 218, 219, 220, 233
Peeren, Esther, 191, 240–241, 243, 245
Porter, James, 20, 22, 208

Quijano, Aníbal, 208, 217

Rajan, Rajeswari Sunder, 22, 208
Ranciére, Jacques, 14, 24, 29–33, 35, 57, 61, 125, 126, 207, 209, 210, 211, 233
Rankine, Claudia, 186, 244
Roberts, Deborah, 213
Roberts, Neil, 210–211
Rokem, Freddie, 44, 213

Segato, Rita Laura, 127, 150–151, 233, 237
Sexton, Jared, 109, 117, 222
Shakur, Assata, 89, 101, 225
Sharpe, Christina, 154, 186–189, 191, 199, 220, 244
Silko, Leslie Marmon, 178, 191
Snorton, C. Riley, 25, 94–96, 97, 104, 147, 199, 226, 227, 228

Sophocles, 1, 2, 4, 8, 12, 17, 18, 19, 28, 36, 37, 40, 43, 46, 47, 48, 53, 75, 106, 107, 117, 118, 119, 120, 128, 198, 203, 209, 213, 216, 242
Spillers, Hortense, 25, 67, 70–74, 76–78, 94, 96, 100, 145, 183, 199, 208, 218, 219, 220, 221, 222
Spivak, Gayatri, 21, 178, 208, 216, 240
Steiner, George, 22, 208, 242

Taylor, Diana, 149, 237

Valencia, Sayak, 115, 139, 152, 199, 230
Veracini, Lorenzo, 155, 238
Vergès, Françoise, 156–157, 209, 238
Vidal-Naquet, Pierre, 48, 214, 216
 and Pierre Vernant, 212, 215

Warren, Calvin, 103, 227
Wilderson, Frank, 89, 101, 226, 227
Whitehead, David, 42, 212
Wolfe, Patrick, 61, 208, 218, 241
Wynter, Sylvia, 61, 208, 218

Yusoff, Kathryn, 162–163, 238, 239, 242

Žižek, Slavoj, 174, 199, 220, 241, 244
Zupančič, Alenka, 88, 220, 224, 225

Subject Index

Aesthetic, 20, 23, 24, 29, 33, 35, 41, 43, 115, 140, 142, 144, 167, 183, 186, 187, 188, 209, 210, 211, 226, 233, 236
Alien, 2, 10–12, 14, 16, 19, 20–23, 25, 33, 42, 43, 61, 105, 111, 117, 123, 126, 173, 180, 192, 197, 199, 206
Anarchy/An-*arkhê*, 14 24, 30, 34, 196, 197
Anthropocene, 154–160, 163, 164, 165, 167, 171, 172, 176, 179, 182, 238, 239, 242
Antigone (*see also* Sophocles)
  and *Antígona en el infierno*, by Rolando Steiner, 232
  and *Antígona González*, by Sara Uribe, 26, 114, 116, 128, 138, 142–143, 199, 230, 234, 236
  and *Antígona: las voces que incendian el desierto*, by Perla de la Rosa, 237
  and *Antigone*, by Jean Anouilh, 26, 117–122, 128, 144, 199, 232
  and *Antigone in Ferguson*, by Bryan Doerries, 105–106, 228
  and *Antigone in New York*, by Janusz Glowacki, 229
  and *Argia*, by Juan Cruz Varela, 114
  and *La fiesta de los moribundos*, by César Rengifo, 229
  and *Los escogidos*, by Patricia Nieto, 26, 114, 116, 128, 138, 143, 146–147, 199, 230, 234, 236, 237
  and *Widows*, by Ariel Dorfman, 26, 114, 115, 116, 128, 142, 144, 146, 149, 208, 209, 230, 234, 236, 237
  and *Yup'ik Antigone,* by Dave Hunsaker, 105–106, 228
Abya Yala, 17, 133, 159, 172, 189, 207
Americas, 4, 5, 7, 9–12, 14, 16–20, 21, 22, 23, 25, 26, 27, 51, 57, 59, 60, 61, 62, 63, 69, 109, 110, 111, 112, 115, 116, 124, 127, 132, 133, 135, 138, 154, 155, 157, 158, 163, 164, 165, 172, 173, 176, 178, 179, 180, 181, 182, 189, 190, 196, 197, 198, 207, 217, 228, 229, 230, 235
  and Latin America, 25, 26, 107, 109, 110, 111–117, 124, 128–140, 141, 142, 144, 149, 154, 198, 209, 230, 232, 234
  and North America, 59, 60, 62, 68, 96, 98, 99, 105, 198, 218

Blackness/Black people, 4, 5, 9–12, 17, 20, 25, 27, 62, 67–74, 76–78, 90, 94–98, 100–105, 106–110, 112, 117, 132, 134, 138, 146–147, 153, 154, 158, 159, 162, 163, 173, 177, 181–188, 191, 192, 197, 199, 207, 208, 209, 217, 218, 219, 220, 221, 225, 226, 227, 228, 229, 231, 235, 236, 237, 238, 239, 242, 244

Burial, 1, 2, 6–8, 15, 19, 36, 38, 40, 46, 50, 56, 57, 63, 66, 76, 81, 82, 97, 98, 99, 104, 106, 121, 122, 128, 136, 144, 145, 147, 151, 153, 154, 159–164, 165, 169, 170, 171, 172, 188, 190, 195, 196, 197, 199, 214, 229, 232

Chile, 26, 107, 109, 111, 113–117, 128, 129, 139, 149, 229, 231, 232, 234, 236

Citizenship/Citizen, 1, 3, 4, 7–12, 13, 15, 16, 21, 23, 24, 27, 32, 33, 38, 43, 47, 48, 49, 51, 54, 55, 56, 59, 60, 61, 62, 63, 67, 73, 76, 93, 105, 109, 110, 111, 112, 113, 119, 120, 121, 123, 162, 168, 176, 184, 186, 196, 197, 198, 199, 200, 201, 204, 206, 209, 211, 217, 219, 229, 232, 233, 237

Colombia, 26, 110, 111, 113–117, 128, 129, 131, 132, 134, 139, 149, 151, 153, 229, 230, 231, 234, 235, 236

and Puerto Berrío, 116, 129, 143, 144, 146, 147, 229

Corpse, 2, 15, 17, 20, 56, 57, 42, 86, 89, 92, 94, 96, 97, 98, 105, 106, 118, 122, 126, 128, 130, 135, 136, 137, 145, 146, 147, 150, 192, 195, 196, 197, 199, 207, 214, 229, 235, 244

Death (*see also* social death), 2, 3, 6, 15, 16, 24, 38, 44, 55, 56, 62, 64, 65, 76, 80–84, 85, 86, 87, 88, 89, 90, 92, 96, 97, 98, 99, 103, 104, 107, 113, 118, 121, 122, 123, 124, 127, 130, 135, 136, 137, 139, 141, 146, 147, 150, 151, 152, 156, 158, 160, 161, 163, 176, 179, 181, 183, 184, 185, 188, 192, 196, 197, 198, 199, 215, 220, 223, 224, 230, 231, 232, 234, 235, 244, 245

and deathliness, 97, 98, 137, 140, 184, 185, 187

Death Drive, 25, 83–86, 99, 100, 102, 103, 199, 227

Decolonial, 5, 16, 19, 22, 23, 25, 26, 59, 79, 109, 126, 143, 154, 163, 171, 173, 180, 182, 189, 190, 191, 228, 245, 201, 208, 209, 216, 233, 238

and Cacophony, 140–141

and Mourning, 27, 144, 145, 152, 153, 154, 159, 177, 182, 192

and Rumination, 20, 23, 27, 28, 79, 178, 190, 196, 199

Deconstruction, 5, 6, 19, 20, 21, 26, 27, 37, 40, 78, 154, 155, 158, 159, 160, 164–168, 171–175, 178, 182, 197, 212, 240, 241

Democracy/Demos, 2, 3, 4, 5, 6, 7, 9, 13, 14, 17, 23, 24, 26, 29–40, 41, 42, 47, 50, 51, 54, 56, 57, 60, 64, 92, 99, 114, 115, 116, 118, 120, 121, 122, 135, 138, 140, 150, 154, 163, 174, 196,

198, 199, 205, 209, 210, 211, 212, 215, 216, 224, 225, 227, 233, 236, 243
and Democratic theory, 6, 14, 19, 24, 27, 32, 38, 40, 43, 56, 57, 59, 140, 154, 197, 209, 211, 212

Enforced Disappearances, 26, 113–116, 129, 130–135, 138, 139, 149, 151, 154, 158, 231, 234, 235, 236
Ethical, 27, 35, 36, 58, 64–66, 79, 81–84, 85–90, 93, 102, 103, 122, 154, 159, 161–163, 165, 166, 169, 175, 191, 221, 224, 225, 240

Feminism, 1, 5, 6, 19, 24, 25, 27, 36, 57, 59, 60, 62, 63, 64, 66, 67, 68, 70, 77, 78, 79, 89, 90, 91, 93, 94, 99, 107, 149, 154, 161, 162, 197, 199, 205, 207, 209, 218, 219, 220, 222, 226, 227, 228, 237, 239
Forced Choice, 79, 81–89, 224
Fungibility, 90, 94–96, 98, 100, 102, 121, 130, 147, 170
Fugitivity, 90, 94, 95, 98, 103, 154, 185, 187, 238

Indigeneity/Indigenous people, 4, 10, 11, 12, 17, 20, 25, 26, 27, 60, 61, 62, 67, 69, 70, 71, 73, 76, 78, 79, 90, 96–106, 110, 112, 113, 116, 117, 124, 125, 132, 133, 134, 138, 154–159, 162, 173, 177, 180, 181–185, 188, 189, 191, 192, 199, 207, 215, 218, 220, 228, 229, 230, 231, 235, 242, 245

Materialism, 27, 41, 69, 71, 94, 137, 159, 173, 175, 176, 177, 178, 180, 188, 200, 222
Maternal, 149–151, 199, 223, 237
Melodrama, 117, 118, 120, 121, 140, 236
Metoikia/Metic, 1–7, 8–12, 13–16, 19, 21, 23, 24, 26, 27, 29, 31, 32, 33, 34, 36, 37, 38, 39, 40, 41, 42–50, 51, 53, 55, 56, 57, 59, 60, 61, 88, 93, 95, 106, 109, 110, 111, 112, 113, 116, 123, 124, 130, 131, 136, 153, 154, 162, 168, 176, 178, 180, 195–201, 204, 205, 209, 212, 213, 214, 215, 217, 218, 219, 221, 222, 232, 233
México, 26, 110, 113–117, 127–132, 139, 149, 150, 151, 153, 231, 232, 233, 236, 237
Modernity, 5, 8, 9, 10, 12, 14, 16, 19, 23, 27, 31, 57, 59, 61, 62, 67, 72, 73, 80, 94, 95, 97, 98, 100, 106, 114, 115, 118, 119, 121, 123, 125, 129, 130, 131, 132, 134, 137, 146, 156, 163, 164, 165, 172, 176, 177, 195, 198, 200, 208, 218, 219, 226, 227, 229, 231, 233, 235
and Postmodernity, 8, 26, 27, 106, 109, 113–115, 128–131, 132, 138, 140, 149, 161, 177, 198, 204, 205, 213, 230, 232, 239
Mourning (*see also* decolonial mourning), 1, 12, 17, 19, 26, 27, 63, 88, 102, 105, 130, 144, 147, 149, 152, 153, 157, 159, 166, 167, 173, 175, 176, 177, 178, 180, 181–192, 193, 197, 201, 212, 215, 224, 234, 243, 244
and Melancholia, 184–188, 243, 244

Mo'nin (*see also* wake), 154, 159, 181, 185

Native (*see also* indigenous), 3, 10, 11, 12, 14, 16, 19, 22, 25, 44, 45, 47, 48, 56, 61, 70, 98, 99, 105, 106, 117, 123, 126, 133, 163, 173, 180, 181, 197, 191, 197, 199, 201, 208, 220, 227, 228, 242

Necropolitics, 11, 117, 122, 124–128, 132, 139, 150, 152, 162, 177, 182, 192, 196, 197, 233, 235, 237

and Necrodialectic, 129–130

Political, 1–11, 12–17, 18, 20, 23, 24, 27, 29, 30, 31, 32, 33, 34, 35, 36–42, 45, 47, 48, 49, 50, 51, 52, 53, 56, 58, 59, 63, 64, 66, 67, 79, 90, 91, 93, 94, 95, 96, 99, 101, 102, 104, 105, 109, 111, 112, 114, 116, 117, 118, 119, 121, 122, 123, 124, 125, 133, 136, 138, 142, 143, 144, 145, 146, 147, 149, 150, 153, 154, 157, 158, 159, 160, 163, 164, 165, 169, 175, 176, 178, 179, 180, 183, 187, 188, 189, 191, 192, 193, 195–201, 203, 205, 206, 209, 210, 211, 213, 215, 215, 221, 226, 227, 234, 235, 236, 237

and Membership, 1–11, 15, 16, 19, 22, 32, 43, 45, 48, 60, 117, 196–201, 215

and Theory, 1, 5, 7, 9, 12, 20, 27, 30, 33, 51, 60, 70, 204, 208, 210, 232

Preposterous History, 5, 11, 16, 17, 23, 27, 57, 121, 135, 158, 203

Psychoanalysis, 6, 66, 67–73, 79, 80, 81, 85, 86, 89, 90, 109, 164, 168, 219, 223, 224, 225, 232, 239, 240, 244

Queer, 5, 6, 19, 24, 25, 27, 57, 59, 60, 62–66, 67, 69, 70, 73, 74, 75, 77, 78, 79, 91, 92, 94, 99–104, 105, 107, 154, 167, 197, 199, 209, 221, 226, 227, 228, 241

and *quare*, 25, 102–105, 147, 199, 228

and two-spirit, 25, 102–105, 147, 199, 228

Race/Racialized (*see also* racialized logic of value), 4, 9, 11, 12, 14, 16, 19, 26, 27, 57, 60, 61, 67, 68, 69, 72, 77, 79, 89, 93, 94, 95, 96, 100, 101, 103, 104, 105, 112, 113, 114, 116, 123, 125, 126, 127, 138, 140, 152, 157, 159, 162, 165, 169, 172, 175, 179, 182, 183, 187, 188, 189, 190, 192, 196, 197, 198, 206, 207, 208, 209, 218, 220, 222, 226, 227, 228, 229, 2238, 43, 244

Racial Capitalocene, 26, 27, 155–159, 163, 165, 167, 172, 176, 177, 178, 179, 188, 189, 191, 192, 198, 199, 209, 238, 242, 243

Racial/Sexual Capitalism, 14, 19, 27, 60, 104, 123, 125, 153, 154, 158, 164, 173, 177, 179, 184, 189, 193, 197, 198, 207, 235

Settler Colonialism/Settler, 10, 11, 14, 15, 16, 18, 19, 25, 26, 27, 60, 62, 67, 69, 70, 73, 77, 78, 96,

Subject Index 275

97, 98, 99, 103, 105, 106, 107, 114, 117, 123, 126, 130, 132, 146, 155, 156, 158, 159, 162, 164, 165, 172, 173, 176, 177, 179, 180, 181, 182, 184, 185, 187, 188, 189, 191, 192, 196, 198, 199, 200, 201, 206, 208, 209, 2218, 221, 227, 228, 229, 238, 241, 243
and Capitalism, 11, 12, 17, 61, 162, 182, 188, 206
and Critique, 5, 123, 176, 189, 197, 199, 209
and Logic of elimination, 10, 11, 25, 26, 61, 62, 70, 98, 103, 105, 106, 107, 113, 114, 115, 117, 124, 126, 128, 132, 133, 134, 138, 150, 152, 153, 154, 155, 170, 173, 178, 179, 182, 197, 198, 208
and Logic of exclusion, 10, 25, 26, 61, 62, 70, 72, 88, 105, 107, 110, 114, 115, 117, 124, 125, 126, 128, 132, 138, 141, 152, 153, 154, 162, 173, 178, 179, 182, 197, 198, 199
Sexuality, 4, 13, 14, 33, 51, 57, 60, 67, 68, 69, 70, 71, 69, 75, 76, 77, 79, 80, 94, 96, 100, 101, 103, 104, 107, 125, 126, 150, 151, 159, 161, 162, 164, 165, 167, 168, 169, 170, 196, 198, 207, 217, 220, 222, 223, 226, 228
Slavery/Enslaved, 1–7, 8–12, 13–15, 18, 21, 23, 24, 25, 26, 29, 30, 31, 39, 40, 49, 50–58, 59–62, 67–77, 87, 88, 89, 93–102, 103, 105, 106, 109, 110, 112, 113, 114, 121, 123, 124, 126, 130, 133, 135, 136, 138, 140, 141, 145, 146, 147, 150, 154, 156, 157, 158, 162, 170, 171, 176, 177, 187, 191, 195–201, 203, 205, 210, 211, 215, 217, 218, 219, 220, 223, 227, 229, 231, 233, 237, 240, 241
and Afterlife, 11, 12, 77, 87, 97, 98, 100, 103, 106, 112, 113, 115, 117, 122, 124, 126, 127, 130, 153, 154, 173, 178, 184, 187, 189, 197, 198, 218, 220, 231, 239, 242
Social Death, 24, 25, 59, 60, 62, 67, 68, 72, 75, 95, 97–103, 112, 113, 121, 124, 133, 141, 197, 218, 219, 224, 232, 233, 237, 238
Sovereignty, 26, 118, 119, 122, 125, 132–138, 229, 234, 235
Specter, 26, 27, 154, 155, 158, 159, 172–182, 191, 234, 240, 241, 242, 243, 245

Tragedy, 1, 4, 5, 6, 9, 12, 16, 17, 18, 20, 24, 32–41, 44, 47, 51, 53, 75, 81, 82, 83, 90, 91, 107, 117, 118, 120, 121, 135, 140, 167, 172, 197, 198, 199, 203, 204, 205, 206, 209, 210, 211, 212, 214, 215, 221, 223, 240, 242, 245

Value, 4, 9, 14, 27, 68, 93, 95, 145, 146, 151, 152, 177, 183, 184, 199, 207, 222, 225
and Racialized logic of, 12, 14, 16, 23, 146, 174, 201

Wake, 154, 186–188, 244

www.ingramcontent.com/pod-product-compliance
Lightning Source LLC
Chambersburg PA
CBHW020641230426
43665CB00008B/263